THE EFFECTIVENESS OF THE KÖBLER LIABILITY IN NATIONAL COURTS

Over the last 15 years, *Köbler* liability has resulted in the allocation of damages on only five occasions. Why is that? And what are the practical implications of the *Köbler* judgment in the Member States?

This book offers a unique analysis of the state liability principle for breaches of EU law by national courts – not from the usual EU-focused point of view but from the practical view of the Member State – and thus follows the track set by earlier books in the 'EU Law in the Member States' series. It thoroughly examines the national jurisprudential and legislative acceptation of the state liability principle and explores the existence of alternative remedies available in the Member States in case of such breaches. The conclusions, based on a systematic assessment of 300 national judgments from the 28 Member States, lead to a reconsideration of the role of the *Köbler* doctrine in the system of judicial remedies against violation of EU law by national supreme courts.

After the pronouncement of the ECJ judgment in *Köbler*, legal scholars and practitioners have forecast the eradication of the principle of *res judicata* and the endangering of judicial independence. The judgment caused a lot of ink to flow; according to the ECJ's records, at least 100 studies are directly devoted to the analysis of this decision. This book is, however, the first to offer a comprehensive analysis on the genuine life of the *Köbler* liability in the Member States.

Volume 6 in the series EU Law in the Member States

EU Law in the Member States

Located at the cross-section between EU law, comparative law and socio-legal studies, *EU Law in the Member States* explores the interaction of EU law and national legal systems by analysing comparative evidence of the impact landmark EU measures – from CJEU decisions and secondary legislation to soft law – have had across different Member States. The nature and operation of EU law has traditionally been analysed in a highly 'centralised' way, through the lenses of Brussels and Luxembourg, and in terms of the Treaty and its interpretation by the Court of Justice. Beneath this orthodoxy, however, lies the complex world of the genuine life of EU law in the Member States. Judicial and administrative practices across the Union's 28, and then 27 Member States considerably qualify and sometimes even challenge the long-standing assumption that doctrines such as the direct effect and supremacy of EU law ensure a uniform and effective application of its provisions.

Each volume brings together leading academics, national experts and practitioners in order to draw conclusions both for EU law generally and the specific area in question on the basis of Member State reports and broader horizontal papers, and will be of interest to generalist EU lawyers and specialists in each field across the Member States. Academic audiences will benefit from the tight integration of national case studies and doctrinal analysis, whilst practitioners and policy-makers will find systematically presented comparative evidence and commentary.

Series Editors
Jeremias Prassl
Michal Bobek

Volume 1: *Viking, Laval* and Beyond
Edited by Mark Freedland and Jeremias Prassl

Volume 2: Central European Judges under the European Influence: The Transformative Power of the EU Revisited
Edited by Michal Bobek

Volume 3: Air Passenger Rights, Ten Years On
Edited by Jeremias Prassl and Michal Bobek

Volume 4: The Eurosceptic Challenge
Edited by Clara Rauchegger and Anna Wallerman

Volume 5: The Impact of European Institutions on the Rule of Law and Democracy: Slovenia and Beyond
Matej Avbelj and Jernej Letnar Cernic

The Effectiveness of the Köbler Liability in National Courts

Zsófia Varga

·HART·
OXFORD · LONDON · NEW YORK · NEW DELHI · SYDNEY

HART PUBLISHING

Bloomsbury Publishing Plc

Kemp House, Chawley Park, Cumnor Hill, Oxford, OX2 9PH, UK

1385 Broadway, New York, NY 10018, USA

HART PUBLISHING, the Hart/Stag logo, BLOOMSBURY and the Diana logo are trademarks of Bloomsbury Publishing Plc

First published in Great Britain 2020

A catalogue record for this book is available from the British Library.

Library of Congress Cataloging-in-Publication data

Names: Varga, Zsófia, author.

Title: The effectiveness of the Köbler liability in national courts / Zsófia Varga.

Description: Oxford, UK ; New York, NY : Hart Publishing, an imprint of Bloomsbury Publishing, 2020. | Series: EU law in the member states ; volume 6 | Includes bibliographical references and index.

Identifiers: LCCN 2020027274 (print) | LCCN 2020027275 (ebook) | ISBN 9781509939190 (hardback) | ISBN 9781509939213 (ePDF) | ISBN 9781509939206 (Epub)

Subjects: LCSH: Government liability—European Union countries. | Administrative responsibility—European Union countries. | Damages—European Union countries. | Res judicata—European Union countries. | Court of Justice of the European Union. | Courts—European Union countries.

Classification: LCC KJE5786 .V37 2020 (print) | LCC KJE5786 (ebook) | DDC 342.408/8—dc23

LC record available at https://lccn.loc.gov/2020027274

LC ebook record available at https://lccn.loc.gov/2020027275

ISBN: HB: 978-1-50993-919-0
ePDF: 978-1-50993-921-3
ePub: 978-1-50993-920-6

Typeset by Compuscript Ltd, Shannon

Acknowledgements

I WOULD LIKE to convey special thanks to my former colleagues at the Research and Documentation Directorate of the Court of Justice of the European Union. I would certainly never have started such a comparative research project had I not had the privilege of working, between 2011 and 2017, within this extraordinary team composed of competent lawyers from each Member State. Knowing that I had the possibility to turn to them for help was an important incentive in carrying out this research. They contributed to this research project in two essential ways. On the one hand, through their daily work, especially with the establishment of the Court of Justice's former publication, 'Reflets', which provided information about notable legal developments in the legal systems of the Member States. On the other hand, they were helpful in responding to my questions and directing my attention to important developments. Therefore, I owe special thanks to Paweł Bańczyk from Poland, Erwin Beysen from Belgium, Elizabeth Borg from Malta, Marina Borkoveca from Latvia, Maria Helena Cardoso Ferreira from Portugal, Keiva Marie Carr from Ireland, Anna Czubinski from France, Ingrid Dussard from Belgium, Patrick Embley from the United Kingdom, Anthea Galea from Malta, Anke Geppert from Germany, Ramona Grimbergen from the Netherlands, Andrea Grgić from Croatia, Victoria Hanley-Emilsson from the United Kingdom, Ave Hussar from Estonia, Sally Janssen from Belgium, Sven Gael Kaufmann from Germany, Petra Komadina from Croatia, Diana Kušteková from the Czech Republic, Giovanna Lanni from Italy, Cornelia Leeb from Austria, Michael George Loizou from Cyprus, Monika Mazur from Poland, Valéria Magdová from Slovakia, Loris Nicoletti from Belgium, Garyfalia Nikolakaki from Greece, María Pilar Núñez Ruiz from Spain, Jerker Olsson from Sweden, Veera Pedersen from Finland, Ragne Piir from Estonia, Suzana Prisacariu from Romania, Cristina Maria Prunaru from Romania, Sabina Ruffo from Italy, Lina Satkutė from Lithuania, Saša Sever from Slovenia, Jens Holm Steenberg from Denmark, Nadezhda Todorova from Bulgaria, Loïc Wagner from France, Johannes Windisch from Austria, as well as to Sabine Hackspiel, Philippe Singer and Professor Rüdiger Stotz for having recruited me into this team. Of course, all mistakes remain mine.

This book is essentially based on my PhD thesis which I completed at the Eötvös Loránd University, Budapest in 2016. Therefore, I would also like to express my sincere gratitude to Professor Réka Somssich, supervisor of my doctoral thesis, for her support and advice, as well as to Professor Ernő Várnay who has been the most tenacious mentor of my academic activities for almost a decade now.

I owe special thanks to my family: my mother, on whom I can always count on; my father, the sharpest legal mind I have ever known; my husband, who made it possible for me to pursue my research projects during our family time; and Júlia and Péter who give a sense to everything I do.

The manuscript was closed on 1 August 2018 and following that date only the most important developments in ECJ and ECtHR case-law could be taken into account. All views expressed in this book are my own.

Comments are welcome at: zsofia.varga@hotmail.com

Contents

Acknowledgements .... *v*
Case-Law .... *xv*
i. Court of Justice of the European Union .... *xv*
ii. European Court of Human Rights .... *xxv*
iii. National Case-Law .... *xxvi*
Legal Acts .... *xli*
i. European Union .... *xli*
ii. ECHR .... *xlii*
iii. National Acts .... *xlii*

1. Introduction 1
I. Theoretical Background 1
II. National Courts and Remedial Competence 5
III. ECJ Case-Law on State Liability for Breach of EU Law by Courts 7
A. The *Köbler* Case 8
B. The *Traghetti del Mediterraneo* Case 9
C. The *Ferreira da Silva e Brito e.a.* Case 10
D. The *Tomášová* Case 12

2. Conclusions from the Past 14
I. Difficulties Hindering the Application of the *Köbler* Principle 14
II. Problems Inherent to the Principle 15
A. Criterion of the Manifestly Serious Breach 15
i. The ECJ Judgment 15
a. Violation of the Applicable EU Law 17
b. Factors to be Considered 19
ii. Procedural Obligations of Member State Courts to Apply EU Law 20
a. Procedural Rule of Reason and Limitations to the Ex Officio Application of EU Law 20
(1) Procedural Rule of Reason 20
(2) National Procedural Autonomy and the *Köbler* Doctrine 21
b. Application of EU Provisions with Direct Effect 23
(1) Principle and Limits of Direct Effect 23
(2) Manifest Infringement of the Direct Effect Principle 25

c. Disapplication of National Legal Provisions Contrary to EU Law 26
(1) Principle and Limits of Primacy 26
(2) Manifest Infringement of the Disapplication Obligation 28
d. Conforming Interpretation of the National Rule with EU Law 29
(1) Principle and Limits of Conforming Interpretation 29
(2) Manifest Infringement of the Consistent Interpretation Obligation 32
e. Obligation to Give a Correct Interpretation to the Substantive Norm or Rule 33
(1) Obligation and Limits of the Correct Interpretation Principle 33
(2) Manifest Infringement of the Correct Interpretation Obligation 33
f. Interim Conclusions Regarding the Gravity of the Violation of the Procedural Obligations 34
g. Obligation to Submit a Request for a Preliminary Ruling to the ECJ 35
(1) Preliminary Remarks 35
(2) Obligation to Make a Reference for a Preliminary Ruling 35
(3) Simple or a Serious Breach of the Referral Duty 38
(4) Development of the ECJ Case-Law on the Violation of the Referral Duty and the Consequences Thereof 38
(5) Conclusion on the Violation of the Referral Duty 40
iii. Manifest Infringement of the Applicable Law and Impact of a Breach of the Referral Duty 41
a. Analysis 41
(1) Manifest Breach of the Applicable Law 41
(2) Impact of the Violation of the Referral Duty on the Gravity of the Breach 44
b. Conclusion on the Impact of the Breach of the Referral Duty on the Infringement 45
iv. Case-Law of the Member State Courts 46
a. Unsuccessful Liability Claims 46
(1) Absence of Manifest Infringement as a Result of the Ambiguity of the EU Law Provision 46
(2) Absence of Violation of the Referral Duty 48

(3) Absence of Violation of Sustantive EU Law 50
(4) Absence of Violation of the Referral Obligation as well as of the Substantive EU Law 52
b. Successful Liability Claims 53
(1) Infringement of EU Law by Several Branches of Government...54
(2) Liability Established Following the ECJ Preliminary Ruling in the Case 55
(3) Specific National Rules Favourable to the Establishment of Judicial Liability.....................56
(4) Establishment of Liability by a Lower-Instance Court..57
v. Conclusion on the Manifest Infringement.......................58
B. Difficulties in Establishing Causality 59
i. Concurrent Liability of Several Branches of Government..60
ii. Causation in the Case of Multiple Breaches....................62
a. Theory...62
b. ECJ Case-Law on Multiple Breaches: The *Commission v Italy* Case 63
c. Tendency to Avoid the Inculpation of the Judiciary 64
iii. The Principle of Mitigation of Damages 64
a. Duty of Mitigation..64
b. ECJ Case-Law on the Effectiveness Principle: The *Metallgesellschaft* and *Fuß* Cases......................65
c. ECJ Case-Law on the Equivalence Principle: The *Transportes Urbanos* Case 67
d. Principle of National Procedural Autonomy 67
e. ECJ Case-Law on the National Procedural Autonomy Principle: The *Tomášová* Case 68
iv. National Case-Law on Liability Claims for Breach of Rights under the VAT Directives 69
a. Liability Actions Based on Legislative Omission........70
b. Liability Actions Based on a Breach by the Tax Administration...72
c. Liability Actions Based on a Breach by the Judiciary 73
d. Liability Action Based on a Breach by Several Branches of Government 75
e. Conclusion on the Allocation of the Responsibility 76

v. The Situation of Sole Breach by one Member State Body 77
a. Liability of the Legislature....77
b. Liability of the Administration 78
c. Liability of the Judicature....78
(1) ECJ Judgment on Purely Judicial Violation of Substantive EU Law: The *Commission v Spain* Case 79
(2) ECJ Judgment on Purely Judicial Violation of the Referral Duty: The *Commission v France* Case....79
(3) ECJ Judgment on Purely Judicial Violation of the Charter: The *EU v Gascogne e.a.* Cases....80
vi. Conclusion on Concurrent Liability of Several Breaches of Government 80
III. National Legislative Restrictions and Recognition of the Principle by National Courts 81
A. Overview of the National Legislative Restrictions 82
B. National Case-Law....83
i. Regimes Compatible with EU Law 83
a. Denmark....83
b. Latvia 84
c. Spain 84
d. Sweden 87
ii. Acknowledgement of the Köbler Principle Through National Case-Law....87
a. Belgium....88
b. Bulgaria 90
c. Germany....92
d. France....93
e. Lithuania 96
f. The Netherlands 97
g. Austria....99
h. Portugal....100
i. Finland 102
j. United Kingdom....103
iii. Acknowledgement of the *Köbler* Principle Through Legislation....104
a. Italy....104
b. Poland 105
iv. Member States Refusing the Application of the *Köbler* Principle....108
a. Czech Republic....109
b. Hungary 110
c. Ireland 112

v. Member States Without any Sign of Accommodation or Refusal ... 113
a. Cyprus ... 113
b. Croatia ... 114
c. Estonia ... 114
d. Greece ... 114
e. Luxembourg ... 115
f. Malta ... 115
g. Romania ... 115
h. Slovakia ... 116
i. Slovenia ... 116
C. Consequences of the Köbler Judgment on National Rules ... 117
i. Duplication of Liability Regimes and Spill-Over Effect ... 117
ii. Conclusion on National Restrictions ... 118
IV. Alternative Remedies in Use in the Member States ... 119
A. Retrial on the Ground of Violation of EU Law ... 119
i. Theory on Retrial ... 119
ii. ECJ Case-Law on Retrial ... 120
iii. Judgment of the ECtHR in the *Dangeville* Case ... 124
iv. Member States' Positions ... 125
a. Overview of the Legislative Provisions ... 125
b. Retrial Available in Extraordinary Situations ... 127
(1) Denmark ... 127
(2) Cyprus ... 127
(3) Lithuania ... 127
(4) Malta ... 129
(5) Finland ... 129
(6) Sweden ... 131
c. Retrial Available Based on Violation of EU Law under Certain Circumstances ... 131
(1) Bulgaria ... 131
(2) Poland ... 132
(3) Romania ... 133
(4) Slovakia ... 134
(5) United Kingdom ... 135
(d) Retrial not Available Based on Violation of EU Law ... 136
(1) Belgium ... 136
(2) Czech Republic ... 136
(3) Germany ... 137
(4) Estonia ... 137
(5) Ireland ... 138
(6) Greece ... 138
(7) Spain ... 138

(8) France 139
(9) Croatia 139
(10) Italy 139
(11) Latvia 140
(12) Luxembourg 140
(13) Hungary 140
(14) The Netherlands 141
(15) Austria 142
(16) Portugal 142
(17) Slovenia 142
e. Conclusion on the Remedy of Retrial 143
(1) Comparative Analysis of National Rules 143
(2) Relationship between State Liability and Retrial 145
(3) Prior or Subsequent Judgment 147
B. Constitutional Complaint on the Ground of Infringement of the Lawful Judge Principle 148
i. Right to One's Lawful Judge and the Obligation to Make a Preliminary Reference to the ECJ 148
ii. ECtHR Case-Law on the Obligation to Make a Preliminary Reference 151
iii. Lawful Judge Cases Before the Member State Courts 156
a. Czech Republic 156
b. Germany 157
c. Austria 162
d. Slovenia 164
e. Slovakia 165
f. Spain* 166
iv. Member States Reluctant to Apply the Lawful Judge Principle to the ECJ 167
a. Hungary 168
v. Conclusion on the Remedy of Constitutional Complaint 169
C. Special Remedies 171
i. *Amtshaftungsanspruch* under Austrian Law 171
ii. *Anhörungsrüge* under German Law 172
iii. *Domvilla* under Swedish Law 172
iv. *Vollstreckungsabwehrklage* and *Drittwiderspruchsklage* under German Law 172
v. *Recours dans l'intérêt de la loi* under French Law 173
vi. *Wytyk* under Polish Law 173
vii. Recovery of Tax Declared Incompatible with EU Law 173
D. Conclusion on Alternative Remedies 174
V. Conclusions on the History of the Köbler Liability 175

3. Perspectives for the Future ... 177
I. Adequate Liability Standard Instead of Manifest Infringement ... 177
II. Effective Remedial System Instead of Effective Remedies ... 179
A. Foundations of the State Liability Principle ... 180
B. Effectiveness and Effective Judicial Protection ... 181
C. ECJ Case-Law on Alternative Remedies ... 182
D. Doctrinal Views on Alternative Remedies ... 188
E. ECtHR Case-Law on Effective Judicial Protection ... 189
F. Conclusion on the Effective Remedial System ... 189
III. Violation of the Referral Duty as a Separate Ground for Liability ... 191
A. ECJ Case-Law and the Doctrine ... 191
i. ECJ Case-Law on the Violation of the Referral Duty ... 191
ii. Doctrinal Views ... 193
iii. National Case-Law ... 194
B. Analysis ... 195
i. Referral Duty as a Procedural Obligation Imposed on the National Courts ... 196
ii. Referral Duty as a Substantive Norm of the Treaty ... 197
a. Right to Have a Request for a Preliminary Ruling Submitted to the ECJ ... 198
(1) ECtHR Case-Law ... 198
(2) National Case-Law ... 199
(3) ECJ Case-Law Developments ... 200
IV. Damages Liability on the Grounds of Violation of the Charter ... 201
A. Referral Duty and the Charter ... 201
i. Right to Statements of Reasons for a Refusal to Submit a Referral to Preliminary Ruling ... 203
a. ECtHR Case-Law ... 203
b. National Case-Law ... 204
c. Case-Law and Doctrine ... 205
ii. Right to an Effective Judicial Protection ... 208
a. Case-Law and Doctrine ... 208
B. Undue Delay in Proceedings ... 208
C. Conclusion on Liability for Violation of the Referral Duty and of the Charter ... 211

4. Findings ... 213
I. Conclusions from the Past ... 213
A. Genuine Life of *Köbler* Doctrine Before National Courts ... 213
B. Impact and Importance of the *Köbler* Principle ... 215
C. Other Means of Remedies in Use ... 215

II. Perspectives for the Future 216
A. Harmonisation of National Remedies at EU Level.................216
B. Effective Judicial Protection in the Event of Violation of EU law by Member State Courts.......................................217
C. Violation of the Duty to Refer a Preliminary Question to the ECJ as a Ground for a Liability Claim........................218

Annex...220
Bibliography 222
Index..239

Case-Law

i. Court of Justice of the European Union

Opinion 1/09 of 8 March 2011, EU:C:2011:123 .... 5, 200, 212
Opinion 2/13 of the Court of 18 December 2014, EU:C:2014:2454 .... 154, 200, 212
Judgment of 11 September 2014 in *A*, C-112/13, EU:C:2014:2195 26
Judgment of 15 September 2011 in *Accor*, C-310/09, EU:C:2011:581 40
Judgment of 4 July 2006 in *Adeneler and Others*, C-212/04, EU:C:2006:443 31
Judgment of 27 June 2013 in *Agrokonsulting-04*, C-93/12, EU:C:2013:432 .... 181, 189
Judgment of 26 February 2013 in *Åkerberg Fransson*, C-617/10, EU:C:2013:105 .... 26, 131, 202
Judgment of 18 March 2010 in *Alassini and Others*, C-317/08 to C-320/08, EU:C:2010:146 182
Judgment of 23 April 2009 in *Angelidaki and Others*, C-378/07 to C-380/07, EU:C:2009:250 31
Judgment of 15 March 2017 in *Aquino*, C-3/16, EU:C:2017:209 ....7, 36, 78, 191–92
Judgment of 26 September 1996 in *Arcaro*, C-168/95, EU:C:1996:363 ...... 24, 32
Judgment of 17 July 2008 in *Arcor AG and others*, C-152/07 to C-154/07, EU:C:2008:426 24
Judgment of 14 December 2016 in *ASML Netherlands BV*, C-283/05, EU:C:2006:787 207
Judgment of 15 January 2014 in *Association de mediation sociale v Union locale des syndicats CGT and Others*, C-176/12, EU:C:2014:2.....27
Judgment of 6 October 2009 in *Asturcom Telecomunicaciones*, C-40/08, EU:C:2009:615 21
Opinion of Advocate General van Gerven in *Banks*, C-128/92, EU:C:1993:860 23
Judgment of 15 April 2010 in *Barth*, C-542/08, EU:C:2010:193 21
Judgment of 6 November 2018 in *Bauer and Willmeroth*, C-596/16 and C-570/16, EU:C:2018:871 27
Judgment of 17 December 1998 in *Baustahlgewebe v Commission*, C-185/95 P, EU:C:1998:608 210
Judgment of 19 January 1982 in *Becker*, 8/81, EU:C:1982:7 24
Judgment of 17 March 2016 in *Bensada Benallal*, C-161/15, EU:C:2016:175 21
Judgment of 3 May 2005 in *Berlusconi and Others*, C-387/02, C-391/02 and C-403/02, EU:C:2005:270 .... 24, 28, 32, 58

Opinion of Advocate General Kokott in *Berlusconi and Others*, C-387/02, C-391/02 and C-403/02, EU:C:2004:624 28
Judgment of 29 April 2004 in *Björnekulla*, C-371/02, EU:C:2004:275....31
Judgment of 10 July 1997 in *Bonifaci and Others et Berto and Others*, C-94/95 and C-95/95, EU:C:1997:348....183
Judgment of 5 March 1996 in *Brasserie du pêcheur and Factortame*, C-46/93 and C-48/93, EU:C:1996:79 ....8, 61, 89, 180, 208
Opinion of Advocate General Tesauro in *Brasserie du pêcheur and Factortame*, C-46/93 and C-48/93, EU:C:1995:407....182
Judgment of 24 September 1998 in *Brinkmann*, C-319/96, EU:C:1998:429....196
Judgment of 26 March 1996 in *British Telecommunications*, C-392/93, EU:C:1996:131 20
Judgment of 27 March 1974 in *BRT v SABAM*, 127/73, EU:C:1974:25....23
Judgment of 8 June 2000 in *Carra and Others*, C-258/98, EU:C:2000:301....26
Judgment of 16 December 2008 in *Cartesio*, C-210/06, EU:C:2008:723....36
Judgment of 27 October 2009 in *ČEZ*, C-115/08, EU:C:2009:660....30
Judgment of 30 April 1996 in *CIA Security International*, C-194/94, EU:C:1996:172....27
Judgment of 6 October 1982 in *Cilfit and Others*, 283/81, EU:C:1982:335....36–40, 42–45, 52–53, 150, 152–53, 156, 161, 164, 169–70, 193, 197–200, 203, 208
Judgment of 4 April 2017 in *Claire Staelen v European Ombudsman*, C-337/15 P, EU:C:2017:256....208
Judgment of 21 November 2002 in *Cofidis*, C-473/00, EU:C:2002:705.... 21, 23
Judgment of 14 January 1997 in *Comateb and Others*, C-192/95 to C-218/95, EU:C:1997:12.... 3, 173, 182
Judgment of 9 December 2010 in *Combinatie Spijker Infrabouw-De Jonge Konstruktie and Others*, C-568/08, EU:C:2010:751....67
Judgment of 16 December 1976 in *Comet*, 45/76, EU:C:1976:191 .... 6, 181
Judgment of 19 March 2009 in *Commission v Finland*, C-10/08, EU:C:2009:171....103
Judgment of 4 April 1974 in *Commission v France*, 167/73, EU:C:1974:35 25
Judgment of 8 October 2018 in *Commission v France*, C-416/17, EU:C:2018:811....39–40, 43, 79, 177, 192, 201
Opinion of Advocate General Wathelet in *Commission v France*, C-416/17, EU:C:2018:626 192
Judgment of 26 April 2005 in *Commission v Ireland*, C-494/01, EU:C:2005:250....39
Order of 6 August 2009 in *Commission v Ireland*, C-455/08, EU:C:2009:491....147

Judgment of 25 October 1979 in *Commission v Italy*, 159/78, EU:C:1979:243 ... 25
Judgment of 9 December 2003 in *Commission v Italy*, C-129/00, EU:C:2003:656 ... 63
Judgment of 29 June 2006 in *Commission v Italy*, C-487/04, EU:C:2006:435 ... 25
Judgment of 24 November 2011 in *Commission v Italy*, C-379/10, EU:C:2011:775 ... 105
Judgment of 1 April 2004 in *Commission v Jégo-Quéré*, C-263/02 P, EU:C:2004:210 ... 66, 200
Judgment of 29 June 2010 in *Commission v Luxembourg*, C-526/08, EU:C:2010:379 ... 122
Judgment of 22 December 2010 in *Commission v Slovakia*, C-507/08, EU:C:2010:802 ... 120, 122, 145–46
Judgment of 6 October 2005 in *Commission v Spain*, C-204/03, EU:C:2005:588 ... 72
Judgment of 12 November 2009 in *Commission v Spain*, C-154/08, EU:C:2009:695 ... 79, 86
Opinion of Advocate General Bobek in *Commission v Zagoriou*, C-217/16, EU:C:2017:358 ... 123
Judgment of 18 July 2013 in *Consiglio Nazionale dei Geologi and Autorità garante della concorrenza e del mercato*, C-136/12, EU:C:2013:489 ... 7, 36, 191
Judgment of 4 December 1997 in *Daihatsu Deutschland*, C-97/96, EU:C:1997:581 ... 24, 77
Judgment of 24 March 2009 in *Danske Slagterier*, C-445/06, EU:C:2009:178 ... 21, 65, 67
Judgment of 21 December 2011 in *Danske Svineproducenter*, C-316/10, EU:C:2011:863 ... 196
Judgment of 22 December 2010 in *DEB*, C-279/09, EU:C:2010:811 ... 181–82, 189, 202, 207
Judgment of 4 June 1992 in *Debus*, C-13/91 and C-113/91, EU:C:1992:247 ... 26
Judgment of 8 April 1976 in *Defrenne*, 43/75, EU:C:1976:56 ... 23
Judgment of 12 June 2014 in *Deltafina v Commission*, C-578/11 P, EU:C:2014:1742 ... 80, 210
Opinion of Advocate General Jacobs in *Denkavit Internationaal and Others*, C-2/94, EU:C:1996:85 ... 182
Judgment of 27 March 1980 in *Denkavit italiana*, 61/79, EU:C:1980:100 ... 147
Judgment of 16 July 2009 in *Der Grüne Punkt – Duales System Deutschland v Commission*, C-385/07 P, EU:C:2009:456 ... 80, 210
Judgment of 19 April 2016 in *DI*, C-441/14, EU:C:2016:278 ... 19, 27, 30–32
Judgment of 16 July 2015 in *Diageo Brands*, C-681/13, EU:C:2015:471 ... 192

Judgment of 8 October 1996 in *Dillenkofer and Others*, C-178/94, C-179/94 and C-188/94 to C-190/94, EU:C:1996:375 ....20, 196
Judgment of 24 January 2012 in *Dominguez*, C-282/10, EU:C:2012:33 ....28, 30–31
Judgment of 17 September 1997 in *Dorsch Consult*, C-54/96, EU:C:1997:413........................196
Judgment of 3 October 2013 in *Duarte Hueros*, C-32/12, EU:C:2013:637........................21, 31
Judgment of 6 October 2015 in *East Sussex County Council*, C-71/14, EU:C:2015:656........................21
Judgment of 1 June 1999 in *Eco Swiss*, C-126/97, EU:C:1999:269 21
Judgment of 17 April 2018 in *Egenberger*, C-414/16, EU:C:2018:257........................27
Judgment of 7 March 1996 in *El Corte Inglés*, C-192/94, EU:C:1996:88 ....24, 28, 77, 196
Judgment of 5 October 2010 in *Elchinov*, C-173/09, EU:C:2010:581 26
Judgment of 26 September 2000 in *Engelbrecht*, C-262/97, EU:C:2000:492........................30
Judgment of 13 July 1989 in *Erichem Base*, 380/87, EU:C:1989:318........................24
Judgment of 22 May 2014 in *Érsekcsanádi Mezőgazdasági*, C-56/13, EU:C:2014:352........................67
Judgment of 2 May 2006 in *Eurofood IFSC Ltd*, C-341/04, EU:C:2006:281........................207
Judgment of 13 December 2018 in *EU v Gascogne Sack Deutschland and Gascogne*, C-138/17 P and C-146/17 P, EU:C:2018:1013 ....80, 211
Opinion of Advocate General Wahl in *EU v Gascogne Sack Deutschland and Gascogne*, C-138/17 P, C-146/17 P, C-150/17 P, C-174/17 P, C-222/17 P 210
Judgment of 13 December 2018 in *EU v Kendrion*, C-150/17 P, EU:C:2018:1014........................80, 211
Judgment of 24 September 1998 in *EvoBus Austria*, C-111/97, EU:C:1998:434........................196
Judgment of 14 July 1994 in *Faccini Dori*, C-91/92, EU:C:1994:292........................24, 28, 77, 196
Judgment of 19 June 1990 in *Factortame and Others*, C-213/89, EU:C:1990:257........................6
Judgment of 3 September 2009 in *Fallimento Olimpiclub*, C-2/08, EU:C:2009:506........................21, 120, 122, 145–46
Judgment of 10 June 2010 in *Fallimento Traghetti del Mediterraneo SpA v Presidenza del Consiglio dei Ministri*, C-140/09, EU:C:2010:335........................56, 194
Judgment of 2 December 1997 in *Fantask and Others*, C-188/95, EU:C:1997:580........................173
Opinion of Advocate General Jacobs in *Fantask and Others*, C-188/95, EU:C:1997:321........................3, 182

Judgment of 15 November 2016 in *Fernand Ullens de Schooten*, C-268/15, EU:C:2016:874. .... 7, 121
Opinion of Advocate General Bot in *Ferreira da Silva e Brito e.a.*, C-160/14,EU:C:2015:390 36
Judgment of 9 September 2015 in *Ferreira da Silva e Brito e.a.*, C-160/14, EU:C:2015:565 .... 10–11, 19, 36, 38, 82–83, 101–02, 119
Judgment of 19 November 2009 in *Filipiak*, C-314/08, EU:C:2009:719 26
Judgment of 23 October 2014 in *flyLAL-Lithuanian Airlines* AS, C-302/13, EU:C:2014:2319 205–06
Judgment of 19 June 2014 in *FLS Plast v Commission*, C-243/12 P, EU:C:2014:2006 .... 80, 210
Judgment of 30 April 2014 in *FLSmidth v Commission*, C-238/12 P, EU:C:2014:284 .... 80, 210
Judgment of 20 November 2008 in *Folesev*, C-18/08, EU:C:2008:647 23
Judgment of 11 July 1989 in *Ford España*, 170/88, EU:C:1989:306 25
Judgment of 12 July 1990 in *Foster*, C-188/89, EU:C:1990:313 24
Judgment of 12 July 2012 in *Fra.bo*, C-171/11, EU:C:2012:453 23
Opinion of Advocate General Mischo in *Francovich and Others*, C-6/90 and C-9/90, EU:C:1991:221 182
Judgment of 19 November 1991 in *Francovich and Others*, C-6/90 and C-9/90, EU:C:1991:428 .... 6, 21, 67, 175, 180, 196
Judgment of 14 October 2010 in Fuß, C-243/09, EU:C:2010:609 .... 65–66, 187
Judgment of 10 January 2017 in *Gascogne Sack Deutschland and Gascogne v EU*, T-577/14, EU:T:2017:1 .... 80, 210
Judgment of 26 November 2013 in *Gascogne Sack Deutschland v Commission*, C-40/12 P, EU:C:2013:768 .... 80, 210
Judgment of 17 November 2011 in *Gaydarov*, C-430/10, EU:C:2011:749 205
Judgment of 25 July 2018 in *Georgsmarienhütte and Others*, C-135/16, EU:C:2018:582 200
Judgment of 15 November 2012 in *Gothaer Allgemeine Versicherung and Others*, C-456/11, EU:C:2012:719 122
Judgment of 6 October 1970 in *Grad, 9/70*, EU:C:1970:78 23
Judgment of 26 November 2013 in *Groupe Gascogne v Commission*, C-58/12 P, EU:C:2013:770 .... 80, 210
Judgment of 17 July 1997 in *GT-Link*, C-242/95, EU:C:1997:376 69
Judgment of 24 June 2004 in *Handlbauer*, C-278/02, EU:C:2004:388 23
Judgment of 10 November 1992 in *Hansa Fleisch Ernst Mundt*, C-156/91, EU:C:1992:423 23
Judgment of 23 May 1996 in *Hedley Lomas*, C-5/94, ECR EU:C:1996:205 .... 61, 89

Opinion of Advocate General Léger in *Hedley Lomas*, C-5/94, EU:C:1995:193 182
Judgment of 15 October 1987 in *Heylens and Others*, 222/86, EU:C:1987:442 .... 62, 189
Judgment of 7 August 2018 in *Hochtief*, C-300/17, EU:C:2018:635 66
Order in *Hochtief Aktiengesellschaft*, C-362/18, EU:C:2019:1100 7
Judgment of 15 October 2009 in *Hochtief and Linde-Kca-Dresden*, C-138/08, EU:C:2009:627 196
Judgment of 29 July 2019 in *Hochtief Solutions AG Magyarországi Fióktelepe*, C-620/17, EU:C:2019:630 .... 7, 112, 141, 193
Opinion of Advocate General Bobek in *Hochtief Solutions AG Magyarországi Fióktelepe*, C-620/17, EU:C:2019:340 193
Order of 6 December 2004 in *i-21 Germany and Arcor*, C-392/04 and C-422/04, EU:C:2004:83 121
Judgment of 19 May 2011 in *Iaia and Others*, C-452/09, EU:C:2011:323 196
Judgment of 8 March 2012 in *Iberdrola*, T-221/10, EU:T:2012:112 183
Judgment of 9 October 2014 in *ICF v Commission*, C-467/13 P, EU:C:2014:2274 .... 80, 210
Judgment of 15 April 2008 in *Impact*, C-268/06, EU:C:2008:223 .... 24, 31, 182, 184
Judgment of 10 July 2014 in *Impresa Pizzarotti*, C-213/13, EU:C:2014:2067 .... 119–20, 122–23, 146
Judgment of 3 October 2013 in *Inuit Tapiriit Kanatami and Others v Parliament and Council*, C-583/11 P, EU:C:2013:625 .... 186, 200
Judgment of 11 January 2007 in *ITC*, C-208/05, EU:C:2007:16 30
Judgment of 3 May 2002 in *Jégo-Quéré v Commission*, T-177/01, EU:T:2002:112 .... 66, 186
Judgment of 15 May 1986 in *Johnston*, 222/84, EU:C:1986:206 .... 24, 62, 181, 189
Judgment of 22 December 2010 in joined cases *Gavieiro and Torres*, C-444/09 and C-456/09, EU:C:2010:819 184–85
Judgment of 27 February 1980 in *Just*, 68/79, EU:C:1980:57 .... 21, 69
Judgment of 16 March 2006 in *Kapferer*, C-234/04, EU:C:2006:17 .... 21, 120, 122, 141, 146
Judgment of 30 April 2014 in *Kásler and Káslerné Rábai*, C-26/13, EU:C:2014:282 30
Judgment of 12 February 2008 in *Kempter*, C-2/06, EU:C:2008:78 147
Judgment of 26 November 2013 in *Kendrion v Commission*, C-50/12 P, EU:C:2013:771 .... 80, 210
Judgment of 1 February 2017 in *Kendrion v EU*, T-479/14, EU:T:2017:48 .... 80, 210
Judgment of 11 November 2015 in *Klausner Holz Niedersachsen*, C-505/14, EU:C:2015:742 .... 121–22, 145

Order of 8 October 1998 in *Köbler*, C-382/97, EU:C:1998:471 8
Judgment of 30 September 2003 in *Köbler*, C-224/01,
EU:C:2003:513 ....7, 11, 16, 18–19, 25, 34, 38, 42, 52, 58, 81, 92, 141
Opinion of Advocate General Léger in *Köbler*, C-224/01,
EU:C:2003:207 ....20, 41, 193, 204
Judgments of 5 July 2007 in *Kofoed*, C-321/05, EU:C:2007:408 .... 24, 32
Judgment of 8 October 1987 in *Kolpinghuis Nijmegen*, 80/86,
EU:C:1987:431 .... 24, 32
Judgment of 24 October 1996 in *Kraaijeveld and Others*, C-72/95,
EU:C:1996:404 ....21, 190
Judgment of 15 January 2013 in *Križan and Others*, C-416/10,
EU:C:2013:8 181
Judgment of 19 January 2010 in *Kücükdeveci*, C-555/07,
EU:C:2010:21 .... 27, 32, 167
Judgment of 13 January 2004 in *Kühne & Heitz*, C-453/00,
EU:C:2004:17 ....121, 132, 137, 141, 147, 190
Judgment of 4 July 2000 in *Laboratoires Pharmaceutiques Bergaderm SA*,
C-352/98, EU:C:2000:361 208
Judgment of 17 May 1972 in *Leonesio*, 93/71, EU:C:1972:39 23
Judgment of 1 December 1998 in *Levez*, C-326/96, EU:C:1998:577 183–84
Judgment of 15 October 2002 in *Limburgse Vinyl Maatschappij and Others v Commission*, C-238/99 P, C-244/99 P, C-245/99 P, C-247/99 P, C-250/99 P to C-252/99 P and C-254/99 P, EU:C:2002:582..... 210
Opinion of Advocate General Léger in *Linster*, C-287/98, EU:C:2000:3 28
Judgment of 19 July 2012 in *Littlewoods Retail Ltd and Others*,
C-591/10, EU:C:2012:478 67
Judgment of 18 July 2007 in *Lucchini*, C-119/05, EU:C:2007:434........ 119, 121–22, 134, 140, 145
Judgment of 4 June 2002 in *Lyckeskog*, C-99/00, EU:C:2002:329 36
Judgment of 14 April 2015 in *Manea*, C-76/14, EU:C:2015:216.................... 147
Judgment of 22 November 2005 in *Mangold*, C-144/04, EU:C:2005:709 .... 27, 32
Judgment of 11 July 2002 in *Marks & Spencer*, C-62/00 EU:C:2002:435 24
Judgment of 13 November 1990 in *Marleasing*, C-106/89,
EU:C:1990:395.. 30–31
Judgment of 26 February 1986 in *Marshall*, 152/84, EU:C:1986:84........... 24, 77
Judgment of 10 July 1997 in *Maso and Others*, C-373/95,
EU:C:1997:353...182–83
Judgment of 5 October 2010 in *McB*, C-400/10, EU:C:2010:582 207
Judgment of 26 November 2015 in *MedEval*, C-166/14, EU:C:2015:779 66
Judgment of 22 June 2010 in *Melki and Abdeli*, C-188/10 and C-189/10,
EU:C:2010:363...26

Judgment of 8 March 2001 in *Metallgesellschaft and Others*, C-397/98 and C-410/98, EU:C:2001:134 ....65–66, 69, 187
Judgment of 22 November 2012 in *MM*, C-277/11, EU:C:2012:744.... 206
Judgment of 16 July 2009 in *Mono Car Styling*, C-12/08, EU:C:2009:466....31, 182
Judgment of 5 November 2014 in *Mukarubega*, C-166/13, EU:C:2014:2336.... 206
Judgment of 4 February 1988 in *Murphy and Others*, 157/86, EU:C:1988:62 30
Judgment of 7 September 2006 in *N*, C-470/04, EU:C:2006:525 20
Judgment of 15 February 2001 in *Nachi Europe*, C-239/99, EU:C:2001:101.... 183
Judgment of 4 October 2018 in *Nikolay Kantarev v Balgarska narodna banka*, C-571/16, EU:C:2018:807 ....7, 66, 91
Opinion of Advocate General Bobek in *Oana Mădălina Călin*, C-676/17, EU:C:2019:94.... 123
Judgment of 27 June 2000 in *Océano Grupo Editorial and Salvat Editores*, C-240/98 to C-244/98, EU:C:2000:346....23
Judgment of 6 October 2015 in *Orizzonte Salute*, C-61/14, EU:C:2015:655.... 181
Judgment of 1 June 2006 in *P & O European Ferries (Vizcaya) and Diputación Foral de Vizcaya v Commission*, C-442/03 P and C-471/03 P, EU:C:2006:356 122
Judgment of 12 March 1996 in *Pafitis and Others*, C-441/93, EU:C:1996:92....27
Judgment of 10 July 1997 in *Palmisani*, C-261/95, EU:C:1997:351....67
Judgment of 4 June 2009 in *Pannon GSM*, C-243/08, EU:C:2009:350.... 21, 23
Judgment of 14 December 1995 in *Peterbroeck*, C-312/93, EU:C:1995:437 21
Judgment of 5 October 2004 in *Pfeiffer and Others*, C-397/01 to C-403/01, EU:C:2004:584 ....24, 27–28, 31
Opinion of Advocate General Ruiz-Jarabo Colomer in *Pfeiffer and Others*, C-397/01 to C-403/01, EU:C:2003:245....28
Opinion of Advocate General Ruiz-Jarabo Colomer in *Pfeiffer and Others*, C-397/01 to C-403/01, EU:C:2004:227....28
Judgment of 15 July 1963 in *Plaumann v Commission*, 25/62, EU:C:1963:17 186
Judgment of 29 October 2009 in *Pontin*, C-63/08, EU:C:2009:666..... 184
Judgment of 16 June 2005 in *Pupino*, C-105/03, EU:C:2005:386....24, 30, 32
Judgment of 5 April 1978 in *Ratti*, 148/78, EU:C:1979:110 .... 24, 30
Judgment of 7 July 1981 in *Rewe-Handelsgesellschaft Nord and Rewe-Markt Steffen*, 158/80, EU:C:1981:163 ....6, 21, 67, 181
Judgment of 16 December 1976 in *Rewe-Zentralfinanz and Rewe-Zentral*, 33/76, EU:C:1976:188 .... 21, 67
Judgment of 21 June 1974 in *Reyners*, 2/74, EU:C:1974:68....23

Judgment of 12 September 2006 in *Reynolds Tobacco and Others v Commission*, C-131/03 P, EU:C:2006:541 187
Judgment of 25 January 2007 in *Robins and Others*, C-278/05, EU:C:2007:56 20
Judgment of 8 March 2007 in *Roquette Frères*, C-441/05, EU:C:2007:150....... 183
Judgment of 21 May 1976 in *Roquette Frères v Commission*, 26/74, EU:C:1976:69 69
Judgment of 28 March 1996 in *Ruiz Bernáldez*, C-129/94, EU:C:1996:143..........27
Judgment of 22 January 1976 in *Russo*, 60/75, EU:C:1976:9 .... 21, 67
Judgment of 28 July 2011 in *Samba Diouf*, C-69/10, EU:C:2011:524 185
Judgment of 9 November 1983 in *San Giorgio*, 199/82, EU:C:1983:318........ 173
Judgment of 28 October 2010 in *SGB Belgium*, C-367/09, EU:C:2010:648......23
Judgment of 15 December 1976 in *Simmenthal*, 106/77, EU:C:1978:49 ...... 6, 26
Judgment of 11 December 2012 in *Sina Bank*, T-15/11, EU:T:2012:661 183
Judgment of 29 April 2015 in *Staelen v European Ombudsman*, T-217/11, EU:T:2015:238...207–08
Judgment of 18 January 2001 in *Stockholm Lindöpark*, C-150/99, EU:C:2001:34 .... 20, 69, 183
Judgment of 22 April 1997 in *Sutton*, C-66/95, EU:C:1997:207 .... 3, 182
Judgment of 6 October 2015 in *Târşia*, C-69/14, EU:C:2015:662...... 21, 119–20, 123, 134, 146, 173, 185
Opinion of Advocate General Jääskinen in *Târşia*, C-69/14, EU:C:2015:269...134, 146, 185
Order of 6 December 2006 in *Test Claimants in the FII Group Litigation*, C-446/04, EU:C:2006:761 .... 20, 69
Judgment of 13 March 2007 in *Test Claimants in the Thin Cap Group Litigation*, C-524/04, EU:C:2007:161 .... 20, 65
Order of 23 April 2008 in *Test Claimants in the CFC and Dividend Group Litigation*, C-201/05, EU:C:2008:239 .... 20, 65
Judgment of 29 March 2011 in *ThyssenKrupp Nirosta v Commission*, C-352/09, EU:C:2011:191 122
Judgment of 30 June 2016, in *Toma and Biroul Executorului Judecătoresc Horaţiu-Vasile Cruduleci*, C-205/15, EU:C:2016:499........202, 207
Judgment of 28 July 2016 in *Tomášová*, C-168/15, EU:C:2016:602..... 12–13, 20, 42–43, 68–69, 82, 113, 116, 186, 190–91
Opinion of Advocate General Wahl in *Tomášová*, C-168/15, EU:C:2016:260.. 12, 69
Judgment of 6 September 2012 in *Trade Agency*, C-619/10, EU:C:2012:531..205–07
Judgment of 13 June 2006 in *Traghetti del Mediterraneo*, C-173/03, EU:C:2006:391 .... 9–10, 44, 53, 55, 82, 93, 101, 105, 107–08, 187, 194

Judgment of 26 January 2010 in *Transportes Urbanos y Servicios Generales*, C-118/08, EU:C:2010:39 ......67, 71–72, 123
Judgment of 9 March 1994 in *TWD Textilwerke Deggendorf*, C-188/92, EU:C:1994:90 183
Judgment of 13 March 2007 in *Unibet*, C-432/05, EU:C:2007:163 ......7, 66, 182, 185, 189
Judgment of 28 January 1999 in *Unilever*, C-77/97, EU:C:1999:30 27
Judgment of 26 September 2000 in *Unilever*, C-443/98, EU:C:2000:496 27
Judgment of 25 July 2002 in *Unión de Pequeños Agricultores v Council*, C-50/00 P, EU:C:2002:462 187
Opinion of Advocate *General Jacobs in Unión de Pequeños Agricultores v Council*, C-50/00 P, EU:C:2002:197 66
Judgment of 23 October 2014 in *Unitrading*, C-437/13, EU:C:2014:2318 67
Judgment of 7 June 2007 in *van der Weerd and Others*, C-222/05 to C-225/05, EU:C:2007:318 21
Judgment of 4 December 1974 in *van Duyn*, 41/74, EU:C:1974:133 26
Judgment of 5 February 1963 in *van Gend & Loos*, 26/62, EU:C:1963:1 23
Judgment of 14 December 1995 in *van Schijndel and van Veen*, C-430/93 and C-431/93, EU:C:1995:441 21
Order of 14 October 2008 in *VB Pénzügyi Lízing and Pannon GSM*, C-137/08 and C-243/08, EU:C:2008:564 23
Order of 28 June 2011 in *Verein Deutsche Sprache v Council*, C-93/11 P, EU:C:2011:429 187
Judgment of 11 July 1991 in *Verholen and Others*, C-87/90 to C-89/90, EU:C:1991:314 21
Judgment of 11 December 2007 in *Viking*, C-438/05, EU:C:2007:772 23
Judgment of 10 April 1984 in *von Colson and Kamann*, 14/83, EU:C:1984:153 30–31
Judgment of 18 September 2014 in *Vueling Airlines*, C-487/12, EU:C:2014:2232 30
Judgment of 12 December 1974 in *Walrave and Koch*, 36/74, EU:C:1974:140 23
Judgment of 7 January 2004 in *Wells*, C-201/02, EU:C:2004:12 ......21, 67
Judgment of 16 October 2014 in *Welmory*, C-605/12, EU:C:2014:2298 196
Opinion of Advocate General Wahl in X *and van Dijk*, C-72/14 and C-194/14, EU:C:2015:319 36
Judgment of 24 October 2018 in *XC e.a.*, C-234/17, EU:C:2018:853 ......21, 121–23, 127, 181, 187, 201, 212
Judgment of 4 June 2013 in *ZZ*, C-300/11, EU:C:2013:363 205

ii. European Court of Human Rights

Arlewin v Sweden, Judgment of 1 March 2016, no 22302/10........................154
Baydar v The Netherlands, Judgment of 24 April 2018, no 55385/14......154–55, 199, 203–04, 207
Bosphorus Hava Yolları Turizm ve Ticaret Anonim Şirketi v Ireland [GC], Judgment of 30 June 2005, no 45036/98, ECHR 2005-VI 152, 154, 199, 203
Cappello v Italy, Judgment of 27 February 1992, no 12783/87, Series A no 230-F 209
Cipolletta v Italy, Judgment of 11 January 2018, no 38259/09 209
Cocchiarella v Italy [GC], Judgment of 29 March 2006, no 64886/01, ECHR 2006-V 189
Coëme and Others v Belgium, Judgment of 22 June 2000, nos 32492/96 32547/96 32548/96 33209/96 33210/96, ECHR 2000-VII.........................204
Desmots v France, Decision of 23 March 1999, no 41358/98, ECHR 2001-XI (extracts)...152
Dhahbi v Italy, Judgment of 8 April 2014, no 17120/09 ....152, 154, 203
Divagsa Company v Spain, Decision of 12 May 1993, no 20631/92... 37, 151–52
Dotta v Italy, Decision of 7 September 1999, no 38399/97 152
Ferreira Santos Pardal v Portugal, Judgment of 30 July 2015, no 30123/10. ....34, 57, 101, 153
Gazsó v Hungary, Judgment of 16 July 2015, no 48322/12 209
Greneche and Others v France, Decision of 15 October 2013, no 34538/08 152
Harisch v Germany, Judgment of 11 April 2019, no 50053/16 .... 152, 155, 199, 203
Herma v Austria, Decision of 8 December 2009, no 54193/07......................152
Hornsby v Greece, Judgment of 19 March 1997, no 18357/91........... 43, 45, 151
İlhan v Turkey [GC], Judgment of 27 June 2000, no 22277/93, ECHR 2000-VII...189, 209
Kaya v Turkey, Judgment of 19 February 1998, no 158/1996/777/978, Reports 1998-I, 329–30 ....189, 209
Kudła v Poland [GC], Judgment of 26 October 2000, no 30210/96, ECHR 2000-XI...189, 209
Lukenda v Slovenia, Judgment of 6 October 2005, no 23032/02, ECHR 2005-X 189
McFarlane v Ireland [GC], Judgment of 10 September 2010, no 31333/06 209
Micallef v Malta [GC], Judgment of 15 October 2009, no 17056/06 90
Negrea and Others v Romania, Judgment of 24 July 2018, no 53183/07 209
Peter Moosbrugger v Austria, Decision of 25 January 2000, no 44861/98........ 152

Repcevirág Szövetkezet v Hungary, Judgment of 30 April 2019, no 70750/14 .... 111, 155, 199, 203–04
Rutkowski v Poland, Judgment of 7 July 2015, no 72287/10 209
Ryon and Others v France, Decision of 15 October 2013, no 33014/08 152
SA Dangeville v France, Judgment of 16 April 2002, no 36677/97, ECHR 2002-III 70, 124
San Leonard Band Club v Malta, Judgment of 29 July 2004, no 77562/01, ECHR 2004-IX 129
Sanofi Pasteur v France, Judgment of 13 February 2020, no 25137/16. .... 153, 155–56
Schipani v Italy, Judgment of 21 July 2015, no 38369/09 .... 38, 153, 156, 199, 203
Schweighofer and Others v Austria, Decision of 24 August 1999, nos 35673/97, 35674/97, 36082/97 and 37579/97 152
Scordino v Italy (no 1) [GC], Judgment of 29 March 2006, no 36813/97, ECHR 2006-V 209
Sindicatul pro Asistenţă Socială v Romania, Decision of 6 March 2014, no 24456/13 152
Somorjai v Hungary, Judgment of 28 August 2018, no 60934/13 152
Stichting Mothers of Srebrenica v The Netherlands, Decision of 11 June 2013, no 65542/12, Reports of Judgments and Decisions 2013 152
Sürmeli v Germany [GC], Judgment of 8 June 2006, no 75529/01, ECHR 2006-VII 209
Ullens de Schooten and Rezabek v Belgium, Judgment of 20 September 2011, nos 3989/07 and 38353/07 .... 152, 154, 199, 203
Valada Matos das Neves v Portugal, Judgment of 29 October 2015, no 73798/13 209
Vilho Eskelinen and Others v Finland [GC], Judgment of 19 Avril 2007, no 63235/00 209
Vocaturo v Italy, Judgment of 24 May 1991, no 11891/85, § 17, Series A no 206-C 209
Wallishauser v Austria (no 2), Judgment of 20 June 2013, no 14497/08 152
Živulinskas v Lithuania, Decision of 12 December 2006, no 34096/02 204

iii. National Case-Law

Belgium

Hof van beroep te Brussel, arrest, 23/12/2015 78
Cour de Cassation, arrêt, 19/12/1991, no 215 .... 88, 176

Cour de Cassation, arrêt, 14/01/2000, C980477F 88
Cour de Cassation, arrêt, 05/06/2008, no 347 88
Cour de Cassation, arrêt, 23/06/2008, C.05.0012.F/1,
Fruytier Scierie/Province de Luxembourg et Région wallonne 71
Cour de Cassation, arrêt, 25/03/2010, no 219 88–89
Cour constitutionnelle, arrêt, 30/06/2014, no 99/2014 .... 87, 89, 117, 176
Cour constitutionnelle, arrêt, 23/02/2017, no 29/2017 89

Bulgaria

Varhoven kasatsionen sad, Reshenie, 09/02/2012, no 1155/2011 131
Varhoven administrativen sad, Reshenie, 03/07/2012, no 9588 132
Sofiyski gradski sad, Reshenie, 03/01/2014, Pretsiz-2
EOOD/Varhoven administrativen sad, no 1782/2013 .... 46, 52–53, 74–75, 87, 91, 176
Varhoven kasatsionen sad, Opredelenie, 08/05/2015, no 269 .... 87, 91, 176
Okrazhen sad Yambol, Reshenie, 04/11/2015, no 407/2014 .... 14, 55, 76, 92
Varhoven kasatsionen sad, Opredelenie, 03/02/2016, no 45 91
Apelativen sad – Burgas, Reshenie, 26/04/2016, no 96/2016 .... 14, 54–55, 60, 75–76, 87, 91–92, 215

Czech Republic

Nejvyšší správní soud, rozsudek ze dne, 29/09/2005, 2 Afs 92/2005-45 30
Ústavní soud, usnesení ze dne 21/02/2006, Pl ÚS 19/04 26
Ústavní soud, usnesení ze dne 02/12/2008, Pl ÚS 12/08 26
Ústavní soud, nález ze dne 31/01/2012, Pl ÚS 5/12 29
Ústavní soud, nález ze dne 08/01/2009, II ÚS 1009/08 .... 156, 200, 205
Nejvyšší správní soud, rozsudek ze dne, 27/10/2010, 7
Afs 79/2010-94 137
Ústavní soud, nález ze dne 29/11/2011, II ÚS 1658/11 .... 157, 200, 205
Nejvyšší soud, rozsudek ze dne, 20/08/2012, 28 Cdo 2927/2010,
ECLI:CZ:NS:2012:28. CDO.2927.2010.1 109
Nejvyšší soud, usnesení ze dne, 10/12/2012, 30 Cdo 3036/2015,
ECLI:CZ:NS:2015:30.CDO.3036.2015.1 109
Ústavní soud, usnesení ze dne 02/12/2013, IV ÚS 136/13 109
Nejvyšší soud, rozsudek ze dne, 02/03/2016, 30 Cdo 4622/2015,
ECLI:CZ:NS:2016:30. CDO.4622.2015.1 .... 59, 109

Denmark

Vestre Landsret, dom af 09/11/2005, *Cimber Air A/S/Skatteministeriet*,
TfS 2005.957 72
Højesteret, Judgment, 06/12/2016, *Dansk Industri (DI) acting for Ajos A/S v the estate left by* A, 15/2014, UfR 2017.824 H 31–32, 42, 118, 162

Germany

Bundesverfassungsgericht, Beschluß, 22/10/1986, 2 BvR 197/83....................158
Bundesverfassungsgericht, Beschluß, 08/04/1987, 2 BvR 687/85......118, 160, 162
Bundesverfassungsgericht, Beschluß, 09/11/1987, 2 BvR 808/82...................158
Bundesverfassungsgericht, Beschluß, 05/08/1998, 1 BvR 264/98,
ECLI:DE:BVerfG:1998:rk19980805. 1bvr026498 158–59
Bundesverfassungsgericht, Beschluss, 09/01/2001, 1 BvR 1036/99,
ECLI:DE:BVerfG:2001:rk20010109. 1bvr103699 160
Bundesverfassungsgericht, Beschluss, 10/05/2001, 1 BvR 481/01,
ECLI:DE:BVerfG:2001:rk20010510. 1bvr048101 158–59
Bundesverfassungsgericht, Beschluss, 30/01/2002, 1 BvR 1542/00,
ECLI:DE:BVerfG:2002:rk20020130. 1bvr154200 158–59
Bundesgerichtshof, Urteil, 09/10/2003, III ZR 342/02..................................147
Oberlandesgericht Köln, Urteil, 31/03/2004, 6 U 158/03..............................137
Bundesverfassungsgericht, Beschluss, 29/07/2004, 2 BvR 2248/03,
ECLI:DE:BVerfG:2004:rk20040729. 2bvr224803 160
Bundesgerichtshof, Beschluss, 28/10/2004, III ZR 294/03 ....46, 52, 87, 92–93, 176
Bundesfinanzhof, 13/01/2005, V R 35/03 73
Bundesfinanzhof, 21/04/2005, V R 16/04 73
Bundesverfassungsgericht, Beschluss, 27/04/2005, 1 BvR 223/05,
ECLI:DE:BVerfG:2005:rk20050427. 1bvr022305 161
Oberlandesgericht Köln, Urteil, 02/06/2005, 7 U 29/04..................................71
Oberlandesgericht Karlsruhe, Urteil, 09/03/2006, 12 U 286/05.......................93
Bundesverfassungsgericht, Beschluss, 14/07/2006, 2 BvR 264/06,
ECLI:DE:BVerfG:2006:rk20060714. 2bvr026406 158–59
Oberlandesgericht Frankfurt, Urteil, 13/03/2008, 1 U 244/07..........................93
Bundesverfassungsgericht, Beschluss, 06/05/2008, 2 BvR 2419/06,
ECLI:DE:BVerfG:2008:rk20080506. 2bvr241906 159
Bundesverwaltungsgericht, Urteil, 09/06/2009, 1 C 7.08,
NVwZ 2009, 1431, ECLI:DE:BVerwG: 2009:090609U1C7.08.0....... 44, 46–47, 87, 92, 176
Bundesverwaltungsgericht, Urteil, 22/10/2009, 1 C 26.08 173
Bundesverfassungsgericht, Beschluss, 25/02/2010, 1 BvR 230/09,
ECLI:DE:BVerfG:2010:rk20100225. 1bvr023009 ....161, 170
Bundesverfassungsgericht, Beschluss, 06/07/2010, 2 BvR 2661/06,
ECLI:DE:BVerfG: 2010:rs20100706.2bvr266106..............................158–59
Bundesverfassungsgericht, Beschluss, 30/08/2010, 1 BvR 1631/08,
ECLI:DE:BVerfG:2010: rk20100830.1bvr163108 161
Bundesverfassungsgericht, Beschluss, 10/11/2010, 1 BvR 2065/10,
ECLI:DE:BVerfG:2010: rk20101110.1bvr206510 158–59
Landgericht Wiesbaden, Urteil, 07/02/2011, 13 O 119/06 173
Kammergericht Berlin, Urteil, 24/06/2011, 9 U 233/10..................................70

Bundesverfassungsgericht, Beschluss, 21/11/2011, 2 BvR 516/09, ECLI:DE:BVerfG:2011: rk20111121.2bvr051609 160
Bundesverfassungsgericht, Beschluss, 15/12/2011, 2 BvR 148/11, ECLI:DE:BVerfG:2011:rk20111215. 2bvr014811 .... 158, 160
Bundesgerichtshof, Beschluss, 26/04/2012, III ZR 215/11 71
Bundesverfassungsgericht, Beschluss, 19/12/2017, 2 BvR 424/17, ECLI:DE:BVerfG:2017: rs20171219.2bvr042417 161

Estonia

Riigikohtu halduskolleegiumi, kohtuotsus, 28/11/2012, no3-3-1-37-12 114
Riigikohtu halduskolleegiumi, kohtuotsus, 31/10/2013, no 3-3-1-84-12 114
Riigikohtu üldkogu, 10/03/2008, no 3-3-2-1-0 146
Riigikohtu halduskolleegiumi, 22/02/2010, no 3-3-2-1-10 146

Ireland

Blackhall v Grehan [1995] 3 IR 208 138
Supreme Court, judgment, *Kathleen Byrne v Ireland the the Attorney General* [1972] 112
Court of Chancery, 20/07/1943, *Henderson v Henderson* [1843] Hare 99 .... 112–13, 138
House of Lords, judgment, 12/02/1974, *Sutcliffe v Thackrah* [1974] AC 727 112
Supreme Court, judgment, 30/07/1986, *Pine Valley Developments Ltd v Minister for the Environment* [1987] ILRM 747 112
Circuit Court, judgment, 29/10/1990, *Dublin Bus v The Motor Insurance Bureau of Ireland* (MIBI) 112
High Court, judgment, 03/02/1995, *Tate v Minister for Social Welfare* [1995] 1 ILRM 507, 1 IR 418 112
High Court, judgment, 25/02/2009, *Kemmy v Ireland & Anor* [2009] IEHC 178 112
High Court, judgment, 07/03/2013, *BUPA Ireland Ltd & anor v The Health Insurance Authority & ors* [2013] IEHC 103 112
Supreme Court, judgment, 13/07/2017, *Ogieriakhi v Minister for Justice & Equality and ors*, 51/2015, [2017] IESC 52 112
High Court, judgment, 17/10/2017, *Cronin v Dublin City Sheriff & anor* [2017] IEHC 685 .... 22, 109, 113, 138

Greece

Άρειος Πάγος (Areios Pagos), 256/1996 114
Συμβούλιο της Επικρατειας (Symvoulio tis Epikrateias) 2744/2000 114
Άρειος Πάγος (Areios Pagos), 14/12/2004, 1845/2005, NOMOS 138, 146

Trimeles Dioikitiko Protodikeio Peiraia, apofasi tis 06/10/2010, 4768/2010.....30
Άρειος Πάγος (Areios Pagos), 16/03/2011, 484/2011, NOMOS.....................138
Άρειος Πάγος (Areios Pagos), 24/02/2012, 353/2012, NOMOS.......114, 138, 146

Spain

Tribunal Constitucional de España (Sala Segunda), Sentencia 58/2004, 19/04/2004, *Generalidad de Cataluña y Administración General del Estado/Herederos de Manuel Martínez Calderón*, Recurso de amparo 4979–1999.....166
Tribunal Constitucional de España (Sala Segunda), Sentencia, 19/06/2006, 194/2006, *Gobierno de Canarias/Real Club Náutico de Gran Canaria*, Recurso de amparo 6182–2004.....166
Tribunal Supremo, Sala de lo Contencioso-Administrativo, Secciòn 6ª, auto de 01/02/2008, *Transportes Urbanos y Servicios Generales SAL/Consejo de Ministros*.....72
Tribunal Supremo, Sala de lo Contencioso-Administrativo, Secciòn 6ª, auto de 17/09/2010, Transportes Urbanos y Servicios Generales SAL/Consejo de Ministros, no de Recurso 153/2007.....71
Tribunal Supremo, Sala de lo Contencioso, Secciòn 6ª, Sentencia, 29/05/2015, no de Recurso 664/2013, ECLI:ES:TS:2015:2413.....86
Tribunal Supremo, Sala de lo Contencioso, Secciòn 1, Sentencia, 19/12/2016, no de Recurso 16/2016, ECLI:ES:TS:2016:5705.....139
Tribunal Supremo, Sentencia, 01/09/1991.....147
Tribunal Supremo, Sala de lo Civil, Secciòn 1, Sentencia, 18/02/2016, no de Recurso 67/2013, ECLI:ES:TS:2016:515.....139
Tribunal Supremo, Sala de lo Civil, Sentencia, 23/01/2004, *José Luis Mazon Costa/Magistrados del Tribunal Constitucional*, No 51/2004.....85, 117
Audiencia Nacional, Sentencia, 10/02/2009, no de Recurso 553/2007, ECLI:ES:AN:2009:415.....86
Audiencia Nacional, Sentencia, 23/04/2009, no de Recurso 362/2007, ECLI:ES:AN:2009:1823.....85
Audiencia Nacional, Sentencia, 30/04/2009, no de Recurso 542/2007, ECLI:ES:AN:2009:2167.....86
Audiencia Nacional, Sentencia, 04/06/2009, no de Recurso 798/2007, ECLI:ES:AN:2009:2686.....86
Audiencia Nacional, Sentencia, 23/06/2009, no de Recurso 546/2007, ECLI:ES:AN:2009:3209.....86
Tribunal Constitucional de España (Pleno), Sentencia, 20/10/2010, 78/2010, Recurso de amparo 8427-2006.....167
Audiencia Nacional, Sentencia, 04/12/2012, no de Recurso 622/2011, ECLI:ES:AN:2012:4581.....84, 86
Audiencia Nacional, Sentencia, 04/11/2013, no de Recurso 133/2013, ECLI:ES:AN:2013:4519.....86

Audiencia Nacional, Sentencia, 30/10/2014, no de Recurso 710/2012, ECLI:ES:AN:2014:4466 86
Tribunal Constitucional de España (Pleno), Sentencia, 05/11/2015, 232/2015, Recurso de amparo 1709-2013 167

France

Conseil d'État, 10ème et 9ème sous-sections réunies, 29/03/2006, décision, 274923, *Centre d'exportation du livre francais et Ministre de la culture et de la communication*, ECLI:FR:CE SSR:2006:274923.20060329, publié au recueil Lebon 139
Conseil d'État, 3ème et 8ème sous-sections réunies, décision, 19/03/1986, 46105, *SA Cabinet Jacques Dangeville*, publié au recueil Lebon 26, 124
Conseil d'État, 3ème sous-section jugeant seule, décision, 30/12/2009, 303506, *Société Phytoservice*, inédit au recueil Lebon 94
Conseil d'État, 4ème et 5ème chambres réunies, décision, 21/09/2016, 394360, ECLI:FR:CECHR:2016:394360.20160921, *Société Lactalis Ingrédients*, mentionné dans les tables du recueil Lebon 94, 103
Conseil d'État, 4ème sous-section jugeant seule, décision, 27/03/2013, 351528, *Société Phytoservice*, ECLI:FR:CESJS:2013:351528.20130327, inédit au recueil Lebon 65, 94
Conseil d'État, 5ème et 4ème sous-sections réunies, décision, 18/06/2008, 295831, *Gestas/Garde des sceaux Ministre de la justice*, ECLI:FR:CESSR:2008:295831.20080618, publié au recueil Lebon 46, 87, 94, 176
Conseil d'État, 8ème et 3ème sous-sections réunies, 10/12/2012, décision, *Rhodia*, no 317074, ECLI:FR:XX:2012:317074.20121210, mentionné dans les tables du recueil Lebon 39
Conseil d'État, 8ème et 3ème sous-sections réunies, 10/12/2012, décision, *Accor*, no 317075, ECLI:FR:CESSR:2012:317075.20121210, inédit au recueil Lebon 39
Conseil d'État, Assemblé, décision, 26/10/2001, 197018, *Ternon*, ECLI:FR:CEASS:2001:197018.20011026, publié au recueil Lebon 139
Conseil d'État, Assemblée, arrêt, 30/10/1996, 141043,*SA Jacques Dangeville*, ECLI:FR:CEASS:1996:141043.1996103, publié au recueil Lebon 81, 124
Conseil d'État, Assemblée, arrêt, 30/10/1996, 45126, *SA Cabinet Revert et Badelon*, ECLI:FR:CEASS:1996:45126.19961030, publié au recueil Lebon 81, 124
Conseil d'État, Assemblée, décision, 28/06/2002, 239575, *Garde des Sceaux, Ministre de la justice/M Magiera*, ECLI:FR:CEASS:2002:239575.20020628, publié au recueil Lebon 210
Conseil d'État, Assemblée, décision, 29/12/1978, 96004, *Darmont*, ECLI:FR:CEASS:1978:96004.19781229, publié au recueil Lebon 93–94, 210

Cour administrative d'appel de Douai, 3e chambre, décision, 09/06/2011, 10DA00077, inédit au recueil Lebon 70
Cour administrative d'appel de Nantes, 4ème chambre, 30/03/2012, 11NT00536, *Ministère du budget des comptes publics et de la réforme de l'État*, inédit au recueil Lebon 81
Cour administrative d'appel de Nantes, 5ème chambre, décision, 25/07/2017, 16NT03263, *SNC Lactalis Ingrédients*, inédit au recueil Lebon 44, 48, 95
Cour administrative d'appel de Paris, Section plénière, arrêt, 01/07/1992, 89PA02498, *Société Jacques Dangeville*, publié au recueil Lebon 81, 124
Cour d'appel de Paris, Pôle 2 Chambre 1, arrêt, 06/05/2015, 13/05638, *SCA Acolyance Société coopérative agricole*.....14, 51, 53, 57, 96
Cour d'appel de Paris, Pôle 2 Chambre 1, arrêt, 16/03/2010, 08/17093..... 50, 95
Cour d'appel de Paris, Pôle 2 Chambre 1, arrêt, 22/09/2015, 2014/01386 95
Cour d'appel de Paris, Pôle 2 Chambre 1, arrêt, 31/10/2017, 15/20011, *Sàrl Dugong investissement*.....210
Cour de cassation, Assemblée Plénière, arrêt, 18/11/2016, 15-21.438, *Société Acolyance, société Cohesis distribution*, ECLI:FR:CCASS:2016:AP00630, publié au bulletin.....14, 46, 51, 58, 89, 96, 109
Cour de cassation, Chambre criminelle, arrêt, 25/10/2016, 16-80.366, *Société Laboratoires de Biologie Réunis*, ECLI:FR:CCASS:2016: CR05288, publié au bulletin 162
Cour de cassation, Première chambre civile, arrêt, 26/10/2011, 10-24.250, *Société Mc Cormick Guadeloupe*, publié au bulletin 46, 49, 87, 176
Cour de cassation, Première chambre civile, arrêts, 26/10/2011, 10-24.251 to 10-24.262, inédit au bulletin..... 49, 95
Tribunal administrative de Rennes, décision, 16/12/2010, 0903640 81
Tribunal de conflict, décision, 31/03/2008, 08-03631, publié au bulletin.....94
Tribunal de grande instance de Paris, 1re chambre 1re section, 07/05/2008, 04/13911, *Ministère Public* 46, 176

Croatia

None .....

Italy

Corte di Cassazione, Prima sezione civile, sentenza, 26/07/2002, no 11046.....209
Corte di Cassazione, Sezione tributaria, sentenza, 14/07/2004, *Società Sief e altra/Amministrazione delle finanze dello Stato* 26

Corte di Cassazione, Sezioni unite civili, sentenza, 19/05/2008, no 12641 140
Tribunale di Genova, ordinanza, 31/03/2009, no 1329, *Fallimento Traghetti del Mediterraneo/Repubblica italiana* 14, 53, 55, 87, 105, 194, 215
Tribunale di Roma, Seconda sezione civile, sentenza, 23/03/2011, no 639, *Lucchini SpA/Ministero Attività produttive* 140
Corte di Cassazione, Prima sezione civile, sentenza, 25/05/2015, no 10749........ 105
Corte di Cassazione, Sezione terza penale, sentenza, 15/09/2015, no 2210...... 26
Corte Costituzionale, sentenza, 03/04/2017, no 164/2017 105

Cyprus

None ....

Latvia

Augstākās tiesas Senāts, 18/12/2013, Lietā nr C04330607, nr SKC-3/2013........ 30
Latvijas Republikas Augstākās tiesas, Senāta Administratīvo lietu departamenta, spriedums, 14/11/2011, Lietā nr SJA-35/2011.................. 140
Latvijas Republikas Augstākās tiesas, Senāta Civillietu departamenta, spriedums, 24/11/2010, Lietā nr SKC-233/2010 84

Lithuania

Lietuvos Respublikos Konstitucinis Teismas, Nutarimas, 19/08/2006, Bylos Nr 23/04 96–97
Lietuvos vyriausiojo administracinio teismo, 10/04/2008, nutartis administracinėje byloje Nr P444-129/2008 .... 97, 128, 143
Lietuvos vyriausiojo administracinio teismo, 24/04/2008, nutartis administracinėje byloje STV Lietuvos valstybė, byla Nr AS444-199/2008 .... 87, 145
Lietuvos vyriausiojo administracinio teismo, 31/07/2009, nutartis administracinėje byloje STV Lietuvos Respublika, atstovaujama Lietuvos Respublikos Konstitucinio Teismo, bylos Nr AS502-363/2009 128–29
Lietuvos apeliacinis teismas, 23/06/2014, Byla 2A-871/2014 97
Vilniaus apygardos teismas, 21/01/2015, Byla 2A-1116-392/2015 97

Luxembourg

Cour d'appel (Grand-Duché de Luxembourg), jugement, 13/01/2010, *Heiko Koelzsch/Etat du Grand-duché de Luxembourg* 176
Cour d'appel (Grand-Duché de Luxembourg), jugement, 21/03/2012, *Heiko Koelzsch/Etat du Grand-duché de Luxembourg* 115

Hungary

Debreceni Ítélőtábla, ítélet, 01/06/2010, Pf.II.20.884/2009/4 110
Fővárosi Törvényszék, ítélet, 29/05/2012, 2.P.24.000/2010/19 110
Fővárosi Törvényszék, végzés, 3.Kf.650.165/2013/3 141
Fővárosi Ítélőtábla, ítélet, 31/10/2013, 9.Pf.22.126/2012/4 209
Fővárosi Törvényszék, ítélet, 05/11/2013, 4.P.23.616/2013/15 110
Kúria, ítélet, 11/12/2013, Pfv.III.22.112/2012/13 .... 22, 74, 108, 111, 155, 176
Kúria, ítélet, 28/02/2014, Pfv.III.21.591/2013/5 .... 108, 111
Alkotmánybíróság, végzés, 19/05/2014, no 3165/2014 (V 23) 111, 155, 168
Alkotmánybíróság, végzés, 07/07/2014, no 3203/2014 (VII 14) 141
Alkotmánybíróság, végzés, 15/12/2014, no 3007/2015 (I 12) 168
Alkotmánybíróság, végzés, 16/12/2014, no 3004/2015 (I 12) 168
Kúria, ítélet, 28/01/2015, Pfv.V.20.320/2014/38 209
Alkotmánybíróság, végzés, 09/02/2015, no 3036/2015 (II 20) 168
Alkotmánybíróság, végzés, 09/02/2015, no 3037/2015 (II 20) 168
Kúria, ítélet, 15/04/2015, Kfv.II.38.010/2014/15 26
Alkotmánybíróság, határozat, 14/07/2015, no 26/2015 (VII 21) 168
Fővárosi Törvényszék, végzés, 18/11/2015, 1.Kpkf.670.333/2015/7 141
Alkotmánybíróság, végzés, 4/12/2016, no 3082/2016 (IV 18) 168
Fővárosi Ítélőtábla, ítélet, 30/05/2017, 5.Pf.20.282/2017/5/II 108, 111, 118
Győri Ítélőtábla, ítélet, 29/06/2017, Pf.III.20.109/2017/5/I 108

Malta

Constitutional Court, judgment of 10 October 1991, *Frank Cachia v the honourable Prime Minister* 129

Netherlands

Hoge Raad, Uitspraak, 03/12/1971, NJ 1971, 137, ECLI:NL:HR:1971:AB6788 97
Hoge Raad, arrest van 29/03/2000, *X/Staatssecretaris van Financiën*, ECLI:NL:HR:2000:AA5297 73
Hoge Raad, Uitspraak, 07/05/2004, ECLI:NL:HR:2004:AO0082 98
Afdeling bestuursrechtspraak van de Raad van State, 27/10/2004, AB 2004, 427 141
Raad van State, 07/12/2005, AB 2006/67 30
Centrale Raad van Beroep, 17/11/2006, AB 2007, 7 141
Raad van State, 05/12/2007, AB 2008, 18 30
Rechtbank' s-Gravenhage, Uitspraak, 05/03/2010, ECLI:NL:RBSGR:2010:BL6948 .... 87, 98
Gerechtshof' s-Gravenhage, Uitspraak, 15/02/2011, ECLI:NL:GHSGR:2011:BP6841 .... 46, 87, 176

Raad van State, 29/05/2011, JB 2001/179 30
Hoge Raad, Uitspraak, 24/06/2011, ECLI:NL:HR:2011:BM9272 141
Gerechtshof' s-Gravenhage, Uitspraak, 03/06/2015,
ECLI:NL:RBDHA:2015:6222 .... 46, 51, 98

Austria

Verwaltungsgerichtshof, Erkenntnis, 21/09/2009, 2008/16/0148,
VwSlg 8471 F/2009 142
Verfassungsgerichtshof, Erkenntnis, 11/12/1995, B 2300/95,
VfSlg 14390/1995 .... 163, 172
Verfassungsgerichtshof, Erkenntnis, 30/09/1996, B 3067/95,
VfSlg 14607/1996 163
Oberster Gerichtshof, Beschluß, 27/05/1997, 5 Ob 160/97h,
ECLI:AT:OGH0002:1997:0050OB00160.97H.0527.000 .... 163, 172
Verfassungsgerichtshof, Erkenntnis, 26/06/1997, B 3486/96,
VfSlg 14889/1997 163
Verfassungsgerichtshof, Urteil, 24/02/1999, B 1625/98 26
Verfassungsgerichtshof, Erkenntnis, 30/11/1999, B 889/97,
VfSlg 15657/1999 163
Verfassungsgerichtshof, Erkenntnis, 08/03/2001, B 707/00,
VfSlg 16118/2001 163
Oberster Gerichtshof, Beschluß, 25/06/2002, 1 Ob 126/02i,
RS0116558, ECLI:AT:OGH0002:-2002:RS0116558 .... 163, 172
Oberster Gerichtshof, Urteil, 26/11/2002, 1 Ob 216/02z, RS0117101,
ECLI:AT:OGH0002:-2002:0010OB-00216.02Z.1126.000 .... 163, 172
Verfassungsgerichtshof, Erkenntnis, 30/09/2003, B 614/01 au,
VfSlg 16988/2003 163
Verfassungsgerichtshof, Erkenntnis, 10/10/2003, A36/00,
VfSlg 17019/2003 .... 87, 99, 176
Verfassungsgerichtshof, Erkenntnis, 12/12/2003, A2/01 ua,
VfSlg 17095 .... 49, 100
Verfassungsgerichtshof, Erkenntnis, 14/06/2004, A17/03,
VfSlg 17214/2004 .... 49, 99
Verfassungsgerichtshof, Erkenntnis, 13/10/2004, A5/04,
VfSlg 17330/2004 .... 48, 87, 99, 194
Oberster Gerichtshof, Urteil, 22/10/2007, 1 Ob 90/07b,
ECLI:AT:OGH0002:2007:RS0123075 .... 163, 172
Verfassungsgerichtshof, Erkenntnis, 12/06/2008, A13/07,
VfSlg 18448/2008 .... 49, 99
Verfassungsgerichtshof, Erkenntnis, 29/09/2008, A2/07,
VfSlg 18557/2008 .... 49, 99
Verfassungsgerichtshof, Erkenntnis, 22/09/2009, A14/08,
VfSlg 18866 .... 49, 100

Verfassungsgerichtshof, Beschluss, 02/05/2011, A4/10, VfSlg 19361.........49, 100
Oberster Gerichtshof, Beschluss, 12/06/2012, 4 Ob 83/12b, RS0127996, ECLI:AT:OGH0002:2012:0040OB00083.12B.0612.000........142
Verfassungsgerichtshof, Urteil, 09/10/2012, G 64/10...................................209
Verfassungsgerichtshof, Beschluss, 19/06/2013, A2/2013 ua, VfSlg 19757..49, 88, 100, 195, 209
Verfassungsgerichtshof, Beschluss, 21/11/2013, A9/2013 ua.....................49, 100
Verfassungsgerichtshof, Beschluss, 23/03/2015, E444/2015, G135/2015, A 2/2015...49, 100
Verfassungsgerichtshof, Beschluss, 11/06/2015, A1/2015.........................49, 100
Verfassungsgerichtshof, Beschluss, 11/06/2015, A3/2015.........................49, 100
Oberster Gerichtshof, Entscheidung, 22/10/2015, 10 ObS 148/14h, ECLI:AT:OGH0002:2015:010-OBS00148.14H.1022.000..........................26
Verfassungsgerichtshof, Beschluss, 19/11/2015, A8/2015.........................49, 100

Poland

Trybunał Konstytucyjny, *Gender Equality in the Civil Service Case*, Orzecznictwo Trybunalu Konstytucyjnego 19 (1997) 380, English translation in *East European Case Reports of Constitutional Law* 5 (1998) 271...30
Trybunał Konstytucyjny, 04/12/2001, SK 18/00, OT ZU 2001/8/256.............105
Sąd Najwyższy, Wyrok, 12/10/2006, I CNP 41/06.......................................108
Naczelny Sąd Administracyjny, Wyrok, 04/12/2008, I FSK 1655/07..............132
Sąd Najwyższy, Uchwała, 19/05/2009, III CZP 139/09.................................108
Sąd Najwyższy, Postanowienie, 22/10/2009, I UZ 64/09...............................132
Wojewódzki Sąd Administracyjny w Rzeszowie, Wyrok, 03/12/2009, I SA/Rz 619/09...133
Sąd Najwyższy, Wyrok, 08/12/2009, I BU 6/09.............................. 88, 108, 176
Naczelny Sąd Administracyjny, Wyrok, 24/03/2010, I FSK 242/09................133
Naczelny Sąd Administracyjny, Wyrok, 05/08/2010, I FSK 1355/2009, Lexis.pl nr 2374744..133
Naczelny Sąd Administracyjny, Postanowienie, 21/12/2010, I FNP 1/10, I FNP 5/10 and I FNP 8/10...107
Naczelny Sąd Administracyjny, Wyrok, 18/03/2011, I FSK 398/2010, LexPolonica nr 2537725...133
Naczelny Sąd Administracyjny, Wyrok, 26/08/2011, I GNP 1/11.............46, 107
Trybunał Konstytucyjny, 27/09/2012, SK 4/11...107
Naczelny Sąd Administracyjny, Wyrok, 28/02/2013, I FNP 10/12.................107
Wojewódzki Sąd Administracyjny w Olsztynie, Wyrok, 19/09/2013, I SA/Ol 486/13, LEX nr 1389573..133
Naczelny Sąd Administracyjny, Wyrok, 19/12/2013, II GNP 2/13, LEX nr 1427455...107

Wojewódzki Sąd Administracyjny w Łodzi, Wyrok z 13/02/2014, I SA/Łd 1300/13, LEX nr 1510263 133
Wojewódzki Sąd Administracyjny w Łodzi, Wyrok z 05/03/2014, I SA/Łd 1357/13, LEX nr 1443319 133
Naczelny Sąd Administracyjny, Wyrok 03/06/2014, II FSK 1545/12 25
Naczelny Sąd Administracyjny, Wyrok, 11/06/2014, I GNP 2/14 .... 46, 52, 106–07, 176
Naczelny Sąd Administracyjny, Wyrok, 26/06/2014, I FNP 5/14 .... 22, 46, 59, 88, 107
Naczelny Sąd Administracyjny, Wyrok 07/08/2014, II FSK 1980/12 25
Trybunał Konstytucyjny, Wyrok, Kp 3/08, OTK ZU 2009/2A/9 148

Portugal

Supremo Tribunal de Justiça, Acórdão, 27/11/2007, X/Estado Português, Processo: 07A3954 77
Tribunal Central Administrativo Sul 21/02/2008 78
Tribunal da Relação de Guimarães, Acórdão, 23/04/2009, 9180/07.3TBBRG.G1 .... 53, 57, 88
Supremo Tribunal de Justiça, Acórdão, 03/12/2009, Revista no 9180/07.3TBBRG.G1.S1 .... 33, 53, 57, 101, 153, 176
Supremo Tribunal de Justiça, Acórdão 24/02/2015, Processo 2210/12.9TVLSB.L1.S1 .... 101, 104
Tribunal Constitucional, Acórdão, 09/07/2015, no363/2015, Processo no 185/15 .... 88, 101, 104, 176

Romania

Curtea de Apel Timişoara, Secţia contencios administrativ şi fiscal, 06/10/2012, Decizia civilă nr 1851. .... 133, 143
Tribunalul Suceava, Secţia de contencios administrativ şi fiscal, 19/05/2011, Număr dosar 4671/86/2011, confirmed in appeal by Curtea de Apel Suceava, Secţia a II-a civilă, 10/11/2011, Număr dosar 4671/86/2011 134
Tribunalul Suceava, Secţia de contencios administrativ şi fiscal, 19/05/2011, Număr dosar 4674/86/2011, confirmed in appeal by Curtea de Apel Suceava, Secţia a II-a civilă, 13/10/2011, Număr dosar 4674/86/2011 134

Slovenia

Vrhovno sodišče Republike Slovenije, VSS 2/95, načelno pravno mnenje, občna seja VSS, 14.12.1995 116
Vrhovnega sodišča Republike Slovenije, Sodba, 13/11/2003, II Ips 556/2002, ECLI:SI:VSRS:2003:-II.IPS.556.2002 .... 59, 116

Vrhovnega sodišča Republike Slovenije, Sodba, 12/01/2005, II Ips 714/2003, ECLI:SI:VSRS:2005:-II.IPS.714.2003 .... 59, 116
Upravno sodišče Republike Slovenije, Odločba, 17/06/2008, U 14/2007 143
Ustavno sodišče Republike Slovenije, Sklep, 24/11/2009, Up-282/09, ECLI:SI:USRS:2009:Up.282.09 164
Ustavno sodišče Republike Slovenije, Odločba, 21/11/2013, Up-1056/11, ECLI:SI:USRS:-2013:Up.1056.11 .... 164, 200, 205

Slovakia

Ústavný súd Slovenskej republiky, uznesenie zo dňa 29/05/2007, III ÚS 151/07-14 .... 165, 205
Ústavný súd Slovenskej republiky, uznesenie zo dňa 03/07/2008, IV ÚS 206/08-50 .... 165, 205
Najvyšší súd Slovenskej republiky, uznesenie zo dňa 20/01/2011, 3 Cdo 10/2010 165
Krajský súd Banská Bystrica, Uznesenie, 18/12/2012, no 15Co/259/2012, 6612206417, ECLI:SK:KSBB:2012:6612206417.2 135
Krajský súd Banská Bystrica, Uznesenie, 27/06/2013, no 41Cob/9/2013, 6211200027, ECLI:SK:KSBB:2013:6211200027.4 135
Krajský súd Trnava, Uznesenie, 09/07/2013, no 24Co/196/2013, 2209209082, ECLI:SK:KSTT:2013:2209209082.1 135
Okresný súd Prešov, Rozsudok, 08/10/2013, no 8C/420/2012, 8112240798, ECLI:SK:OSPO:-2013:8112240798.2 135
Okresný súd Rožňava, Uznesenie, 20/12/2013, no 10C/581/2012 135
Okresný súd Prešov, Uznesenie, 12/03/2015, 7C 6/2010-316 .... 12, 176

Finland

Korkein oikeus, tuomio, 02/04/2007, 626, KKO:2007:34, Diaarinumero: H2006/18 130
Korkein oikeus, tuomio, 02/04/2007, 627, KKO:2007:35, Diaarinumero: H2006/166 130
Korkein hallinto-oikeus, tuomio, 07/12/2009, 2806, KHO:2009:99, Diaarinumero: 4221/2/08 130
Korkein hallinto-oikeus, tuomio, 30/06/2010, 1561, KHO:2010:44, Diaarinumero: 1043/2/09 130
Korkein hallinto-oikeus, tuomio, 11/04/2011, 1018, KHO:2011:38, Diaarinumero: 3059/2/06 130
Korkein hallinto-oikeus, tuomio, 28/11/2012, 3320, KHO:2012:104, Diaarinumero: 26/3/11 .... 94, 102
Korkein oikeus, tuomio, 05/07/2013, A Oy, KKO:2013:58, Diaarinumero S2012/143 .... 14, 53–54, 60, 74–76, 88, 103, 176, 215

Helsingin käräjäoikeus, tuomio, 30/09/2013 103
Korkein hallinto-oikeus, tuomio, 27/12/2013, 4057, KHO:2013:199, Diaarinumero: 2356/2/13 .... 130, 145
Helsingin hovioikeus, tuomio, 28/11/2014 103
Korkein oikeus, tuomio, 05/03/2016, 1011, KKO:2016:28, Diaarinumero S2015/88 .... 14, 53, 74, 103, 215

Sweden

Justitiekanslern, Beslut, 06/04/2009, Flexlink AB, drn 2409-08-40 .... 14, 53, 56, 74, 87–88, 176, 215

United Kindgdom

Court of Appeal (England), Civil Division, judgment, 08/03/2000, *The Queen/Durham County Council and others, ex parte Rodney Huddleston* 26
Court of Appeal (England), Civil Division, judgment, 12/05/2010, *Cooper/Her Majesty's Attorney General* [2010] EWCA Civ 464 .... 44, 46–47, 59, 88, 104, 176
Court of Appeal, judgment, 29/06/2010, *R v Budimir (Nikolas)* [2011] 2 WLR 396 136
Supreme Court, judgment, 15/12/2010, *R (on the application of Edwards) v Environment Agency* [2010] UKSC 57 [2011] 1 WLR 79 136

Legal Acts

i. European Union

Charter of Fundamental Rights of the European Union
[2012] OJ C326, 391–407 ....5, 80, 123, 177, 187, 195, 198, 201–212, 219
Art. 41 of the Charter 201
Art. 47 of the Charter 79, 181, 185, 189, 202, 205, 206, 207, 209, 210, 211, 218, 301
Art. 47(1) of the Charter 189
Art. 50 of the Charter 160
Art. 51 of the Charter 210
Art. 51(1) of the Charter 202, 205
Art. 52(1) of the Charter 182
Art. 52(3) of the Charter 207
Art. 53 of the Charter 189
Art. 53(2) of the Charter 207
Art. 4 of the Charter
Council Directive 2000/78/EC of 27 November 2000 establishing a general framework for equal treatment in employment and occupation [2000] OJ L303, 16–22 27
Recommendations to national courts and tribunals in relation to the initiation of preliminary ruling proceedings [2018] OJ C257, 1–7 206
Treaty establishing the European Community (Amsterdam consolidated version) [1997] OJ C340, 173–306
Art. 4(3) TEU 29, 55, 60, 81, 92
Art. 19 TEU 186
Art. 19(1) TEU 6, 181, 207
Treaty on the Functioning of the European Union [2012] OJ C326, 47–390
Art. 49 TFEU 39
Art. 63 TFEU 39
Art. 256(1) TFEU 210
Art. 258 TFEU 79, 218
Art. 260 TFEU 86, 218
Art. 263 TFEU 183, 186
Art. 267 TFEU 123, 150, 154, 159, 164, 171, 200

Art. 267(3) TFEU 11, 17, 35, 36, 37, 38, 39, 40, 42, 43, 44, 45, 52, 56, 80, 105, 110, 158, 161, 162, 175, 191, 192, 194, 195, 196, 197, 198, 200, 206, 207, 208, 211, 216
Art. 268 TFEU 187
Art. 288 TFEU 17, 24, 25, 29, 196, 197, 219
Art. 340 TFEU 180, 187, 210

ii. ECHR

Convention for the Protection of Human Rights and Fundamental Freedoms 123
Art. 6 ECHR
Art. 6(1) ECHR 207, 209
Art. 13 ECHR 209
Recommendation No R (2000) 2 of the Committee of Ministers to member states on the re-examination or reopening of certain cases at domestic level following judgements of the European Court of Human Rights (Adopted by the Committee of Ministers on 19 January 2000 at the 694th meeting of the Ministers' Deputies) 126

iii. National Acts

Belgium

Arrêté du Régent déterminant la procédure devant la section du contentieux administratif du Conseil d'État, 23/08/1948, dernière modification par la AR 2017-12-25 136
Arts40 à 50 on *Opposition, tierce opposition* (opposition) 136
Arts 50bis à 50sexies on *Recours en révision* (revision) 136
Code civil, 21/03/1804, Livre III, dernière modification par L 2018-07-22
Arts 1382–83 on *Les délits et les quasi-délits* (torts and quasi-torts) 88
Code judiciaire, 10/10/1967, Première partie, dernière modification par L 2018-05-25
Arts 23–28 on *Res judicata de la chose jugée* (res judicata) 136
Code judiciaire, 10/10/1967, Quatrième partie, dernière modification par L 2018-07-22
Arts 1113–14 on *Rétractation* (revocation – in the meaning of retrial) 136
Arts 1140–47 on *Prise à partie* (inculpation of judges) 88
Loi spéciale sur la Cour constitutionnelle (Special Act on the Constitutional Court), 06/01/1989, dernières modifications par diverses règles du 25-12-2016 136

Bulgaria

Aministrativen protsesualen kodeks / Административнопроцесуален кодекс (Administrative Procedure Code), prom SG no 30, 11.04.2006, last amend SG no 42, 22.05.2018
Art 99 on *Основания за възобновяване* (grounds for resumption).......... 131
Art 203 on *Производствазаобезщетения* (public liability) 90
Art 239 on *Основанизаотмяна* (grounds for revocation) 126, 131–32, 146
Grazhdanski protsesualen kodeks/Граждански процесуален кодекс – GPK (Civil Procedure Code), prom SG no 59, 20.07.2007, last amend SG no 42, 22.05.2018
Art 303 on *Основания за отмяна* (grounds for revocation) 126, 131, 146
Konstitutsiya na Republika Balgariya / Конституция на Република България (Constitution of the Republic of Bulgaria), prom SG no 56, 13.07.1991, las amend SG no 100, 18.12.2015
Art 7 on *Отговорността на държавата* (state liability) 90
Zakon za otgovornosta na darzhavata i obshtinite za vredi/Закон за отговорността на държавата и общините за вреди – ZODOV (Law on the liability of the state and municipalities), prom SG no 60, 5.08.1988, last amend SG no 7, 19.01.2018
Art 2 on *Отговорност за дейност на правозащитните органи* (liability for actions of the judicial authorities) 90–91
Zakon za zadalzheniata i dogovorite/Закон за задълженията и договорите – ZZD (Law on the Obligations and Contracts), prom SG no 275, 22.11.1975, last amend SG no 42, 22.05.2018
Arts 45–49 on *Непозволено увреждане* (liability for damages) 91

Czech Republic

Listina základních práv a svobod (Charter of Fundamental Rights and Basic Freedoms) Předpis č 2/1993 Sb, Novely 162/1998 Sb, Znění od 01.01.1999
Čl 38 odst.1 on *Pravo na zákon ného sudce* (right to a lawful judge) 148, 150, 156
Občanský soudní řád (Code of Civil Justice), Předpis č 99/1963 Sb, Novely 365/2017 Sb, Znění od 01.01.2018
§ 159a(4) on *Res iudicata* 137
§§ 228–29 on *Obnova řízení* (review of proceedings) 137
Ústava České republiky (Constitution of the Czech Republic), Předpis č 1/1993 Sb, Novely 98/2013 Sb, Znění od 01.06.2013
Čl 1(1) on *Právní stát* (rule of law).. 157
Čl 87, d) on *Ústavní stížnost* (constitutional complaint).................150, 156
Zákon daňový řád (Code of Fiscal Procedure), Předpis č 280/2009 Sb, Novely 94/2018 Sb, Znění od 05.06.2018
§§ 117–20 on *Obnova řízení* (review of proceedings) 137
§§ 121–24a on *Přezkummé řízení* (revision)... 137

Zákon o odpovědnosti za škodu způsobenou při výkonu veřejné moci rozhodnutím nebo nesprávným úředním postupem a o změně zákona České národní rady č 358/1992 Sb, o notářích a jejich činnosti (notářský řád) (Law on liability for damage caused in the exercise of public authority decision or incorrect official procedure), Předpis č 82/1998 Sb, Novely 105/2013 Sb, 303/2013 Sb, Znění od 01.01.2014

§ 8(1) on *Nezákonné rozhodnutí* (unlawful decisions) 109

Zákon o Ústavním soudu (Act on the Constitutional Court), Předpis č 182/1993 Sb, Novely 90/2017 Sb, Znění od 13.04.2017

§ 64 on *Řízení o zrušení zákonů a jiných právních předpisů* (proceedings for the annulment of laws) 150, 156

§ 72 on *Ústavní stížnost* (constitutional complaint) 150, 156

§ 119 on *Obnova řízení* (review of proceedings) 125, 137, 146

Zákon soudní řád správní (Code of Administrative Justice), Předpis č 150/2002 Sb, Novely 225/2017 Sb, 365/2017 Sb, Znění od 01.01.2018

§ 111 on *Obnova řízení* (retrial) 137

Zákon správní řád (Code of Administrative Procedure), Předpis č 500/2004 Sb, Novely 225/2017 Sb, Znění od 01.01.2018

§§ 94–99 on *Přezkummé řízení* (revision) 137

§§ 100–02 on *Obnova řízení* (review of proceedings) 137

Denmark

Bekendtgørelse af lov om rettens pleje (Retsplejeloven) (Administration of Justice Act), Herved bekendtgøres lov om rettens pleje, jf lovbekendtgørelse nr 1257 af 13. oktober 2016, med de ændringer, der følger af § 1 i lov nr 674 af 8 juni 2017, LBK nr 1101 af 22/09/2017 Gældende, Offentliggørelsesdato: 30/09/2017, Justitsministeriet

§ 399 on *Ekstraordinær genoptagelse og anke* (extraordinary revison and appeal) 127

§§ 975–78 on Genoptagelse (resumption) 127

Betænkning nr 214 om statens og kommunernes erstatningsansvar (Act on the Liability of Central and Local State bodies) Afgivet af det af det ved Justitsministeriet skrivelse af 24 februar 1952 nedsatte udvalg, Denmark. Justitsministeriet, 16. 83

Germany

Bundesverfassungsgerichtsgesetz (BVerfGG) (Law on the Federal Constitutional Court), Bundesverfassungsgerichtsgesetz in der Fassung der Bekanntmachung vom 11 August 1993 (BGBl I S 1473), das zuletzt durch Artikel 2 des Gesetzes vom 8 Oktober 2017 (BGBl I S 3546) geändert worden ist

§ 13, Abs 8bis on *Verfassungsbeschwerde* (constitutional complaint) 150, 157

§ 90, Ab. 1 on *Verfahren in den Fällen des § 13 Nr 8a* (procedure in the cases of § 13 8a) 150, 157
§ 95, Abs 2 on *Verfassungsbeschwerde* (constitutional complaint) 150, 157
Bürgerliches Gesetzbuch (BGB) (German Civil Code), Bürgerliches Gesetzbuch in der Fassung der Bekanntmachung vom 2 Januar 2002 (BGBl I S 42, 2909; 2003 I S 738), das zuletzt durch Artikel 6 des Gesetzes vom 12 Juli 2018 (BGBl I S 1151) geändert worden ist
§ 839, Abs 2 on *Richterspruchprivileg*/Spruchrichterprivileg (judicial immunity) 47, 92–93
Grundgesetz für die Bundesrepublik Deutschland (GG) (Basic Law for the Federal Republic of Germany), Grundgesetz für die Bundesrepublik Deutschland in der im Bundesgesetzblatt Teil III, Gliederungsnummer 100-1, veröffentlichten bereinigten Fassung, das zuletzt durch Artikel 1 des Gesetzes vom 13 Juli 2017 (BGBl. I S. 2347) geändert worden ist
Art 34 *on Amtshaftungsanspruch* (state responsibility) 47, 92–93
Art 93, Abs 1, Nr 4a on *Verfassungsbeschwerde* (constitutional complaint) 150, 157
Art 101, Abs 1, S 2 on *Recht auf den gesetzlichen Richter* (right to a lawful judge) 148, 150, 157
Strafgesetzbuch (StGB) (Criminal Code), Strafgesetzbuch in der Fassung der Bekanntmachung vom 13 November 1998 (BGBl I S 3322), das zuletzt durch Artikel 1 des Gesetzes vom 30. Oktober 2017 (BGBl I S 3618) geändert worden ist
§§ 331–58 *Straftaten in Amt* (Offences committed in public office) 92
Verwaltungsgerichtsordnung (VwGO) (Code of Administrative Court Procedure), Verwaltungsgerichtsordnung in der Fassung der Bekanntmachung vom 19 März 1991 (BGBl I S 686), die zuletzt durch Artikel 7 des Gesetzes vom 12 Juli 2018 (BGBl. I S. 1151) geändert worden ist
§ 152a on *Anhörungsrüge* (violation of the right to be heard) 172
§ 153 on *Wiederaufnahme des Verfahrens* (resumption of proceedings) 137
Verwaltungsverfahrensgesetz (VwVfG) (Federal Administrative Procedure Act) Verwaltungsverfahrensgesetz in der Fassung der Bekanntmachung vom 23 Januar 2003 (BGBl I S 102), das zuletzt durch Artikel 11 Absatz 2 des Gesetzes vom 18 Juli 2017 (BGBl I S 2745) geändert worden ist
§ 51 on *Wiederaufgreifen des Verfahrens* (resumption of the procedure) 137
Zivilprozessordnung (ZPO) (Code of Civil Procedure), Zivilprozessordnung in der Fassung der Bekanntmachung vom 5 Dezember 2005 (BGBl I S 3202; 2006 I S 431; 2007 I S 1781), die zuletzt durch Artikel 2 des Gesetzes vom 12 Juli 2018 (BGBl I S. 1151) geändert worden ist
§ 580 on *Restitutionsklage* (action for retrial) 126, 137

§ 767 on *Vollstreckungsabwehrklage* (action raising an objection to the claim being enforced) 172
§ 771 on *Drittwiderspruchsklage* (action to prevent the enforcement of a judgment) 173

Estonia

Eesti Vabariigi põhiseadus (PS, The Constitution of the Republic of Estonia) 28.06.1992 (RT 1992, 26, 349; RT I, 15.05.2015, 2), Redaktsiooni jõustumise kp: 13.08.2015
§ 24 (lawful judge) 148
§ 25 (right to compensation) 114
Halduskohtumenetluse seadustik (HKMS, Code of Administrative Court Procedure), 27.01.2011 (RT I, 23.02.2011, 3, RT I, 28.11.2017, 1) Redaktsiooni jõustumise kp: 01.01.2018
§ 240(2) 8) on *Teistmine* (retrial) 126, 137
Haldusmenetluse seadus (HMS, Administrative Procedure Act), 06.06.2001 (RT I 2001, 58, 354; RT I, 28.12.2017, 2), Redaktsiooni jõustumise kp: 01.02.2018
§§ 64–70 on *Haldusakti* muutmine ja kehtetuks tunnistamine (administrative amendment and repeal) 137
§§ 71–74 on *Vaidemenetlus* (internal review) 137
Kriminaalmenetluse seadustik (KrMS, Code of Criminal Procedure), 12.02.2003 (RT I 2003, 27, 166, RT I, 31.05.2018, 22), Redaktsiooni jõustumise kp: 10.06.2018
§ 366(7) on *Teistmise alused* (retrial) 126
Riigivastutuse seadus (RVastS, State Liability Act) 02.05.2001 (RT I 2001, 47, 260; RT I, 17.12.2015, 1), Redaktsiooni jõustumise kp: 01.07.2016
§ 7 on *Vastutuse alused* (basis of liability) 146
§ 15(1) on *Riigivastutus* (state responsibility) 114, 137
Tsiviilkohtumenetluse seadustik (TsMS, Code of Civil Procedure), 20.04.2005 (RT I 2005, 26, 197, RT I, 04.07.2017, 4), Redaktsiooni jõustumise kp: 01.03.2018
§ 702(2) 8) on *Teistmine* (retrial) 126, 137

Ireland

None

Greece

Εισαγωγικός Νόμος του Αστικού Κώδικα (Introductory Law to the Greek Civil Code), Προεδρικό Διάταγμα 456/1984: Αστικός Κώδικας και Εισαγωγικός Νόμος (ΦΕΚ 164/A/1984), 24-10-1984
Αρθρο: 105 on state liability 114

Κώδικας Διοικητικής Δικονομίας (Code of Administrative Justice), Έτος: 1999, ΦΕΚ: A 97 19990517, Τέθηκε σε ισχύ: 17.07.1999
Αρθρο: 197 on *Δεδικασμένο* (res judicata) Ημ/νία: 17.07.1999, Ημ/νία Ισχύος: 17.07.1999 138
Κώδικας Διοικητικής Διαδικασίας (Code of Administrative Procedure), ΦΕΚ: A 45 19990309, Τέθηκε σε ισχύ: 09.03.1999, Ημ. Υπογραφής: 05.03.1999, Ο παρών Κώδικας κυρώθηκε με το πρώτο άρθρο του N 2690/1999 (ΦΕΚ Α‘ 45)
Αρθρο: 25 on *Ειδική διοικητική προσφυγή – Ενδικοφανής προσφυγή* (special administrative appeal) 138
Κώδικας Ποινικής Δικονομίας (Code of Criminal Procedure), ΦΕΚ: A 182 19500817, Τέθηκε σε ισχύ: 01.01.1951
Αρθρο: 525(1) on *Επανάληψη της Διαδικασίας* (retrial) 126, 138
Κώδικας Πολιτικής Δικονομίας (Code of Civil Procedure), ΦΕΚ: A 182 19851024, Τέθηκε σε ισχύ: 16.09.1968 Ημ. Υπογραφής: 10.10.1985
Αρθρο: 538 on *Αναψηλάφηση* (reopening), Ημ/νία: 01.01.2016, Το παρόν άρθρο τίθεται όπως αντικαταστάθηκε με το άρθρο τρίτο του άρθρου 1 του ν.4335/2015 (ΦΕΚ Α΄87/23.7.2015) 138
Αρθρο: 544 on Αναψηλάφηση (reopening), Ημ/νία: 01.01.2016, Ο αριθμός 6) του παρόντος τίθεται όπως αντικαταστάθηκε με το άρθρο τρίτο του άρθρου 1 του ν.4335/2015 (ΦΕΚ Α΄87/23.7.2015) 138

Spain

Constitución Española de 1978 (Spanish Constitution), última actualización publicada el 27/09/2011
Art 24 on *Derecho a la tutela judicial efectiva* (right to effective judicial protection) 29, 148, 166
Art 53 on *De las garantías de las libertades y derechos fundamentales* (protection of fundamental rights) 150, 166
Art 121 on *Los daños causados por error judicial* (damages caused by judicial error) 84–85
Arts 161–62 on *Del Tribunal Constitucional* (Constitutional Court) 166
Art 161.1.b) on *Del recurso de amparo por violación de los derechos y libertades* (recurso de amparo for violation of fundamental rights) 150
Ley 29/1998, de 13 de julio, reguladora de la Jurisdicción Contencioso-administrativa (Law on administrative judicial procedures), 'BOE' núm 167, de 14/07/1998, Última actualización publicada el 19/07/2017
Art 31.2 on *Objeto del recurso* contencioso-administrativo – Pretensiones de las partes (object of the appeal – claim of the parties) 84
Art 102 *on Revisión de sentencias* (retrial) 138

Ley 38/2003, de 17 de noviembre, General de Subvenciones (Law on subventions), 'BOE' núm 276, de 18/11/2003, Última actualización publicada el 04/07/2018
Arts 36–42 on *Del reintegro* (refund) 138
Ley 39/2015, de 1 de octubre, del Procedimiento Administrativo Común de las Administraciones Públicas (Common Administrative Procedures) 'BOE' núm 236, de 02/10/2015, Texto original publicado el 02/10/2015, Última actualización publicada el 22/06/2018
Art 47 on *Nulidad y anulabilidad* (nullity) 138
Art 106 on *Revisión de oficio* (review ex officio) 138
Ley 40/2015, de 1 de octubre, de Régimen Jurídico del Sector Público (Legal Regime of Public Administrations) 'BOE' núm 236, de 2 de octubre de 2015, Última actualización publicada el 04/07/2018
Art 32 on *De la responsabilidad patrimonial de las Administraciones Públicas* (liability of the public administration) 84, 138
Real Decreto de 14 de septiembre de 1882 por el que se aprueba la Ley de Enjuiciamiento Criminal (Criminal procedure code), 'BOE' núm 260, de 17/09/1882, Última actualización publicada el 06/10/2015
Art 954 on *Recurso de revisión* (action for retrial) 138
Real Decreto de 24 de julio de 1889 por el que se publica el Código Civil (Civil Code), 'BOE' núm 206, de 25/07/1889, Última actualización publicada el 29/06/2017
Art 1902 on *De las obligaciones que nacen de culpa o negligencia* (liablity arising from fault or negligence) 84
Ley Orgánica 2/1979, de 3 de octubre, del Tribunal Constitucional (Organic law on the Constitutional Court), 'BOE' núm 239, de 05/10/1979, Última actualización publicada el 17/10/2015
Arts 41–44 on *De la procedencia e interposición del recurso de amparo constitucional* (role of the constitutional recurso de amparo) 150, 166
Ley Orgánica 6/1985, de 1 de julio, del Poder Judicial (Organic law on the judiciary), 'BOE' núm 157, de 02/07/1985, Última actualización publicada el 28/10/2015 138–39
Arts 292–96 on *Responsabilidad patrimonial del Estado por el funcionamiento de la Administración de Justicia* (state liability for the administration of justice) 84–85
Ley 1/2000, de 7 de enero, de Enjuiciamiento Civil (Civil Procedure Code), 'BOE' núm 7, de 08/01/2000, Última actualización publicada el 12/06/2018
Arts 509–10 *La revisión de sentencias firmes* (review of final judgments) 138

Ley Orgánica 7/2015, de 21 de julio, por la que se modifica la Ley Orgánica 6/1985, de 1 de julio, del Poder Judicial (Organic Law 7/2015, of July 21, amending the Organic Law 6/1985, of July 1, of the Judiciary) 'BOE' núm 174, de 22 de julio de 2015 139
Art único 3 *on De la revisión de sentencias* (review of judgments) 138

France

Code de justice administrative (Code of Administrative Justice), version consolidée au 19 juillet 2018
Art L211-1, modifié par Loi no 2011-1862 du 13 décembre 2011 – Art 48, on *Les tribunaux administratifs et les cours administratives d'appel – Attributions contentieuses* (the administrative courts – jurisdiction) 94
Art L311-1, modifié par Loi no 2011-1862 du 13 décembre 2011 – Art. 48, on *La compétence* (competency of administrative courts) 94
Art R421-1, modifié par le décret no 2016-1480 du 2 novembre 2016 – Art 10, on *L'introduction de l'instance de premier ressort – les délais* (introduction of a first instance appeal – deadine) 139
Code de l'organisation judiciaire (Code of Judicial Organisation), version consolidée au 20 juin 2018
Art L111-5, créé par ordonnance no 2006-673 du 8 juin 2006 on *L'impartialité des juridictions judiciaires* (objectivity of the judge) 148
Art L141-1,codifié par l'ordonnance no 2006-673 du 8 juin 2006, modifié par la loi no 2016-1547 du 18 novembre 2016 – Art 1, on *Responsabilité du fait du fonctionnement du service public de la justice* (state responsibility for damage caused by the malfunctioning of justice) 58, 93–94
Code civil (Civil Code), version consolidée au 3 janvier 2018
Arts 1240–42, modifié par ordonnance no 2016-131 du 10 février 2016 – Art 2, on *La responsabilité extracontractuelleen général* (liability in tort) 93
Code pénal (Criminal Code), version en vigueur au 9 juin 2018
Art 112-1 on the *Principe de la non-rétroactivité des lois pénales nouvelles plus sévères* (principle of retroactivity in mitius) 58

Croatia

Ustav Republike Hrvatske (Constitution of the Republic of Croatia), pročišćeni tekst NN 56/90, 135/97, 8/98, 113/00, 124/00, 28/01, 41/01, 55/01, 76/10, 85/10, 05/14
članak 129 on *Ustavni sud Republike Hrvatske* (Croatian Constitutional Court) 150

Ustavni zakon o Ustavnom sudu Republike Hrvatske (Act on the Constitutional Court of the Republic of Croatia), pročišćeni tekst zakona NN 99/99, 29/02, 49/02 151
članak 62–64 on *Ustavna tužbu* (constitutional complaint) 150
Zakon o parničnom postupku (Civil procedure Act) pročišćeni tekst zakona NN 53/91, 91/92, 58/93, 112/99, 88/01, 117/03, 88/05, 02/07, 84/08, 123/08, 57/11, 148/11, 25/13, 89/14
članak 382(2)(3) on *Revizija* (retrial) 127, 139
Zakon o sudovima (Courts Act) pročišćeni tekst zakona, NN 28/13, 33/15, 82/15, 82/16
članak 105 on *Odgovornost za štetu* (responsibility for damage) 114

Italy

Regio Decreto 16/03/1942, no 262, 'Approvazione del testo del Codice civile' GU 04/04/1946, no 79, Codice Civile (Civil Code), Vigenti al 31/07/2018
Art 2043 on *Risarcimento per fatto illecito* (liability in tort) 104
Art 2909 on *Cosa giudicata* (res judicata) 139
Regio Decreto, 28/10/1940, no 1443, GU 28/10/1940, no 253, Codice di procedura civile (Civil Procedure Code), Vigenti al 31/07/2018
Art 395 on *Casi di revocazione* (grounds for retrial) 139
Costituzione della Repubblica italiana (Constitution of the Italian Republic), GU 27/12/1947, no 298,Vigenti al 31/07/2018
Art 24. on *Il diritto attivo e passivo alla difesa in tribunale* (judicial protection and liability for judicial errors) 104
Legge, 27/02/2015, no 18, GU 04/03/2015 no 52, Disciplina della responsabilità' civile dei magistrati (Regulations governing the civil liability of judges), Entrata in vigore del provvedimento 19/03/2015
Art 2 on *Responsabilità per dolo o colpa grave* (liability for wilful default or gross negligence) 105
Legge, testo coordinato 07/08/1990, no 241, GU 18/08/1990, Legge sul procedimento amministrativo (Code of the Administrative Procedure), Vigenti al 31/07/2018
Art 21-nonies on *Annullamento d'ufficio* (annulment ex officio) 139
Legge, 13/04/1988, no 117, GU 15/04/1988 n 88, Risarcimento dei danni cagionati nell'esercizio delle funzioni giudiziarie e responsabilità civile dei magistrati (Compensation for damage caused in the exercise of judicial functions and the civil liability of judges), Vigenti al 31/07/2018
Art 2, Aggiornato il 19/3/2015 on *Responsabilita' per dolo o colpa grave* (liability for wilful default or gross negligence) 9, 56, 104–05, 194

Legge, 24/03/2001, no 89, GU 03/04/2001, n 78, Previsione di equa riparazione in caso di violazione del termine ragionevole del processo e modifica dell'articolo 375 del codice di procedura civile (Provisions on equitable compensation for breach of the reasonable time of the process and the amendment of Art 375 of the Code of Civil Procedure), Vigenti al 31/07/2018
Art 2 on *Diritto all'equa riparazione* (right to a fair compensation)........209

Cyprus

Constitution of the Republic of Cyprus, 16/08/1960..................................150
Art 146.6. ....113, 151

Latvia

Administratīvā procesa likums (Administrative Procedure Law) 25.10.2001, 'Latvijas Vēstnesis' 164 (2551), 14.11.2001, Grozījumi Administratīvā procesa likumā 02.02.2017. likums/LV, 36 (5863), 16.02.2017, Stājas spēkā 01.03.2017
92 pants on *Tiesības uz atlīdzinājumu* (right to redress)..........................84
353 pants 6) on *Lietas jauna izskatīšana sakarā ar jaunatklātiem apstākļiem – Jaunatklātie apstākļi* (rehearing of cases due to newly discovered circumstances – newly discovered facts) 140
Civilprocesa likums (Civil Procedure Law) 14.10.1998, 'Latvijas Vēstnesis' 326/330 (1387/1391), Grozījumi Civilprocesa likumā 01.03.2018. likums/LV, 53 (6139), 14.03.2018, Stājas spēkā 01.07.2018
479 pants 6) on *Lietas jauna izskatīšana sakarā ar jaunatklātiem apstākļiem – Jaunatklātie apstākļi* (rehearing of cases due to newly discovered circumstances – newly discovered facts) 140
Kriminālprocesa likums (Criminal Procedure Law) 21.04.2005, 'Latvijas Vēstnesis' 74 (3232), 11.05.2005., Grozījumi Kriminālprocesa likumā 28.09.2017. likums/LV, 203 (6030), 12.10.2017, Stājas spēkā 15.06.2018
655 pants (2) 5) on *Lietas jauna izskatīšana sakarā ar jaunatklātiem apstākļiem – Jaunatklātie apstākļi* (rehearing of cases due to newly discovered circumstances – newly discovered facts) 126
Latvijas Republikas Satversme (Constitution of the Latvian Republic) 15.02.1922, 'Latvijas Vēstnesis', 43, 01.07.1993, Grozījums Latvijas Republikas Satversmē 19.05.2016. likums/LV, 104 (5676), 31.05.2016, Stājas spēkā 14.06.2016
92 pants on *Tiesības uz atlīdzinājumu* (right to redress)..........................84
Satversmes tiesas likums (Constitutional Court Law) 05.06.1996, 'Latvijas Vēstnesis', 103 (588), 14.06.1996, Grozījumi Satversmes tiesas likumā 16.03.2017. likums/LV, 59 (5886), 21.03.2017, Stājas spēkā 30.03.2017
17 pants on *Tiesības iesniegt pieteikumu par lietas ierosināšanu* (right to file an application) 150

Valsts pārvaldes iestāžu nodarīto zaudējumu atlīdzināšanas likums (Law on the Compensation of Damage Caused by Public Administration), 02.06.2005, 'Latvijas Vēstnesis', 96 (3254), 17.06.2005, Grozījumi Valsts pārvaldes iestāžu nodarīto zaudējumu atlīdzināšanas likumā 15.02.2018. likums/LV, 41 (6127), Stājas spēkā 01.03.2018 84

Lithuania

Lietuvos Respublikos administracinių bylų teisenos įstatymas (Law of the Republic of Lithuania on Administrative Proceedings) 1999 m sausio 14 d Nr VIII-1029, Suvestinė redakcija nuo 2018-07-16
156 straipsnis on *Proceso atnaujinimo pagrindai* (reopening of proceedings) 126–28, 143
Lietuvos Respublikos civilinio proceso kodekso patvirtinimo, įsigaliojimo ir įgyvendinimo įstatymas. Civilinio proceso kodeksas (Civil Procedure Code) 2002 m vasario 28 d Nr IX-743, Suvestinė redakcija nuo 2018-07-01
279(4) straipsnis on *Sprendimo įsiteisėjimas* (binding effect of judgments) 97
366 straipsnis on *Proceso atnaujinimo pagrindai* (reopening of proceedings), Straipsnio punkto pakeitimai: Nr XII-2751, 2016-11-08, paskelbta TAR 2016-11-17, i. k. 2016-26956 126–28
Lietuvos Respublikos civilinis kodeksas (Civil Code of the Republic of Lithuania) patvirtintas 2000 m liepos 18 d įstatymu Nr VIII-1864, Suvestinė redakcija nuo 2018-07-17
6.272 straipsnis on *Atsakomybė už žalą, atsiradusią dėl ikiteisminio tyrimo pareigūnų, prokuroro, teisėjo ir teismo neteisėtų veiksmų* (Liability for damage caused by the investigating officers, prosecutors, judges and courts) 96–97
Lietuvos Respublikos Konstitucija (Constitution of the Republic of Lithuania) 25.10.1992, Suvestinė redakcija nuo 2014-01-24
30 straipsnis on *Asmuo, kurio konstitucinės teisės ar laisvės pažeidžiamos, turi teisę kreiptis į teismą. Asmeniui padarytos materialinės ir moralinės žalos atlyginimą nustato įstatymas* (right for judicial protection and compensation for violation of fundamental rights) 96–97

Luxembourg

Code civil, 01.01.2004, consolidé au 01.03.2018
Arts 1382–83 on *Des délits et des quasi-délits* (torts and quasi-torts) 115
Loi du 1er septembre 1988 relative à la responsabilité civile de l'Etat et des collectivités publiques (Law on the liability of the state and state bodies) 01.09.1988, modifiée le 7.07.1994

Art 1, alinéa 1 on *Responsabilité pour le dommage causé par le fonctionnement défectueux du service public* (liability for damage caused by the malfunction of the public service) 115
Nouveau Code de Procédure Civile (New Civil Procedure Code), 17.08.1998, modifié le 27.06.2018
Art 617 on *Rétractation* (revocation – in the meaning of retrial) 140
Règlement grand-ducal du 8 juin 1979 relatif à la procédure à suivre par les administrations relevant de l'Etat et des communes, 08.06.1979, acte de base non modifié
Art 8 on *Retrait rétroactif d'une décision* (revocation with retroactive effect of a decision) 140

Hungary

A bíróságok szervezetéről és igazgatásáról szóló 2011 évi CLXI törvény (Law on the organisation and administration of the courts) 2018 július 31-én hatályos állapota
Art 2 § (1) on *jogerő* (res judicata) 110
A polgári perrendtartásról szóló 1952 évi III törvény (Act on Civil Procedure Code) 2018 december 31-ig hatályos állapota (this act was repealed by the New Act on Civil Procedure Code with effect of 01/01/2018)
260 §, utolsó módosítás a 2008: XXX törvény 40 §-a alapján on *perújítás* (retrial) 140–41
A polgári perrendtartásról szóló 2016 évi CXXX törvény (New Act on Civil Procedure Code) 2018 július 31-én hatályos állapota
393 § on *perújítási okok* (grounds for retrial) 126, 141
Az Alkotmánybíróságról szóló 2011 évi CLI. törvény (Act on the Constitutional Court) 2018 július 31-én hatályos állapota
26–27 §§ on *alkotmányjogi panasz* (constitutional complaint) 168
Magyarország Alaptörvénye (Constitution of the Hungary) 2018 július 31-én hatályos állapota
XXVIII cikk on *törvényes bíróhoz való jog* (right to a lawful judge) 168

Malta

Civil Code, Cap 16 of the Laws of Malta, 11/02/1870, last amended by act XXVII of 2018
Arts 1030–33 on Torts and quasi-torts 115
Code of Organization and Civil Procedure, Cap 12 of the Laws of Malta, 01/08/1855, as amended by act XI of 2018
Art 811(e) on Grounds for new trial 129
Constitution of Malta, as amended by act XXII of 2018
Art 46 on Enforcement of protective provisions 115, 151

The Netherlands

Algemene wet bestuursrecht (Awb, General Administrative Law Act),
Wet van 4 juni 1992, houdende algemene regels van bestuursrecht,
Geldend van 12-07-2018
Arts 4:48, 4:49 on *Intrekking en wijziging* (withrawal and amendment) 141
Art 8:88 on *Schadevergoeding* (compensation)..................................98, 142
Art 8:119 on *Herziening* (retrial) 141
Burgerlijk Wetboek (BW, Boek 6, Civil Code), 01/01/1992,
Geldend van 01-09-2017
Art 6:162 on *Onrechtmatige daad* (tortious act)................................. 97–98
Tweede Kamer (House of Representatives), 12/08/2005, 2004–2005,
29279, no 28 .... 98, 142, 147
Wetboek van Burgerlijke Rechtsvordering (BES, Code of Civil Procedure),
Geldend van 01-09-2017
Art 382 on *Herroeping van vonnissen* (revocation of decisions)....... 97, 127, 141

Austria

Allgemeines Verwaltungsverfahrensgesetz (AVG, General Administrative
Procedure Act) 1991, BGBl Nr 51/1991 zuletzt geändert durch
BGBl I Nr 161/2013
§ 68 on *Abänderung und Behebung von Amts wegen* (amendment
and revocation ex officio)...142
§ 69 on *Wiederaufnahme des Verfahrens* (reopening of proceedings).......142
Amtshaftungsgesetz (AHG, Public Liability Act), BGBl Nr 20/1949
zuletzt geändert durch BGBl I Nr 122/2013
§ 2(3) *Staatshaftungsanspruch* (state liability claim).........................99, 171
Bundesabgabenordnung (BAO, Federal Tax Act), BGBl Nr 194/1961
zuletzt geändert durch BGBl I Nr 32/2018
§ 299 (revocation of decisions) 142
§ 303 on *Wiederaufnahme des Verfahrens* (reopening of proceedings).....142
Bundes-Verfassungsgesetz (B-VG, Federal Constitutional Law),
BGBl Nr 1/1930 zuletzt geändert durch BGBl I Nr 22/2018
Art 23 on *Amtshaftung/Staatshaftung* (liability of public authorities) 99
Art 83(2) on the *Recht auf den gesetzlichen Richter*
(right to a lawful judge) 148, 150, 162
Art 137 on *Verfassungsgerichtsbarkeit* (constitutional jurisdiction) 99
Art 144 on *Verfassungsgerichtshof* (Constitutional Court) 150, 162
Verfassungsgerichtshofgesetz (VfGG, Constitutional Court Act),
BGBl Nr 85/1953 zuletzt geändert durch BGBl I Nr 22/2018
Art 82 on *Bei Beschwerden wegen Verletzung in verfassungsgesetzlich
gewährleisteten Rechten oder Verletzung in Rechten wegen
Anwendung einer gesetzwidrigen Verordnung, einer gesetzwidrigen
Kundmachung über die Wiederverlautbarung eines Gesetzes*

(Staatsvertrages), eines verfassungswidrigen Gesetzes oder eines rechtswidrigen Staatsvertrages (Art 144 B-VG) (complaints for infringement of constitutionally guaranteed rights or infringement of rights due to an unlawful order, an unlawful declaration of re-promulgation of a law (state contract), an unconstitutional law or an illegal state contract (Art 144 B-VG)) 150

Zivilprozessordnung (ZPO, Code of Civil Procedure), RGBl Nr 113/1895 zuletzt geändert durch BGBl I Nr 32/2018

Arts 530–31 on *Wiederaufnahme des Verfahrens* (reopening of proceedings) 142

Poland

Kodeks cywilny (Civil Code), Ustawa z dnia 23 kwietnia 1964 r, Dz.U.2018.0.1025 t.j.

Art 417[1] on *Szkoda wynikająca z aktu normatywnego, prawomocnego orzeczenia lub ostatecznej decyzji* (damage resulting from a normative act, or final decision)........ 105–06, 108

Kodeks postępowania cywilnego (Code of Civil Procedure), Ustawa z dnia 17 listopada 1964 r, Dz.U.2018.0.1360 t.j.

Art 403 on *Inne podstawy żądania wznowienia postępowania* (other grounds for retrial) 132

Art 424[1] on *Skarga o stwierdzenie niezgodności z prawem prawomocnego orzeczenia* (action to declare a final decision unlawful) 106, 147

Art 424[1a] on *Niedopuszczalność skargi o stwierdzenie niezgodności z prawem prawomocnego orzeczenia* (inadmissibility of an action for declaration of unlawfulness of a final decision) 106

Art. 424[1b] on *Odszkodowanie z tytułu szkody wyrządzonej przez wydanie orzeczenia niezgodnego z prawem* (compensation for damages) 106

Konstytucja Rzeczypospolitej Polskiej (Constitution of The Republic of Poland), z dnia 2 kwietnia 1997 r, Dz.U.2009.114.946 t.j.

Art 45 on *Prawo do sprawiedliwego procesu* (right to fair trial) 148

Art 77 on *Prawo do wynagrodzenia szkody* (right to compensation) 105

Ordynacja podatkowa (Tax Code), Ustawa, z dnia 29 sierpnia 1997 r, Dz.U.2018.0.800 t.j.

Art 240, § 1, pts 9 and 11 on *Przesłanki wznowienia postępowania* (grounds for retrial) 132

Prawo o postępowaniu przed sądami administracyjnymi (Regulations of Proceedings in Administrative Court), Ustawa z dnia 30 sierpnia 2002 r, Dz.U.2018.0.1302 t.j.

Art 285a on *Skarga o stwierdzenie niezgodności z prawem prawomocnego orzeczenia* (action of declaration of unlawfulness of a final judgment) 59, 106–08

Ustawa o skardze na naruszenie prawa strony do rozpoznania sprawy w postępowaniu sądowym bez nieuzasadnionej zwłoki (on complaint about the violation of the party's right to hear the case without undue delay), Ustawa z dnia 17 czerwca 2004 r, Dz.U.2018.0.75 t.j. 106

Ustawa o zmianie ustawy – Kodeks cywilny oraz niektórych innych ustaw (Act amending the Civil Code and other acts), Ustawa z dnia 17 czerwca 2004 r, Dz.U. 2004.162 poz.1692.......... 106

Portugal

Código de Processo Civil (Civil Procedure Code) Lei no 41/2013, de 26 de Junho, Contém as seguintes alterações: DL no 114/2017, de 29/12, 7ª versão

Art 696° f), on *Revisão – fundamentos de recurso* (review – grounds of appeal).......... 142

Código de Processo nos Tribunais Administrativos (Administrative Court Procedure Code), Lei no 15/2002, de 22 de Fevereiro, Contém as seguintes alterações: DL no 214-G/2015, de 02/10, 6ª versão

Art 154° on *Recursos extraordinários* (extraordinary appeals).......... 142

Constituição da República Portuguesa (Constitution of the Portuguese Republic), Contém as seguintes alterações: Lei no 1/2005, de 12/08, 8ª versão

Art 22° on *Responsabilidade das entidades públicas* (liability ot public authorities).......... 100

Lei no 67/2007, de 31 de Dezembro, Aprova o Regime da Responsabilidade Civil Extracontractual do Estado e Demais Entidades Públicas (Non-contractual liability of the state and other public bodies), Contém as seguintes alterações: Lei no 31/2008, de 17/07, 2ª versão

Art 7° on *Responsabilidade exclusiva do Estado e demais pessoas colectivas de direito público* (exclusive liability of the State and other legal persons governed by public law) 100

Art 12° on *Responsabilidade civil por danos decorrentes do exercício da função jurisdicional – Regime geral* (liability for damages resulting from the exercise of the judicial function) 100

Art 13° on *Responsabilidade por erro judiciário* (liability for judicial errors).......... 11, 100–02, 104

Art 14° on *Responsabilidade dos magistrados* (liability of judges).......... 100

Art 15° on *Responsabilidade no exercício da função político-legislativa* (liability in the exercie of political-legislative function) 100

Romania

Codul civil al României (Civil Code), Lege Nr 287/2009, modificată prin Lege nr 138/2014
Art 1357 on *Răspunderea civilă* (civil liability) ... 116
Art 1358 on *Criterii particulare de apreciere a vinovăţiei* (criteria for appreciation of fault) ... 116
Art 1359 on *Repararea prejudiciului constând în vătămarea unui interes* (reparation of damages) ... 116
Codul de procedurăcivilă (Civil Procedure Code) Lege Nr 134/2010, actualizat prin OUG nr 4/2013 ... 127
Art 509(1) on *Revizuirea* (retrial) ... 127
Constituţia României, M.Of. nr 767 din 31/10/2003, modificată şi completată prin Legea nr 429/2003 de revizuire a Constituţiei României
Art 20(2) on *Tratatele internaţionale privind drepturile omului* (international treaties on human rights) ... 134
Art 52 on *Dreptul persoanei vătămate de o autoritate publică* (rights for compensation caused by a public authority) ... 116
Art 148 on *Integrarea în Uniunea Europeană* (accession to the European Union) ... 134
Legea nr 554/2004 contenciosului administrative (Law on Administrative Disputes), M.Of. nr 1154 din 7.12.2004, actualizată prin Decizie CCR nr 898/2015 ... 127
Art 21(2) on *Revizuirea* (retrial) ... 133–34
Legea nr 303/2004 privind statutul judecătorilor şi procurorilor (Law on the statute of judges and prosecutors), M.Of. nr. 826/2005 rep, actualizata prin Legea nr 300/2011
Art 96(4) on *Răspunderea judecătorilor si procurorilor (liability of judges and prosecutors)* ... 116

Slovenia

Obligacijski zakonik – OZ (Obligations Code) Uradni list RS, št 97/07 – uradno prečiščeno besedilo in 64/16 – odl US in 20/18 – OROZ631
131 člen on *Podlage za odgovornost* (basis of liability) ... 116
148 člen on *Odgovornost pravne osebe za škodo, ki jo povzroči njen organ* (liability of legal persons for damage caused by its governing body) ... 116
Ustava Republike Slovenije – URS (Constitution of the Republic of Slovenia), Uradni list RS, št 33/91-I, 42/97 – UZS68, 66/00 – UZ80, 24/03 – UZ3a, 47, 68, 69/04 – UZ14, 69/04 – UZ43, 69/04 – UZ50, 68/06 – UZ121, 140,143, 47/13 – UZ148, 47/13 – UZ90,97,99 in 75/16 – UZ70a

23 člen on the principle of *Pravica do sodnega varstva* (right to justice) or *naravni sodnik* (natural judge)..............148, 150, 164
26 člen on *Pravica do povračila škode* (right to compensation)..........59, 116
160 člen on *Pristojnosti ustavnega sodišče* (competence of the Constitutional Court)..150, 164

Zakon o splošnem upravnem postopku – ZUP (General Administrative Procedure Act), Uradni list RS, št 24/06 – uradno prečiščeno besedilo, 105/06 – ZUS-1, 126/07, 65/08, 8/10 in 82/13
260 člen on *Obnova postopka* (reopened proceedings – in the meaning of review of proceedings) 143
274–77 člen on *Razveljavitev odločbe po nadzorstveni pravica* (annulment or revocation of administrative decisions by the higher administrative organ)..143

Zakon o upravnem sporu – ZUS-1 (Administrative Dispute Act) Uradni list RS, št 105/06, 107/09 – odl. US, 62/10, 98/11 – odl. US, 109/12 in 10/17 – ZPP-E
67(3) člen on *Odločba* (judicial decision)..116
96 člen on *Obnova postopka* (reopened proceedings)............................142

Zakon o ustavnem sodišče – ZUstS (Constitutional Court Act), Uradni list RS, št 64/07 – uradno prečiščeno besedilo in 109/12 200
24 člen on *Zahteva in pobuda za začetek postopka* (submission of a complaint)..150, 164
50 člen on *Ustavna pritožba* (constitutional complaint) 150, 164

Slovakia

Civilný sporový poriadok (Code of Civil Procedure) Zákon č 160/2015 Z z, v znení č 87/2017 Z z, Účinnosť od 01.05.2017
§ 397 e) on *Prípustnosť žaloby na obnovu konania* (admissibility of an action for retrial)......................................134, 143

Občiansky súdny poriadok (Code of Civil Procedure), Zákon č 99/1963 Zb, v znení č 194/2016 Z z, repealed by Civilný sporový poriadok (Code of Civil Procedures) Zákon č160/2015 Z z.
§ 228(1) e) on *Obnova konania* (retrial) 134, 143

Ústava Slovenskej republiky (Constitution of the Slovak Republic), Ústavný zákon č 460/1992 Zb, v znení č 137/2017 Z z, Účinnosť od 01.06.2017
Čl 46 on *Právo na súdnu a inú právnu ochranu* (right to judicial protection) 148, 150, 165
Čl 48 ods 1 on *Právo nebyť odňatý zákonnému sudcovi* (the right not be deprived of one's lawful judge) 148, 150, 165
Čl 127 on *Ústavný súd Slovenskej republiky* (Constitutional Court of the Republic of Slovakia)...150, 165

Zákon Národnej rady Slovenskej republiky o organizácii Ústavného súdu Slovenskej republiky, o konaní pred ním a o postavení jeho sudcov (Law on the Organisation of the Constitutional Court) Zákon č. 38/1993 Z z, v znení č. 55/2017 Z z, Účinnosť od 01.06.2017
§ 18 h) on *Konania pred ústavným súdom* (proceedings before the Constitutional Court) 150
§ 49 on *Konanie o sťažnostiach* (complaint procedure) 150, 165

Finland

Hallintolainkäyttölaki (Administrative Judicial Procedure Act) 26.7.1996/586, Säädöksiä seurattu 7.8.2015/891
11 luku, 63 § (1)(2) on *Purku* (annulment) 129–30
11 luku, 64 § (2) on *Purun hakeminen* (demande d'annulment) 131
Suomen perustuslaki (Constitution of Finland), 11.6.1999/731, Säädöksiä seurattu 4.11.2011/1112
118 § on *Vastuu virkatoimista* (liability) 102
Oikeudenkäymiskaari (Code of Judicial Procedure), 1.1.1734/4, Säädöksiä seurattu 12.01.2017/803
31 luku, 7–10 § on *Lainvoiman saaneen tuomion purkaminen* (reversal of final judgments) 129–31
Vahingonkorvauslaki (Tort Liability Act), 31.5.1974/412, Säädöksiä seurattu 3.12.2010/1051
3 luku, 5§ on *Työnantajan ja julkisyhteisön korvausvastuu* (Vicarious liability of employers and public corporations) 102

Sweden

Förordning om handläggning av skadeståndsanspråk mot staten (Regulation on the processing of claims against the state), 1995-12-07, SFS 1995:1301, t.o.m. SFS 2018:1203 87
Förvaltningsprocesslag (Administrative Court Procedure Act), 1971-06-04, SFS 1971:291, t.o.m. SFS 2017:901
36 § on *Särskilda regler om överklagande hos Högsta förvaltningsdomstolen* (special rules on the appeal before the Supreme Administrative court) 57
37b § on *Resning* (relief for a substantive defect in the judgment) 131
Lag om justitiekanslerns tillsyn (Act on the Chancellor of Justice's supervision), 1975-12-15, SFS 1975:1339, t.o.m. SFS 2010:1412 87
Rättegångsbalk (Civil Court Procedure Act), 1942-07-18, SFS 1942:740, t.o.m. SFS 2018:1252
58. kap, § 1 on *Resning* (relief for a substantive defect in the judgment) 131
59. kap on *Domvilla* (miscarriage of justice) 172

Skadeståndslag (Tort Liability Act), 1972-06-02, t.o.m. SFS 2018:23
3 kap, 7 § on *Skadeståndsansvar för annans vållande och för det allmänna* (liability for another's negligence) or *utomobligatoriskt ansvar* (extracontractual liability) 87
Skattebetalningslag (Tax Law), 1997-06-12, SFS 1997:483, t.o.m. SFS 2011:1511
21 kap, § 3 on *Omprövning* (reconsideration) 131

United Kingdom

Civil Procedure Rules, 97th Update,
Rule 52.30 on Reopening of final appeals....... 135–36
Crown Proceedings Act 1947, 1947 c 44 (Regnal 10 and 11 Geo 6)
Section 2 on Liability of the Crown in tort 103–04

1

Introduction

I. THEORETICAL BACKGROUND

THE COURT OF Justice of the European Union (ECJ) held in the judgment in *Köbler* that Member States are obliged to make good the damage caused to individuals in cases where the infringement of EU law stems from a decision of a Member State court adjudicating at last instance. The conditions of this liability are, in principle, the same as those which govern state liability under EU law in general; that is, where the rule of law infringed is intended to confer rights on individuals, the breach is sufficiently serious (manifest), and there is a direct causal link between that breach and the loss or damage sustained by the injured parties. Under the remedial rules of the Union, state liability is the only generally available remedy for a violation of EU law by national supreme courts. The importance of *Köbler* lies in the fact that Member State courts play a key role in the application of EU law.[1] As EU law is primarily given effect by national courts, individuals have to claim the full enforcement and protection of their rights derived from EU law before national benches. It is, therefore, essential that the national courts fulfil their obligations in this regard and apply EU law correctly.

Since this seminal ECJ judgment, delivered in 2003, the principle of state liability for breaches of EU law by national courts has received considerable attention in scholarly writing. These works have already provided an in-depth analysis of several central issues. In that regard, the focus has been placed on the acceptance of state liability for judicial breaches of EU law as a matter of principle.[2] Liability due to judicial errors has been criticised with regard to the principles of res judicata and the procedural autonomy of the Member States in particular. Moreover, the criterion of manifest breach of the EU norm has also been thoroughly analysed. It has notably been subject to criticism by several scholars;[3] and Scherr has already offered a detailed analysis of this criterion from a comparative law perspective.[4] Hofstötter has put the *Köbler* decision

[1] Bobek 2017: 140–43; De Visser 2004: 61–62; Lenaerts et al 2014: 13–14; Šadl 2016: 68; Temple Lang 1997: 3.

[2] Breuer 2004; Cabral and Chaves 2006: 123; Classen 2004: 816–17; Jans 2004: 176; Komárek 2005a: 77; Wattel 2004: 186–87.

[3] Beutler 2009: 792; Golecki and Wojciechowski 2009: 195–97; Komárek 2005b: 17; Rodríguez 2004–05: 614–15; Valutytė 2011: 37, 47.

[4] Scherr 2008; Scherr 2012: 565–88.

into a wider context, offering a comprehensive study of the non-compliance by national courts with their EU obligations.[5] Similarly, the potential consequences of a particular judicial breach of EU law under national law of several Member States have been presented in a publication edited by Coutron.[6] To conclude, *Köbler* has already been studied extensively. However, the focus of these works has remained theoretical, as they primarily offer an analysis of the doctrine in relation to the legal concept of state liability for judicial acts. This book does not seek to analyse issues that have already been the subject of such a detailed examination.

Nevertheless, much less attention has so far been placed on the application of this much-criticised doctrine by national courts and on the real impact of *Köbler* on national remedies. Even though there has been a great deal of speculation that the *Köbler* doctrine might remain mere theory,[7] more than 15 years after the ECJ judgment, there is no analysis available to confirm or disprove this assumption.[8]

Even so, there are some studies on the application by national courts of the state liability doctrine in general, including EU law violations by the legislature and the executive. These papers incorporate national case-law regarding breaches of EU law by the judiciary. In this regard, the study by Granger from 2007[9] must be mentioned; this offered a comprehensive analysis of the *Francovich* case-law, covering the judicial follow-up of this judgment in the 15 'old' Member States, on the basis of research conducted at the TMC Asser Institute.[10] Granger has also published another paper on this matter, which depicts *Francovich* liability before national courts 25 years after the seminal ECJ judgment.[11] A similar research project has been carried out at the European University Institute, which resulted in the publication of a research paper by Condon and van Leeuwen. This paper deals with the application of the *Francovich* doctrine in ten Member States.[12] National cases have also been described by Claes in her in-depth work on the mandate of national courts in the European Constitution.[13] Moreover, in 2012, Lock provided an assessment of the case-law of German, English and Welsh courts in order to examine the effectiveness of the state liability principle as a means of enforcing EU law, compared to the infringement procedure.[14] In his study, he pointed out the need for more detailed research in this regard,

[5] Hofstötter 2005.
[6] Coutron 2014.
[7] Beutler 2009: 789–90; Loth 2017: 49; Nassimpian 2007: 826; Wattel 2004: 182.
[8] Two articles (Varga 2016a; Varga 2017b) based on the same research as the present book have already been published; these shed some light on the application of the *Köbler* judgment before the national courts.
[9] Granger 2007.
[10] Betlem et al 2007.
[11] Granger 2017: 95.
[12] Condon and Van Leeuwen 2016.
[13] Claes 2006.
[14] Lock 2012: 1675–702.

such as noted by Condon and Leeuwen in the abstract in their paper and by Granger in her study published in 2017.[15]

Ten years after the *Köbler* judgment, Bobek contended that very little or nothing at all is known about whether the ECJ's case-law is followed by national courts. In 2013, he argued that the Member States' liability for judicial breaches of EU law is unfeasible in national judicial practice, and, to his knowledge, there has been not a single decision in any of the Member States which would have awarded damages following the *Köbler* guidance.[16] In 2016, Broberg mentioned only one national judgment as a known example where a claimant has been awarded compensation based on the *Köbler* doctrine.[17]

It is noteworthy that although the ECJ confirmed the autonomous character of the liability remedy,[18] it does not operate in a vacuum. Besides the features inherent to the *Köbler* liability (such as the criterion of a manifest breach), it is also the legal environment in which this principle operates that has a profound influence on its practical application. Therefore, the *Köbler* doctrine should be considered in a wider context of remedies for violation of EU law by national courts. Consequently, there are many questions to be clarified about the relationship between *Köbler* liability and other national remedies. Several authors – eg Anagnostaras, Eeckhout, van Gerven, Kornezov, Leczykiewicz, and Wattel[19] – have already analysed the position of state liability in the system of remedies available in national courts. I support their view that the European and national judicial legal environment in which the doctrine operates must necessarily be taken into account in order to provide a useful and comprehensive analysis of *Köbler* liability.[20]

The aim of this book is thus to offer an analysis on the genuine life of the *Köbler* principle in the Member States, and to assess whether it has proved to be – and if not, why not – an efficient method to ensure the effectiveness of EU law and of the protection of individuals' rights over the past 15 years. The research behind this book is primarily based on published case-law regarding the legal consequences of violation of EU law by national courts of last instance.[21] Analysing the national case-law has allowed an examination of judicial practice regarding the topic in question, not only the theory,[22] and made it

[15] Granger 2017: 127; Condon and van Leeuwen 2016: 226.

[16] Bobek 2013: 197, 201, 209, 215–17.

[17] Broberg 2016: 250.

[18] (ECJ) Judgments in *Sutton*; in *Comateb and Others*; opinion of AG Jacobs in *Fantask and Others*.

[19] Anagnostaras 2001a: 355–83; Anagnostaras 2007; Eeckhout 1998: 66–70, 72; Van Gerven 2000: 506–20; Kornezov 2014a; Leczykiewicz 2012; Leczykiewicz 2015; Wattel 2008.

[20] Tridimas 2006: 500–03.

[21] The obvious drawback of this method is that not all cases are published and translated; therefore, the research cannot be exhaustive. Moreover, linguistic barriers made it necessary to rely on indirect sources, without the possibility to verify the primary source.

[22] See Schmitt 2005, quote cited in Procházka 2013: 340.

possible to observe developments in the field of national remedies against EU law violations.[23] In addition, besides analysing the effectiveness of the *Köbler* doctrine in the past, the book also looks for possible future applications of the doctrine. As such, this book focuses on the position of this remedy in the decentralised system of the application of EU law, both from a retrospective and a prospective point of view.

The structure of the book is as follows. Chapter 1 is the introduction, divided into three sections. The first section explains the theoretical background. The second section offers an overview of the context of the application of EU law and a brief description of the competence of the EU and the Member States regarding remedies. The third section provides a presentation of the ECJ case-law on state liability for violation of EU law by Member State courts.

Chapter 2, focusing on the experiences from the past, deals with the difficulties hindering the application of *Köbler* liability before national benches. In this respect, the research shows that since the pronouncement of the ECJ judgment in 2003, there have been about 60 reported cases from the 28 Member States concerning the application of the *Köbler* principle. Even if we take into consideration the fact that not all cases have been reported, the number of actions remains quite low. Moreover, in all of these cases, damages have only been awarded in five occasions so far.[24] This raises the question as to why *Köbler* liability is not a frequently used method to remedy violations of individuals' rights protected under EU law.

Therefore, chapter 2 analyses various limitations in order to verify their role in hindering the application of the *Köbler* liability in the practice. This chapter is divided into four sections, of which the first one introduces the topic. The second section analyses the problems arising from the nature of the *Köbler* principle and from the conditions inherent to it. The two main topics covered in this section relate to the criterion of 'manifest infringement of the applicable law' and to the difficulties in establishing causality between the damages suffered and the act of the national supreme court. The third section of chapter 3 deals with the limitations arising from factors that are external to the *Köbler* liability, such as the national legislative restrictions and the resistance of the national courts to apply the *Köbler* doctrine. The fourth section presents alternative actions available for individuals in various Member States which pursue the same objectif as *Köbler* liability, namely to remedy a violation of EU law committed by a national supreme court. In this respect, two main alternative remedies are presented, retrial and constitutional complaint. Through the presentation of these remedies and the analysis of their association with the *Köbler* doctrine, this section examines whether they can offer broadly equivalent protection to that afforded

[23] To better understand national regimes and to complete the list of cases, I have also relied on comparative legal studies. The following research papers have proved to be helpful in identifying relevant case-law: Betlem et al 2007; Beutler 2009: 792; Coutron 2014; Granger 2007; Hofstötter 2005; Kornezov 2014a; Lock 2012: 1675; Scherr 2008; Scherr 2012.

[24] See s 2.II.A.iv.b.

by state liability. The fifth section draws conclusions on the application of the *Köbler* principle between 2003 and 2018 in the then 28 Member States.

Then, building on the conclusions drawn from the application of the *Köbler* liability in the past, as well as on recent legal developments, the book examines perspectives for the possible future application of *Köbler* liability. In this respect, chapter 3 concentrates on questions regarding a development and an eventual extension of the scope of application of *Köbler* liability in the future. In particular, after an introduction, in the second section, it addresses the question as to whether the standard of liability as imposed in *Köbler* is adequate. Then, in the third section, it examines whether EU law should require Member States to offer specific remedies (eg *Köbler* liability) or, instead, an effective remedial system to ensure the application of EU law and the judicial protection of individual rights. Finally, in the fourth and fifth sections, the book explores whether the breach of the obligation to refer a preliminary question to the ECJ can be considered as separate ground for liability, and, similarly, whether damages liability can be established on the grounds of infringement of the Charter.

Chapter 4 draws some conclusions on various questions regarding the practice and the past of the liability doctrine, such as: To what extent is the *Köbler* doctrine applied by national courts? What are the main difficulties which hinder the application of the principle in the practice? In what situations can a breach be considered a manifest violation of the applicable law? Is it the breach of a substantive EU rule or the violation of the procedural obligation regarding its application that triggers liability? What is the real, practical importance of this principle? Can the *Köbler* liability be substituted by alternative means of remedy? Then, various other questions regarding the prospective part of this book will also be addressed: To what extent is the harmonisation of national remedies necessary? Is it up to EU law or that of Member States to determine the remedies available in cases of violation of EU law by Member State courts? What is the required standard of effective judicial protection in this regard? Can liability incur on the sole basis of violation of the duty to refer a preliminary question to the ECJ? Is it possible that liability may occur for breach of fundamental rights, such as the violation of the right to a fair trial in the future?

II. NATIONAL COURTS AND REMEDIAL COMPETENCE

Before starting the empirical analysis, it is essential to understand the legal context in which the *Köbler* principle operates. One special feature of EU law is that it is primarily applied and enforced by national courts and authorities, and not by EU institutions.[25] In this respect, the application of EU law is obligatory

[25] (ECJ) Opinion 1/09, para 69; Anagnostaras 2000; Anagnostaras 2002: 665; Becker 2007: 1036; Dougan 2004: 2; Fennelly 2013: 63; Prechal 2006b: 429; Temple Lang 2007: 1484; Tridimas 2013: 375–78; Tridimas 2015: 404; Van Cleynenbreugel 2012b: 90.

for national bodies under the conditions established in the EU treaties and in the case-law of the ECJ.[26]

In particular, as for Member State courts, they are EU courts of general jurisdiction, with the power and obligation to apply rules of EU law. In fact, supremacy and direct effect, in combination with the *Simmenthal* doctrine, established a system of decentralised judicial review.[27] National judges, in their capacity of 'agents of compliance' of EU law have, therefore, a duty to see that EU law is respected and applied correctly in the Member State.[28]

Also, in the absence of common EU procedural rules,[29] the application of these norms is ensured through the national procedural framework.[30] This principle, called the principle of national procedural autonomy, was laid down by the ECJ in a series of important judgments in the 1970s.[31]

In the earlier stages of the EU's development, the ECJ had remained content to respect national autonomy, intervening only when domestic rules either discriminated against claims based on EU law or rendered the exercise of EU rights virtually impossible. Consequently, there was hardly any interference by the ECJ regarding the standard of remedies to be provided. The ECJ made it clear that it was for national courts to apply the most appropriate of the various measures available under national law when these courts were called upon to enforce EU law.[32] Similarly, national courts were not required to create new remedies.[33] Later, the ECJ became increasingly concerned about the vulnerability of rights without remedies, which led to more demanding standards of effective judicial protection being expected of the national legal systems. Moreover, due to the extension of EU law beyond fundamental freedoms and 'liberalising rules', rights were no longer guaranteed by the mere invocability of a directly applicable provision in the proceedings. On the contrary, their protection required the disapplication of national law and, furthermore, appropriate remedies for bringing action.[34] In the early 1990s, the ECJ delivered several judgments which show a tendency in the ECJ's case-law to regard the existence of a remedy as an adjunct to rights conferred on individuals by EU provisions.[35]

[26] Caranta 1995: 704; Van Cleynenbreugel 2012a: 91.

[27] Weiler 1991; Dyèvre 2016.

[28] Bobek 2010: 130–32; Lenaerts 2007: 1659; Nollkaemper 2012: 157, 160–63; Temple Lang 1997: 3.

[29] Two main exceptions can be mentioned in this regard. First, according to Art 19(1) TEU, 'Member States shall provide remedies sufficient to ensure effective legal protection in the fields covered by Union law.' Second, there are several secondary pieces of legislation which contain remedial provisions. These rules apply, however, for certain sectors only. For further information on the secondary legislation containing special damages remedial rules, see Wilman 2015: 14–19; Wilman 2016.

[30] Eeckhout 1998: 66; Van Cleynenbreugel 2012a: 91.

[31] (ECJ) Judgment in *Comet*, paras 13, 15.

[32] Prechal 1997: 4; Van Gerven 2000: 503.

[33] (ECJ) Judgment in *Rewe-Handelsgesellschaft Nord and Rewe-Markt Steffen*, para 44.

[34] Arnull 2011; Biondi and Farley, 2009: 1–8; Bobek 2012: 305–09; Dougan 2000: 104; Dougan 2004: 28–34, 392–93; Eilmansberger 2004: 1206–19; Micklitz 2012: 364–65.

[35] (ECJ) Judgments in *Factortame and Others*, paras 19–22; in *Francovich and Others*, paras 33–36. See also Tomkins 2003: 282–83; Van Gerven 2000: 521.

The ECJ has gradually developed its doctrine on remedies available under EU law. These remedies comprise restitution of money paid contrary to EU rules, interim relief and liability in damages for breaches of EU law by the state.[36] In several instances, the ECJ even made it clear that a certain type of remedy must be available to the aggrieved parties – in the sense that individuals must have the right to seek a particular remedy.[37] Therefore, by reconsidering its case-law on national procedural rules, the ECJ established positive procedural obligations on Member States' legal orders.[38]

Member State liability for breach of EU law is referred to in the literature as a new type of remedy, which stems directly from EU law, and which constitutes a clear exception to the principle of procedural – for that matter 'remedial' – autonomy.[39] Here, the ECJ has clearly authorised the creation of a novel remedy, and even specified the conditions under which damages must be granted.[40] In this regard, ECJ has derived liability not only from the *effet utile* rule, but also from the principle of effective judicial protection.[41] In 2003, the ECJ extended the principle of state liability for breach of EU law by national courts. The principal justification for this extension was the central importance of national courts in the effective application of EU law, particularly in the protection of individuals' EU rights.[42] Liability for court decisions is, according to the ECJ, accepted in nearly all national legal systems and in international law as well, including in the ECHR.[43]

III. ECJ CASE-LAW ON STATE LIABILITY FOR BREACH OF EU LAW BY COURTS

So far there have been four judgments in which the ECJ dealt with substantial issues concerning state liability for judicial acts.[44]

[36] Eilmansberger 2004: 1231. Van Gerven (2000: 520) adds to the list the general remedy of setting aside national measures and Prechal (1997: 7) qualifies as remedy the obligation to have available some form of judicial review.

[37] Prechal 1997: 7.

[38] Becker 2007: 1053; Galetta 2010: 38–41; Van Cleynenbreugel 2012a: 90–91; (ECJ) judgment in *Unibet*.

[39] Harlow 2000: 80; Tomkins 2003: 283–84; Tridimas 2001: 301.

[40] See Leczykiewicz 2012: 2.

[41] Caranta 1995: 710; Dougan 2000a: 233–67, 298–306.

[42] (ECJ) Judgment in *Köbler*, paras 33–34.

[43] Classen 2004: 815; Pfander 2006: 297; Wissink 2005: 419–42.

[44] There have been other requests for preliminary rulings in which national courts asked questions regarding state liability for judicial acts. In these cases, either the ECJ has not answered the questions on its merits for procedural reasons or it simply reiterated the already well-known general principles regarding the establishment of liability and the assessment of the gravity of the violation. See (ECJ) judgments in *Consiglio Nazionale dei Geologi and Autorità garante della concorrenza e del mercato*; in *Aquino*; in *Fernand Ullens de Schooten*; in *Nikolay Kantarev v Balgarska narodna banka*; in *Hochtief Solutions AG Magyarországi Fióktelepe*; and order in *Hochtief Aktiengesellschaft*.

A. The *Köbler* Case

The first case was *Köbler*. As the facts of the case are well known by now, they will be only briefly recalled here. Mr Köbler worked as a professor at an Austrian university and claimed that he was entitled to a salary increase under Austrian laws, which provided a bonus for 15 years of prior service. The university denied the claim, saying that his prior service had occurred within another EU Member State. The professor brought the case before the Verwaltungsgerichtshof (VwGH, Austrian Administrative Court). The court referred a question for preliminary ruling to the ECJ concerning the interpretation of the principle of freedom of movement of workers. While the case was pending, the ECJ handed down a decision in an analogous case.[45] Upon learning of the decision, the VwGH withdrew his reference, and, ultimately, dismissed the claim. Since no further appeal lay against that judgment, the professor brought an action for damages against Austria before the Landesgericht für Zivilrechtssachen Wien (Regional Civil Court, Vienna). He claimed to be entitled to compensation due to the VwGH's breach of EU law in denying his free-movement claim without making a preliminary reference. The Landesgericht für Zivilrechtssachen Wien referred the issue to the ECJ, asking, among others, whether the principle of state liability for violation of EU law was also applicable where the violation was committed by a national supreme court.

In its decision, the ECJ upheld state liability in theory but rejected the claimant's action on the merits. The ECJ stated that its doctrine on state liability applies to all Member State actions, including those of the judiciary. Therefore, the state can be held liable for breach of EU law by national supreme courts. Moreover, regarding the conditions for liability, the ECJ did not distinguish between the branches of government that had committed the violation of EU law. As a result, the three conditions for state liability already established in *Francovich* and in *Brasserie du pêcheur and Factortame* also apply to judicial violations. Nevertheless, concerning the condition of 'sufficiently serious breach', the ECJ stated that liability can be incurred only in the exceptional case where a court adjudicating at last instance had 'manifestly' disregarded the applicable law.[46] This solution was adopted considering the specific nature of the judicial function and to the legitimate requirement of legal certainty. Therefore, in situations where the violation of EU law is attributable to a Member State court, the general condition of state liability concerning the gravity of the

[45] (ECJ) Order in *Köbler*.

[46] The cases of 'manifest disregard of the applicable law' are nevertheless defined by the same factors already stipulated by the ECJ when defining 'manifest and grave disregard of the limits on the discretion of a Member State or a Community institution' in prior cases of state liability. The ECJ merely added one factor – non-compliance by the court in question with its obligation to make a reference for a preliminary ruling. In our search for the practical importance and the real impact of the *Köbler* principle, this factor is of paramount importance. See (ECJ) judgment in *Brasserie du pêcheur and Factortame*.

breach, namely the 'sufficiently serious breach of EU law' is met where the national court commits a 'manifest infringement of the applicable law'.

The ECJ then stated that the contested Austrian provision constituted an obstacle to freedom of movement for workers, which is prohibited under EU law. According to the ECJ's settled case-law, it is, in principle, up to the national courts to determine whether the criteria for establishing liability are satisfied. Nonetheless, in the *Köbler* case, having all the materials needed to examine the requisite criteria, the ECJ decided to make this evaluation itself. The ECJ concluded that even if the contested judgment had been based on an incorrect reading of the prior ECJ judgment, and therefore constituted an infringement of EU law, this infringement itself could not be described as manifest.

B. The *Traghetti del Mediterraneo* Case

The second case before the ECJ concerning state liability for judicial acts was *Traghetti del Mediterraneo*.[47] In this case, the question arose whether Italian rules, which severely restricted the possibility to hold the state liable for judicial errors, were compatible with the principle of effectiveness of EU law and, especially, with the *Köbler* judgment.

In the underlying proceedings, a maritime transport undertaking operating regular ferry services in Italian seas blamed its competitor for having breached EU competition law and claimed damages for these infringements before the Italian courts. The courts dismissed this action as they concluded that there had not been any violation of EU law. The Corte Suprema di Cassazione (Italian Supreme Court of Cassation) rejected the claim at last instance without making a reference for preliminary ruling to the ECJ on the interpretation of the EU competition rules relevant to the case. It concluded that the interpretation of EU rules by the Italian courts in the underlying proceedings had been consistent with the ECJ case-law. Afterward, the company brought a liability action before the Tribunale di Genova (Genova District Court) against the state for compensation for the damage suffered because of the erroneous application of EU competition law by the Corte Suprema di Cassazione and for the failure to request a preliminary ruling from the ECJ in the main proceedings. The Italian state raised a question of inadmissibility, claiming that the interpretation of provisions of law in the exercise of judicial functions cannot give rise to state liability under the national rules.[48]

Consequently, the question arose in the liability proceedings whether these rules were compatible with the principle of effectiveness of the EU law and, especially, with the *Köbler* liability. Therefore, the Tribunale di Genova submitted a

[47] (ECJ) Judgment in *Traghetti del Mediterraneo*.
[48] (IT) Legge, 13/04/1988, no 117, Art 2. This provision was modified in 2015 and the amendments entered into force on 19 March 2015.

request for preliminary ruling to the ECJ on this matter. Examining the Italian rules, the ECJ argued that the exclusion of all state liability, on the ground that the infringement of EU law arises from an interpretation of provisions of law, would be tantamount to rendering the principle laid down in the *Köbler* judgment meaningless. An analogous conclusion was drawn regarding a legislation which, in a general manner excludes all state liability where the infringement attributable to a court of that state arises from its assessment of the facts and evidence.[49]

Therefore, the ECJ found that EU law

> precludes national legislation which excludes State liability, in a general manner, for damage caused to individuals by an infringement of Community law attributable to a court adjudicating at last instance by reason of the fact that the infringement in question results from an interpretation of provisions of law or an assessment of facts or evidence carried out by that court. Community law also precludes national legislation which limits such liability solely to cases of intentional fault and serious misconduct on the part of the court, if such a limitation were to lead to exclusion of the liability of the Member State concerned in other cases where a manifest infringement of the applicable law was committed, as set out in paragraphs 53 to 56 of the *Köbler* judgment.[50]

C. The *Ferreira da Silva e Brito e.a.* Case

The third ECJ judgment on state liability for judicial acts concerned another type of restriction of state liability for judicial acts, which is applied by several Member States.[51] In the case of *Ferreira da Silva e Brito e.a.*, a Portuguese court asked the ECJ whether national rules requiring the reversal of the contested judicial decision as a precondition for a liability claim are compatible with the *Köbler* principle.[52]

The factual background of the case before the ECJ can be summarised as follows. Mr Ferreira da Silva e Brito was dismissed as a part of a collective redundancy when the company employing him was wound up. He and other employees brought an action against the collective redundancy before the Portuguese courts, seeking reinstatement and payment of their remuneration. The Supremo Tribunal de Justiça (Portuguese Supreme Court) held, without submitting a request for a preliminary ruling to the ECJ, that the collective redundancy was not unlawful and dismissed the action. The employees then brought an action against the state before the Varas Cíveis de Lisboa (Court

[49] (ECJ) Judgment in *Traghetti del Mediterraneo*, paras 36, 37, 40.

[50] (ECJ) Judgment in *Traghetti del Mediterraneo*, para 46.

[51] For restrictions in national laws hindering the establishment of state liability for judicial wrongs, see s 2.III.A.

[52] (ECJ) Judgment in *Ferreira da Silva e Brito e.a.* For an analysis of the case, see Silveira and Fernandes 2016, and for different aspects of the case, see s 2.II.A.ii.g(4).

of First Instance, Lisbon), claiming compensation for their material loss. They maintained that the judgment of the Supremo Tribunal de Justiça was manifestly unlawful since it had misinterpreted the EU law and the Supremo Tribunal de Justiça had failed to comply with its obligation to refer questions concerning the interpretation of EU law to the ECJ.

In this context, the Varas Cíveis de Lisboa submitted a request for preliminary ruling to the ECJ. It asked, among other things, whether the Supremo Tribunal de Justiça had an obligation to refer a question to the ECJ.[53] In this respect, the ECJ stated that

> in circumstances such as those of the case before the referring court, which are characterised both by conflicting lines of case law at national level … and by the fact that that concept frequently gives rise to difficulties of interpretation in the various Member States, a national court or tribunal against whose decisions there is no judicial remedy under national law must comply with its obligation to make a reference to the Court, in order to avert the risk of an incorrect interpretation of EU law.

Moreover, the Portuguese court also asked a question on the compatibility with the *Köbler* principle of national rules requiring the prior reversal of the decision that caused the loss or damage, as a precondition of the liability action.[54]

Examining this provision, the ECJ concluded that a rule of that kind may indeed make it excessively difficult to obtain reparation for the loss or damage caused by the infringement of EU law, given that the situations in which decisions of the Supremo Tribunal de Justiça may be subject to review are extremely limited.[55] Therefore, the ECJ concluded that EU law and the principles regarding state liability

> preclud[e] a provision of national law which requires, as a precondition, the setting aside of the decision given by that court or tribunal which caused the loss or damage, when such setting aside is, in practice, impossible.[56]

Noteworthy is that despite the above-described conclusions, the ECJ did not explicitly apply the criteria formulated in *Köbler*, nor did it examine the fulfilment of the conditions of state liability in the judgment.[57]

[53] On another aspect of the case, which concerns the application of the *acte clair* doctrine, see Broberg 2011; Kornezov 2016.

[54] (PT) Lei no 67/2007, Artigo 13° N °2.

[55] (ECJ) Judgment in *Ferreira da Silva e Brito e.a.*, paras 51–52.

[56] (ECJ) Judgment in *Ferreira da Silva e Brito e.a.*, para 60. See also Silveira and Fernandes 2016: 655.

[57] Silveira and Fernandes (2016: 651) deduce, however, from the ECJ judgment, which concluded that an infringement of Art 267(3) TFEU had taken place, that the national court has manifestly infringed EU law within the meaning of the *Köbler* judgment. Krommendijk (2017: 58) is more prudent in his conclusion, when he observes that the violation of the referral could potentially give rise to state liability. On this topic, see s 3.III.

D. The *Tomášová* Case

In the fourth case, the ECJ was invited to pronounce on several questions regarding the application of the *Köbler* doctrine. The alleged violation of EU law consisted in the failure by the national court, in proceedings for enforcement of an arbitration award, to assess of its own motion whether the terms of the consumer contract at issue were unfair.

The background to the dispute is as follows. Ms Tomášová signed a contract for a consumer loan with a financial institution. Under the arbitration clause, stipulated in the contract and formulated beforehand by the supplier, she had to submit to arbitration proceedings before they could turn to a court of the state. When a dispute arose between the parties, the arbitrator decided in favour of the supplier, and the state enforcement court, the Okresný súd Prešov (Prešov District Court), authorised enforcement of the arbitrator's decision. Afterward, Ms Tomášová asked the court to order the Slovak Republic to pay her compensation, on the ground of breach of EU law committed by the Okresný súd Prešov in the enforcement proceedings. She contended that several clauses of the contract were unfair and should have been disregarded according to the applicable EU directive. She argued that the enforcement court had breached EU law when it had authorised the enforcement without assessing, of its own motion, whether the terms of the consumer contract were unfair. The court hearing the liability claim submitted a request for preliminary ruling and asked the ECJ whether the national court could incur liability even if a person deemed to have suffered damages had not exhausted all national legal remedies.[58] It also asked a question on the scope of the possible compensation claim. In addition, it sought guidance from the ECJ on the question whether, given the circumstance of the case, the violation of EU law committed by the national court could be considered as manifest.

As for the first and second aspects, the ECJ stated, succinctly, that the scope of compensation and the relationship between a liability action and the other actions available under national law fall within the concept of national procedural autonomy.

Therefore, the ECJ found that

> the conditions of the compensation of damages …, such as the identification and assession of the harm and the the relationship between an action of compensation for damages and the other actions available under national law are determined by the national laws subject to observance of the principles of equivalence and effectiveness.[59]

[58] (SK) Okresný súd Prešov, Uznesenie, 12/03/2015.

[59] (ECJ) Judgment in *Tomášová*, paras 40–41; opinion of AG Wahl in *Tomášová*, paras 85–86.

As for the third aspect, namely whether the state may be held liable because the national enforcement court failed to assess of its own motion whether the terms of the contract at issue were unfair, the ECJ responded in the negative. In this regard, it stated that such liability may only incur if the violation was committed by a national court adjudicating at last instance, which belonged to the national court to verify. It then pointed out that in order for liability to be incurred, the national court has to commit a manifest infringement of the applicable law or the established ECJ case-law. Nevertheless, the obligation of the national court to assess of its own motion whether the clauses of a consumer contract are unfair became established ECJ case-law only after the main proceedings. Therefore, the national court has not committed a manifest infringement of the applicable EU law, neither has it infringed the established ECJ case-law by its decision. Consequently, the conditions of state liability were not fulfilled in the case.[60]

[60] (ECJ) Judgment in *Tomášová*, paras 23–36.

2

Conclusions from the Past

I. DIFFICULTIES HINDERING THE APPLICATION OF THE *KÖBLER* PRINCIPLE

BASED ON THE research conducted, since the pronouncement of the ECJ judgment in 2003, there have been about 60 reported cases from the 28, and now 27 Member States concerning the application of the *Köbler* principle.[1] Even if we take into consideration the fact that not all cases have been reported, the number of actions remains quite low. Moreover, in all of these cases, damages have only been awarded in five occasions so far.[2] This raises the question as to why *Köbler* liability is not a frequently used method to remedy violations of individuals' rights protected under EU law. There seem to be multiple explanations for this, starting from the problems inherent in the conditions of *Köbler* liability, through the challenges in national laws and the resistance by national courts to apply the principle, to the existence of better alternatives for the parties.

The following sections focus on these limitations in order to verify their role in hindering the application of the *Köbler* liability. To begin with, the second section examines problems relating to the conditions of liability, such as the 'manifest infringement of applicable law' criterion and the difficulties in establishing causality. The third section then analyses whether the principle is accepted in national laws in practice. In this regard, the domestic legislative restrictions and the positions of national courts regarding the application of the principle are presented. In this context, the question of the extent to which the *Köbler* liability is applied in domestic judicial practice is thoroughly examined. Next, in the fourth section, the alternative remedies available under national

[1] The results of the research conducted on the subject-matter of this chapter were first published in Varga 2016a; Varga 2016c.

[2] (FI) Korkein oikeus, tuomio, 05/07/2013, reported by Pedersen in Reflets no 3/2013: 22–23; Korkein oikeus, tuomio, 05/03/2016; (IT) Tribunale di Genova, ordinanza, 31/03/2009, reported by Gencarelli 2014: 279; (SE) Justitiekanslern, Beslut, 06/04/2009, reported by Göransson 2014: 493–95; (BG) Apelativen sad – Burgas, Reshenie, 26/04/2016, confirming the judgment of Okrazhen sad Yambol, Reshenie, 04/11/2015, reported by Todorova in Reflets no 1/2016: 14. It is noteworthy that the decision of the Tribunale di Genova was not a definitive judgment. There has also been a sixth decision rendered by an appeal court which was, however, reversed at last instance. See (FR) Cour d'appel de Paris, arrêt, 06/05/2015; Cour de Cassation, arrêt, 18/11/2016.

laws for violations of EU law by Member State courts are presented. Finally, the fifth section draws a conclusion on the efficacy of this remedy in protecting the individual's rights and in ensuring the effective application of EU law.

II. PROBLEMS INHERENT TO THE PRINCIPLE

Research reveals that on the rare occasions where *Köbler* liability has been relied on, compensation has almost never been awarded. This raises the question as to whether the conditions in EU law triggering liability are adequate. In this regard, two issues deserve particular attention: the first one is the criterion of 'manifest breach of applicable law'; and the second one is the difficulty of linking a breach of EU law to the judiciary's action.

A. Criterion of the Manifestly Serious Breach

The focus of this subsection is the criterion established by the ECJ regarding the gravity of the breach of EU law by the national court.[3] As already mentioned, academic writers have widely criticised this element of judicial liability since the pronouncement of the *Köbler* judgment.[4] This section aims to examine the conditions under which the criterion of manifest breach of applicable law can be, at least on theoretical grounds, fulfilled. Then it will also assess the national judicial practice in this respect.

This subsection is divided into five parts. The first describes the criterion of 'manifest infringement of the applicable law'. The second examines the procedural obligations of Member State courts regarding the application and the correct interpretation of EU law in order to identify scenarios eventually amounting to such a qualified infringement. The third analyses the impact of the violation of the referral duty on the gravity of the breach of EU law and presents a theory on possible manifest infringements. The fourth section then summarises the relevant case-law of the national courts regarding *Köbler* claims. The fifth section concludes.

i. The ECJ Judgment

Academics predicted shortly after the pronouncement of the ECJ judgment that the practical effect of *Köbler* would depend on how the ECJ interprets the term a 'manifest breach'.[5]

[3] The content of this chapter was published previously as an article: see Varga 2016b.

[4] Beutler 2009: 792; Golecki and Wojciechowski 2009: 195–97; Komárek 2005b: 17; Rodríguez 2004–05: 614–15; Valutytė 2011: 37, 47.

[5] Tridimas 2007: 154–55.

In this regard, it seems to be useful to recall the relevant paragraphs of the *Köbler* judgment. According to the ECJ, state liability for damage caused by Member State bodies is governed by the same conditions irrespective of which body is responsible for the infringement.[6] However, the ECJ added that the specific nature of the judicial function and the legitimate requirements of legal certainty justify a more restricted interpretation of 'a sufficiently serious breach' when it comes to a breach committed by a Member State court adjudicating at last instance:

> State liability for an infringement of Community law by a decision of a national court adjudicating at last instance can be incurred only in the exceptional case where the court has manifestly infringed the applicable law.[7]

In order to determine whether this condition is satisfied, various factors must be taken into account, including

> the degree of clarity and precision of the rule infringed, whether the infringement was intentional, whether the error of law was excusable or inexcusable, the position taken, where applicable, by a Community institution and non-compliance by the court in question with its obligation to make a reference for a preliminary ruling under the third paragraph of Art 234 EC.[8]
>
> In any event, an infringement of Community law will be sufficiently serious where the decision concerned was made in manifest breach of the case law of the Court in the matter.[9]

Therefore, in situations where the violation of EU law is attributable to a Member State court, the general condition of state liability concerning the gravity of the breach, namely the 'sufficiently serious breach of EU law', is met where the national court commits a 'manifest infringement of the applicable law'.

The ECJ has summarised its conclusions in the operative part of the judgment in the following words:

> [T]he principle that Member States are obliged to make good damage caused to individuals by infringements of Community law for which they are responsible is also applicable where the alleged infringement stems from a decision of a court adjudicating at last instance where the rule of Community law infringed is intended to confer rights on individuals, the breach is sufficiently serious and there is a direct causal link between that breach and the loss or damage sustained by the injured parties. In order to determine whether the infringement is sufficiently serious when the infringement at issue stems from such a decision, the competent national court, taking into account the specific nature of the judicial function, must determine whether that infringement is manifest. It is for the legal system of each Member State to designate the court competent to determine disputes relating to that reparation.

[6] (ECJ) Judgment in *Köbler*, paras 51–52. See also Jans and Duijkersloot 2015: 465–71.
[7] (ECJ) Judgment in *Köbler*, para 53.
[8] (ECJ) Judgment in *Köbler*, para 55.
[9] (ECJ) Judgment in *Köbler*, para 56. On the question whether it means building a judicial hierarchy in the EU, see eg Komárek 2005a: 92–94; Komárek 2005b.

What is interesting for the purposes of the present analysis is to examine whether, and under what circumstances, the breach of EU law qualifies as manifest. According to the doctrine, two factors are most relevant. The first one is the clarity and precision of the law in the area where the violation has taken place. The second one is the disregard of the duty to make a reference. The problems that transpire from the practical application of these two criteria are, however, deeper than they first seem.[10] Before studying these relevant factors, it is noteworthy to define the term 'violation of the applicable [EU] law' in the context of state liability.

a. Violation of the Applicable EU Law

Due to the decentralised enforcement of EU law, EU norms are primarily applied and enforced by national courts and authorities.[11] One might think that Member State bodies, including courts, are obliged to apply these *substantive* EU rules in every case.[12] However, the non-application or the misinterpretation of such norms does not amount to a violation of EU law in every situation. This is because substantive EU norms do not have to be applied directly and obligatorily by Member State authorities in every situation.[13] As a matter of fact, the application of substantive EU rules is obligatory for Member State bodies only under the conditions developed in the case-law of the ECJ.[14] This means that *substantive* EU norms must only be enforced if correspondent *procedural* EU obligations are imposed on Member State bodies with regard to the application of EU law in the specific case.[15] Hence, the violation (misinterpretation or non-application) of the substantive provision qualifies as a breach of EU law only where *a procedural obligation to apply this norm exists* in the case at hand.[16] Once the national court has the obligation to *apply* the substantive norm, it also has to ensure that it is *correctly* understood and applied. This means that in such

[10] Anagnostaras 2006: 744.

[11] Anagnostaras 2000; Anagnostaras 2002: 665; Becker 2007: 1036; Lenaerts 2007: 1659; Lenaerts et al 2014: 3, 13–14; Lock 2012: 1675; Temple Lang 2007: 1484; Temple Lang 1997: 3; Van Cleynenbreugel 2012a: 90.

[12] In this work, 'substantive EU norms' covers written provisions in the treaties and in the secondary legislation which may or may not have direct effect, and which may or may not confer substantive rights on individuals. The term 'substantive EU norms' may also include rules and principles established in the ECJ case-law.

[13] Consider, for example, the absence of horizontal direct effect of non-implemented directives.

[14] Anagnostaras 2000; Biondi and Farley 2009: 3–8; Caranta 1995: 704; Nassimpian 2007: 821; Van Cleynenbreugel 2012a: 91.

[15] In this book, the expression 'procedural obligations' encompasses various forms of duties of Member State bodies to give effect to substantive EU norms. While most of these obligations have been developed in the ECJ case-law, the exceptions are the obligation of the legislation to transpose a directive into the domestic legal order, which is enshrined under Art 288 TFEU and the obligation of the courts to make a reference for preliminary ruling to the ECJ, which is found in Art 267(3) TFEU. See also Van Cleynenbreugel 2012a: 90–91, 94; Galetta 2010: 1–2.

[16] See also Dougan 2017: 127; Prechal 2006a: 301.

situations, either the misinterpretation or the non-application of the substantive norm qualifies as a breach of EU law.

It is therefore important to distinguish between the substantive EU rules and the procedural EU obligations. It is also necessary to recall the procedural duties of national courts, as *Köbler* liability arises in the event of violation of these obligations. The well-known procedural duties of national courts regarding the application of EU law[17] are as follows: (1) to apply directly effective EU law and protect the rights this confers on individuals; (2) to leave unapplied national rules that are contrary to EU law; (3) and to interpret and apply national laws as far as possible to make them compatible with EU law. Considering the above, we can add to this list the obligation of national courts (4) to ascertain that the content of the substantive provision is *correctly* understood and applied in the case. Moreover, if the national court encounters doubt regarding the above obligations, it is required (5) to submit a request for preliminary ruling to the ECJ.[18] These procedural obligations have their own limits, however; and they apply only if certain conditions are fulfilled.

Accordingly, the five main scenarios that may lead to the violation of EU law in the terms of the *Köbler* judgment are the scenarios in which the national court, in breach of its corresponding procedural obligations: (1) does not apply an EU norm that has direct effect; (2) continues to apply a national rule that is contrary to the EU law; (3) does not give an interpretation to the national law that is consistent with the EU norm; (4) misinterprets the substantive EU norm; or (5) does not refer a preliminary question to the ECJ.[19]

In any case, the breach of these procedural obligations should result in a breach of the substantive EU norm which confers rights on individuals, so that state liability arises. These infringements are, typically, the following: in scenarios (1)–(3), the non-application of the substantive norm; in scenario (4), the misinterpretation of the substantive norm; and in scenario (5), either the non-application or the misinterpretation of the substantive norm.[20] Moreover, the violation of the above – *substantive* and *procedural* – EU rules by a national

[17] In this work, the expression 'application of EU law' is used in a general way, and refers to any form of measures contributing to ensure the application of the substantive EU norm – regardless of which Member State body is responsible for its execution. See also Becker 2007: 1037. For a more comprehensive list, see Claes 2006: 58–59; Fennelly 2013: 64–78; Sjöstrand 2013; Temple Lang 2007.

[18] As a supplementary obligation, we can add to this list obligation (6) to decide on the request in reasonable time.

[19] Tridimas 2007: 155.

[20] Scenario (4) shows that there is no clear distinction between the procedural obligations and the substantive EU norms. In this work, the expression of 'violation of EU law' by national courts is used in a general sense, as in the ECJ judgment in *Köbler*. It can take the form of violation of a substantive EU rule ('misinterpretation of a substantive EU norm'), of breach of a procedural obligation ('non- or mistaken application of the substantive EU norm'), or of infringement of the duty to request a preliminary ruling from the ECJ. The two former violations are referred to, together, as 'misinterpretation or misapplication of EU law'. The benefit of using this expression is that it focuses not on the violation of the substantive EU norm but on the violation of the obligation to apply it – which is what triggers liability. See also Prechal 2006a: 301.

court is not enough to entail liability for the state. According to the ECJ, liability for judicial breaches 'can only arise in the exceptional case where the court has manifestly infringed the applicable law'. This raises the questions whether, and if so, under what circumstances, a breach can be qualified as manifest. To answer these questions, it is important to go through the relevant factors the ECJ enumerated in *Köbler* regarding the evaluation of the gravity of the breach.[21]

b. Factors to be Considered

According to the ECJ, various factors must be taken into account in order to determine whether the breach of EU law by the Member State court is manifest. These factors are as follows.

Degree of clarity and precision of the rule infringed: This factor refers to the *substantive* EU norm which confers rights to individuals and which is not, or is incorrectly, applied in the procedure. If this norm is clear, it means that the content and the extent of the right conferred to individuals are obvious, and the national courts should not encounter problems concerning its interpretation. However, the clarity of the substantive norm is independent from the question as to whether it should be applied in the national proceedings. This latter issue relates to the procedural obligation – that is to say, to the obligation of the national court regarding the application of the substantive EU norm.

The question whether the infringement was intentional, whether the error of law was excusable or inexcusable and the position taken, where applicable, by an EU institution: These criteria are primarily related to the violation by the Member State court of its *procedural* obligation regarding the application and/or the correct interpretation[22] of a substantive norm. Therefore, they should be analysed in relation to the procedural obligation which the Member State court breaches when it refuses to apply, or when it does not interpret correctly, the substantive EU norm.

Non-compliance by the national court with its obligation to make a reference for a preliminary ruling: In my opinion, the referral duty cannot be isolated from the procedural obligation of the Member State court to apply and ensure the correct interpretation of EU law. On the contrary, the obligation to make a reference for preliminary ruling emerges only in situations where either the interpretation of the substantive norm and/or its application in the national proceedings[23] is ambiguous. It is, however, unclear whether the consideration of this factor actually raises or lowers the standard of liability. A separate section will be dedicated to this issue.[24]

[21] (ECJ) Judgment in *Köbler*, para 55.
[22] (ECJ) Judgment in *Ferreira da Silva e Brito e.a.*, para 45.
[23] (ECJ) Judgment in *DI*, para 15.
[24] See s 2.II.A.iii.b.

Moreover, it is important not to forget that, in state liability, the general factor to evaluate the gravity of the breach of EU law is whether the Member State body has *manifestly and gravely disregarded the limits on the exercise of its powers*. In *Tomášová*, this criterion has been slightly reformulated as *the scope of the room for assessment that the infringed rule allows for national authorities*.[25] Therefore, the margin of discretion at the Member State body's disposal when deciding whether and how to apply EU law is of paramount importance.[26] This criterion is in particular relevant when considering the freedom of choice of the national court on how to respect its procedural obligation to apply EU law and whether to make a preliminary reference.[27] Besides, the ECJ emphasised in *Köbler* that the *manifest breach of its case-law in the matter* amounts to a manifest breach. This appears to be the logical consequence of the restricted margin of discretion of the court regarding the interpretation and the application of the EU law.

ii. Procedural Obligations of Member State Courts to Apply EU Law

The next part of this paper will present an analysis of the procedural obligations mentioned above in order to identify scenarios of a 'manifest infringement of the applicable EU law' by the national courts.[28] In this regard, consideration will be given to the obligations (1) to apply directly effective EU law; (2) to leave unapplied national rules that are contrary to EU law; (3) to interpret and apply national laws as far as possible to make them compatible with EU law; (4) to ensure that the content of the substantive provision is *correctly* understood and applied in the case; and (5) to make a preliminary reference to the ECJ.

a. Procedural Rule of Reason and Limitations to the Ex Officio Application of EU Law

(1) Procedural Rule of Reason

Before starting this analysis, it must be recalled that, in the decentralised system of enforcement of EU law, Member States enjoy national procedural autonomy,[29]

[25] (ECJ) Judgment in *Tomášová*, para 25.

[26] See also (ECJ) opinion of AG Tesauro in Joined Cases *Brasserie du pêcheur and Factortame*, para 78; judgments in *British Telecommunications*, para 42; in *Dillenkofer and Others*, para 25; in *Stockholm Lindöpark*, para 39; in *N*, para 64; in *Robins and Others*, para 70; in *Test Claimants in the Thin Cap Group Litigation*, para 118; orders in *Test Claimants in the FII Group Litigation*, para 212; in *Test Claimants in the CFC and Dividend Group Litigation*, para 121.

[27] See also (ECJ) Opinion of AG Léger in *Köbler*, paras 133–40; Jans and Duijkersloot 2015: 446–51.

[28] Even though the procedural obligations of national court regarding the application of EU law apply to all jurisdictional instances, only breaches committed by national courts of last instance are relevant for the purposes of the present analysis, as only a breach of EU law by these courts can trigger liability for the state and only these courts are under an obligation to make a reference for preliminary ruling.

[29] On the principle of national procedural autonomy, see De Búrca 1997: 37–46; Galetta 2010: 33–74; Hoskins 1996; Kakouris 1997; Micklitz and de Witte 2012; Wallerman 2016a; Wattel 2008.

which is only limited by the principles of equivalence and effectiveness.[30] Nevertheless, as far as effectiveness is concerned, the procedural rule of reason may even prevail over this principle. According to this latter principle, national procedural provisions hindering the application of EU law – or, in other terms, the *execution of procedural obligations of national courts* regarding the application of EU law – may be justified and accepted.[31]

In this regard, the ECJ has consistently held that every case in which the question arises as to whether a national procedural provision makes the application of EU law impossible or excessively difficult must be analysed by reference to the role of that provision in the procedure. In that context, it is necessary to take into consideration, where relevant, the principles which lie at the basis of the national legal system, such as the protection of the rights of the defence, the principle of legal certainty and the proper conduct of the proceedings.[32]

Therefore, the procedural obligations of the national courts analysed below may be subjected to national procedural rules. One of the most relevant procedural limitations on the execution of the procedural obligations by the Member States courts concerns the ex officio application of EU law.[33] Other such limitations may include, for example, the statute of limitations,[34] the restriction regarding the pleas that can be raised for the first time before a national court of appeal,[35] and the restraint scope of judicial review of decisions of administrative authorities.[36]

(2) National Procedural Autonomy and the *Köbler* Doctrine

The principle of national procedural autonomy, and especially the rule according to which there is no obligation for the national judges to apply EU law ex officio, have an impact on the application of the *Köbler* doctrine. In several cases the liability action was dismissed on the ground that the consideration of EU law in the main proceedings was not an obligation imposed on the national judge, as the claimant has not relied on arguments based on EU law either.

From the case-law, see in particular (ECJ) judgments in *Russo*; in *Rewe-Zentralfinanz and Rewe-Zentral*; in *Rewe-Handelsgesellschaft Nord and Rewe-Markt Steffen*; in *San Georgio*, para 13; in *Just*, para 25; in *Francovich and Others*, para 41; in *Wells*, para 67; in *Danske Slagterier*, para 31.

[30] (ECJ) Judgments in *Duarte Hueros*, para 31; in *Peterbroeck*, para 12; in *Wells*, para 67.

[31] (ECJ) Judgments in *van Schijndel and van Veen*, para 19; in *van der Weerd and Others*, para 33; in *Peterbroeck*, para 14.

[32] (ECJ) Judgments in *Fallimento Olimpiclub*, para 27; in *Kapferer*, para 41; in *Târşia*, paras 36–37, in *XC e.a.*, para 49.

[33] (ECJ) Judgments in *Asturcom Telecomunicaciones*; in *Cofidis*; in *Eco Swiss*; in *Kraaijeveld and Others*; in *Pannon GSM*; in *Peterbroeck*; *van Schijndel and van Veen*; in *Verholen*. For further information, see eg Engström 2008; Heukels 1996; Jans and Marseille 2008; Lenaerts et al 2014: 131–36; Prechal 1998: 690–93; Prechal and Shelkoplyas 2004; Tridimas 2006: 461–66; Van Dam and van Eijsden 2009: 17.

[34] (ECJ) Judgment in *Barth*, paras 17, 20, 17, 20, 27–30.

[35] (ECJ) Judgment in *Bensada Benallal*, paras 24, 29, 31, 35.

[36] (ECJ) Judgment in *East Sussex County Council*, paras 55, 58.

In this regard, three examples will be provided, one is a judgment of the Hungarian Kúria (Supreme Court, Hungary), the second was delivered by the Polish Naczelny Sąd Administracyjny (Supreme Administrative Court, Poland), and the third one is a judgment rendered by the Irish High Court.

In its judgment rendered in a *Köbler* liability action in 2013, the Hungarian Kúria emphasised that the alleged illegality of proceedings before the administrative judge must be evaluated in the light of the national procedural rules, and, especially, in the light of the principle under which the parties delimit the scope of the case.[37] In this regard, the Kúria pointed out that the claimant himself had not invoked arguments based on EU law in the proceedings before the administrative court. According to the Kúria, since the court is bound by the pleas raised by the parties, the administrative court had not committed any breach when it had not considered the EU law.

In the second judgment delivered in 2014, the Polish Naczelny Sąd Administracyjny held that if the claimant had not invoked EU law in the prior proceedings, it was not possible to claim of violation of EU law in a subsequent liability action.[38] The Naczelny Sąd Administracyjny emphasised that an action to declare a final judgment unlawful cannot substitute, supplement or be filed before an appeal on points of law.

Finally, in its judgment rendered in 2017, the High Court dismissed an action containing several claims, including a claim for damages, based on the principle preventing the party from raising legal points that could have been raised in the earlier proceedings.[39] According to the High Court, 'there was not any ECJ authority directly suggesting that an exception to the principle of finality should be made' because the court has an obligation to assess the unfair terms of the contract of its own motion. It also pointed out that the claimant was entitled to present any and all arguments in the main proceedings, including those founded upon EU law, but failed to do so.

These cases demonstrate that the absence of the obligation for national courts to apply EU law ex officio in the underlying, contested proceedings has a strong connection, when it comes to a subsequent liability action, with the duty of the parties to mitigate their damages and to rely on arguments on EU law relevant to the case themselves. In addition, the first two cases show a correct interpretation and application of the procedural rule of reason and of the limitation to the obligation of national judges to apply EU law in the main proceedings. The third judgment rendered by the Irish High Court does not seem compatible with the effectiveness principle, as the national court failed

[37] (HU) Kúria, ítélet, 11/12/2013, reported by Varga in Reflets no 2/2014: 30. For different aspects of the case see ss 2.II.B.iv.c and 2.III.B.iv.b.

[38] (PL) Naczelny Sąd Administracyjny, Wyrok, 26/06/2014, reported in database JuriFast. See also s 2.III.B.iii.b.

[39] (IR) High Court, judgment, 17/10/2017. For different aspects of the case, see s 2.III.B.iv.c.

to apply EU law on its own motion in an action that fell under the scope of application of the unfair contract terms directive. In terms of ECJ case-law, in cases regarding consumer protection, an obligation to apply EU rules ex officio is imposed on national judges.[40]

b. Application of EU Provisions with Direct Effect

(1) Principle and Limits of Direct Effect

The first obligation of national courts emanates from the seminal judgment in *van Gend & Loos*, which introduced the doctrine of direct effect into the EU legal order. In this landmark case, the ECJ established that certain EU rules are capable of producing direct effects and creating individual rights, which national courts must protect.[41] In other words, direct effect enables individuals to invoke EU provisions immediately before a national court. From the point of view of the procedural obligation of Member State courts, direct effect means that national courts *are bound to enforce and apply directly those provisions of EU law that have direct effect*.[42]

Not all EU provisions, however, have direct effect. According to the threshold criteria developed by the ECJ, a substantive EU norm has to be clear, sufficiently precise and unconditional in order to produce such effect.[43] The test seems to be whether the EU law provision contains an understandable and justiciable rule of behaviour, which can be applied by the national courts,[44] or whether this norm is 'sufficiently operational in itself to be applied by a court'.[45] EU law provisions that are not directly effective are those from which the extraction of an immediately applicable rule is impossible.[46]

It also depends on the type of the EU legislative act containing the EU norm whether the latter has direct effect.[47] Treaty[48] and regulation[49] provisions are presumed to be directly effective, even in horizontal situations governing relationships between individuals.[50] Decisions addressed to a Member State might produce direct effect with respect to individuals within the Member State in question, provided that the conditions for direct effect are fulfilled.[51] This direct

[40] (ECJ) Judgments in *Océano Grupo Editorial and Salvat Editores*, paras 27–28; in *Cofidis*, paras 32–33; order in *VB Pénzügyi Lízing and Pannon GSM*, para 48.

[41] (ECJ) Judgment in *van Gend & Loos*.

[42] See eg Da Cruz Vilaça 2013: 281–89, Bobek 2017: 149–53.

[43] The clarity of the substantive norm and of the procedural obligation to apply it are, therefore, separate issues. See also Dougan 2004: 56–59.

[44] Bobek 2017: 145.

[45] (ECJ) Opinion of AG van Gerven in *Banks*, para 27.

[46] Bobek 2017: 146.

[47] For a detailed presentation on this issue, see Jans and Verhoeven 2015: 87–109 and Kofler 2014.

[48] (ECJ) Judgments in *Reyners*; in *Defrenne*; in *Walrave and Koch*; in *Viking*.

[49] (ECJ) Judgments in *Leonesio*, para 5; in *SGB Belgium*, para 32; in *Handlbauer*, para 25.

[50] (ECJ) Judgments in *BRT v SABAM*; in *Defrenne*; in *Walrave and Koch*; in *Fra.bo*, para 31.

[51] (ECJ) Judgments in *Grad*, para 5; in *Hansa Fleisch Ernst Mundt*, paras 12 and 13; in *Folesev*, para 11.

effect is, however, limited to vertical situations, namely when an individual relies on the EU norm against a Member State.

Directive provisions have direct effect only if the Member State has not transposed the directive into the national legal system by the deadline.[52] Moreover, as a main rule, neither an individual nor the state can rely directly on an unimplemented directive against an individual.[53] As a main rule, only against the state[54] are individuals given the right to rely directly on a directive.[55] For this function of the direct effect it is, however, irrelevant whether the individual was conferred a substantive right by the directive.[56] In addition, the Member State is precluded from enforcing the non-implemented directive against its own nationals; therefore, the reverse vertical direct effect of directives is also excluded.[57]

There might be situations, therefore, where it is not evident whether the substantive EU norm has indeed direct effect. If there is any doubt, the Member State court has to make a reference for a preliminary ruling to the ECJ, which is the competent court to decide on the direct effect of the substantive EU norm.[58]

Taking into account the previous reflection, a question arises as to under what circumstances violating the obligation to apply directly a substantive EU provision in the national proceedings amounts to a manifest breach of EU law. To address this issue, it is important to distinguish between two situations, namely where there is no ECJ judgment available on the matter, and where it is established case-law that the norm at question has direct effect.

In the first situation, a mistake in interpretation or application of a directly effective EU provision and the violation of the referral duty will – at least partially – coincide. Therefore, the question arises whether it is the non-application or misapplication of the norm, or the violation of the referral obligation which may entail state liability. This scenario will be developed further in the section devoted to the violation of the obligation to make a reference for preliminary ruling.[59]

[52] (ECJ) Judgments in *Van Duyn*; in *Arcor AG and Others*, para 40; in *Pfeiffer and Others*, Cpara 103; in *Marks & Spencer*, para 25; and, more recently, in *Impact*, para 57.

[53] (ECJ) Judgments in *Marshall*; in *Faccini Dori*; in *El Corte Inglés*; in *Daihatsu Deutschland*; as well as, eg Dougan 2000b: 586–87; Prechal 1990.

[54] The notion of state should be interpreted broadly, and an individual can rely on the directive against the state regardless of the capacity in which the latter is acting, whether as an employer or as public authority. See (ECJ) judgments in *Marshall*, para 49; in *Johnston*; in *Foster*, paras 17, 20; as well as Leczykiewicz 2015: 219–20.

[55] The vertical direct effect is justified by reference to Art 288 TFEU. See also Bobek 2017: 150, Dougan 2000b: 586.

[56] (ECJ) Judgments in *Becker*; in *Ratti*, para 23; but, on the contrary position, judgment in *Erichem Base*, para 11. See on this matter Leczykiewicz 2015: 217.

[57] (ECJ) Judgments in *Kolpinghuis Nijmegen*, paras 9 and 13; in *Arcaro*, para 42; in *Kofoed*, para 45; in *Pupino*, and in *Berlusconi and Others*. For further analysis on this matter, see also Bobek 2017: 156–58; Craig 1997: 526–28; Drake 2005: 337–38, 348; Hilson and Downes 1999: 127–29; Leczykiewicz 2015: 221–22; Ryan 2000: 149.

[58] Similarly, in case of doubt about the obligation to disapply a national rule, the national courts are required to send a request for preliminary ruling to the ECJ. See Piqani 2016: 27.

[59] See s 2.II.A.iii.

In the second situation, the procedural obligation of the national court to apply the substantive EU norm is straightforward. When it is obvious that the EU provision has direct effect, the national court has no room for discretion but has to apply the substantive rule. Any Member State court that refuses to do so appears to commit a manifestly serious infringement of the applicable law.[60]

There is, however, a limitation to this statement, regarding the problem of causal link and the identity of the tortfeasor. This is most typically an issue in the context of the direct effect of directives. The direct effect of directives matters only if the national legislation has already failed to transpose the directive into the national legal order – in violation of its clear duty established in Article 288 TFEU. One may therefore ask whether it is not the legislation that is responsible for such a breach of EU law in the first place.[61] Even if less evident at first sight, the problem may be similar with regard to the primary legislation. In situations concerning primary legislation, the necessity to invoke and apply directly substantive EU provisions originates from the fact that the national rules have not been harmonised with EU law,[62] and the responsibility for such inconsistency lies with the national legislation.

It is, however, true that there are situations where the infringement by the national court of its obligation to apply directly effective EU norms correctly is independent from the obligations of the legislative and administrative bodies. In this case – considering that other conditions are fulfilled – a manifest breach can eventually give rise to a clear judicial violation, and, consequently, the liability of the state according to *Köbler*.[63]

(2) Manifest Infringement of the Direct Effect Principle

Thus, even if it appears obvious that national supreme courts are obliged to apply substantive EU norms that have direct effect, the violation of such an obligation will not necessarily amount to a manifest disregard of the applicable law. Only under rare occasions does it seem to be possible to qualify a breach as manifest to entail liability for the state under the *Köbler* doctrine. In this regard, it seems necessary that the direct effect of the norm be a matter already decided by the ECJ and, additionally, the national court has an obligation to apply it (ex officio or due to the parties' request) in the specific case. Considering the above

[60] (ECJ) Judgment in *Köbler*, para 56.

[61] See s 2.II.B; also Anagnostaras 2006: 747.

[62] See (ECJ) judgments in *Commission v France*, 167/73, para 41; in *Commission v Italy*, 159/78, para 22; in *Ford España*, para 19; in *Commission v Italy*, C-487/04, para 33.

[63] Such a situation can emerge when the legislation has implemented, albeit incorrectly, the EU directive in the national legal order and its breach cannot be considered as serious in terms of *Francovich* liability. The Polish Supreme Administrative Court has confirmed that in the event of incorrect implementation of a directive, the EU provision can be directly relied on and should be directly applied before the national courts. See (PL) Naczelny Sąd Administracyjny, Wyrok, 03/06/2014; Naczelny Sąd Administracyjny, Wyrok, 07/08/2014, both cases reported by Czubinski and Jurago in Reflets no 3/2014: 38.

arguments, we can conclude that the national court appears to commit a manifest infringement of its procedural duty to apply directly a provision of EU law that has direct effect only in a situation where the direct effect of this substantive norm has already been confirmed by the ECJ,[64] or where the national court denies, in general, the existence of the principle of direct effect itself in a situation where it would be applicable.

For the sake of demonstration, historical judgments rendered at a time when the direct effect as a principle had not yet been widely accepted by national courts can be cited as examples for a manifest infringement of the direct effect principle. One such case is a decision of the Conseil d'État (French Supreme Administrative Court) from 1986, by which this court explicitly held that a directive, which had not yet been implemented by national law, could not be relied on before the national courts in any case.[65] This national judgment clearly went against the findings of the ECJ judgment in *van Duyn*, which had already established the direct effect of directives.[66] This French decision therefore denied the existence of direct effect of the directives as a principle, in clear contradiction to the established ECJ doctrine. Therefore, it could be considered as a manifest violation of the EU law and in particular of the principle of direct effect.

c. Disapplication of National Legal Provisions Contrary to EU Law

(1) **Principle and Limits of Primacy**

The principle of primacy, along with the direct effect, is another feature that makes EU law unique.[67] The ECJ originally established this principle in the *Simmenthal* judgment.[68] Due to the doctrine of primacy, EU law takes precedence over conflicting national law.[69] It is not necessary, in this regard, that the EU norm confers right on the individual.[70] According to Bobek, there are three main features of primacy. First, primacy over national law means primacy in application in the individual case at hand, but does not affect the validity of the national

[64] Broberg (2016: 250) recalls that according to the (then) AG Jacobs, a Member State would only be held liable under the *Köbler* ruling in a case of bad faith.

[65] (FR) *Conseil d'État*, décision, 19/03/1986.

[66] (ECJ) Judgment in *Van Duyn*, para 12.

[67] Prechal 2000: 1047.

[68] (ECJ) Judgment in *Simmenthal*, paras 21 and 24. See also (ECJ) judgments in *A*, para 36; in *Åkerberg Fransson*, para 45; in *Carra and Others*, paras 16–17; in *Debus*, para 32; in *Elchinov*, paras 25, 39, 31–32; in *Filipiak*, para 81; in *Melki and Abdeli*, para 43.

[69] For national judicial practice regarding the primacy principle, see (AT) VfGH, Urteil, 24/02/1999, reported in Reflets no 1/2000: 5; OGH, Entscheidung, 22/10/2015, reported by Leeb in Reflets no 1/2016; (UK) Court of Appeal (England), judgment, 08/03/2000, reported in Reflets no 1/2001: 12; (IT) Corte di Cassazione, sentenza, 14/07/2004, reported by Iannone in Reflets no 1/2005: 16; Corte di Cassazione, sentenza, 15/09/2015, reported by Ruffo in Reflets no 1/2016: 28; (CZ) Ústavní soud, usnesení ze dne 21/02/2006, reported by Škvařilová and Navrátilovà in Reflets no 1/2007: 23; Ústavní soud, usnesení ze dne 02/12/2008, reported by Škvařilová in Reflets no 2/2009: 20; (HU) Kúria, ítélet, 15/04/2015. For a presentation of the development of the jurisprudence of the national courts, see Claes 2015: 188–99; Slaughter et al 1998.

[70] Leczykiewicz 2015: 217.

law in question. Second, the primacy of EU law over national rules is unreserved and absolute in two dimensions: hierarchical and temporal. Third, the primacy empowers all national judges to leave unapplied incompatible national laws.[71]

It means that national courts are under the procedural obligation *to refuse of their own initiative to apply any conflicting provision of a national rule* if it is necessary to give the full effect of EU law.[72]

At first sight, the conflict between the national provision and the EU rule appears to be the only criterion necessary to trigger the duty of the national court to leave the domestic rule unapplied. However, there are – not always clear – limits to this obligation. In fact, two differing concepts can be deduced from the case-law.[73]

According to the first theory, the obligation to leave a conflicting national rule unapplied is independent of whether the EU rule fulfils the threshold criteria of direct effect and whether the legal relationship between the parties is horizontal or vertical.[74] Consequently, the principle of direct effect is neither necessary, nor even relevant, regarding the duty of the Member State court to leave a conflicting national rule unapplied. For example, the *CIA Security*,[75] *Unilever Italia*,[76] *Pafitis*,[77] *Ruiz Bernáldez*[78] and *Unilever*[79] cases were decided based on this first concept. All cases concerned horizontal situations, characterised by the absence of the relevant EU directive having direct effect.[80] Nevertheless, this has not prevented the ECJ from concluding that the national court had the obligation to leave the conflicting national rule unapplied to give effect to EU law.[81]

Moreover, in several other decisions, the ECJ stated that the general principle prohibiting all discrimination on grounds of age, as given expression in Directive 2000/78, precludes national legislation which is in violation of this principle even in disputes between private parties.[82] This means that the national courts are obliged to interpret the national provision at issue in a manner that is consistent with the directive. If such interpretation is not possible, because of

[71] Bobek 2017: 160–61.

[72] See also Colgan 2002; Dougan 2019: 1460–70; Tridimas 1994, 2001; and, from the case-law (ECJ) judgments in *Melki* and in *A v B*.

[73] Dougan 2007: 933, 951. See also Dougan 2004: 59–62.

[74] In Dougan's (2007: 933, 951; 2004: 59–62) classification, this concept is the 'primacy model' of the application of EU law, based on civil law traditions and on the importance principles, as opposed to remedies. See also Bobek 2017: 147, 157; Timmermans 2016.

[75] (ECJ) Judgment in *CIA Security*. See also Dougan 2000b: 594; Leczykiewicz 2015: 231–32.

[76] (ECJ) Judgment in *Unilever*, C-443/98. See also Dougan 2001.

[77] (ECJ) Judgment in *Pafitis and Others*. See also Dougan 2000b: 595–96.

[78] (ECJ) Judgment in *Ruiz Bernáldez*. See also Dougan 2007: 949; Leczykiewicz 2015: 237–38.

[79] (ECJ) Judgment in *Unilever*, C-77/97. See also Dougan 2000b: 594–95.

[80] See Bobek 2017: 151–53; Hilson and Downes 1999: 126–27.

[81] Prechal (2005: 1454, 1458) points out that exclusionary direct effect is often seen as a matter of supremacy rather than direct effect. See (ECJ) judgment in *Pfeiffer and Others*.

[82] (ECJ) Judgments in *Mangold*, para 78; in *Kücükdeveci*, para 27; in *DI*, paras 27, 31–37. See also, regarding the horizontal direct effect of the (judicially created) general principles, judgments in *Association de mediation sociale v Union locale des syndicats CGT and Others*; in *Bauer and Willmeroth*; in *Egenberger*; as well as, from the doctrine, Lazzerini 2014; Leczykiewicz 2015: 240–44; Muir 2011.

the contra legem limit, the national courts have to disapply the national provisions that do not comply with the principle. In these judgments, the ECJ has implicitly recognised the horizontal direct effect of unimplemented directives in exclusionary situations.[83]

According to the second theory, the national court is not required to leave the conflicting national rule unapplied in the absence of direct effect of the relevant EU provision.[84] This conclusion results from the limits of the direct effect principle and, mainly, from the rule that excludes the horizontal direct effect of directives. Therefore, the obligation of national courts is limited to the duty to interpret the national rule as far as possible in conformity with the EU provision. The traditional case-law concerning the absence of directives' horizontal direct effect reflects this position.[85]

The doctrine struggles to find a rationale for the coexistence of these approaches and has not yet managed to isolate the decisive factors governing the choice between the two concepts.[86] Moreover, there have been cases before the ECJ where the Advocate Generals and the ECJ had differing opinions as to which concept to follow. For example, in the *Pfeiffer*[87] and *Berlusconi*[88] cases, the ECJ insisted on the absence of the horizontal direct effect of the EU directives, despite the proposals of Advocate General Ruiz-Jarabo Colomer[89] and Advocate General Kokott[90] to treat these cases as exclusionary situations. Finally, in the terms of the ECJ judgments, the Member State courts were not required to leave the national rule unapplied, but to apply the conforming interpretation rule and to do 'whatever lies within its jurisdiction' in order to give full effect to EU law.

(2) Manifest Infringement of the Disapplication Obligation

The scope of the obligation to leave national rules unapplied is not always clearly defined. One may assume that the breach of this duty can qualify as a manifest infringement only if it contradicts specific case-law of the ECJ on the matter. In particular, it appears to be necessary for the ECJ to have already pronounced on the requirement to leave unapplied the specific national legislative measure at issue.

[83] This distinction was first introduced in (ECJ) opinion of AG Léger in *Linster*. See also, for a good historical overview, Regueiro 2002.

[84] According to Dougan (2007: 933, 951; 2004: 59–62), this is the 'trigger model' of the application of EU law, based on common law traditions and on the importance remedies, as opposed to principles.

[85] (ECJ) Judgments in *Faccini Dori*, paras 20–25; in *El Corte Inglés*, paras 15–17; and, more recently, in *Dominguez*, para 42.

[86] Bobek 2017: 152; Claes 2015: 183; Dougan 2000b, 2007; Hilson and Downes 1999: 126–27; Leczykiewicz 2015: 231–47; Prechal 1997: 3–13.

[87] (ECJ) Judgment in *Pfeiffer and Others*, paras 100–01, 106–19. See also Klamert 2006: 1259; Prechal 2005.

[88] (ECJ) Judgment in *Berlusconi and Others*.

[89] (ECJ) Opinions of AG Ruiz-Jarabo Colomer in Joined Cases *Pfeiffer and Others*; judgment in *Pfeiffer and Others*.

[90] (ECJ) Opinion of AG Kokott in Joined Cases *Berlusconi and Others*.

In order to demonstrate a such infringement, a decision of the Ústavní soud (Czech Constitutional Court) is presented. Noteworthy is that this judgment did not give rise to a subsequent *Köbler* liability claim.

In a judgment handed down in 2012, the Ústavní soud clearly departed from the ECJ judgment regarding the obligation to leave unapplied a national rule in order to give effect to EU law.[91] The violation committed appears, therefore, to qualify as a manifest infringement in the terms of *Köbler*. The judgment was rendered following a request for a preliminary ruling submitted by the Nejvyšší správní soud (Czech Supreme Administrative Court) in the *Landtová* case, in which the ECJ interpreted the EU law rules applicable to the case. It arrived at the conclusion that national rules, as established and applied by the the Ústavní soud, were contrary to EU law. In subsequent, distinct proceedings, the Ústavní soud claimed, however, that the ECJ acted ultra vires and refused to follow the ECJ decision and to disapply the national rules that had been found to be contrary to EU law by the ECJ.

Regarding the disapplication obligation, mention should be made of the former case-law by the Spanish Tribunal Constitucional (Constitutional Court, Spain), according to which the disapplication of a national legal provision requires that a prior request for preliminary ruling be sent to the ECJ in the specific case. According to the court, in case of infringement of this referral duty, the right of the parties to a due process[92] may be compromised.[93] This case-law, which has already been amended, denied the right of national ordinary courts to disapply, by their own initiative and without consulting the ECJ, any national rule hindering the application of EU law.

d. Conforming Interpretation of the National Rule with EU Law

(1) Principle and Limits of Conforming Interpretation

The third obligation of national courts to be addressed here is the application of the rule of conforming interpretation.[94] This obligation originally grew out of ex Articles 10 and 249 TEC.[95] Several judgments from national courts show

[91] (CZ) Ústavní soud, nález ze dne 31/01/2012. For an analysis of the case, see Dyèvre, A (2012) 'The Czech Ultra Vires Revolution: Isolated Accident or Omen of Judicial Armageddon?' VerfBlog, 2012/2/29, verfassungsblog.de/czech-ultra-vires-revolution-isolated-accident-omen-judicial-armageddon; Komárek, J (2012) 'Playing With Matches: The Czech Constitutional Court's Ultra Vires Revolution' VerfBlog, 2012/2/22, verfassungsblog.de/playing-matches-czech-constitutional-courts-ultra-vires-revolution/; Zbíral 2012.

[92] (ES) Constitución Española, Art 24.

[93] On this matter, see s 2.IV.B.i.

[94] The term 'conforming interpretation' is used by Fennelly (2013: 68). Wallerman (2016a) uses the term 'harmonious interpretation', while other academics use the term 'consistent interpretation' or even 'concurring interpretation' for the same concept.

[95] Dougan 2007: 946. Art 10 TEC was replaced, in substance, by Art 4(3) TEU. Art 249 TEC corresponds to Art 288 TFEU.

the acceptance of this doctrine by Member State courts.[96] As Tridimas points out, the failure by Member State courts to interpret national law in conformity with non-directly effective provisions of EU law may, in principle, trigger state liability.[97]

The ECJ has established this doctrine, also referred to as the 'indirect effect' of EU law, in the *von Colson*[98] and *Marleasing*[99] judgments. According to the principle, Member State courts have to give – as far as possible – an interpretation to the national norm which makes it consistent with the EU rules. Both national provisions adopted in order to implement a directive and those adopted before or after the directive for other reasons than its implementation are covered by the obligation of conforming interpretation.[100] This obligation applies even during the implementation period of directives; however, during this period, the obligation does not possess the force to disapply national law, neither substantive nor procedural.[101] Moreover, the interpretative obligation[102] of national courts may arise either when the substantive EU norm does not have direct effect, and therefore cannot be directly applied, or where the substantive EU norm has direct effect. As for the latter, in several judgments, the ECJ has argued that national courts have to leave unapplied national rules only where the result required under (directly applicable) EU law cannot be achieved by adopting a consistent interpretation of the domestic law.[103]

Due to the general principles of law, such as legal certainty, there are limits to the indirect effect of EU norms. In particular, Member State courts are not required to interpret national rules contra legem.[104] As a matter of fact, this obligation is quite vague, and its interpretation in not unanimous in the ECJ case-law either.

[96] On this principle, see eg Betlem 2002, 1995; Drake 2005; Dougan 2007: 946–47; Franklin 2018; Galetta 2010: 22–30; Haket 2015; Hilson and Downes 1999: 127–29; Jans and Verhoeven 2015; Prechal 1990: 468–72. (PL) Trybunal Konstytucyjny, *Gender Equality in the Civil Service Case* (1997) Orzecznictwo Trybunalu Konstytucyjnego 19: 380, reported by Bobek 2008: 53; (CZ) Nejvyšší správní soud, rozsudek, 29/09/2005, reported by Bobek 2008: 54; (EL) Trimeles Dioikitiko Protodikeio Peiraia, apofasi tis 06/10/2010, reported by Apostolidis and Afroditi-Ioanna in Reflets no 1/2012: 18–19. See also (LV) Augstākās tiesas Senāts, 18/12/2013, reported by Borkoveca in Reflets no 1/2014: 33–35.

[97] Tridimas 2007: 157.

[98] (ECJ) Judgment in *von Colson and Kamann*, para 28.

[99] (ECJ) Judgment in *Marleasing*, para 8.

[100] (ECJ) Judgment in *Marleasing*, para 13.

[101] Klamert 2006: 1274. See also (ECJ) judgment in *Ratti*, para 23; Leczykiewicz 2015: 217.

[102] The term 'interpretative obligation' is borrowed from Drake 2005.

[103] From these judgments it transpires that consistent interpretation should have the priority and only if that is not possible, direct effect is the next option. See in this regard (ECJ) judgments in *ČEZ*, paras 138, 140; in *DI*, paras 35–37; in *Dominguez*, para 23; in *Engelbrecht*, paras 38–40; in *ITC*, paras 68–70; in *Murphy and Others*, para 11; in *Vueling Airlines*, para 47–49.

[104] (ECJ) Judgments in *Pupino*, para 47; in *Kásler and Káslerné Rábai*, para 65. See also Haket 2015: 239–40; Jans and Verhoeven 2015: 80–87; and (NL) Raad van State, 29/05/2011, Raad van State, 07/12/2005, Raad van State, 05/12/2007, all reported by Prechal 2011: 62.

In *von Colson*, the ECJ laid down the interpretative obligation for national courts 'in so far as [they are] given discretion … under national law'.[105] After this judgment it was suggested that EU law may set limits to certain methods of interpretation. Therefore, in *Marleasing*, the ECJ concluded that national courts are obliged to interpret national law in the light of the directive only 'as far as possible'. It seems that, initially, the conforming interpretation obligation was to be applied in accordance with the national rules prescribing interpretational methods.[106]

Concerning the contra legem interpretation limit, in *Impact*, the ECJ ruled that the conforming interpretation obligation cannot require the referring court to allow the retrospective effects of a national implementing act if the national legislation contains a general rule preluding the retrospective application of legislation unless there is a clear an unambiguous indication to the contrary.[107]

Nevertheless, in the terms of the judgment in *Björnekulla*, national courts have to disregard an interpretation in light of the *travaux préparatoires* for the national rule, and they are obliged to employ all available national methods of construction – not by virtue of national law – to fulfil the interpretation obligation.[108] Moreover, according to the judgment in *DI*, the national court cannot claim that it is impossible for it to interpret the national provision in a manner that is consistent with EU law for the mere reason that the judicial practice has consistently interpreted that provision in a manner that is incompatible with EU law.[109]

On several occasions, after having reminded that national courts are not required to interpret national law contra legem, the ECJ, however, emphasised that these courts are required to do whatever lies within their jurisdiction, to ensure the compatibility of the national law with the EU provision.[110] This line of case-law, which aims to remedy the limitations of the direct effect principle, appears to impose, de facto, an obligation on national courts to disapply domestic rules that are contrary to EU law.[111] This obligation is imposed expressis verbis in the judgment *DI*.[112]

As for another limit to this obligation, the consistent interpretation cannot lead to the imposition of obligations on individuals. This limitation finds its origin in the principle of the absence of horizontal direct effect of directives.

[105] (ECJ) Judgment in *von Colson and Kamann*, para 28.

[106] Prechal 2005: 1458.

[107] (ECJ) Judgment in *Impact*, paras 100–01.

[108] (ECJ) Judgment in *Björnekulla*, para 13; Klamert 2006: 1259–60.

[109] (ECJ) Jugdment in *DI*, paras 33–34. On the repercussions of this judgment, see (DN) Højesteret, Judgment, 06/12/2016.

[110] (ECJ) Judgments in *Adeneler and Others*, para 111; in *Angelidaki and Others*, para 200; in *Dominguez*, para 27; in *Duarte Hueros*, para 42; in *Marleasing*, paras 7, 13; in *Mono Car Styling*, paras 64–65; in *Pfeiffer and Others*, paras 100–01, 106–19.

[111] See also Prechal 2005: 1458.

[112] (ECJ) Judgment in *DI*, paras 35–37.

There are, however, exceptions to this latter rule in the ECJ's case-law.[113] In all, the respect of the scope of application and the limits of this duty may be unclear in several cases.[114]

(2) Manifest Infringement of the Consistent Interpretation Obligation

In conclusion, the violation of the conforming interpretation principle appears to be manifest only if it constitutes an obvious breach of the established case-law on the particular question at hand. It means that not only the EU rule relevant to the case but also the national provision concerned by the ECJ precedent need to be the same as the ones in the case at hand. Such infringement may occur in particular where a national supreme court refuses to give effect to an ECJ judgment on the interpretation of a specific national legislative provision.

A good illustration for a situation where the national supreme court breached its unambiguous obligation to apply the consistent interpretation principle was provided by the Højesteret (Danish Supreme Court) in 2016.[115] Similarly to the above-presented *Landtová* case, this judgment has not given rise to a *Köbler* liability claim either.

In this case, the Højesteret submitted a referral for preliminary ruling to the ECJ, asking, in substance, for an interpretation of EU law and the obligations of national courts when applying EU law. It argued that in a horizontal case, the national law has to be interpreted in conformity with EU law only as far as possible. The Højesteret explained that due to the consistent and abundant national case-law regarding the interpretation of the Danish norm applicable to the case in hand, it would be contra legem to interpret it in conformity with a previous ECJ judgment. Therefore, it was unwilling to disapply the national rule. In its preliminary ruling the ECJ stated that the requirement to interpret national law in conformity with EU law entails the obligation for national courts to change their established case-law, if this is based on an interpretation of national law that is incompatible with the objectives of a directive. That meant, in essence, that the ECJ required the Højesteret either to interpret the national provision in line with the EU law in the case at hand or to disapply the conflicting national provision. In its final judgment rendered in the proceedings following the preliminary ruling, the Højesteret rejected both options and did not follow the judgment of the ECJ. The court explained that, due to the state of Danish law and the established judicial practice, as well as to the contra legem

[113] (ECJ) Judgments in *Arcaro*, para 42; in *Berlusconi and Others*; in *Kofoed*, para 45; in *Kolpinghuis Nijmegen;* in *Pupino*. On this matter see Drake 2005: 338; Leczykiewicz 2015: 238–39. Also, in *Mangold*, *Kücükdeveci* and *DI*, the ECJ was not concerned about imposing obligations on individuals either. On this matter, see also Craig 1997: 526–28; Bobek 2017: 156–58; Drake 2005: 337–38, 348; Hilson and Downes 1999: 127–29; Leczykiewicz 2015: 221–22; Ryan 2000: 149.

[114] Jans and Verhoeven 2015: 120–22.

[115] (DN) Højesteret, Judgment, 06/12/2016, rendered following (ECJ) Judgment in *Ingeniørforeningen i Danmark, acting on behalf of Ole Andersen v Region Syddanmark*. For an annotation to the case, see Holdgaard et al 2018.

limitation, it was not possible for it to interpret the national provision in line with EU law. From the perspective of the present book, such reticence to follow the ECJ's explicit judgment amounts to a manifest violation of the applicable law. In fact, the Højesteret's decision clearly goes against the established, specific ECJ case-law.

e. Obligation to Give a Correct Interpretation to the Substantive Norm or Rule

(1) Obligation and Limits of the Correct Interpretation Principle

Given its obvious nature, the obligation of national courts to ensure that the content of the substantive provision or a jurisprudential rule is correctly understood and applied in the case is not usually enlisted as an autonomous procedural obligation of national courts.[116] Contrary to the three obligations above that aim to ascertain that the EU norm is *applied* in a case, this obligation relates to the *content* of the substantive norm. Therefore, the misinterpretation of the substantive norm is usually considered as a mere violation of that norm, and is not linked to any procedural obligation. Nevertheless, it does not change the fact that the national court is under an obligation to ensure the correct interpretation of the norm. As the procedural obligations of national courts are of primary importance with regards to this analysis, it is necessary to consider this obligation separately.

Contrary to the above three obligations related to the application of the substantive norm, this procedural obligation is not restricted by any criteria or limit. In each case where a substantive norm is applicable, it should be understood and applied correctly. The problem in this regard is that the interpretation of a legal norm might be (and often is) ambiguous.

(2) Manifest Infringement of the Correct Interpretation Obligation

Therefore, the misinterpretation of a substantive norm appears to amount to a manifest infringement only where its interpretation is evident from the ECJ's case law. As ECJ judgments can also be at the origin of substantive EU provisions, a national judgment which is clearly incompatible with a previous ECJ judgment can also trigger liability of the state.

In this regard, for demonstration purposes, it is possible to refer to a judgment rendered in 2009 by the Portuguese Supremo Tribunal de Justiça, which dismissed a liability claim against Portugal for breach of the EU law by the same court.[117] In this case, the Supremo Tribunal de Justiça held that there was no

[116] Claes 2006: 58–59; Fennelly 2013: 64.

[117] (PT) Supremo Tribunal de Justiça, Acórdão, 03/12/2009, available at Network of the presidents of the supreme judicial courts of the European Union, reported by Da Cunha Rodríguez and de Jesus Patricio 2014: 400–04. For different aspects of the case see, ss 2.II.A.iv.b(4) and 2.III.B.ii.h.

rule in Portuguese law under which the liability of the state for judicial breaches could be established, since the national law had not yet been in force at the time of the facts.[118]

This interpretation appears to be a clear violation of the *Köbler* judgment which has previously established state liability as a matter of EU, and not national, law.

f. Interim Conclusions Regarding the Gravity of the Violation of the Procedural Obligations

As can be seen from the above analysis, in every scenario of violation by a Member State court of its procedural obligation to apply or correctly interpret a substantive EU rule, the gravity of the breach depends on the existence of relevant ECJ case-law. Therefore, to address the issue of a manifest breach, it is important to distinguish between two situations, namely where there is an ECJ judgment available on a question of application or interpretation of the substantive norm; and where there is no established case-law on the specific matter.

In the first situation, the duty to apply and the interpretation to give to the substantive EU norm are straightforward. It appears, therefore, that the national court commits a manifest violation in situations where it is established in case-law that, under circumstances similar to the case at hand, (1) the substantive norm has direct effect and therefore should be applied; or (2) the national provision should be left unapplied; or (3) the national provision should be interpreted in a certain way to ensure its consistent interpretation with EU law; or (4) the substantive EU norm should be interpreted in a certain way. This conclusion is in line with the statement of the ECJ in *Köbler*, according to which 'in any event, an infringement of Community law will be sufficiently serious where the decision concerned was made in manifest breach of the case law of the Court on the matter'.[119]

It is noteworthy that, on the practical side, the above-presented examples show that a manifest infringement that is such a clear violation of a specific ECJ case-law does not usually happen as a result of a mistake in the interpretation of the rules but much more as a deliberate decision on the part of the national court not to follow ECJ case-law.[120] This is so because an infringement is considered manifest if there is ECJ case-law that is clear and deals with a specific question, implying that there is not much margin of appreciation left to the national court concerning its application and interpretation.

In the second situation, a misinterpretation or non-application of the EU provision and the violation of the referral duty will – at least partially – coincide.

[118] The case was brought before the ECtHR, which, however, established a violation of Art 6(1) ECHR due to the divergence in the domestic case-law as to the administibility of state liability claims, leading to a violation of the principle of legal certainty. See (ECtHR) judgment in *Ferreira Santos Pardal v Portugal*.

[119] (ECJ) Judgment in *Köbler*, para 56.

[120] See, in this regard, Anagnostaras 2006: 744–45; Broberg 2016: 250; and s 2.II.A.v.

Therefore, the question arises whether it is the misinterpretation or non-application of the norm, or the violation of the referral obligation, that may entail state liability. This scenario will be developed further in the next point devoted to the violation of the obligation to make a reference for preliminary ruling.

g. Obligation to Submit a Request for a Preliminary Ruling to the ECJ

(1) Preliminary Remarks

According to some authors, the impact of the failure to make a reference for a preliminary ruling on the *Köbler* liability proved to be the thorniest question of all.[121] This issue concerns the relationship between the two (sets of) obligations set before national courts: namely to apply and correctly interpret the substantive EU norm; and to make a preliminary ruling in case of doubt about the correct interpretation or application of the norm.

Hereinafter, this chapter does not distinguish between the different procedural obligations, analysed above, regarding the application and the correct interpretation of the substantive norm.[122] On the contrary, the *obligation to make a reference for a preliminary ruling* (or *referral duty*) is opposed to the *obligation to apply and correctly interpret the substantive norm*, whatever the procedural obligation of the Member State court is in this regard. Therefore, the breach of this latter duty is referred to under the general terms of *mistaken application or interpretation of EU law* from now on.

Although the ECJ has clearly established that failure to make a referral when under an obligation to do so constitutes an important liability factor, it remains silent on the circumstances which would actually lead to a successful claim.[123] That has left two important questions unanswered: whether the breach of the referral duty is sufficient in itself to trigger liability of the Member State;[124] and what the impact of the breach of this obligation would be on the gravity of the infringement of EU law.

Before attempting to answer these questions, several preliminary points need to be addressed. It is necessary to examine the constitutive elements of the *violation of the obligation to make a reference for preliminary ruling*. In this respect, the following point concentrates on the scope of the referral duty, on the violation of this obligation and on its qualification as a manifest breach.

(2) Obligation to Make a Reference for a Preliminary Ruling

There are several rules in EU law determining the conditions under which courts of last instance are obliged to submit a question for preliminary ruling to the ECJ. The primary rule in this regard can be found in Article 267(3) TFEU.

[121] Drake 2010: 79; Nassimpian 2007: 824.
[122] See s 2.II.A.ii.
[123] Nassimpian 2007: 826; see also Anagnostaras 2006: 739.
[124] This topic will be addressed later, see s 3.III.

Under this provision, if a question on the interpretation of the EU law is raised before a court against whose decisions there is no judicial remedy,[125] this court is bound to bring the matter before the ECJ. However, the ECJ has set a threefold limit to this general obligation in the *Cilfit* judgment.[126] Therefore, national supreme courts are exempted from the obligation to make a reference in the following situations: first, if the question is not relevant; second, if the question raised is materially identical to a question that has already been subject to a preliminary ruling in a similar case (*acte éclairé*); and third, if the correct application of the EU law is so obvious that it leaves no scope for any reasonable doubt (*acte clair*).[127]

In fact, it is much more difficult to provide a clear definition of a breach of the referral duty than expected. It appears logical simply to state that there is a violation of the obligation to make a reference if the rules under which it is obligatory are not respected. These rules are established in Article 267(3) TFEU and in the *Cilfit* judgment. However, it is also possible to evaluate the violation of the referral duty against the obligation to state reasons for a decision on not to submit a referral. These two possibilities – to which I will refer, respectively, as the *material element* and the *procedural element* of the referral duty – are further developed below.[128]

First, as already explained, the referral is obligatory under the conditions set in Article 267(3) TFEU and in the *Cilfit* judgment. Due to the subjective nature of these conditions, considerable discretion remains with the national court as to whether or not to make a preliminary reference. In the terms of the ECJ jurisprudence, in principle a reference should be made only where the interpretation of EU law is necessary for the national judge to render their decision.[129] The evaluation of this necessity is inevitably subjective and leaves a considerable margin of discretion with the national court. This margin of discretion makes it difficult to evaluate whether the violation of the referral duty has taken place.

The most problematic in this regard is the application of the *acte éclairé* doctrine, according to which the national court does not have to make a reference if there is established ECJ case-law on the matter. However, the exercise of the judicial function – both by the ECJ and the national court – consists of

[125] Concerning references to courts, the expressions 'court adjudicating at last instance', 'court of last instance' and 'supreme courts' will be used synonymously in this book, each term referring to courts whose decisions cannot be appealed to a higher national court. See also (ECJ) judgments in *Lyckeskog*, para 16; in *Cartesio*, para 79; in *Aquino*, paras 30–38; Lenaerts et al 2014: 96–97.

[126] (ECJ) Judgment in *Cilfit and Others*. See also opinion of AG Wahl in joined cases *X and van Dijk*, para 62; opinion of AG Bot in case *Ferreira da Silva e Brito e.a.*, para 90.

[127] The third exception is called *acte clair*, ie 'clear'. However, a subjective conviction of a national court is not sufficient; a national court must be convinced that the matter is equally obvious to the courts of the other Member States and to the ECJ. See also Broberg 2008; Broberg 2011; Lenaerts et al 2014: 97–101; Kornezov 2016.

[128] See also Broberg and Fenger 2016: 559–601.

[129] (ECJ) Judgments in *Consiglio Nazionale dei Geologi and Autorità garante della concorrenza e del mercato*, para 25; in *Ferreira da Silva e Brito e.a.*, paras 37, 45.

the interpretation of legal norms and the application of the norms to individual cases; and the legal and factual background of different cases will coincide only in the rarest circumstances. This makes it difficult for the national court to evaluate whether the ECJ precedent is applicable to the case before it. Moreover, it will be similarly difficult to assess in hindsight whether the national court was indeed under the obligation to make a referral.[130] The situation is similar concerning the application of the *acte clair* doctrine, which also presupposes the interpretation and the application of legal rules to a concrete situation.[131]

Second, taking the above difficulties into account, it is not surprising that several academics and jurisdictions do not apply the *Cilfit* criteria to assess whether a breach of the referral duty has taken place. Instead, they have chosen a more objective standard, which is the obligation to state reasons for a refusal.[132] According to Classen, the procedural obligation to state reasons can be deduced from Article 267(3) TFEU and the *Cilfit* judgment.[133]

In my opinion, the obligation to request a preliminary ruling from the ECJ is different from the obligation to state reasons for a decision rendered on whether to make a reference. Therefore, the transformation of the former duty to the latter obligation does not seem correct at first sight. Neither Article 267(3) TFEU nor the *Cilfit* judgment make a reference to the obligation to state reasons; instead, they establish the conditions under which a referral is obligatory.[134] However, if we consider the *Cilfit* conditions and their application in practice, such a transformation might be justified. As already explained, the application of the *Cilfit* criteria comprises the interpretation of law and the application of legal rules to a specific case. It follows from the ECJ case-law that misinterpretation of law will only amount to a (sufficiently serious) breach if the infringement is manifest. This rule can be applied to violations of the *Cilfit* criteria as well. It means that if a national court unlawfully deals a case under the *acte clair* or *acte éclairé* doctrines, it will, objectively, infringe its obligation to make a reference. However, if the court justifies its (erroneous) decision, this statement of reasons would turn the breach of law to a misinterpretation of law. Therefore, it is possible to conclude that the (manifest) violation of the referral duty will occur precisely where the national court does not give reasons for its decision on not making a reference. This conclusion can, therefore, be indirectly deduced from ECJ case-law, especially from the *Cilfit* and the *Köbler* judgments.[135]

[130] The 'abuse' of the *acte clair* doctrine by national courts has significant implications for the EU legal order which has traditionally been based on the premise of achieving European integration through the uniform application of EU law. See Drake 2010: 55.

[131] Wattel 2004: 182.

[132] The ECrtHR case-law shows that this court qualifies a refusal by the national court contrary to the principle of fair trial – enshrined under the Art 6(1) ECHR – if it is 'arbitrary', that is to say not motivated. See (ECtHR) decision in *Divagsa Company v Spain*.

[133] Classen 2004: 820–21.

[134] Lacchi 2016: 702.

[135] For a different explanation regarding the relationship between the material and the procedural element of the referral duty, see Lacchi 2015a: 108–11.

The clear advantage of this interpretation is that, since the duty to give reasons for a decision is straightforward, the violation of this obligation can be objectively evaluated – as opposed to where there is a misuse of the *Cilfit* exceptions. However, it remains a problem that such a violation can be established only on rare occasions. In practice, a simple reference to the notions of *acte clair* or *Cilfit* will probably be sufficient to be exempted from liability.[136]

(3) **Simple or a Serious Breach of the Referral Duty**

With the infringement of the referral duty being already difficult to establish, it is even more problematic to distinguish between ordinary and serious breaches. In my view, it is neither possible nor necessary to differentiate between simple and qualified breaches of the referral duty.[137] This conclusion applies irrespective of whether the *Cilfit* criteria or the obligation to state reasons are used as a standard to evaluate the breach of the referral duty.

(4) **Development of the ECJ Case-Law on the Violation of the Referral Duty and the Consequences Thereof**

In the judgment in *Ferreira da Silva e Brito e.a.* the ECJ declared, for the first time, a breach of the *Cilfit* doctrine of *acte clair*. As already described, the Portuguese court asked questions about the interpretation of several rules of EU law, about the referral obligation and also about the *Köbler* principle.[138] Amongst the various questions submitted, one concerned the obligation of the Portuguese Supremo Tribunal de Justiça to refer a question for preliminary ruling to the ECJ when lower courts rendered contradictory decisions on a specific question of EU law. In particular, the referring court asked the ECJ whether the supreme court had breached Article 267(3) TFEU when it erroneously invoked the *acte clair* exception due to the specific circumstances of the case.[139] In this respect, the ECJ stated that

> in circumstances such as those of the case before the referring court, which are characterised both by conflicting lines of case law at national level … and by the fact that that concept frequently gives rise to difficulties of interpretation in the various Member States, a national court or tribunal against whose decisions there is no judicial remedy under national law must comply with its obligation to make a reference to the Court, in order to avert the risk of an incorrect interpretation of EU law.

It is noteworthy that despite the above conclusion, which implies that the ECJ found a violation of the *acte clair* doctrine, the ECJ has not applied the criteria

[136] In its recent case-law, the ECtHR is no longer content with a sole statement of reasons for a decision on non-referral but considers also the content of the reasoning. See Lacchi 2015b: 102–05, 108; (ECtHR) judgment in *Schipani v Italy*.

[137] From the theoretical point of view, one might consider the situation where a national court has first made, and later withdrawn, a reference for preliminary ruling. However, the ECJ did not accept such a distinction in the *Köbler* judgment. See (ECJ) judgment in *Köbler*, paras 117–18.

[138] See s 1.III.C.

[139] For an analysis of the case, see Silveira and Fernandes 2016.

formulated in *Köbler*, nor did it examine the fulfilment of the conditions of state liability in the judgment.[140] Nevertheless, academics refer to this judgment as being an important step in the case-law as it was the first time that the ECJ declared that such a breach of the referral obligation had happened. This judgment also shows us that the violation of the referral duty is assessed by the ECJ by reference to the material elements of this duty, that is by the rules enshrined in Article 267(3) TFEU and in *Cilfit*.

Then, by a judgment rendered at the end of 2018, the ECJ took a step forward and declared a violation of EU law by a Member State, in the context of an infringement action, when the *Cilfit* doctrine was breached by a supreme court.[141] It is noteworthy that in the past, even though there had been numerous occasions where the ECJ adopted a specific position at the pre-litigation stage of the infringement proceedings on these grounds, most of these cases were solved extra-judicially.[142] Moreover, authors argued that an action for infringement with regard to errors committed by national courts would only be possible where the violation is the result of an obvious lack of knowledge or deliberate conduct of a national judge.[143]

However, in the case *Commission v France*, the ECJ rendered its first decision in which it condemned a national supreme court for the breach of its obligation to refer a question for preliminary ruling to the ECJ.[144] This judgment was delivered in infringement proceedings, and therefore the seriousness of the violation was not assessed. Nonetheless, given the groundbreaking nature of this judgment and the important step it may represent regarding an eventual acknowledgement of the possibility of establishing liability for the breach of the violation of the referral obligation, this judgment certainly deserves attention.

In particular, the ECJ found that the substance of the decision of the Conseil d'État breached Articles 49 and 63 TFEU. Then it explained that the Conseil État had chosen to depart from the earlier judgment of the ECJ rendered in *Test Claimants* on the explicit ground that the UK scheme was different from the French scheme. However, according to the ECJ, the fact that the interpretation adopted by the Conseil d'État was contrary to EU law on the substance implies that there must have been a reasonable doubt concerning the correct interpretation of EU law, which means that the *acte éclairé* doctrine could not have been followed and the referral for a preliminary ruling could not have been avoided.

[140] See Krommendijk 2017: 58; Silveira and Fernandes 2016: 651.

[141] (ECJ) Judgment in *Commission v France*, C-416/17.

[142] For a reference to these cases, see Anagnostaras 2001c: 295, nn 45 and 46; Broberg, 2008: 1395; Komárek 2005b: 26, n 75; Prete and Smulders 2010: 9–61; Kornezov 2016; Schmauch, 2005: 445–54; Timmermans 2004: 161–62; Taborowski 2012: 1902–06. See also generally on this matter Várnay 2015: 836–61; Várnay et al 2006: 69–74; Wennerås 2006, 2012.

[143] See (ECJ) judgment in *Commission v Ireland*, C-494/01, para 28; Prete and Smulders 2010: 25; Taborowski 2012: 1896–1900, 1907–08; Wennerås 2006: 36–39.

[144] (FR) Conseil d'État, décisions, 10/12/2012; (ECJ) judgment in *Commission v France*, C-416/17. For an annotation to the case, see Turmo (2019), and for various aspect of the case, see also ss 2.II.B.v.c(2) and 3.III.A.i.

Consequently, when the Conseil d'État decided not to submit a request for a preliminary ruling in a situation where the interpretation of the provisions of EU law was not so obvious as to leave no scope of doubt, it committed a breach of Article 267(3) TFEU.

Several interesting conclusions can be drawn from this judgment. On the one hand, in the contested decision the Conseil d'État has thoroughly considered the EU law aspects of the case and the ECJ precedents in *Accor* and *Test Claimants*. The prior ECJ judgment in the *Test Claimants* case explained the correct interpretation of the relevant EU rules, but the Conseil d'État, after due consideration, explicitly departed from it, saying that it was not applicable to the case before it. In this respect, the Conseil d'État has presented the reasons for such decision. On the other hand, the ECJ assessed the violation of the referral duty against the material elements of this obligation, that is against the *Cilfit* criteria. More precisely, the ECJ concluded that the *acte éclairé* doctrine could not have been applied by the Conseil d'État. Moreover, the ECJ deduced the existence of a reasonable doubt regarding the correct interpretation of EU law from the fact that the Conseil d'État had erroneously interpreted the relevant provision. This confirms the belief that the violation of the substantive EU norm and the referral duty are closely linked and the latter cannot occur without the former.

Certainly, there are relevant distinctions between a liability action and infringement proceedings conducted based on a violation of the referral duty. In this case, being an infringement action, the seriousness of the breach was not considered, contrary to a *Köbler* action. What is also particular in this judgment is that there was no prior motion from a party for a request for preliminary ruling to be submitted, which may also be the reason why there was no explicit reasoning by the Conseil d'État regarding the assessment of a referral obligation either. In addition, as the ECJ case-law had been considered in practice by the Conseil d'État, the ECJ had not condemned the French court for the breach of the formal requirements regarding the referral obligation, but because of the breach of the substantial elements of the duty.

In all, this judgment confirms that development in the specific field of obligations of national courts regarding the application of EU law is not a far-fetched possibility. It also confirms that, as Sarmiento puts it, in EU law, no matter how well established its principles may be, they are revisited over and over again.[145]

(5) Conclusion on the Violation of the Referral Duty

Due to the nature of the obligation to submit a referral and the criteria attached to this obligation, a violation of a manifest breach of a referral duty seems even

[145] Sarmiento, D (2018) 'Judicial Infringements at the Court of Justice: A Brief Comment on the Phenomenal Commission/France (C-416/17)' Blog Despite our Differences, despiteourdifferencesblog.wordpress.com/2018/10/09/judicial-infringements-at-the-court-of-justice-a-brief-comment-on-the-phenomenal-commission-france-c-416-17/.

more difficult to establish than the violation of the other procedural obligations of the national courts. The above judicial breaches regarding the application of EU law having been analysed, it is time to summarise the findings and provide a theory on the breaches that probably qualify as a 'manifest infringement of the applicable law' in the terms of *Köbler*.

iii. Manifest Infringement of the Applicable Law and Impact of a Breach of the Referral Duty

The next topic to examine relates to the circumstances that can lead to a finding of a manifest breach of EU law, taking into account an eventual breach of the referral duty. This analysis will help to shed further light on the impact of the breach of the referral duty on the seriousness of the violation of EU law.

a. Analysis

(1) Manifest Breach of the Applicable Law

Scholars have already provided various theories regarding the scenarios that can lead to a finding of a manifest breach of EU law.[146] They have also evaluated the impact of the breach of the referral duty on a breach of the EU law. My theory is mainly based on Anagnostaras's concept, combined with Advocate General Léger's opinion, Classen's theory and the European Court of Human Rights (ECtHR) case-law.[147]

In order to define a 'manifest infringement of the applicable law', the most relevant distinction to be considered is whether or not there is established ECJ case-law on the matter of law that is central to the dispute. Based on this distinction, it is worth examining the gravity of the *mistaken application or interpretation of EU law*, on the one hand, and the seriousness of the *breach of the obligation to make a preliminary reference* to the ECJ, on the other hand.[148]

The first scenario to be considered is a situation where there is established case-law regarding the application or the interpretation of the substantive EU rule relevant to the case before the national court, but the national court nevertheless renders a judgment that is contrary to these ECJ precedents.[149] This breach will probably qualify as a manifest infringement, sufficient to establish state liability. It results explicitly from the *Köbler* judgment, and has

[146] Anagnostaras 2006: 744–46; Classen 2004: 816–21; Hofstötter 2005: 134–35; Tridimas 2007: 154–57; Tridimas 2006: 526–27.

[147] (ECJ) Opinion of AG Léger in *Köbler*, paras 139–41; Anagnostaras 2006: 744–46; Classen 2004: 819–21.

[148] As opposed to the violation of the obligation to make a preliminary reference, considered as a 'procedural violation', the misinterpretation or misapplication of the EU norm is referred to as a 'substantial violation' by Tridimas 2007: 155.

[149] On this matter, see Várnay and Papp 2010: 354–78.

been confirmed by scholars.[150] Analysing this scenario from a systemic point of view, the following conclusions can be drawn. Such a manifest breach of EU law means that not only was the substantive EU norm clear but also the procedural obligation of the Member State court on how to apply it was obvious.[151] Accordingly, the *mistaken application or interpretation of EU law* amounted to a serious breach. However, it is not evident whether a violation of the duty to refer a preliminary question has eventually occurred.

As a matter of fact, the consideration of the *violation of the referral duty* in this situation will lead to various results depending on what is meant by a violation of this obligation. Two possibilities exist in this regard: either to consider the violation of Article 267(3) TFEU and the misuse of the *Cilfit* exceptions; or to take into account the absence of a statement of reasons for not making a reference. First, if the breach is understood as a violation of Article 267(3) TFEU or a misuse of the *Cilfit* exceptions, strictly speaking, there is no breach of the referral duty. It is because there is no obligation under these rules to make a preliminary reference where the EU law in question is clear and precise, apart from where the national courts intends to derogate from this case-law.[152] Therefore, the question whether there has been a *violation of the referral duty* is not relevant and should be ignored while determining the gravity of the breach of EU law. In fact, taking the (non) violation of the referral duty into account would result in making the conditions of liability less strict. Moreover, accepting that the violation of the referral duty is a decisive condition to finding a manifest breach would even result in exempting the court from liability in the end. Secondly, state liability would be rendered less strict if, when considering the violation of the referral duty, it were defined as the violation of state reasons for a decision of non-referral. In practice, it can even occur that an erroneous statement of reasons is sufficient to exonerate the state from liability.[153] On the other hand, the absence of a statement of reasons will not have much influence on the liability – which should already have been established based on the manifest infringement of the ECJ case-law.

Therefore, if the national court renders a judgment which is manifestly contrary to the established ECJ case-law, such deviance should in itself be enough to entail state liability. It should not be considered whether a violation

[150] (ECJ) Judgment in *Köbler*, para 56, in *Tomášová*, para 26; as well as Anagnostaras 2006: 744; Broberg 2015: 25; Classen 2004: 819; Hofstötter 2005: 134–35; Tridimas 2007: 155.

[151] For a recent example, see (DN) Højesteret, Judgment, 06/12/2016. See also Broberg (2016: 250), making reference to AG Jacobs.

[152] It is possible to argue that a Member State court cannot deviate from the established ECJ case-law – *unless making a reference for a preliminary ruling.*

[153] In this regard, it is sufficient to imagine the situation where the *violation of the EU law* in the strict sense is obvious; however, the national court explains how it has arrived at such an interpretation and why it has not made a referral. If the violation of the duty to refer (ie the duty to state reasons) is a condition to establish a manifest breach, the statement of reasons may be sufficient to exempt the court from liability in such cases.

of referral duty has taken place or not.[154] This is because the obvious mistake in the *interpretation or application of the substantive EU law* is already a manifest infringement of the applicable law, sufficient to trigger liability. If we add one more condition to be satisfied to trigger liability, it can only result in making the conditions[155] of liability less – and not more – strict.

It is noteworthy in this regard that, as already mentioned, national courts attempt to deal with this problem by declaring that it is not possible to deviate from the established ECJ case-law without making a referral.[156] As for the ECJ, it has resolved a similar issue in the recent case *Commission v France* by holding that a deviation from established ECJ case-law implies, by the sole result of deviation, that the interpretation of the substantive EU rule was not obvious, and therefore the request for referral should not have been avoided.[157]

My second scenario is for a situation where there is no established case-law on the matter, and the national court interprets and applies the ambiguous EU provision without making a preliminary reference. It may occur that the interpretation followed by the Member State court turns out to be incorrect only in hindsight, due to the development of the ECJ's jurisprudence. Such a *mistaken application or interpretation of EU law* will certainly not amount in itself to a manifest infringement of the applicable law, as the interpretation of the EU law was not obvious at the time of the deliberation of the national court.[158]

Therefore, is seems relevant to examine whether the eventual *violation of the duty to make a preliminary reference* will have as a result the aggravation of such simple breach.[159] According to *Köbler*, this additional infringement should have to contribute to the finding of the manifest breach. To verify whether this is the case, it is necessary to consider the two possible interpretations regarding the violation of the duty to refer a preliminary question: first, the violation of Article 267(3) TFEU and the misuse of the *Cilfit* exceptions; second, the absence of a statement of reasons for a decision of non-referral.

As for the first possibility, it has already been shown that the main problem is the difficulty in establishing a violation of the *Cilfit* criteria. Presuming that this establishment is theoretically not excluded, such a finding may have the result of qualifying a simple violation of EU law as manifest. As for the

[154] According to Jans (2004: 171), liability of the state depends in the first place on the violation of the EU law in the strict sense, and not on the violation of Art 267(3) TFEU.

[155] In other words, it will raise, and not lower, the threshold of liability of the state.

[156] Hofstötter 2005: 134–35; Tridimas 2007: 155. See the case-law of the BVerfG in s 2.IV.B.iii.b regarding a 'deliberate deviation of the ECJ case law without willingness to make a submission' and Valutytė 2012a: 1175. See also (ECtHR) judgment in *Hornsby v Greece*.

[157] (ECJ) Judgment in *Commission v France*, C-416/17, paras 112, 114.

[158] (ECJ) Judgment in *Tomášová*, para 33.

[159] It is noteworthy that in the *Tomášová* judgment the ECJ did not consider the eventual violation of the referral duty on the side of the national court. It only stated that the violation of EU law arising from a decision given in proceedings for enforcement of an arbitration award, granting an application for recovery of sums in accordance with a clause that had to be considered unfair, did not constitute a manifest serious infringement.

second possibility, taking the eventual violation regarding the obligation to state reasons into consideration might contribute to finding a serious breach. In fact, if the national court does not provide any explanation as to why it has not submitted a request for preliminary ruling to the ECJ, this infringement – together with the *mistaken application or interpretation of EU law* – might result in triggering liability.

Therefore, if the *mistaken application or interpretation of EU law* is not manifest in itself, the *breach of the obligation to refer a preliminary question* may have the result of aggravating the simple breach and making it a manifest violation. However, considering the difficulties regarding the establishment of a violation of the *Cilfit* conditions, this possibility is primarily relevant in situations where the national court omits completely to explain why it has not made a referral.

In fact, there are examples from the national case-law, where the national courts dismissed a liability claim based on the argument that the substantive EU norm applicable to the case was ambiguous, and therefore its violation could not be considered, in any case, a manifest infringement.[160] The practice shows that the national courts can, effectively, use this argument only where they, erroneously, failed to examine an eventual violation of the referral duty.[161]

(2) **Impact of the Violation of the Referral Duty on the Gravity of the Breach**

Finally, we can examine the impact of an eventual breach of the referral obligation on the conditions of *Köbler* liability. The general problem in this regard is that if we consider the *Köbler* judgment as imposing a supplementary condition – namely the *breach of the referral duty* – to the list of liability factors, it could mean that the aggrieved party will have to prove two violations by the court: the *mistaken application or interpretation of EU law* and the *violation of the referral duty*.

Moreover, the violation of Article 267(3) TFEU or the misuse of the *Cilfit* exceptions seems to be even more difficult to establish than the *mistaken application or interpretation of EU law*. This is mainly due to the *Cilfit* criteria, which leaves a considerable margin of discretion with the national court on whether to make a reference and, as a consequence, makes it difficult to establish judicial malpractice in this regard. Thus, in practice, by adding this criterion to the list of liability conditions the ECJ has probably imposed a less strict liability on national courts than would have resulted without taking this criterion into account. This factor has contributed to make the liability conditions more subjective, which is contrary to the recommendations after the economic analysis of *Köbler* and *Traghetti del Meditarraneo*.[162]

[160] See eg (DE) BVerwG, Urteil, 09/06/2009, reported in Jean Monnet Database; (UK) Court of Appeal (England), judgment, 12/05/2010, reported by Embley in Reflets no 2012/3: 21, and Lock 2012: 1682; Cour administrative d'appel de Nantes, décision, 25/07/2017.

[161] See s 2.II.A.iv.a(1).

[162] (ECJ) Judgment in *Traghetti del Mediterraneo*. See also Golecki and Wojciechowski 2009: 189–97.

This is especially problematic where the *mistaken application or interpretation of EU law* is already manifest. In my opinion, in such situations the violation of the referral duty should not be taken into consideration at all. This is an issue on which the doctrine is also especially hesitant. In fact, several academics[163] and national courts[164] have chosen to qualify the deviation from the established ECJ case-law as comprising not only a violation of EU law but also a violation of the duty to refer. In my opinion, this solution can be criticised from the strictly theoretical point of view – even if it is acceptable and reasonable from a practical standpoint.

The one scenario where taking the breach of the referral obligation into account contributes to imposing a stricter liability on the state is a situation where the *mistaken application or interpretation of EU law* by the court was not manifest, due to the absence of established ECJ case-law on the question. If, in such a situation, the national court chooses a wrong interpretation without even considering submitting a preliminary question, that can result in the liability of the state. However, that violation will probably be established only if the national court failed to justify its decision; judicial malpractice regarding Article 267(3) TFEU and the *Cilfit* criteria is difficult to prove. In my view, liability will only occur where the national court ignores the request of the party to make a preliminary reference. In this case, the *mistaken application or interpretation of an ambiguous EU norm* combined with the *breach of the referral duty* might amount to a serious breach of EU law in the sense of *Köbler*.

b. Conclusion on the Impact of the Breach of the Referral Duty on the Infringement

The breach of EU law by the national court is manifest in two situations. First, in situations where the national court has not applied or has misinterpreted the substantive EU rule, without even considering making a reference on the question that has not yet been clarified by the ECJ. Second, where the national court has deliberately deviated from the established ECJ case-law. As for this second scenario, it is irrelevant whether the national court has been under the obligation to make a reference to the ECJ and whether it has breached that obligation. In summary, the *Köbler* doctrine appears to protect individuals against manifest and deliberate violations of EU law in the first place.[165]

[163] Hofstötter 2005: 134–35; Tridimas 2007: 155.

[164] See the case-law of the BVerfG in s 2.IV.B.iii.b regarding a 'deliberate deviation of the ECJ case law without willingness to make a submission' and Valutytė 2012a: 1175. See also (ECtHR) judgment in *Hornsby v Greece*.

[165] Broberg (2016: 250) recalls that according to the (then) AG Jacobs, a Member State would only be held liable under the *Köbler* ruling in the case of bad faith.

iv. Case-Law of the Member State Courts

a. Unsuccessful Liability Claims

Considering all the above arguments, the criterion of 'manifest infringement of the applicable law', combined with the obligation of the national courts to refer a preliminary question to the ECJ, renders the establishment of liability possible only on rare occasions. In fact, the research confirms that in many cases national courts refused the liability claims because they did not find a 'manifest breach of the applicable law'. Their main arguments, based on the absence of a manifest infringement, can be regrouped as follows. In several cases the courts claimed that the interpretation of the EU norm was ambiguous at the time the erroneous decision was made; therefore, the violation of the applicable law was not manifest.[166] Other claims had been dismissed as the national court did not find any violation of the material EU law,[167] or the referral duty, or both[168] in the case at hand. It is noteworthy that in other cases the liability action was not dismissed because of the absence of a manifest infringement of EU law but because of another reasons, linked to the existence of national procedural rules or of alternative remedies available under the national law. These latter cases will be presented in the relevant chapters of this book.

(1) **Absence of Manifest Infringement as a Result of the Ambiguity of the EU Law Provision**

There are several cases in the national judicial practice where the *Köbler* liability was ruled out based on the argumentation that an – eventually – erroneous interpretation of the substantive EU norm was not, in any case, manifest, due to the ambiguity of the norm. It is noteworthy that in such a situation the eventual violation of the obligation to submit a request for a preliminary ruling to the ECJ should have been considered by the national courts, precisely because of the uncertainties on how to interpret the substantive norm. Theoretically, the erroneous interpretation of an ambiguous substantive norm, combined with the violation of the referral duty, could result in state liability. However, for various reasons, the national courts either did not take into account, or ruled out, the violation of the referral duty in those cases.

For the sake of demonstration, three judgments will be presented, one from the German Bundesverwaltungsgericht (BVerwG, Federal Administrative Court,

[166] (FR) Tribunal de grande instance de Paris, 07/05/2008; (DE) BVerwG, Urteil, 09/06/2009; (UK) Court of Appeal (England), judgment, 12/05/2010; (PL) Naczelny Sąd Administracyjny, Wyrok, 26/06/2014.

[167] (FR) Conseil d'État, décision, 18/06/2008; Cour de Cassation, Assemblée Plénière, arrêt, 18/11/2016; (PL) Naczelny Sąd Administracyjny, Wyrok, 26/08/2011.

[168] (BG) Sofiyski gradski sad, Reshenie, 03/01/2014; (DE) BGH, Beschluss, 28/10/2004; (NL) Gerechtshof 's-Gravenhage, Uitspraak, 03/06/2015; Gerechtshof 's-Gravenhage, Uitspraak, 15/02/2011; (PL) Naczelny Sąd Administracyjny, Wyrok, 11/06/2014; (FR) Cour de Cassation, arrêt, 26/10/2011.

Germany), one from the English Court of Appeal, and another from the French Cour d'Appel Administrative de Nantes (Administrative Appeal Court, Nantes).

The BVerwG rendered a decision in 2009, in which it analysed the conditions for judicial liability actions under German and EU law, and the criterion of 'manifest breach'.[169] Even though this case did not concern a liability action, the BVerwG made relevant statements regarding the conditions of *Köbler* liability under German law. In its judgment, the BVerwG pointed out that the scope of application of the *Köbler* liability, as triggered by a breach of EU law by the German judiciary, is wider than liability for breach of official duty in terms of German law.[170] Nonetheless, the BVerwG concluded that the conditions for establishing state liability for a breach of EU law by the judiciary were not met in the case at hand. In fact, the breach of law committed by the defendant was not sufficiently serious to meet the requirement of a manifest breach as the EU provision lacked the required level of clarity and the applicability of that provision to the case of the claimant was thus doubtful.[171] This case is interesting insofar as the BVerwG, obiter dictum, did not rule out the possibility of an eventual infringement of EU law, but only the manifest character of such a violation, based on the ambiguous nature of the substantive EU norm. The eventual violation of the referral duty was, however, not considered.

By its judgment from 2010, the Court of Appeal found that the alleged breach committed by UK courts in earlier proceedings was not sufficiently manifest to engage state liability.[172] In particular, the Court of Appeal found that the contested judgments were contrary to EU law as both the applicable directive and the Treaty provision on the obligation to ask for a preliminary ruling had been breached. As for the gravity of the violation, the Court of Appeal held that the contested judgments, handed down in 1999, were consistent with several judgments made by other Member States' courts in similar cases. Furthermore, the Commission had been notified on the national transposition measures before their entry into force, and these were not the subject of any complaint until 2000, when the ECJ judgments were handed down. Bearing in mind all of these factors, the Court of Appeal ruled that the failure to make a preliminary reference was an excusable error, the fact being that the national courts examined the issue and reached a conclusion different to that of the ECJ. This judgment is another rare example in the national judicial practice of a situation where the violation of EU law was established, but only its manifest nature was ruled out. In this case, the incompatibility of the national rules with EU law became clear only after the domestic decision was delivered, due to a posterior ECJ judgment.

[169] (DE) BVerwG, Urteil, 09/06/2009.

[170] (DE) Grundgesetz für die Bundesrepublik Deutschland, Art 34; Bürgerliches Gesetzbuch, § 839, Abs 2. See also Scherr 2012: 579.

[171] Nevertheless, the BVerwG found the appeal well founded and, by amending the judgment of the Verwaltungsgericht Aachen, granted the claimant the residence status retroactively.

[172] (UK) Court of Appeal (England), judgment, 12/05/2010, reported by Embley in Reflets no 2012/3: 21, and Lock 2012: 1682. See also O'Reilly 2014.

As for the eventual violation of the referral duty, this was dismissed essentially because the national court provided a statement of reasons for its decision.

Similarly, in a decision rendered in 2017, the Cour d'appel administrative de Nantes dismissed a liability action.[173] In this case, the claimant brought an action for damages before the administrative court invoking an ulterior ECJ decision which revealed the incompatibility of a contested prior judgment by the Conseil d'État with EU law. Regarding the alleged violation of the substantive EU rule, the Cour d'appel administrative de Nantes analysed the relevant ECJ judgment and concluded that the contested national decision was not necessarily incompatible with the ECJ decision. The EU provision was ambiguous at least, which excludes any manifest violation. Regarding the alleged failure to submit a request for a preliminary ruling, the Cour d'appel pointed out that French courts had already referred a question to the ECJ on the same matter of law but had not received a precise answer. The Cour d'appel then cited the ECJ case-law, according to which liability may occur only in case of manifest violation of EU law. In all, without deciding definitely on the question as to whether an eventual violation of EU law had occurred, the appeal court ruled out the liability of the state based on the argument, that in any case, the violation of the substantive rule was not manifest.

(2) Absence of Violation of the Referral Duty

In several cases, mainly from Austria, liability actions were dismissed based on the argumentation that there had been no violation of the referral obligation in the case at hand. As EU law requires that a national court hearing a liability claim verify that the refusal to submit a referral was not taken in manifest disregard of EU case-law, the situation where the referral duty is assessed only against the obligation to state reasons can be problematic from the point of view of the effectiveness of the *Köbler* principle. Nevertheless, this was the approach followed by the Austrian Verfassungsgerichtshof (VfGH, Austrian Constitutional Court) and by the French Cour constitutionnelle (Constitutional Court, France).

In a judgment delivered in 2004, the VfGH set the limits of state liability for damages allegedly resulting from a decision of the VwGH on not to refer a question to the ECJ.[174] The VfGH first stated that it was not competent to review the decision of the VwGH, but could, nevertheless, examine the gravity of the violation. It recalled the stricter conditions for state liability resulting from acts committed by a national judiciary, and, applying them to the case at hand, rejected the claim. The VfGH considered that a simple non-referral is not per se a manifest breach. It argued that even though the question at issue had not been specifically decided upon by the ECJ, the outcome could be easily deduced from its case-law. Hence, the VwGH could reasonably conclude that the correct

[173] (FR) Cour administrative d'appel de Nantes, décision, 25/07/2017.
[174] (AT) VfGH, Erkenntnis, 13/10/2004.

application of EU law left no doubt as to the solution to be adopted.[175] This decision highlights an important question regarding the application of the *Köbler* doctrine, namely whether the violation of the referral duty or the violation of the obligation to apply the substantive EU norm triggers state liability. The VfGH investigated only the refusal to ask a preliminary question to the EU, without analysing whether the decision itself – and the national rule on which it had been rendered – was compatible with EU law. Moreover, the VfGH's decision was influenced by the fact that the VwGH had not ignored its duty to refer, but decided not to proceed with a reference after due consideration had been given to the matter.[176]

In a decision from 2013, the VfGH confirmed that the infringement of the duty to make a reference for a preliminary ruling to the ECJ does not as such trigger Austria's liability.[177] The VfGH reiterated that it is not incumbent upon it, in proceedings based on state liability claims, to reconsider its own decisions or the decisions made by other supreme courts. On the contrary, its only task is to determine whether a specific infringement of EU law had been committed. Also, it recalled that a claim concerning the state's liability is well founded only in the event of manifest and sufficiently defined infringement of EU law. Therefore, a breach of the obligation to refer a preliminary question to the ECJ does not as such trigger the liability of the state.[178] Consequently, the complaint was rejected by the VfGH. In conclusion, similarly to the above-presented judgment from 2009, the VfGH examined in this decision the gravity of the breach, taking only the violation of the referral duty into consideration. Moreover, other *Köbler* claims had been rejected on the ground of absence of manifest infringement of referral duty in other proceedings before the VfGH.[179]

In France, in a series of judgments handed down in 2011, the Cour constitutionnelle dealt with the question of whether the failure to make a preliminary reference can be considered a denial of justice in the terms of the French law. In this regard, it examined whether a refusal to submit a request for preliminary ruling can constitute a manifest breach entailing liability of the state for defects in the functioning of the judicial system.[180] In the case at hand, the Cour

[175] Granger 2007: 167.

[176] In fact, the VfGH refused to do so, under cover of the national jurisdictional rule precluding such a review of the substance of the VwGH's assessment. See Betlem et al 2007: 44–45; Granger 2007: 167–68.

[177] (AT) VfGH, Beschluss, 19/06/2013, reported by Frodl in Reflets no 3/2013: 17.

[178] The VfGH confirmed that principle in several subsequent decisions. See (AT) VfGH, Erkenntnis, 14/06/2004; VfGH, Erkenntnis, 12/06/2008; VfGH, Erkenntnis, 29/09/2008, A2/07, VfSlg 18557/2008, reported by Pelzl 2014: 113; in the conference on Liability of Judges in European and National Laws –14–15 December 2012 EUI.

[179] (AT) VfGH, Erkenntnis, 12/12/2003, reported by Beutler 2009: 789; VfGH, Erkenntnis, 22/09/2009; VfGH, Beschluss, 02/05/2011; VfGH, Beschluss, 23/03/2015; VfGH, Beschluss, 21/11/2013; VfGH, Beschluss, 11/06/2015; VfGH, Beschluss, 11/05/2015; VfGH, Beschluss, 19/11/2015.

[180] (FR) Cour de Cassation, arrêt, 26/10/2011; Cour de Cassation, arrêts, 26/10/2011, all reported by Dubos et al 2014: 223–24.

constitutionnelle found, based on the succinct analysis of the relevant EU rules and ECJ case-law, that there was no obligation to submit a preliminary reference at all. Scholars appraise the fact that the French court dismissed the claim using the criterion set in *Köbler*, that is by evaluating the manifest character of the breach, instead of assessing it against the French *faute lourde* condition. However, in the above cases, the French Cour constitutionnelle followed a approach similar to that of the Austrian VfGH. This means that it only assessed whether a violation of the procedural element of the referral duty incurred, without engaging in a substantial appreciation of the adequacy of the contested judgment with the material rules of EU law. Also, it is noteworthy that when analysing the EU substantive rules, the courts hearing the liability claim at first and second instances limited themselves to repeat, in principle, the reasoning of the courts in the underlying contested proceedings. They have not engaged in a detailed examination of the griefs of the claimant on the merits of that assessment.

(3) Absence of Violation of Sustantive EU Law

In other cases, national courts dismissed liability claims as they found that there had been no violation of the substantive EU norm in the case at hand. Such a finding, if correct, can indeed justify a dismissal of a liability action. However, when ruling out a *Köbler* liability claim based on an argumentation that there had been no violation of the material EU law in the case at hand, lower courts often rely on the simple fact that an assessment of the EU rule had been made, without reassessing the merits of the decision based on material EU law. Therefore, there is no substantial analysis regarding the compatibility of the judgment with EU law, which can be problematic from the point of view of the effectiveness of EU law and of the *Köbler* judgment. As examples, a decision by the French Cour d'appel de Paris (Appeal Court, Paris) and a judgment by the Dutch Gerechtshof 's-Gravenhage (District Court, The Hague) will be presented. In addition, a summary of a decision rendered by the French Cour de cassation (Court of Cassation, France) will be provided, in which there is a such assessment, albeit erroneous.

In a decision delivered in 2010, the Cour d'appel de Paris dismissed a claim seeking compensation for a breach of EU law committed by the Cour de cassation.[181] In this judgment, the appeal court held that all acts or series of acts which prevent the system of justice from fulfilling its function and operating properly constitute a *faute lourde*. It also added that such qualification is, nonetheless, only possible if the EU law violation is manifest according to the criteria established in *Köbler*. Regarding the alleged breach in the case at hand, the court concluded that the contested judgment had not fulfilled these conditions, as the Cour de cassation had thoroughly analysed the EU rules and

[181] (FR) Cour d'appel de Paris, arrêt, 16/03/2010.

reached the conclusion that they were not applicable, ratione temporis, to the case. This judgment is interesting insofar it does not go into detail regarding the assessment of the interpretation of the EU norm as it had been made in the contested decision. Instead, it limits itself to the assessment of the procedural elements of a fair trial, such as whether there had been an appropriate statement of reasons.[182]

Furthermore, in a judgment rendered in 2015, the Gerechtshof 's-Gravenhage applied the *Köbler* conditions to decide on a liability claim based on an alleged violation committed by the Hoge Raad der Nederlanden (Supreme Court of the Netherlands).[183] The Gerechtshof 's-Gravenhage rejected the liability claim, stating that the contested ruling had not violated EU law, since the supreme court based its judgment on an extensive and defensible analysis or ECJ case-law. The Gerechtshof 's-Gravenhage also observed that the claimants made their request for a preliminary reference only at an advanced stage of the proceedings, and failed to ask detailed questions. The observations presented regarding the decision by the Cour d'Appel de Paris on the reticence of the national lower courts to reassess the merits of a judgment rendered by national supreme court apply to the Dutch court's decision as well. The above two decisions confirm speculations that when assessing whether a superior court's decision caused a manifest infringement of EU law, it is unlikely that a lower court will recognise such a breach.[184]

Similarily interesting is a judgment delivered in 2016, by which the Cour de cassation annulled a judgment of the Cour d'appel de Paris that established state liability,[185] affirming that there had not been any violation of EU law in the case at hand.[186] According to the succint argumentation of the Cour de cassation, there is no legal provision or ECJ decision stating that the principle of retroactivity *in mitius* prohibits the prosecution of false declarations made in order to receive financial advantage relating to the importation of goods into the EU before the creation of the common market. This statement appears at least debatable in the view of the substantive EU case-law applicable to the matter. As Guiot points out correctly, given the ECJ case-law on the principle of retroactivity, the Cour de cassation should have considered, at least, submitting a request for a preliminary ruling to the ECJ regarding the interpretation of this principle.

[182] See also the case-law of the constitutional courts when assessing a constitutional complaint based on the violation of the right to a fair trial as a result of the breach of the referral duty. See s 2.IV.B.iii.

[183] (NL) Gerechtshof 's-Gravenhage, Uitspraak, 03/06/2015, reported by Loth 2017: 49.

[184] Classen 2004: 813–18; Lacchi 2016: 685.

[185] (FR) Cour d'appel de Paris, arrêt, 06/05/2015.

[186] (FR) Cour de Cassation, arrêt, 18/11/2016. For an interesting analysis of this judgment, see Guiot, F-V (2016) 'La Cour de cassation et la responsabilité de l'État du fait des décisions de justice: une nouvelle illustration des faiblesses de la subsidiarité juridictionnelle', Réseau Universitaire européen dédié à l'étude du droit de l'Espace de liberté, sécurité et justice (ELSJ) www.gdr-elsj.eu/2017/01/23/informations-generales/cour-de-cassation-responsabilite-de-letat-decisions-de-justice-nouvelle-illustration-faiblesses-de-subsidiarite-juridictionnelle/.

The fact that it had failed to do so raises the question of whether the Cour de cassation had not committed – besides an eventual violation of substantive EU law – a violation of Article 267(3) TFEU.

(4) Absence of Violation of the Referral Obligation as well as of the Substantive EU Law

In several decisions, national courts adjudicating on liability claims assessed both the eventual violation of the referral duty and that of the substantive EU law in order to render their decisions. As examples, a judgment of the German Bundesgerichtshof (BGH, Federal Court of Justice), a judgment of the Polish Naczelny Sąd Administracyjny and a judgment of the Bulgarian Sofiyski gradski sad (Sofia City Court) will be presented.

In its decision from 2004, the BGH expressly acknowledged the possibility to hold the state liable for miscarriages of justice based on the principles developed by the ECJ in *Köbler*.[187] However, after reiterating the conditions set up by the ECJ, the BGH concluded that there had been no manifest infringement in the case. It especially rejected the interpretation of EU law offered by the claimants and concluded that the regional court had correctly applied EU law in the previous proceedings. In the BGH's opinion, this was so obvious that, based on the standards set in *Cilfit*,[188] there had been no need for the administrative courts to refer the case to the ECJ for a preliminary ruling.[189] In all, the liability claim was dismissed following a combined analysis of the interpretation of the substantive EU law and of the referral obligation in the case at hand.

Similarily, in a judgment from 2014, the Naczelny Sąd Administracyjny held that the refusal by the same court to make a preliminary reference in the previous proceedings had not breached any EU rule, as the interpretation of the EU norm was not ambiguous.[190] The Naczelny Sąd Administracyjny found that there had not been any violation of EU law either. It also pointed out that the national courts of last instance enjoy certain discretion as to whether to make a request or not. In particular, if the interpretation of the EU rule is not doubtful, the court does not have to make a referral, even if one of the parties proposes such a submission.

Finally, in 2014, the Sofiyski gradski sad handed down a judgment regarding an eventual violation of EU law by the Varhoven administrativen sad (Supreme Administrative Court, Bulgaria).[191] As for the alleged breach of a directly applicable provisions of EU law, the Sofiyski gradski sad found the judgment of the Varhoven administrativen sad to be correct in the light of ECJ case-law. As for

[187] (DE) BHG, Beschluss, 28/10/2004, reported by Beutler 2009: 788–89; Dittert 2014: 77–78; Lock 2012: 1683–84.

[188] (ECJ) Judgment in *Cilfit and Others*.

[189] Beutler 2009: 788–89.

[190] (PL) Naczelny Sąd Administracyjny, Wyrok, 11/06/2014, reported by Mazur in Reflets no 3/2014: 38. See also Mikłaszewicz 2014: 382; and for different aspects of the case, s 2.III.B.iii.b.

[191] (BG) Sofiyski gradski sad, Reshenie, 03/01/2014, reported by Todorova in Reflets no 1/2014: 16.

the alleged violation of the obligation to refer a question to the ECJ, the Sofiyski gradski sad pointed out that the national court is only required to make a reference if there is a real difficulty of interpretation or validity regarding EU law.[192] Because in the case at hand the relevant provisions of the directive had already been interpreted on several occasions by the ECJ and were therefore sufficiently clear, a referral for a preliminary ruling to the ECJ would have been devoid of any value. As a result, the Sofiyski gradski sad rejected the liability claim lodged against Bulgaria. This case confirms again that, in the event of a judicial breach, it is often difficult to distinguish between the violation of the obligation to apply a substantive EU norm – by virtue of the direct effect doctrine or the consistent interpretation rule or by setting aside the contrary national law – and the obligation to make a preliminary reference to the EU.

b. Successful Liability Claims

In addition to the numerous judgments that resulted in the dismissal of a liability claim, it is also possible to identify a few cases where the *Köbler* liability actions were successful. These judgments confirm, however, that a finding of a 'manifest infringement of the applicable law' is more the exception than the rule.

In fact, all five cases in which such a breach had been found are specific for a certain reason. In three of them, the domestic rules were found to be contrary to EU law; and not only their application by the national supreme courts.[193] In the fourth case, the national decision was made in the proceedings that gave rise to the preliminary ruling in *Traghetti del Mediterraneo*.[194] Finally, in the fifth case, damages have been awarded not in ordinary liability proceedings before the civil court but in a specific procedure for damages in Sweden.[195] It is noteworthy that there are two other judgments, rendered by the Portuguese Tribunal da Relação de Guimarães (Court of Second Instance of Guimarães)[196] and by the French Cour d'appel de Paris,[197] which also established the liability of the state, but these decisions were subsequently annulled by the Supremo Tribunal de Justiça,[198] and by the Cour de cassation.[199]

The analysis of these judgments shows that a finding of a manifest infringement requires, in practice, a prior clear statement by the ECJ regarding the violation of EU law in relation to the national rule to be applied in the case, either in an infringement action or in a preliminary ruling proceeding.

[192] (ECJ) Judgment in *Cilfit and Others*.

[193] (FI) Korkein oikeus, tuomio, 05/07/2013 and Korkein oikeus, tuomio, 05/03/2016; (BG) Apelativen sad – Burgas, Reshenie, 26/04/2016.

[194] (IT) Tribunale di Genova, ordinanza, 31/03/2009.

[195] (SE) Justitiekanslern, Beslut, 06/04/2009.

[196] (PT) Tribunal da Relacao de Guimaraes, Acórdão, 23/04/2009.

[197] (FR) Cour d'appel de Paris, arrêt, 06/05/2015.

[198] (PT) Supremo Tribunal de Justiça, Acórdão, 03/12/2009.

[199] (FR) Cour d'appel de Paris, arrêt, 06/05/2015.

(1) Infringement of EU Law by Several Branches of Government

In several successful *Köbler* actions, there has been a general violation of EU law by several branches of government, leading together to the finding of a serious breach. In this respect, in a Finnish case from 2013, the defendant was the state, and in a Bulgarian case from 2016, all the three branches of government. Therefore, the civil courts adjudicating on the state liability claims had the possibility to address the breach of EU law by the state as an entity, without the need to narrow the scope of the examination to the judgments of the national supreme courts. Also, at the time the contested judgments were made, there had already been serious doubts about the compatibility of the national legislation with the EU rules in both cases.[200] Thus several branches of government contributed to the damage caused by the application of national rules contrary to EU law in the claimants' cases.

In a judgment rendered in 2013 the Korkein oikeus (Finnish Supreme Court) has awarded damages in favour of the claimant for the violation of his rights conferred by EU rules.[201] The case concerned a decision of the fiscal administration, confirmed by the Korkein hallinto-oikeus (Finnish Supreme Administrative Court), imposing the payment of VAT and other taxes on the claimant. In the liability proceedings lodged against the state before the Korkein oikeus, the adjudicating court referred to previous ECJ judgments to find that the Finnish system was discriminatory and contrary to EU rules. Therefore, it ordered compensation for the prejudice suffered as the result of the application of the unlawful national fiscal rules in the claimant's case.[202] It is noteworthy that this judgment is not clear on the question of whether the violation of EU law was attributable to the legislature, to the tax administration or to the administrative court. In spite of that, there are indications showing that Finland was especially held liable for the erroneous decision of the Korkein hallinto-oikeus. In particular, the Korkein oikeus emphasised that the state liability principle applies even to damages incurred as a result of the decision of a Member State's supreme court.[203]

Contrary to Finnish law, the defendant in a state liability action is the specific state body responsible for the breach under the Bulgarian rules. Therefore, the consideration of multiple breaches by several state bodies is only possible if the claimant sues more branches of government, such as in the case below.

In its judgment from 2016, the Apelativen sad – Burgas (Court of Appeal, Burgas, Bulgaria) confirmed the judgment of the Okrazhen sad Yambol (Regional Court, Yambol, Bulgaria) which had established joint and several liability of

[200] In the Bulgarian case the Commission had already initiated infringement proceedings, and in the Finnish case the ECJ had already rendered a judgment declaring the Finnish regulation non-compliant with EU law.

[201] (FI) Korkein oikeus, tuomio, 05/07/2013.

[202] For diffent aspects of the case, see s 2.II.B.iv.d.

[203] (FI) Korkein oikeus, tuomio, 05/07/2013, point 24.

the Varhoven kasatsionen sad, as well as national administrative and legislative bodies for the damage sustained by a company due to the application of a national act contrary to EU law.[204] In particular, the Okrazhen sad Yambol pointed out that the European Commission had already initiated infringement proceedings against Bulgaria claiming violation of EU law due to the contested provision of the national law. Therefore, as the Okrazhen sad Yambol argued, the Bulgarian Parliament had infringed its obligation of cooperation enshrined under Article 4(3) TEU by not having amended the national law. In addition, the national administrative authority had also contributed to the damage by having rendered its decision on the basis of the national provision contrary to EU law. Moreover, the Okrazhen sad Yambol also held the Varhoven kasatsionen sad responsible for the breach. In this regard, the first-instance court argued that in the proceedings on the revision of the administrative decision, the supreme court should have referred a preliminary question to the ECJ. After finding that all three branches of the state had contributed to the damage incurred, the Okrazhen sad Yambol held them jointly and severally liable to pay compensation to the company. As the defendants appealed against this decision, the case was brought before the Apelativen sad – Burgas. The court of appeal dismissed the appeals and confirmed the judgment of the Okrazhen sad Yambol. The second-instance court concluded that the conditions of state liability were established, the violation of EU law was sufficiently serious, and that all three branches of government were responsible for the damages suffered by the claimant.

(2) Liability Established Following the ECJ Preliminary Ruling in the Case

State liability has also been established in the case that gave rise to ECJ judgment in *Traghetti del Mediterraneo*. In the preliminary ruling, the ECJ found that the Italian rules restricting the possibility to hold the state liable for breaches of EU law by the national courts had been contrary to EU law.[205] Noteworthy is that in its judgment, the ECJ had not evaluated the gravity of the breach but left this assessment to the national court.

Following the ECJ judgment in *Traghetti del Mediterraneo*, the Italian Tribunale di Genova, the court which made the preliminary reference, declared that a violation of EU law had taken place due to the refusal by the Corte Suprema di Cassazione to submit a request for preliminary ruling.[206] Then the Tribunale di Genova ordered the continuation of the proceedings in order to decide on the claim for compensation in separate proceedings.[207] In this regard,

[204] (BG) Apelativen sad – Burgas, Reshenie, 26/04/2016; Okrazhen sad Yambol, Reshenie, 04/11/2015. For different aspects of the case, see s 2.II.B.iv.d.

[205] (ECJ) Judgment in *Traghetti del Mediterraneo*.

[206] (IT) Tribunale di Genova, ordinanza, 31/03/2009. For a more detailed presentation and for different aspects of the case, see ss 1.III.B, 2.III.B.iii.a and 3.III.A.iii.

[207] Unfortunately, it was not possible to identify the decision rendered in these proceedings. All information provided originates from the order of the Tribunale di Genova, which was published in the journal *Il Diritto Marittimo* 2010: 665–70.

the Tribunal di Genova argued that the request for preliminary ruling would have been necessary in the underlying case, as the compatibility of the national rules with the EU requirements had not been obvious at the time of those proceedings. Consequently, the Tribunal di Genova found that the conditions of state liability were fulfilled according to the *Köbler* criteria. First, individuals have the right to see their rights conferred by EU law being observed, and the preliminary ruling procedure serves the correct application of EU law. Second, the violation of the obligation to submit a request for preliminary ruling constitutes a breach of EU law according to the *Köbler* judgment. Third, there had been a causal relationship between the damages suffered as a result of an unfair competition and the refusal to submit a request for preliminary ruling. Had the Corte Suprema di Cassazione submitted a request for preliminary ruling during the main proceedings, the outcome of the case could have been different.[208] In short, the Tribunal di Genova declared the state liable for a breach of Article 267(3) TFEU by the national supreme court in its decision rendered in 2009.[209]

(3) Specific National Rules Favourable to the Establishment of Judicial Liability

In a case from Sweden, the establishment of liability for judicial breach of EU law was possible due to the existence of flexible national rules allowing the Justitiekanslern (Office of the Chancellor of Justice) to award damages on a discretionary basis.

In its decision of 2009, the Justitiekanslern awarded compensation for damages suffered by the claimant due to judicial decisions contrary to EU law.[210] In this case the claimant brought a liability claim before the Justitiekanslern, requesting compensation for the damages suffered as a result of previous proceedings in which the Swedish courts, first, had rendered a decision contrary to EU law, and, afterwards, had denied revision of that judgment based on an ECJ judgment delivered in the meantime. The Justitiekanslern found that the erroneous interpretation of EU law in the first set of proceedings could not be considered manifest. It pointed out that the national court had analysed in detail the available ECJ case-law and the erroneous interpretation attributed to the directive was excusable. Yet the Justitiekanslern found that the violation of law by the Regeringsrätten (Supreme Administrative Court of Sweden), consisting of declaring the appeal against the contested judgment inadmissible in the first round of proceedings, was a manifest breach allowing for compensation. The Justitiekanslern emphasised that, at that time, the Regeringsrätten had already had information on the relevant ECJ judgment. Therefore, in the light of this

[208] It is notable that, as for the violation of the substantive EU rules, the Tribunal di Genova decided to submit another request for preliminary ruling to the ECJ, in which it asked a question regarding the compatibility of the national provisions on state aids with EU rules. See (ECJ) judgment in *Fallimento Traghetti del Mediterraneo SpA v Presidenza del Consiglio dei Ministri*.

[209] (IT) Legge, 13/04/1988, Art 2. See also Scherr 2012: 581.

[210] (SE) Justitiekanslern, Beslut, 06/04/2009.

new ECJ jurisprudence, the appeal should have been declared admissible. By declaring the appeal inadmissible, the Regeringsrätten committed a manifest breach of EU law, and the claimant was therefore entitled to compensation. The decision of the Justitiekanslern shows that incompatibility with an ECJ judgment is a sufficient basis for granting an appeal before the Regeringsrätten.[211]

(4) **Establishment of Liability by a Lower-Instance Court**

It is noteworthy to mention that there have been a few reported cases where national courts established state liability for violation committed by a national court. These decisions were, however, overturned by a higher-instance court. In this respect, we can refer to a judgment rendered by the Portuguese Tribunal da Relação de Guimarães, albeit this does not contain extensive substantial analysis regarding *Köbler* liability, and a judgment delivered by the French Cour d'appel de Paris.

By a judgment rendered in 2009, the Tribunal da Relação de Guimarães established the liability of the state for a violation of EU law committed by the Supremo Tribunal de Justiça. In the liability action, the claimant invoked the failure on the side of the Supremo Tribunal de Justiça to interpret national rules in conformity with EU law. The Tribunal da Relação de Guimarães declared the claim well founded on the basis of the ECJ case-law regarding state liability, and therefore ordered the state to pay compensation.[212] The court argued that the state can be held liable for the breach of EU law by its courts, even in the absence of a national law on judicial liability. The defendant appealed against this judgment before the Supremo Tribunal de Justiça, which overturned the decision.[213] The supreme court held that the state was not liable for a breach of EU law in this particular case. It has also pointed out that there was no rule in Portuguese law under which the liability of the state for judicial breaches could be established, since the national law had not yet been in force at the time of the facts.[214]

In another judgment delivered in 2015, the Cour d'appel de Paris found a violation of EU law by an earlier judgment of the Cour de cassation.[215] In the underlying case, following the establishment of their liability in criminal proceedings, the claimant organisation brought the case before the Human Rights Committee of the United Nations. The Committee found a violation

[211] (SE) Förvaltningsprocesslag, 36 §.

[212] (PT) Tribunal da Relacao de Guimaraes, Acórdão, 23/04/2009.

[213] (PT) Supremo Tribunal de Justiça, Acórdão, 03/12/2009, available at Network of the presidents of the supreme judicial courts of the European Union, reported by Da Cunha Rodríguez and de Jesus Patricio 2014: 400–04.

[214] This case was brought before the ECtHR which, however, established a violation of Art 6(1) ECHR due to the divergence in the domestic case-law as to the admissibility of state liability claims, leading to a violation of the principle of legal certainty. See the analysis of the *Ferreira Santos Pardal* judgment in s 2.III.B.ii.h. See also (ECtHR) judgment in *Ferreira Santos Pardal v Portugal*.

[215] (FR) Cour d'appel de Paris, arrêt, 06/05/2015.

of the Covenant,[216] by reason of the interpretation by the Cour de cassation of the principle of retroactivity *in mitius* in the main proceedings. Subsequently, the claimant introduced a liability action against the state for the *faute lourde* committed by the Cour de cassation. At first instance, the Cour d'appel de Paris found that the breach of law by the Cour de cassation constituted a *faute lourde* in the terms of the national rules[217] and the damages suffered were to be compensated.[218] The court emphasised that in general the content of a judicial decision cannot be challenged by way of a state liability action once it has become final. However, as an exception to this rule, it is possible to obtain damages when the content of a judgment is in manifest breach of EU law. Referring to the decision of the Human Rights Committee, to the ECJ case-law which declared the principle of retroactivity *in mitius* a general principle of law,[219] as well as to the national provisions confirming this principle,[220] the Cour d'appel concluded that the violation was manifest. According to academics, the Cour d'appel de Paris was the first decision stating clearly that the Cour de cassation had erred in law.[221] Nevertheless, the Cour de cassation reversed this decision, adopting a contestable interpretation of EU law.[222]

v. Conclusion on the Manifest Infringement

In this subsection, I have examined several questions regarding the establishment of a manifest infringement of the applicable law in the terms of *Köbler*. The main conclusions are as follows.

Research and theoretical reflection confirm that only in rare circumstances is it possible to find a manifest breach of EU law committed by a national supreme court. On a theoretical level, the breach of EU law by a national court is considered manifest in two situations. The first is where the national court has made a mistake in the interpretation or application of the substantive EU rule, without even considering making a reference on a question that has not yet been clarified by the ECJ. The other scenario is where the national court has deliberately deviated from the established ECJ case-law. It seems, therefore, that it is of primary importance whether there is an established ECJ jurisprudence on the matter central to the dispute. It is what the ECJ also pointed out in paragraph 56 of the *Köbler* judgment.

[216] International Covenant on Civil and Political Rights, adopted by the United Nations General Assembly with resolution 2200A (XXI) on 19 December 1966, Art 15.

[217] (FR) Code de l'organisation judiciaire, Art L141-1.

[218] The Cour d'appel de Paris ordered the state to pay to the successors in law of the cooperative organisation €15,000 and €2,000 for the moral damages suffered and €100,000 for the pecuniary damages.

[219] (ECJ) Judgment in *Berlusconi and Others*.

[220] (FR) Code pénal, Art 112-1.

[221] Guiot 2016.

[222] See also s 2.II.A.iv.a(3) on the decision of the Cour de Cassation, arrêt, 18/11/2016.

On a practical level, the national courts adjudicating on liability claims for violation of EU law also experience problems in finding a manifest infringement. According to the research conducted, only on five occasions has such liability been established so far. These decisions were usually preceded by an ECJ decision which had already found a violation of EU law due to the national legislative rules or judicial practice either in infringement or in preliminary ruling proceedings. Without such clear previous decisions, it appears quite easy for a national court to dismiss a liability claim, on the grounds that either there had been no manifest violation of the substantive EU norm due to the ambiguity of the rule, or there had been no violation of the referral duty as the norm was not clear. As the conditions of *Köbler* liability are not clear under EU law either, it is not surprising that the argumentation of the national courts does not follow a systematic or coherent line of reasoning. The study of the national decisions demonstrates that there is uncertainty on the question as to whether the violation of the substantive EU rule or that of the referral duty, or both, is necessary for a finding of a manifest breach.

Finally, it is noteworthy that in several Member States, namely under the Czech, Spanish, Polish, Slovenian and UK rules,[223] the national condition regarding the gravity of the breach is quite severe as well. However, the incompatibility of this condition with the EU requirements is not obvious for two reasons. First, as far as these requirements apply without distinction to national and EU law violations, the principle of equivalence is observed. Second, the ECJ itself set very strict conditions for liability in *Köbler*. As such, it is not obvious whether the strict, albeit subjective, conditions for liability under national laws, even if they may be contrary to the effectiveness principle, are in fact incompatible with the *Köbler* conditions. The position of the legal doctrine is not unanimous in this respect either.[224]

For a discussion as to whether the standard of liability is adequate or should be lowered, see the chapter of the book dedicated to the perspectives of the *Köbler* liability.[225]

B. Difficulties in Establishing Causality

Despite the abundant literature on *Köbler* liability, a dimension of the liability criteria appears to have been neglected. It concerns the difficulty in identifying

[223] (CZ) Nejvyšší soud, rozsudek, 02/03/2016; (ES) Sarmiento 2014: 179; (PL) Naczelny Sąd Administracyjny, Wyrok, 26/06/2014; Prawo o postępowaniu przed sądami administracyjnymi, Art 285a; (SI) Ustava Republike Slovenije, 26 člen; Vrhovnega sodišča Republike Slovenije, Sodba, 12/01/2005; Vrhovnega sodišča Republike Slovenije, Sodba, 13/11/2003; Trstenjak and Plaustajner 2014: 472–73; ACA Europe 2008, National Report of Slovenia; (UK) Court of Appeal (England), judgment, 12/05/2010.

[224] See also Beutler 2009; Nassimpian 2007: 834; Scherr 2008: 585.

[225] See s 3.I.

the state body responsible for the breach, and in linking the breach to the judicature's action. These issues were raised by Anagnostaras in the early 2000s. Considering the doctrine of state liability in general, he stated even before the *Köbler* judgment that 'it is not always easy to determine the capacity – legislative, administrative or judicial – in which the state has committed a given violation'.[226] Later, Rodríguez studied the problem in the context of *Köbler* liability.[227] Since then, the allocation of responsibility in state liability action has not been much discussed in academic writing. Therefore, the present section focuses on this specific issue and investigates whether the practice has encountered such problems as foreseen by the academics mentioned earlier.[228]

i. Concurrent Liability of Several Branches of Government

The research confirms that it is often possible to link the damages sustained by the individual with the activity of more than one branch of government when confronted with national court decisions incorrectly applying EU rules.[229]

As the case law shows, such a situation may arise when it comes to the application of directives in disputes between the state and the individual. In particular, it is the case where the application of directly effective provisions of a directive is at stake before a supreme administrative court, following the failure by the legislature to implement the directive into the national legal order. If the administrative authority and the administrative court give their decisions based on the national rule contrary to the EU law, it will not be easy to determine whether the loss sustained by the individual is primarily due to the conduct of the legislature, the executive or the judiciary.[230] Therefore, we can pose the question that Anagnostaras has already raised: What kind of breach should be established, if the affected party were to bring a liability action on the basis of the loss suffered as a denial of their rights conferred by the directive? A legislative one, based on the failure by the legislature to implement the directive; an administrative one, linked to the failure by the administrative authority to apply the provisions of a directly effective measure; or, a judicial one, originating from

[226] Anagnostaras 2002: 663; Anagnostaras 2001a: 355; Anagnostaras 2001b: 142; Anagnostaras 2001c: 281; Kornezov 2016: 1335.

[227] Rodríguez 2004–05: 614–15.

[228] The first version of this section was published as Varga 2017a.

[229] Anagnostaras 2001b: 142. See, in the context of infringement proceedings, Taborowski 2012: 1886–88, and for examples from the judicial practice, (FI) Korkein oikeus, tuomio, 05/07/2013; (BG) Apelativen sad – Burgas, Reshenie, 26/04/2016.

[230] Even though it is less obvious, the case is not essentially different in the event of the application by the national court of a domestic provision contrary to directly applicable (primary) EU law. Despite the absence of any obligation on the side of the national legislature to adopt implementation measures, it is however obligatory, pursuant to Art 4(3) TEU, to render national law compatible with EU law. Therefore, in the event of infringement of this obligation, one may wonder whether the legislature or the judiciary was (more) in breach of EU law by not having provided a legal framework compatible with EU law for the individual's case.

the refusal by the national court to overturn the administrative decision that are inconsistent with the EU law?

It would mean that in these situations it is theoretically possible for the individual to bring a liability action against the Member State, invoking a violation of EU law by the national legislature or executive instead of suing because of a judicial breach. However, there are two limits to this freedom of choice. First, under a liability law, compensation for damages necessitates the determination of the most proximate cause of the sustained loss.[231] Second, the mitigation principle requires that the individual shall do everything in their power to avoid or mitigate the damage, including availing themselves of all available remedies at their disposal.[232]

Meanwhile, it is not possible to provide any generally applicable test as to the specific circumstances under which the damage will be linked to the one or the other arm of the Member State.[233] The matter will thus be resolved on an ad hoc basis. It means that several individuals can bring a liability action invoking violation by the legislature – and several courts may apply the *Francovich* doctrine – instead of the *Köbler* principles to decide on a state liability claim.

The question emerges whether the determination of the exact capacity in which a violation has been committed makes any difference to the attainment of the objectives pursued under the state liability doctrine. These objectives are twofold: on the one hand, the enhancement of the effectiveness of the EU legal order; and, on the other hand, the protection of the rights it confers upon individuals.[234] In my view, the answer to this question is positive, as the degree of culpability required to trigger state liability differs based on the capacity – legislative, administrative or judicial – in which the state has committed the violation.[235] This distinction would only be irrelevant if one should solely take into account the degree of precision of the infringed rule and the clarity of the law in the field to determine the seriousness of the breach. However, the gravity of the violation will also depend on the discretion that the defaulting national institution enjoys regarding the application of the norm.[236] And, in spite of apparent cohesiveness, legislative, administrative and judicial bodies do not enjoy the same discretion regarding the application of EU law.[237] In this regard, we can consider damages suffered as the result of the non-application of a directly effective provision of the VAT directive, such as the rule providing exemption of VAT payment. As for the legislature, its procedural obligation

[231] Anagnostaras 2001b: 147.

[232] See s 2.II.B.iii.a.

[233] Anagnostaras 2001b: 139.

[234] Anagnostaras 2001b: 143.

[235] For a different point of view, see Anagnostaras 2001b: 147.

[236] See (ECJ) judgments in the *Brasserie du pêcheur and Factortame*, paras 44–49; in *Hedley Lomas*, paras 25, 28.

[237] Rodríguez (2004–05) emphasises that even if the ECJ accepts the rule of state unity in international law, the application of state liability in EU law is diversified.

regarding the application of this substantive norm is clear: it has to implement the directive (together with the provision) into the national legal order. The violation of this obligation automatically gives rise to liability, as the legislature enjoys no discretion in this regard. However, the margin of discretion of the national administration is wider; the violation of its obligations emanating from the direct effect of the same provision does not trigger liability automatically.[238] Instead, liability depends on the clarity of the substantive norm and the way other institutions have interpreted it, among other factors. As for the national supreme court, the standard of culpability is even higher, as liability only arises in the event of manifest disregard of the applicable law.[239] Therefore, the standard of culpability is different as regards a violation of the same substantive norm, as it depends on which branch of government committed the violation. It means that the individual is more likely to receive compensation if they invoke the breach by the legislature or the executive, instead of suing on the basis of a judicial violation.

It appears that, in these situations, *Köbler* liability – combined with an obligation to bring up the issue before the court – actually lowers the standard of protection of individual rights.[240] The solution to this problem could be the application of a real state unity doctrine, which means holding the Member State liable and not a specific state body.[241]

ii. Causation in the Case of Multiple Breaches

a. Theory

As already mentioned, there is a twofold limit that is relevant to identify the branch of government responsible for the breach. The first is the causation element, which is to be established by the national court while linking the claimant's loss with the activity of the defaulting institution. The second is the mitigation principle, which guides the claimant's conduct and influences their choice regarding the branch of government to sue.

In any damages remedy, compensation necessitates the determination of the most proximate cause of the sustained loss.[242] Several scholars predict that, if there is a possibility to link the breach with any Member State institution other than courts, the ECJ, as well as national courts deciding on liability claims, will try to avoid inculpating the judiciary.[243]

[238] If necessary, the administrative authority even has the obligation to set aside any national norm conflicting with the provision of EU law automatically.

[239] See also Anagnostaras 2001b: 147.

[240] See also Rodríguez 2004–05: 617, with reference to (ECJ) judgments in *Johnston*; in *Heylens and Others*.

[241] Rodríguez 2004–05: 615.

[242] See also Anagnostaras 2002: 674; Anagnostaras 2001b: 143–44; Rodríguez 2004–05: 616–17.

[243] Anagnostaras 2001c: 298–99 and n 55; Taborowski 2012: 1888–90, 1908; Timmermans 2004: 161–62; Tridimas 2006: 529–33; Tridimas 2007: 157.

b. ECJ Case-Law on Multiple Breaches: The *Commission v Italy* Case

ECJ case-law seems to confirm this assumption. The responsibility was disconnected from the judicial error in the *Commission v Italy*[244] judgment, delivered by the ECJ in an infringement procedure.[245]

In this case, the Commission brought an action before the ECJ against Italy because the latter maintained in force a law that, as applied by administrative authorities and courts, was in breach of EU law. Although the original law that gave rise to these findings had been amended, further references from Italian courts followed, showing that the law was still applied by Italian courts. The Commission therefore brought the case before the ECJ, initiating an infringement procedure. At the beginning of its statement of reasons, the ECJ confirmed that, in an infringement procedure, a failure to fulfil obligations may be established whichever body of a Member State is responsible for the infringement. The ECJ even stated that the Italian law in question was in itself neutral in respect of EU law, and therefore must be examined in the light of its interpretation by the Italian courts.[246] However, the ECJ shifted its argumentation in the end, concluding that the infringement did not occur as a result of the action of the judiciary, but as a consequence of Italy's failure to amend the law in question. The ECJ stated that the Italian rule was not clear enough, and, hence, it was subject to multiple interpretations, some of them leading to infringements of EU law. As such, the judgment against Italy was not based on an infringement committed by the national supreme court. Instead, it was held that Italy had failed to amend the national law, and administrative practice and national case-law led to the breach of EU law.[247]

Despite this, the judgment is full of indications that the ECJ in essence dealt with judicial conduct and in this way, for the very first time, held a Member State responsible for an infringement committed by its judiciary, albeit in the guise of a breach by the legislation.[248] Moreover, the ECJ included certain paragraphs to accept the possibility of an infringement by a Member State court of last instance.[249] Several academics point out that the judgment in *Commission v Italy* should also be read as a pragmatic solution, motivated by the desire not to impinge excessively on the cooperative relationship between national courts and the ECJ.[250] This is why both state functions – judicial and legislative – have been added in order to establish the infringement and also, just as in *Köbler*, the standard of liability has been slightly raised.[251]

[244] (ECJ) Judgment in *Commission v Italy*, C-129/00. For a detailed analysis of the judgment, see Rossi and Di Federico 2005.
[245] Even if this case was rendered in the context of an infringement proceeding, its findings are important for judicial liability cases as well. See also Taborowski 2012: 1908.
[246] Komárek 2005b: 23–25.
[247] Escudero 2011: 236. See also Timmermans 2004: 161.
[248] Hofstötter 2005: 184.
[249] Escudero 2011: 236–37.
[250] Hofstötter 2005: 184, 187; Komárek 2005b: 25.
[251] Hofstötter 2005: 184, 187.

c. Tendency to Avoid the Inculpation of the Judiciary

Certainly, the ECJ has its own reasons for trying to dissociate liability from the conduct of the national courts. Even if the reasons may be different, one may suppose that the same tendency holds true for Member State courts adjudicating on state liability claims.[252] In fact, given the exceptional nature of judicial and legislative liability in national civil laws,[253] it seems logical that national courts try to associate the breach with the national administration's conduct, if there is a possibility to do so.[254]

iii. The Principle of Mitigation of Damages

a. Duty of Mitigation

Besides the question of causation, the duty of damage mitigation may also be relevant to determine the branch of government against which a liability claim must be brought.[255] The ECJ has recognised the duty of mitigation as a matter of EU law and has extended its application to the state liability field. It means that an aggrieved individual must take all reasonable steps to prevent the occurrence of damage or limit its scale, including the obligation to avail themselves, correctly and in time, of the legal remedies open to them in the national courts.[256]

The question can be raised whether the duty of mitigation prevents the individual from bringing a liability action based on a breach of EU law by the legislature or the administrative body if they have not appealed the allegedly illegal decision before the national (administrative) court. If the exhaustion of substantial remedies is considered as a prerequisite for a liability action, this may force the claimant to challenge the last measure that contributed to their damage. In this situation, they have to claim damages on the ground of an (administrative) court's erroneous judgment, instead of suing for damages on the basis of a breach by the legislature or the administrative body.[257] Moreover, national courts hearing state liability claims may find that a violation of the mitigation duty breaks the chain of causality between the breach committed

[252] Anagnostaras 2001c: 298–99 and n 55; Timmermans 2004: 161–62; Tridimas 2007: 157; Szyszczak 1992: 697.

[253] Półtorak 2014: 189–91.

[254] Anagnostaras 2001b: 145–49.

[255] To avoid confusion, it should be made clear, as Anagnostaras (2001a: 363, 374–75) rightly pointed out, that there are two different questions that can be asked in this regard. The first one is whether the ECJ's case-law developed under the doctrine can ever introduce a hierarchy among the judicial means provided for by the domestic legal systems. This question was dealt with to a certain extent by Dougan (2000a: 111), who arrived at the conclusion that the ECJ had not yet imposed a formal exhaustion of local remedies requirement. The second question, which is analysed above, is whether the national legal orders may impose on individuals the obligation to exhaust all available remedies, before they can finally proceed with their public liability actions.

[256] Jans and Duijkersloot 2015: 437–85.

[257] Anagnostaras 2001a: 365.

by the legislature or the administrative authority and the loss sustained by the claimant.[258] It may also affect the measure of compensation that the claimant will finally receive.

b. ECJ Case-Law on the Effectiveness Principle: The *Metallgesellschaft* and *Fuß* Cases

The ECJ did not, however, apply the mitigation principle in the *Metallgesellschaft* and *Fuß* cases, both about actions for damages directly on the basis of the conduct of the legislature and the administrative body, respectively. In this regard, the main question was whether liability action was permitted without seeking substantive justice on the ground of the direct effect doctrine in an appeal procedure before the competent administrative authority or administrative court.[259]

The *Metallgesellschaft* judgment concerned a liability claim based on a legislative breach since the claimants were obliged to pay certain taxes under UK rules in violation of EU law. It was suggested that the claimants could have avoided the payment by contending their rights conferred by the EU rules before the tax authority. As the national rules were contrary to the EU rules, these claims would have probably been rejected by the tax administration. However, this decision could have been challenged before the competent administrative authority and the national courts, as infringing the principles of direct effect and supremacy. In those proceedings, the administrative court should have considered the above principles of EU law. Having to decide on the above arguments, the national court adjudicating the liability claim made a request for preliminary ruling to the ECJ on whether the failure to follow this procedure constituted a violation of the mitigation principle.[260] The ECJ found that the mitigation duty should not reach the point of overburdening the affected individuals by making the admissibility of their liability claims subject to the previous exhaustion of costly legal actions, regardless of their prospects of success. This would make individual protection excessively difficult and contrary to the principle of effectiveness. The only possibility to challenge the tax authority's refusal on the basis of the principles of direct effect and supremacy was not therefore considered to be enough to establish a violation of the mitigation duty in that case on its own.[261]

The *Fuß* judgment concerned an officer who sought compensation, either in the form of time-off instead of payment or damages, for having worked in excess of the maximum average weekly hours limit laid down by EU law. Under

[258] (FR) Conseil d'État, décision, 27/03/2013.

[259] Both *Metallgesellschaft* and *Fuß* concern therefore procedures for obtaining compensation for breaches of EU law and the compatibility of substantive and procedural requirements in national law that limit access to such liability remedies.

[260] Anagnostaras 2001a: 366–67; Tomkin 2012: 1439.

[261] Anagnostaras 2001a: 366–67. See also (ECJ) judgments in *Metallgesellschaft and Others*, para 106; in *Test Claimants in the Thin Cap Group Litigation*, paras 125–26; in *Danske Slagterier*, para 63; as well as the order in *Test Claimants in the CFC and Dividend Group Litigation*, paras 128–29.

German law, entitlement to compensation could only arise if the claimant had first submitted a request seeking compliance with number of working hours legally allowed. The national court hearing the liability claim referred a preliminary question to the ECJ, asking whether the national provision was compatible with the conditions of state liability under EU law. In particular, it sought guidance on whether EU law precluded making the right to compensation conditional on a claimant having first drawn to the employer's attention the alleged infringement of EU and having requested compliance with that provision. The ECJ noted that aggrieved parties might be expected to show reasonable diligence in limiting the extent of their loss or damage. Nevertheless, it also observed that requiring employees to request compliance with a directly effective provision of EU law as a precondition for obtaining compensation for loss suffered had the effect of shifting the burden of compliance from the authorities to individual workers. In addition, the ECJ considered that workers, being the weaker parties in employment relationships, might be reluctant to claim rights against their employer.[262] Hence the ECJ concluded that a national procedural rule requiring a claimant to make a prior application of compliance with the directive was incompatible with the principle of effectiveness.[263]

It seems to follow from these judgments that the possibility for a claimant to bring a liability claim on the basis of a legislative or administrative breach cannot depend on having challenged the allegedly illegal decision before the competent national (administrative) courts in an appeal proceeding.[264] However, it appears that the above two ECJ judgments did not seek to establish a generally applicable principle, but, on the contrary, the ECJ decided on the basis of the specific factual and legal background of these cases. In *Metallgesellschaft*, the conclusion was probably reached due to the uncertainty in which the claimants were placed by the inconsistent national legislation, and the complexity of the procedures that had to be followed to receive a very uncertain remedy.[265] In their situation, the tax advantage would have been denied in any case.[266] In *Fuß*, the ECJ attributed importance to the fact that, in the employment relationship, the aggrieved party was in the weaker position. However, entitlement to compensation may well be limited or excluded if a party that is considered to be an equal in a contractual relationship becomes aware of a breach or anticipated breach of EU law, and is in a position to take reasonable steps to limit or prevent such a breach but fails to do so.[267]

[262] Tomkin 2012: 1430–31.

[263] (ECJ) Judgment in *Fuß*, especially paras 72, 80–81, 83–87, 90, 99.

[264] See (ECJ) judgment in *Unibet*, paras 40–41, and, in the context of annulment proceedings, the opinion of AG Jacobs in *Unión de Pequeños Agricultores v Council*, para 43; judgments in *Jégo-Quéré v Commission*, para 45; in *Commission v Jégo-Quéré*; Arnull 2011: 54–55.

[265] Anagnostaras 2001a: 366–67.

[266] Anagnostaras 2002: 671.

[267] Tomkin 2012: 1439. See also (ECJ) judgments in *Nikolay Kantarev v Balgarska narodna banka*, paras 140–43; in *MedEval*, paras 39–45; in *Hochtief*, paras 50–58.

c. ECJ Case-Law on the Equivalence Principle: The *Transportes Urbanos* Case

In the *Transportes Urbanos* case,[268] the ECJ examined a national rule requiring the prior exhaustion of remedies in a liability action from the perspective of the principle of equivalence.[269] The judgment concerned Spanish rules that made an action for damages against the state subject to the exhaustion of remedies if the claimant invoked the breach of EU law as a ground for compensation from the state. However, the exhaustion of remedies was not required if they claimed damages for a breach of the Constitution.[270] The compatibility of these rules with EU law was at the core of the preliminary reference before the ECJ. In its judgment, which was based on the facts and questions as presented in the request for preliminary ruling, the ECJ decided that the two actions in question could be considered 'similar', and therefore should both follow the same procedural rules.[271] It held, therefore, that the Spanish rules were contrary to the principle of equivalence.

d. Principle of National Procedural Autonomy

Considering all the above arguments, it does not seem possible to offer general guidance on the extent of the mitigation principle under EU law in the context of state liability. This question appears to fall within the general concept of national procedural autonomy. According to this principle, EU law does not interfere with the nature of the action, or with the domestic arrangements on the hierarchy of the legal means guaranteed by national law for the protection of the infringed rights of individuals.[272] Therefore, Member States are allowed to require the previous exhaustion of all alternative courses of action before a state liability suit can finally be held admissible.[273] The only limitation in this regard is not to compromise the effectiveness of EU law and to respect the principle

[268] (ECJ) Judgment in *Transportes Urbanos y Servicios Generales*. For further discussion of the case, see the annotation by Pérez de Nanclares 2010.

[269] See also from the case-law regarding state liability (ECJ), judgments in *Palmisani*, paras 33–40; in *Combinatie Spijker Infrabouw-De Jonge Konstruktie and Others*, para 92. From other matters of law, see eg (ECJ) judgments in *Unitrading*; in *Érsekcsanádi Mezőgazdasági*; in *Littlewoods Retail Ltd and Others*.

[270] See Plaza 2010: 35, 45.

[271] (ECJ) Judgment in *Transportes Urbanos y Servicios Generales*, see especially paras 33, 36, 43–46, 48. Plaza (2010: 48–49) argues that the result might have been different had the Tribunal Supremo presented in the preliminary ruling all aspects of the national legislation.

[272] On the principle of national procedural autonomy, see eg Brown 1997: 67–71; De Búrca 1997; Galetta 2010: 33–74; Hoskins 1996; Kakouris 1997; Micklitz and de Witte 2012; Wallerman 2016a; Wallerman 2016b: 858–62; Wattel 2008. From the case-law, see in particular the following decisions: (ECJ) judgments in *Russo*; in *Rewe-Zentralfinanz and Rewe-Zentral*; in *Rewe-Handelsgesellschaft Nord and Rewe-Markt Steffen*; in *Francovich and Others*, para 41; in *Wells*, para 67; in *Danske Slagterier*, para 31.

[273] Anagnostaras 2001a: 377, 382; Anagnostaras 2001b: 153; Dougan 2000a: 111.

of equivalence. Therefore, it appears possible for Member States to prohibit liability actions where other means of redress exist, but the individual has failed to use them within the applicable time limits. This may result in an obligation for the individual to appeal the challenged legislative or administrative decision before national (administrative) courts. As for liability actions, this may have a consequence in shifting the responsibility onto national (administrative) courts, therefore favouring the application of *Köbler* claims over *Francovich* actions.[274] In fact, the exhaustion of prior remedies is a condition for judicial liability claims in many Member States. According to Scherr, the mitigation duty, namely the 'primary use of appellate review' is a prerequisite to liability action in most Member States.[275]

However, one should not forget that national rules on public liability claims based on breaches of national law differ, by nature, from actions based on EU law violations. This makes it even more difficult to evaluate the national regimes in the context of violation of EU law. First of all, in several legal systems, legislative and judicial liability is rare or even non-existent. Moreover, there is no relation or hierarchy between the different branches of government concerning their respective liabilities regarding the application of law, with the exception of the system of application of EU law.

In a recent case, the ECJ was invited to pronounce on the question whether a national court may incur liability on the grounds of the *Köbler* doctrine even when the claimant has not exhausted all legal remedies available to them in the national legal order. This was the *Tomášová* case.

e. ECJ Case-Law on the National Procedural Autonomy Principle: The *Tomášová* Case

The *Tomášová* case concerned a liability claim based on an infringement of EU law attributable to a national court. The violation consisted in the failure by the court to assess of its own motion in proceedings for enforcement of an arbitration award whether the terms of the consumer contract at issue were unfair. Had the terms been assessed, the enforcement court would have been obliged to disregard them because of their unfair nature. However, the court instead granted an application for the recovery of sums in accordance with the contested clauses. The consumer lodged a liability claim on the grounds of the decision given in these proceedings for enforcement of an arbitration award. The national court sitting on the liability claim found that the consumer had not exhausted all national remedies, an action for recovery of a sum unduly paid

[274] Rodríguez 2004–05: 617.

[275] According to Scherr (2008: 408–09), the following Member States applied this condition in 2008: Czech Republic, Denmark, Germany, Estonia, Spain, Latvia, Luxembourg, Hungary, Austria, Poland, Romania, Finland and Sweden.

being always available to them. Therefore, it asked the ECJ whether the national court could incur liability even if a person deemed to have suffered damages had not exhausted all national legal remedies available to them. It also asked whether an action for recovery of a sum unduly paid had priority over compensation for damages.

The ECJ stated, succinctly, that the relationship between a liability action and the other actions available under national law, in particular an action for recovery of a sum unduly paid, is determined by the national laws subject to observance of the principles of equivalence and effectiveness.[276]

iv. National Case-Law on Liability Claims for Breach of Rights under the VAT Directives

The case-law on state liability for breach of individual rights conferred by the VAT directives is a good illustration of different issues concerning concurrent liability or joint responsibility by several branches of government.[277] In this matter of law, individuals are often confronted with a simultaneous breach of EU rights by several branches of government. Moreover, the violation of the EU rules granting VAT exemption rights to individuals has already given rise to numerous state liability claims.

It must be mentioned briefly that an action for recovery of unlawfully levied charges is an alternative remedy to the liability claim to make good the infringed pecuniary rights in such cases. Since, according to the ECJ case-law,[278] there is no need to establish a manifest breach of EU law but only a mere violation in a recovery action, this latter can be an even more efficient way than a liability claim to obtain restitution. In the *Metallgesellschaft* and *Test Claimants* judgments, the ECJ held that it is for the national court to qualify the action of the claimant as a recovery or a damages claim.[279] However, it seems that, in *Stockholm Lindöpark*, the ECJ favoured the latter over the former to a certain extent.[280] In this judgment, the ECJ suggested that the liability action did not seem to be necessary, since the claimant could pursue the debts retrospectively by basing its claim directly on the provisions of the misimplemented measure.[281]

[276] (ECJ) Judgment in *Tomášová*, paras 40–41; opinion of AG Wahl in Case *Tomášová*, paras 85–86. See also s 1.III.D.

[277] The term 'joint responsibility' in the context of violations for EU law was used by Nollkaemper (2011) who analysed the joint responsibility between the EU and Member States in his research paper. For the same concept, De Visser (2004: 47) uses the expression 'concurrent liability'.

[278] (ECJ) Judgments in *Roquette Frères v Commission*; in *Just*; in *GT-Link*, paras 58, 60–61.

[279] (ECJ) Judgment in *Metallgesellschaft and Others*; order in *Test Claimants in the FII Group Litigation*.

[280] (ECJ) Judgment in *Stockholm Lindöpark*, especially para 35.

[281] According to Anagnostaras (2001a: 376), the ECJ judgment in *Stockholm Lindöpark* seems to suggest that there would be no objection if national law obliged the claimant to bring its claim under an entitlement action with the availability of a liability suit being reserved for any further loss that could not be recovered under the direct effect doctrine.

Nevertheless, as issues regarding the relationship and the primacy between a recovery and a liability action fall outside the scope of this research, they will not be analysed further.[282]

The following judgments demonstrate that damages caused by violation of individual rights conferred by the VAT directives may give rise to liability claims based on either legislative, administrative or judicial errors. Hence, there is no clear rule to define the branch of government that is to be accused of violation in these cases.[283]

It is noteworthy that in several Member States the defendant in a liability action is the state itself, while in other cases it is the specific branch of government. Certainly, a liability action is necessarily based on a specific illegal act of one or another state body in both scenarios. Nevertheless, national courts adjudicating on state liability claims have presumably more leeway in evaluating the infringement of EU law in its complexity if the defendant is the state itself. On the contrary, the national court judging the liability claim can only decide on a liability of the Member State body sued by the claimant if the defendant is the rebuked state body. Therefore, national procedural rules which foresee liability of the state instead of that of a specific body appear to be more favourable with regard to the application of the liability doctrine.

a. Liability Actions Based on Legislative Omission

In several German cases, the responsibility for violation of EU law was attributed to the national legislature, given the inconsistency of the national rules with the VAT directives. The liability actions were preceded by an ECJ judgment holding that Germany had been in violation of the EU directive since it had exempted state-owned casinos from VAT, whereas privately owned casinos were subject to VAT. Following the ECJ judgment, several claims were brought by former operators of private gambling establishments in order to seek compensation from the state for the VAT unduly paid when the discriminatory German law had been in force. However, the Kammergericht Berlin (Highest State Court, Berlin) and the BGH denied compensation by the state for different reasons.

In its judgment from 2011, the Kammergericht Berlin held that the infringed provision of the directive did not confer rights on individuals but aimed to accomplish neutral taxation.[284] Lock criticises this conclusion and states that, prior to this decision, the ECJ had already held the provision to be directly effective, and explicitly stated that individuals could rely on provisions 'in so far as they define rights which individuals are able to assert against the state'.[285] As for

[282] In this regard, see also the (ECtHR) judgment in *SA Dangeville v France*.

[283] For another interesting example, see (FR) Cour administrative d'appel de Douai, décision, 09/06/2011, reported by Condon and van Leeuwen 2016: 257.

[284] (DE) Kammergericht Berlin, Urteil, 24/06/2011, reported by Lock 2012: 1691–92.

[285] Lock 2012: 1691–92.

a judgment by the BGH, handed down in 2012, the damages claim was refused for a different reason.[286] Referring to the ECJ case-law, the BGH acknowledged that Member States had to respect the principle of fiscal neutrality and could not make the benefit of exemption dependent on the identity of an operator of gambling activities and gambling machines. Nonetheless, the BGH considered that the failure to implement the directive into German law within the required timeframe did not constitute a sufficiently serious breach to trigger state liability. In conclusion, in these cases a previous ECJ judgment had already established the German legislation's inconsistency with EU law. Such a finding usually serves as an incentive for the aggrieved party to raise the liability of the legislature. This can help to explain why the legislative act, and not the administrative decision, was at issue in the proceedings. While, in principle, the German courts accepted the possibility of bringing a liability action on the basis of a legislative breach, with no need for prior contestation of the administrative decision,[287] the Belgian Supreme court arrived at a different solution.

The Belgian Cour de Cassation (Supreme Court, Belgium) handed down a judgment in 2008, based on facts similar to those in the above German cases.[288] A company requested compensation from the state for the VAT paid in the past, the legal basis of which was later declared contrary to the EU directive. The Cour de Cassation found, however, that the claimant company had not lodged an appeal against the administrative decision in time. This omission was enough to break the causal link between the action of the legislature and the damage suffered. The fact that the unlawfulness of the national rule with regard to the EU law had not been established at the time of the facts was irrelevant. The Cour de Cassation held that it should have not prevented the claimant from availing themselves in time of all legal remedies available to them, and to appeal against the administrative decision. The Belgian Court de Cassation thus denied a liability claim where previous administrative remedies had not been exhausted.

In addition, as explained above, the *Transportes Urbanos* case before the Spanish Tribunal Supremo (Supreme Court, Spain) concerned a liability action against the state based on the legislature's act. The case related to the obligation to exhaust the remedies available according to the principle of equivalence. The Tribunal Supremo handed down its final judgment in 2010,[289] following a reference for a preliminary ruling made to the ECJ.[290] The factual background of this case is similar to the one in the Belgian action above. The Transportes Urbanos Company had paid an undue amount of tax because of the incorrect implementation of the EU directive into Spanish law. However, the ECJ judgment that declared the Spanish law contrary to the directive was only delivered after

[286] (DE) BGH, Beschluss, 26/04/2012, reported by Laut in Reflets no 2/2012: 42.
[287] See also (DE) Oberlandesgericht Köln, 02/06/2005, reported by Granger 2017: 117.
[288] (BE) Cour de Cassation, arrêt, 23/06/2008, reported by Rémy in Reflets no 3/2008: 13.
[289] (ES) Tribunal Supremo, auto, 17/09/2010, reported by Plaza 2010:50.
[290] (ECJ) Judgment in *Transportes Urbanos y Servicios Generales*.

the deadline for the company to request the rectification of its self-assessment and the refund of overpayments had already passed. The claim for damages that the company brought before the Council of Ministers was dismissed as, according to the council, the direct causal link between the infringement of EU law and the damages was broken since Transportes Urbanos had failed to request the rectification of the self-assessments in due time. The company challenged the decision before the Tribunal Supremo, which referred a request for preliminary ruling to the ECJ.[291] The ECJ found that, since the prior exhaustion of remedies was not a condition for compensation of damages incurred from a breach of the Constitution under Spanish law, the rule concerning EU liability claims infringed the principle of equivalence.[292] In the end, the Tribunal Supremo held the state liable for the breach of the EU directive by the legislature and ordered it to pay compensation. The court declared that there is a direct causal link between the breach and the damage sustained by the injured person, and it cannot be sustained that such causal relationship is breached because the claimant did not exhaust the administrative and judicial remedies available against the tax decision.

It therefore overruled its previous case-law, under which failure to challenge administrative decisions in due time, applying national laws in breach of EU law, had entailed the breach of the causal link.[293]

b. Liability Actions Based on a Breach by the Tax Administration

The previous cases concerned liability claims due to violation of EU law by the legislature; especially on the ground of the non- or incorrect transposition of the VAT directives. There are, however, other national judgments which show that, in several cases, the actions were instead directed against the tax authority's decision. Three decisions are noteworthy in this regard, one rendered by the Danish Vestre Landsret (Western High Court), another by the German Bundesfinanzhof (Federal Fiscal Court) and the third by the Dutch Hoge Raad.

In a judgment from 2005, Vestre Landsret ordered the Ministry of Taxation to pay damages for the violation of the VAT directive.[294] The liability proceeding was preceded by an ECJ judgment declaring the national implementation measure contrary to EU law. Based on this ECJ decision the Vestre Landsret found that the provision of the VAT directive was clear, and its violation constituted a qualified infringement of EU law engaging the liability of the Ministry

[291] (ES) Tribunal Supremo, auto de 01/02/2008, reported in database JuriFast. See also (ECJ) judgment in *Commission v Spain*, C-204/03, para 26.

[292] (ECJ) Judgment in *Transportes Urbanos y Servicios Generales*, paras 36–37, 44, 48.

[293] Plaza 2010: 50.

[294] (DN) Vestre Landsret, dom af 09/11/2005, reported in the XXIVth Annual Report on monitoring the application of EU law (2006), Annex VI, I-41.

of Taxation. Because of this, it ordered the ministry to compensate the claimant for the tax unduly paid.

The German Bundesfinanzhof handed down a judgment in 2005 with a background that was similar to the above Danish case.[295] The main question was whether a tax decision that proved to be contrary to EU law in the light of subsequent ECJ jurisprudence can give rise to compensation. In this case, the claimant company initiated an action to obtain compensation for the tax that they claimed to have paid unduly. The Bundesfinanzhof, while hearing the case, submitted a request for a preliminary ruling to the ECJ, which gave an interpretation of the directive in favour of the claimant. The Bundesfinanzhof thus had to decide whether the claimant had the right to VAT compensation for the overpaid tax in the light of the subsequent ECJ jurisprudence, and on the basis of the state liability doctrine. The Bundesfinanzhof examined whether the assessment decisions of the Finanzamt (Tax Office) should be considered as a sufficiently serious violation of EU law. It responded in the negative, stating that even the Bundesfinanzhof itself had doubts about the correct interpretation of the directive at the time of the case. It meant that the conditions for state liability were not met and the request was rejected.

The Hoge Raad handed down a judgment in 2000 on a liability claim for the legal costs of bringing a recovery action to have unduly paid taxes reimbursed.[296] Initially, the taxpayer brought a recovery action and had the unduly paid tax reimbursed. However, as they received only the tax reimbursed under national rules, they sought compensation before the Hoge Raad for the legal costs incurred in the recovery action. The Hoge Raad held that there was no infringement of EU law and, thus, no duty to pay compensation for the legal costs. The Hoge Raad stressed that, while the Netherlands had correctly implemented the directive, the recovery at issue was not based on the chargeable events within the meaning of the provision concerned and that, therefore, VAT was not due in that particular case. It is worth noting that the reimbursement of the allegedly unlawfully charged tax had been demanded in the first course of action. The liability claim was only brought afterwards, to seek compensation for the costs that had not been paid in the recovery action.

c. Liability Actions Based on a Breach by the Judiciary

Moreover, several liability actions for violation of rights conferred by the VAT directives were directed against the administrative courts' judgments confirming

[295] (DE) Bundesfinanzhof, 13/01/2005, reported in the XXIIIrd Annual Report on monitoring the application of EU law (2005), Annex VI, I-33; Bundesfinanzhof, 21/04/2005, reported in the XIIIrd Annual Report on monitoring the application of EU law (2005), Annex VI, I-33.

[296] (NL) Hoge Raad, arrest van 29/03/2000, reported in the XVIII Annual Report on monitoring the application of Community law (2000), Annex VI, 54.

the decisions of the tax authority.[297] It is noteworthy to briefly recall the three most telling judgments in this regard, a decision of the Swedish Justitiekanslern, a judgment of the Hungarian Kúria, and a judgment of the Bulgarian Sofiyski gradski sad.

The first decision to mention is the one rendered by the Justitiekanslern in 2009 which awarded compensation for damages suffered due to the violation of EU law by the Regeringsrätten.[298] As already described above, in the underlying proceedings, the claimant company invoked, in vain, the EU directive before the tax authority in order to exercise their right to VAT deduction. The administrative court then confirmed the decision of the fiscal authority, and this judgment became final after the refusal by the Regeringsrätten to declare admissible the appeal lodged against it. Later, the company brought a liability action against the state before the Justitiekanslern, claiming compensation for the damages suffered as a result of the underlying proceedings. Deciding on the liability action against the state, the Justitiekanslern found that the violation of law by the Regeringsrätten was manifest and sufficiently serious to give rise to compensation. It argued that the Regeringsrätten should have declared the appeal admissible, with regard to the new ECJ case-law on this matter. Specifically, the ECJ had rendered a judgment that was favourable to the claimant immediately before the Regeringsrätten's refusal to allow appeal against the first-instance court's judgment. Therefore, the appeal should have been declared admissible in the light of this new ECJ jurisprudence. In this case, the finding of a manifest breach of EU law was due to the new ECJ jurisprudence, which emerged only before the Regeringsrätten's decision. Therefore, the decision of attributing the violation of EU law to this court seems to be reasonable and justified.

In addition, the Hungarian Kúria rendered a judgment in 2013 in a liability action directed against a final judgment of the administrative division of the same court by reason of the breach of the EU rules regarding the right to deduction of the VAT paid.[299] The liability action originated in an administrative dispute between the claimant and the fiscal authority, in which the tax administration denied the right of the claimant to deduct the VAT paid, and the Kúria, as an administrative court of last instance, confirmed this decision. Sitting as an appeal court on the subsequent liability action, the Kúria dismissed the action, invoking domestic procedural rules. In this regard, the Kúria pointed out that the claimant himself had not invoked the directive in the proceedings before the administrative court. According to the court's reasoning, since the

[297] (SE) Justitiekanslern, Beslut, 06/04/2009; (FI) Korkein oikeus, tuomio, 05/07/2013; Korkein oikeus, tuomio, 05/03/2016 (HU) Kúria, ítélet, 11/12/2013; (BG) Sofiyski gradski sad, Reshenie, 03/01/2014.

[298] (SE) Justitiekanslern, Beslut, 06/04/2009. For different aspects of the case, see s 2.II.A.iv.b(3).

[299] (HU) Kúria, ítélet, 11/12/2013. In Hungary, the same supreme court, the Kúria, is competent in civil and administrative matters as well. For different aspects of the case, see ss 2.II.A.ii.a(2) and 2.III.B.iv.b.

court is bound by the pleas raised by the parties, the administrative court had not committed any breach when it had not considered the EU law.

Finally, the Sofiyski gradski sad handed down a judgment in 2014 in a liability claim for violation of EU law by the Varhoven administrativen sad.[300] The claimant rebuked the Varhoven administrativen sad for having confirmed the decision of the fiscal administration rejecting his claim for VAT deduction. The Sofiyski gradski sad rejected the liability action. The court stated that the judgment of the Varhoven administrativen sad was correct in the light of ECJ case-law relative to VAT deductions. Moreover, the provisions of the directive were sufficiently clear, meaning that the Varhoven administrativen sad was not in breach in its obligation to make preliminary reference either. The conclusion is that if the EU directive was correctly implemented into the national legal order, the liability of the legislation and the administration cannot be raised. In this a case, only the jurisdiction can be rebuked for having violated EU law, and, in particular, for failing to interpret the national rules in conformity with the directive.

d. Liability Action Based on a Breach by Several Branches of Government

Moreover, there are cases showing that the contribution to the breach by several branches of government can be considered as a whole when deciding on liability claims. In this respect, two cases are noteworthy. The first one is a judgment of the Finnish Korkein Oikeus of 2013, which is an example of a scenario where the defendant in the liability action is the state; and the second one is a judgment of the Bulgarian Apelativen sad – Burgas of 2016, which demonstrates the establishment of joint and several liability of the three branches of government, all defendants in the liability action.

As already cited amongst the successful liability claims, in a judgment of 2013 the Korkein oikeus awarded damages in favour of the claimant for the violation of their rights conferred by EU rules regarding tax payment in previous administrative proceedings.[301] In its decision, the Korkein oikeus concluded that the infringement of EU law in the primary proceedings was demonstrated to a sufficient extent to make Finland liable. As already mentioned, the judgment is not clear on the question of whether the violation of EU law was attributable to the legislature, to the tax administration or to the administrative court. In this regard, two remarks need to be made. The first one is that the defendant was the state itself, and not the specific state body, the Korkein hallinto-oikeus. That meant that the civil court had the possibility to address the breach of EU law by the state as an entity, without the necessity to narrow the scope of the examination for the judgment of the court. In the case at hand, the entire system as a

[300] (BG) Sofiyski gradski sad, Reshenie, 03/01/2014.

[301] (FI) Korkein oikeus, tuomio, 05/07/2013. For different aspects of the case, see s 2.II.A.iv.b(1).

whole was found contrary to EU law, albeit some paragraphs of the judgment suggest that Finland was especially held liable for the erroneous decision of the Korkein hallinto-oikeus.[302] The second remark is that the ECJ had already made it clear by the time of the proceedings that the Finnish regulation was contrary to EU law. Moreover, the EU provision on neutral taxation was infringed from the beginning of the procedure: the legislature, the tax authority and the administrative court were all in breach in that regard.

As already mentioned amongst the successful liability claims as well, in a judgment dated in 2016, the Apelativen sad – Burgas confirmed the judgment of the Okrazhen sad Yambol, which established joint and several liability of the Varhoven kasatsionen sad, as well as national administrative and legislative bodies for the damage sustained by the claimant company due to the application of a national act contrary to EU law in previous judicial proceedings.[303] Consequently, the liability court ordered the defendants to pay compensation to the claimant. In its judgment the Apelativen sad – Burgas concluded that the conditions of state liability were established, as the violation of EU law was sufficiently serious, and that all three branches of government were responsible for the damages suffered by the claimant. It also held that it was possible under Bulgarian law to establish joint and several responsibility of the three state bodies which all contributed to the breach. The particularity of this case is that the court rebuked all three branches of government for having applied a national law contrary to EU law. It had the possibility to do so as the claimant had claimed such a cumulative breach and sued all three branches of government in the request. This element seems to be a determinant factor in establishing liability for the state. As the three branches of government had infringed their obligations regarding the application of EU law, the court was able to qualify the violation sufficiently serious to trigger liability. Moreover, given the fact that the Commission had already raised doubts on the compatibility with EU law of the national provision at stake, it was easy for the court to find an actual incompatibility.

e. Conclusion on the Allocation of the Responsibility

To summarise, the above judgments show that in cases of violation of rights conferred by non-implemented directives, the damage to the individual can be related to breaches committed by several branches of government. It is therefore not obvious which branch of the state is responsible for the damages suffered. In fact, the loss of the individual can often be related to several branches, depending on the circumstances of the case.

302 In particular, the Korkein oikeus emphasised that the state liability principle applies to damages incurred as a result of the decision of a Member State's supreme court. (FI) Korkein oikeus, tuomio, 05/07/2013, para 24.

303 (BG) Apelativen sad – Burgas, Reshenie, 26/04/2016; Okrazhen sad Yambol, Reshenie, 04/11/2015. For different aspects of the case, see s 2.II.A.iv.b(1).

v. The Situation of Sole Breach by one Member State Body

In order to understand the whole context, it should be emphasised that there exist situations when liability can be clearly attributed to one or another branch of government, notwithstanding the eventual involvement of several branches of government in the breach of EU law. This is so because the infringement of a substantive EU norm does not go together with the infringement of the procedural obligation regarding the application of this EU norm in every situation. Under certain circumstances, Member State bodies are exempt from the obligation to apply the EU norm, for example because of the absence of the direct effect of the provision in the case.[304] The following judgments aim to demonstrate this scenario.

a. Liability of the Legislature

Non-implemented directives do not produce direct effect between private parties.[305] If the consistent interpretation of the EU provision with the national rules is not possible either, the breach can only be attributed to the national legislature. The reason is that administrative and judicial bodies do not have any procedural obligation to apply substantive EU norms that do not have direct effect and are contrary to the national rules. Therefore, even if these bodies infringe a substantive EU norm, they do not infringe any procedural obligation regarding the application of this substantive EU norm. As a result, they cannot be held responsible for violating EU law, even if they seem to be involved in the breach.[306]

A Portuguese judgment rendered by the Supremo Tribunal de Justiça in 2007 regarding the eventual breach of individual rights conferred by the motor insurance directive illustrates this scenario.[307] In this case the Supremo Tribunal de Justiça had to decide whether the claimants were entitled to receive compensation from the state for what they had not received under a previous judgment by the Portuguese court, considered to be contrary to EU law. In this regard, the Supremo Tribunal de Justiça reached the conclusion that the conditions of state liability under EU law had been established. It argued that there had been a clear failure on the part of the state due to the belated implementation of the directive, which implied that the claimants could not rely on the provisions of this directive against a private party in the previous proceedings. A similar decision,

[304] See also Anagnostaras 2001b: 144.

[305] (ECJ) Judgments in *Marshall*; in *Faccini Dori*; 1996 in *El Corte Inglés*; in *Daihatsu Deutschland*.

[306] The situation is more complicated in exclusionary situations, namely when Member State courts are obliged to leave unapplied a national provision that is contrary to the directive. Under these circumstances, even in a vertical situation, the Member State court is not exempted from its obligation to give effect to the EU norm. However, this subject will not be further discussed here. For supplementary explanations regarding exclusionary and substitutionary situations, see eg Bobek 2017: 146–52; Dougan 2007: 937–40, 944–45; Dougan 2019: 1468; Eilmansberger 2004: 1213–15; Hilson and Downes 1999; Prechal 2000: 1050; Van Gerven 1995; Van Gerven 2000.

[307] (PT) Supremo Tribunal de Justiça, Acórdão, 27/11/2007.

on a similar factual and judicial background, was rendered by the Tribunal Central Administrativo in 2008.[308]

In conclusion, in situations where a non-implemented directive cannot produce direct effect between the parties before the national court, the violation of EU law capable of entailing liability of the state can only be attributed to the legislature.

b. Liability of the Administration

Where a directive had been correctly implemented into the national legal order, but the administrative authority applies it in a manner inconsistent with EU law, the liability of the state in the exercise of its executive power can be raised. A decision rendered by the Belgian Hof van beroep te Brussel (Court of Appeal, Brussels) will be presented as an example for the establishment of the liability of the administrative authority; however, in this case, the liability of the Belgian administrative court could have been established too.

By a judgment of 2015, the Hof van beroep te Brussel held the Belgium state liable for the violation of the EU law by a national administrative authority.[309] In this case, the claimant brought a liability action claiming damages for the breach of EU law committed in previous administrative proceedings by the Belgian authorities. Sitting on the liability claim, the Hof van beroep te Brussel found that the decision of the immigration office, confirmed by the administrative court, was contrary to EU law. It, therefore, ordered the Belgian state to pay €5,000 as compensation for the non-pecuniary damage resulting from that decision. In all, the Hof van beroep te Brussel's judgment appears to provide fuller protection then the ECJ's state liability doctrine, as neither the gravity of the breach, nor the eventual harmful effects of the contested decision, had been assessed,[310] moreover, moral damages had also been compensated. It is also interesting that the Hof van beroep te Brussel did not consider the judicial proceedings which followed the administrative decision, or the eventual contribution of the claimant to its own damage due to the deficiencies of the appeal lodged against the decision. On the contrary, the Hof van beroep te Brussel appears to have limited itself to the statement that the administrative authority's decision was unlawful.

c. Liability of the Judicature

On the other hand, there exist situations where the only source of the damage is the act of the judicature.[311] These situations involve breaches, first, when the

[308] (PT) Tribunal Central Administrativo Sul, 21/02/2008.

[309] (BE) Hof van beroep te Brussel, arrest, 23/12/2015, paras 12–28. As the original decision was not available, the conclusions are drawn from the elements of the case which were made public via the proceedings before the ECJ in the *Aquino* case.

[310] As the claimant had in the meantime received the residence permit applied for, the harmful effects of the contested decision were only temporary.

[311] See also Rodríguez 2004–05: 617; Timmermans 2004: 161–62.

national court applies an EU provision correctly implemented into the national legal order in a way that is contrary to EU law; second, when the national court does not comply with its obligation to refer a preliminary question to the ECJ; and third, when the national court infringes a procedural right enshrined in EU law, for example Article 47 of the Charter on the right to receive a judgment within a reasonable time.[312] An example for each scenario will be offered; however, not necessarily from the field of *Köbler* liability. The ECJ judgments cited as examples below have been rendered either in infringement proceedings against a Member State, or in liability actions against EU institutions. They can, however, be used as examples to demonstrate cases of pure judicial breach of EU law.

(1) ECJ Judgment on Purely Judicial Violation of Substantive EU Law: The *Commission v Spain* Case

The ECJ judgment in *Commission v Spain* is the first pure judicial infringement in the history of EU law, according to several legal commentators.[313] In fact, it was the first time ever that the ECJ declared that a Member State was in breach of EU law as a result of a national supreme court decision.

The ECJ delivered its judgment in infringement proceedings brought by the Commission against Spain for failure to fulfil its obligations under the VAT directive. The Spanish law was harmonised with the directive, and the Spanish tax administration applied correctly the ECJ case-law in that matter. It was clear that the infringement was exclusively attributable to the case-law of the court of last instance, without any relation to the legislative or administrative powers. The ECJ established the infringement with a brief reference to the precedent judgment in *Commission v Italy*; however, it did not make any reference to *Köbler*. Academic writers agree that the ECJ has resolved the first purely judicial infringement in the history of EU law with an excessively low profile, as it pronounced in a five-judge chamber judgment, which was not published subsequently. This shows that the court clearly refused to fix its doctrine on infringement for judicial errors of national supreme courts under Article 258 TFEU.

(2) ECJ Judgment on Purely Judicial Violation of the Referral Duty: The *Commission v France* Case

As already presented above, in 2018, the ECJ rendered a judgment in infringement proceedings, in which it condemned the French state for violation of EU law committed by the Conseil d'État.[314] In this judgment, the ECJ found that

[312] (ECJ) Judgment in *Commission v France*, C-416/17. See ss 2.II.A.ii.g(4), 2.II.B.v.c(2) and 3.III.A.i.

[313] (ECJ) Judgment in *Commission v Spain*, C-154/08. For detailed analysis, see Escudero 2011; Do 2010: 145–46; Taborowski 2012: 1891–92.

[314] (ECJ) Judgment in *Commission v France*, C-416/17. For different aspects of the case, see ss 2.II.A.ii.g(4) and 3.III.A.i.

the substance of two decisions of the Conseil d'État was contrary to Treaty provisions.[315] Also, according to the ECJ, the fact that the interpretation adopted by the Conseil d'État was found contrary to EU law on the substance implied that there must had been a reasonable doubt concerning the correct interpretation of EU law, which means that the *acte éclairé* doctrine could not have been applied and the referral for a preliminary ruling could not have been avoided. Consequently, when the Conseil d'État decided not to request a preliminary ruling in a situation where the interpretation of the provisions of EU law was not as obvious as to leave no scope of doubt, it committed a breach of Article 267(3) TFEU.

The factual and legal background that gave rise to this judgment is an example of a situation where the violation of the national supreme court is autonomous and independent – at least so far as the violation of the referral duty is concerned – of a violation of EU law committed by another state organ.[316]

(3) ECJ Judgment on Purely Judicial Violation of the Charter: The *EU v Gascogne e.a.* Cases

In judgments rendered in 2018, the Court upheld, in liability actions against the EU, the allocation of non-material damages imposed by General Court in the context of excessively long proceedings before the General Court in previous proceedings.[317] These judgments confirm previous case-law which had already acknowledged liability of the EU for violation of the right of parties to have their dispute resolved in reasonable time before the EU jurisdiction.[318] The violation by EU or national courts of the parties' procedural rights in judicial proceedings is certainly a breach attributable exclusively to the jurisdiction itself. In this respect, it is generally accepted that the infringement of the right of the parties to have their case heard within a reasonable time amounts to a breach of the right to a fair trial.[319]

vi. Conclusion on Concurrent Liability of Several Breaches of Government

As it follows from the above examples, the case-law confirms that there is no general rule, either in EU law or in the Member States, on which state body to accuse of violation in the event of cumulative breach of EU law by several state

[315] (ECJ) Arts 49 and 63 TFEU.

[316] For further discussion on the violation of the referral duty as a ground for liability, see s 3.III.

[317] (ECJ) Judgments in *Gascogne Sack Deutschland and Gascogne v EU*, T-577/14, paras 78–81, 151–65; in *Kendrion v EU*, T-479/14, paras 121–35; in *EU v Gascogne Sack Deutschland and Gascogne*, C-138/17 P, paras 61–62; in *EU v Kendrion*, C-150/17 P, paras 106–13.

[318] (ECJ) Judgments in *Der Grüne Punkt – Duales System Deutschland v Commission*, para 195; in *Gascogne Sack Deutschland v Commission*, C-40/12 P, paras 89–90; in *Kendrion v Commission*, C-50/12 P, paras 93–94; in *Groupe Gascogne v Commission*, C-58/12 P, paras 82–83; in *FLSmidth v Commission*, para 116; in *Deltafina v Commission*, paras 86–89; in *FLS Plast v Commission*, para 135; in *ICF v Commission*, paras 57–58.

[319] For further discussion as to whether the violation of procedural rights might entail state liability, see s 3.IV.

bodies. One might even suppose that claimants are not aware of the distinction either, and initiate actions without paying attention to the identity of the defendant.[320] Member State courts, influenced by national traditions and left with no ECJ guidance on the question, then sit on the particular claim without putting the violation in a wider context.[321]

The absence of a rule regarding the question of which Member State body's liability should be invoked causes inconsistencies. As the gravity of the breach that must be proved in a procedure against the legislature is lower, and against the courts is higher, a party who avails themselves in time of all of the (administrative) remedies at their disposal before raising the liability of the Member State can find themselves in a disadvantaged situation.

In several Member States, the principle of mitigation and the necessity of direct causal link seem to shift the responsibility from the legislature to the law-applying bodies. This favours the application of the *Köbler* liability and discourages the *Francovich* claim for a legislative breach, resulting in lowering the individual right protection due to the more severe conditions of state liability.

One may observe that the most claimant-friendly judgments have not specifically determined the responsible branch of government but held the state liable for the violation of EU law.[322] From the perspective of EU law, this can be easily justified by the fact that the obligation of sincere cooperation applies to all Member State bodies.[323] Moreover, the ECJ, recognising the state unity doctrine, does not interfere with the national attribution of competences.[324] Therefore, I support the view that considering the liability of the state as a whole can be, at least theoretically, a solution for the problems arising from the inconsistencies between *Francovich* and *Köbler* liability.[325] To be able to apply such a stance, it is, however, necessary that the national law foresee the liability of the state and not that of the state bodies. Otherwise, it is the responsibility of the claimant to be vigilant and sue all branches of government that contributed to the breach.

III. NATIONAL LEGISLATIVE RESTRICTIONS AND RECOGNITION OF THE PRINCIPLE BY NATIONAL COURTS

It is important to remember that one particularly challenging aspect of the application of the *Köbler* liability is that while the ECJ has determined the main

[320] See also Granger 2017: 111–12.

[321] See (FR) Tribunal administrative de Rennes, décision, 16/12/2010; Cour administrative d'appel de Nantes, 30/03/2012.

[322] In this regard, see also (FR) Cour administrative d'appel de Paris, arrêt, 01/07/1992, reported by Granger 2007: 165; Anagnostaras 2001b: 148, and in Jean Monnet Database; Conseil d'État, arrêt, 30/10/1996, English translation in *EC Tax Review* (1997) 190–91, reported by Betlem et al 2007: 47–48, Granger 2007: 165, and in Jean Monnet Database.

[323] (EU) Art 4(3) TEU.

[324] (ECJ) Judgment in *Köbler*, para 32.

[325] It is true that such a solution can eventually meet procedural limitations in Member States where the defendant is, by law, the state body and not the state itself.

conditions of the establishment of such liability, the national procedural rules remain applicable so far as they do not threaten the effective application of the principle. According to the ECJ, the national rules can be applied so long as they do not impose more stringent conditions than the 'manifest infringement of the applicable law' determined in *Köbler*. Therefore, it needs to be assessed, with respect of each domestic legislation, whether the national rules are compatible with *Köbler* liability. In several cases, such as in case of complete exclusion of judicial liability, the incompatibility appears evident. However, in other cases, such as where there is a condition similar to a 'manifest infringement' or a requirement of prior declaration of incompatibility, the assessment has to be made on a case-by-case basis. Such doubts regarding the compatibility of national procedural conditions with the *Köbler* conditions have given rise to requests for preliminary ruling in the already presented post-*Köbler* decisions of the ECJ, notably in the cases *Traghetti del Mediterraneo*, *Ferreira da Silva e.a.* and *Tomášová*.[326]

As already discussed, one of the main concerns of academic writers at the time when the *Köbler* judgment was rendered has been that state liability would be unfeasible in practice, due to the restrictions in national laws regarding judicial liability.[327] This section examines whether these fears were justified and whether the national judges managed to overcome these obstacles.

A. Overview of the National Legislative Restrictions

At this point, it seems relevant to bring up the results of comparative research conducted by Scherr, who in 2008 revealed the restrictions in national laws regarding liability for judicial errors in general.[328] Combining her results with the present findings, the following overview can be offered of the traditional national restrictions on judicial liability.

Almost complete exclusion of liability for judicial activity in purely national cases characterises five national legal systems (Bulgaria, Ireland, Greece, the Netherlands and the UK). The establishment of criminal responsibility of the judge is a precondition for state liability in three Member States (Germany, Estonia and Romania). The liability of the highest national courts is excluded in one state (Austria). The importance of res judicata and the unquestionable nature of final judgments is a major impediment to judicial liability in

[326] For ECJ judgments, see s 1.III.

[327] Breuer 2004: 243–54; Cabral and Chaves 2006: 123; Classen 2004: 816–17; Jans 2004: 176; Komárek 2005a: 77; Wattel 2004: 186–87.

[328] Scherr 2008: 168, 227, 306, 408–09, 414, 417. When analysing the existence of 'liability for judicial acts' or 'judicial liability' in the Member States, it is investigated whether the national legal systems recognise the liability of the state for judicial acts in general. It means that state liability should be guaranteed beyond compensation for violations of the fair trial principle provided under the ECHR and the allocation of damages for illegal arrest or detention and wrongful conviction.

six Member States (France, Croatia, Italy, Luxembourg, Hungary and Ireland). The prior reversal of the contested judgment is a prerequisite for liability under seven national laws (Belgium, Czech Republic, Cyprus, Portugal, Slovakia, Finland and, as far as supreme court liability is concerned, Sweden).[329] The declaration of unlawfulness of the final judgment is required before asking damages from the competent authority in three Member States (Spain, Lithuania and Poland). The construction of these proceedings does not seem, however, necessarily contrary to EU law. In addition, the strict criterion concerning the degree of fault on the part of the judge is a significant obstacle to the allocation of damages in several Member States. This appears to be the case in Slovenian or Spanish law, for example.

However, as a reaction to the *Köbler* judgment, and as far as the erroneous judgment concerns the application of EU law, several Member States' courts and legislatures created exemptions from these overly strict requirements. These cases are the subject of the next subsection of the book.

On the other hand, at first sight, national provisions do not appear to exclude the theoretical possibility to hold the state liable for breaches by supreme courts in two Member States (Denmark and Latvia). The position of Malta is not clear in this regard, as liability of the state is accepted under the general regime of tort law; however, the cases filed to date have only dealt with the executive and legislative arms of the state but not the judiciary. The following overview presents the actual situation in Member States with specific regard to breaches of EU law.

B. National Case-Law

i. Regimes Compatible with EU Law

In several Member States, the national regime of state liability appears to be conforming to the requirements of *Köbler*.

a. Denmark

As liability for judicial acts is accepted in Denmark, the state can be held liable for violation of EU law by the supreme court.[330] In this regard, a simple error in the interpretation of the law is insufficient, as only significant error can trigger liability. Neither the prior reversal of the contested decision is necessary, nor is the res judicata an impediment to liability. Therefore, national conditions on state liability seem to be compatible with the requirements under *Köbler*. Nonetheless, there is no judgment on a *Köbler* claim available yet.

[329] See (ECJ) judgment in *Ferreira da Silva e Brito e.a.*, para 60.
[330] (DN) Betænkning nr 214 om statens og kommunernes erstatningsansvar, 16.

b. Latvia

National provisions do not appear to exclude the possibility of holding the Latvian state liable for breaches of law by the supreme courts.[331] In Latvia, state liability for damages caused by judicial activity has been developed by the case-law. As there is no legislative act on judicial liability, the liability of the state can be raised directly on the basis of the Constitution and the general principles of law, according to a judgment of the Latvijas Republikas Augstākās tiesas (Supreme Court, Latvia) rendered in 2010.[332] In Latvia, fault is not a prerequisite to hold the state liable for actions of its authorities and officials. If these have acted unlawfully, then the state must bear liability for the damages caused to individuals. Due to the general scope of such liability, it can be presumed that it may also embrace violations of EU law.[333] The national regime on judicial liability hence appears to be in line with the *Köbler* requirements, but no case has yet been reported where such liability was established.[334]

c. Spain

In Spain, state liability is the primary remedy to make good damages caused by judicial errors and improper administration of justice. Theoretically, it holds true for breaches of EU law by the courts as well.[335] The claim for compensation must be preceded by a court decision that expressly states the judicial error committed in a final judgment.[336] According to the law on the judiciary, the Tribunal Supremo is competent to establish such violation of law. Only then, based on this prior declaration of judicial error, can the claimant seek pecuniary compensation from the Ministerio de Justicia (Minister of Justice).[337] In line with the case-law, the obvious inattention of the judge in relation to the assessment of facts and a misinterpretation of legal provisions, which cannot be supported by any means of interpretation method, can serve as grounds for compensation.[338] Despite such rules, there is no successful liability action available rendered on

[331] (LV) Latvijas Republikas Satversme, 92.pants; Administratīvā procesa likums, 92.pants. See also ACA Europe 2008, National report of Latvia, question 14. Specific rules on the implementation of state liability are codified in Valsts pārvaldes iestāžu nodarīto zaudējumu atlīdzināšanas likums.

[332] (LV) Latvijas Republikas Augstākās tiesas, Senāta Civillietu departamenta, spriedums, 24/11/2010.

[333] Haba 2015: 70.

[334] It is noteworthy that in Latvia legal norms in the procedural codes declare explicitly that institutions and courts shall take into account the ECJ case-law. See Zukova 2010: 250.

[335] (ES) Constitución Española de 1978, Artículo 121; Real Decreto de 24 de julio de 1889 por el que se publica el Código Civil, Art 1902; Ley 29/1998, de 13 de julio, reguladora de la Jurisdicción Contencioso-administrativa, Art 31.2; Ley 40/2015, de 1 de octubre, de Régimen Jurídico del Sector Público, Art 32; Ley Orgánica 6/1985 del Poder Judicial, Art 292–96.

[336] (ES) Ley Orgánica 6/1985 del Poder Judicial, Art 293. However, if the unlawfulness of the judgment has already been established in the extraordinary remedy of *revisión*, the procedure before the Tribunal Supremo is not required.

[337] See also Sarmiento 2014: 178.

[338] (ES) Audiencia Nacional, Sentencia, 04/12/2012.

the basis of the alleged violation of EU law, although several scholars refer to a judgment by the Tribunal Supremo in this context.

Although the decision of the Tribunal Supremo, pronounced in 2004, does not deal with issues of EU law,[339] it is worth noting that, by relying partially on the *Köbler* principle, the national court extended the reach of ECJ case-law on state liability to purely domestic situations. The liability claim brought before the Tribunal Supremo concerned the rejection, on the grounds of inadmissibility, of a *recurso amparo* introduced by the claimant before the Tribunal Constitucional contesting the recruitment proceedings of legal assistants employed by this court. In its argumentation in favour of applying the common tort liability in the case,[340] the Tribunal Supremo made an explicit reference to the *Köbler* judgment, although the affair in question was unrelated to EU law. It then concluded that the rejection of the *recurso de amparo* constituted a denial of justice, and ordered each of the judges of the Tribunal Constitucional to pay a fine. As the doctrine explains, the Tribunal Supremo's decision shows that some national courts, even the highest ones, are ready to hear tort actions against judicial instances.[341]

In addition, there are several judgments of the Audiencia Nacional (National Court) which assessed the compatibility of the national rules on judicial liability with the *Köbler* conditions. For example, in a judgment delivered in 2009, the Audiencia Nacional found that the Spanish rules are harmonised with the EU requirements.[342] In this respect, the Audiencia Nacional stated that Member States enjoy procedural autonomy to decide on the form of the remedy to be granted, provided that the remedy is compatible with the conditions of efficiency and equivalence. In Spain, such remedy is available, and according to the national rules, the claimant can only introduce its claim before the minister after having sought a prior declaration of judicial error before the Tribunal Supremo. As for the allegations regarding the overly strict conditions of liability, according to the Audiencia Nacional, the deadline of three months to introduce a claim does not render the liability claim practically impossible or excessively difficult. Regarding the condition of a serious breach, the Audiencia National confirmed that the national judicial practice respected the *Köbler* conditions, as EU law requires a manifest error as well. Consequently, the Audiencia Nacional dismissed the appeal against the decision of the Ministerio de Justicia which rejected a liability claim on the grounds that it had not been preceded by a declaration of a judicial error. This case was followed by several other proceedings

[339] (ES) Tribunal Supremo, 23/01/2004, no 51/2004, reported in Reflets no 1/2004: 8, and by Granger 2007:168.

[340] (ES) Código Civil, Art 1902, instead of the application of the special regime of judges' and courts' liability as provided in Constitución Española, Art 121; Ley Orgánica 6/1985 del Poder Judicial, Arts 292–96.

[341] Betlem et al 2007: 62–63.

[342] (ES) Audiencia Nacional, Sentencia, 23/04/2009.

resulting in analogue decisions based on parallel argumentation adopted by the Audiencia Nacional.[343]

Another judgment rendered by the Audiencia Nacional in 2012 follows the same line of reasoning as the judgments mentioned above.[344] Nevertheless, a new element makes this decision worth mentioning. In their liability claim before the Ministerio de Justicia and then before the Audiencia Nacional, the claimant argued that the court adjudicating in their case had committed the same violation of law which had already been found in a ECJ judgment. Therefore, they claimed that the judicial error resulted directly from the ECJ judgment in *Commission v Spain*,[345] and a procedure before the Tribunal Supremo was not necessary. Adjudicating on the claim on second instance, the Audiencia Nacional dismissed the appeal because of the absence of prior declaration of a judicial error by the Tribunal Supremo. To answer the claimant's arguments, it pointed out that the ECJ judgment could not be considered as a prior declaration of judicial error in the case, and could not therefore replace the decision by the Tribunal Supremo, which is a prerequisite for compensation under the national rules.

In addition, by its judgment pronounced in 2015, the Tribunal Supremo dismissed the appeal on points of law introduced by the claimant against the decision of 2012 of the Audiencia Nacional, analysed above.[346] The court emphasised that the question as to whether the claimant suffered damages because of a violation of EU law by the national supreme court was different from the one as to whether the ECJ judgment was correctly implemented. As for the first aspect, the ECJ judgment in *Commission v Spain* was executed correctly, in accordance with Article 260 TFEU, as the national legislator amended the Spanish law following the decision. The Tribunal Supremo pointed out that the liability claim needs to be assessed, however, according to the *Köbler* criteria, taking into account the principle of national procedural autonomy of the Member States. In Spain, in the event of judicial errors, the prior declaration of error is a prerequisite for any compensation. Therefore, in the case at hand, even if the claimant had not been party to the proceedings which resulted in the ECJ decision in *Commission v Spain*, they could have claimed compensation by asking a prior declaration of judicial error of the final judgment rendered in their case. Moreover, the ECJ judgment in *Commission v Spain* could not serve directly as a basis for compensation, as it did not assess whether the conditions for liability had been met. Therefore, the prior declaration of judicial error by the *Tribunal Supremo* cannot be replaced by the ECJ judgment.

[343] (ES) Audiencia Nacional, Sentencia, 30/04/2009; Audiencia Nacional, Sentencia, 04/06/2009; Audiencia Nacional, Sentencia, 23/06/2009; Audiencia Nacional, Sentencia, 10/02/2009; Audiencia Nacional, Sentencia, 04/11/2013; Audiencia Nacional, Sentencia, 30/10/2014.

[344] (ES) Audiencia Nacional, Sentencia, 04/12/2012.

[345] (ECJ) Judgment in *Commission v Spain*, C-154/08.

[346] (ES) Tribunal Supremo, Sentencia, 29/05/2015.

Notwithstanding the recognition of state liability for judicial errors in Spain, no decision has yet been identified in the available databases that resulted in the establishment of liability of the state for a violation of EU law by Spanish courts. Moreover, even if fault is not a condition for liability, it results from the case-law of the Tribunal Supremo that the mistake has to be serious and flagrant in order to give rise to compensation. In this regard, Sarmiento even questions the compatibility of this criterion with the *Köbler* principle.[347]

d. Sweden

Under Swedish law, the acts of the two supreme courts (Högsta domstolen, the Supreme Court of Sweden and Regeringsrätten) are exempted from the general scheme of state liability.[348] Claims for compensation raised against an act of these organs are only admissible if the contested judgment has been previously reversed (according to the terms used in the Swedish law, 'withdrawn' or 'annulled'). Nevertheless, there exists another, informal way to request damages for erroneous judgments. This special procedure before the Justitiekanslern has even given rise to pecuniary compensation for violation of EU law in a final judgment.[349]

In all, even though the traditional avenue to receiving damages under Swedish law is overly restrictive as regards the *Köbler* requirements, there is no limitation on the possibility to receive damages before the Justitiekanslern.[350] In the light of the case-law, this procedure appears to provide sufficient protection of individual rights against the violation of EU law by Swedish supreme courts.

ii. Acknowledgement of the Köbler Principle Through National Case-Law

Research shows that 11 Member States where state liability for judicial acts is restricted have already accepted to hold, at least theoretically, the state liable for breaches of EU law by national supreme courts (Belgium, Bulgaria, Germany, France, Italy, Lithuania, the Netherlands, Austria, Portugal, Finland and the UK).[351] Moreover, recent requests for preliminary ruling submitted by certain

[347] Sarmiento 2014: 188–90.

[348] (SE) Skadeståndslag, 3 kap, 7 §. This restriction applies to the final judgments of the supreme courts, the Högsta domstolen and Regeringsrätten. See also Scherr 2008: 188–90; Scherr 2012: 578.

[349] (SE) Justitiekanslern, Beslut, 06/04/2009. For different aspects of the case, s see 2.II.A.iv.b(3).

[350] (SE) Lag om justitiekanslerns tillsyn; Förordning om handläggning av skadeståndsanspråk mot staten.

[351] (BE) Cour constitutionnelle, arrêt, 30/06/2014; (BG) Sofiyski gradski sad, Reshenie, 03/01/2014; Varhovenkasatsionensad,Opredelenie,08/05/2015;Apelativensad–Burgas,Reshenie,26/04/2016;(DE) BVerwG, Urteil, 09/06/2009; BGH, Beschluss, 28/10/2004; (FR) Conseil d'État, décision, 18/06/2008; Cour de Cassation, Première chambre civile, arrêt, 26/10/2011; (IT) Tribunale di Genova, ordinanza, 31/03/2009; (LT) Lietuvos vyriausiojo administracinio teismo, 24/04/2008, nutartis administracinėje byloje; (NL) Gerechtshof 's-Gravenhage, Uitspraak, 15/02/2011; Rechtbank' s-Gravenhage, Uitspraak, 05/03/2010; (AT) VfGH, Erkenntnis, 10/10/2003; VfGH, Erkenntnis, 13/10/2004;

Hungarian and Slovak courts may suggest that these courts are inclined to accept the theory of state liability as well.

It is noteworthy that almost every national court judging the above cases had to set aside domestic rules on liability for judicial activity to be able to establish liability of the state on the basis of the *Köbler* doctrine.[352] Therefore, in most of these Member States, the *Köbler* principle has been transposed into the national legal order through judicial practice.[353] This has been the case in Belgium (condition of prior reversal of the contested judgment), Bulgaria (exclusion of liability), Germany (liability for judicial errors only for criminal offences), France (no liability for final judgments), Lithuania (condition of prior declaration of unlawfulness of the final judgment), the Netherlands (exclusion of liability for judicial activity), Austria (exclusion of liability of supreme courts), Portugal (condition of prior reversal of the contested judgment), Finland (condition of prior reversal of the contested judgment or conviction or condemnation for damages of the judge), the UK (absolute immunity of courts); and, partially, in Hungary (exclusion of liability for the content of a final judgment) and Italy (exclusion of liability for judicial activity) as well.

a. Belgium

Traditionally, the Civil Code of Belgium is interpreted in a way that sets out the prior reversal of the contested decision as a condition for state liability.[354] However, the jurisprudence has changed this interpretation as a consequence of the *Köbler* principle.

In a judgment delivered in 2000, the Cour de Cassation (Court of Cassation, Belgium) concluded that all violation of a directly effective provision of an international agreement by the national administration in the exercise of its legislative function constitutes, in itself, a fault.[355] According to this judgment, there is no a need to submit the liability of the state to the *Francovich* conditions, or to examine whether a manifest breach occurred. This case-law was developed further, and its scope was extended to cover violations committed in the exercise of judicial functions.[356]

VfGH, Beschluss, 19/06/2013; (PL) Naczelny Sąd Administracyjny, Wyrok, 26/06/2014; Sąd Najwyższy, Wyrok, 08/12/2009; (PT) Tribunal da Relacao de Guimaraes, Acórdão, 23/04/2009; Tribunal Constitucional, Acórdão, 09/07/2015; (FI) Korkein oikeus, tuomio, 05/07/2013; (SE) Justitiekanslern, Beslut, 06/04/2009; (UK) Court of Appeal (England), Civil Division, judgment, 12/05/2010. However, the position of Spanish courts is not unanimous in this regard.

[352] See also Granger 2017: 106.

[353] See also Nollkaempler 2012: 161, 162, 167.

[354] (BE) Code civil, Art 1382–83; Code judiciaire, Arts 23, 1140–47. See also Houyet 2014: 128–37, 142; ACA Europe 2008, National report of Belgium, question 14, points 121–24; Cour de Cassation, arrêt, 19/12/1991, reported in ACA Europe 2008, National report of Belgium, question 14, points 119.

[355] (BE) Cour de Cassation, arrêt, 14/01/2000, reported in ACA Europe 2008, National report of Belgium, question 14, point 123.

[356] (BE) Cour de Cassation, arrêt, 05/06/2008; Cour de Cassation, arrêt, 25/03/2010.

In a judgment pronounced in 2010, the Cour de Cassation declared that the principle according to which the violation of a national or international rule having direct effect is sufficient to trigger liability of the state applies to errors made by the judiciary too.[357] This judgment, however, did not assess the violation in the case at hand on the substance, as the decision was based on the interpretation of the condition of the prior reversal of the contested judgment, a prerequisite for a judicial liability action in Belgian judicial practice. Even though this condition is maintained in this decision, it is interpreted in a way that is favourable to the claimant. In fact, the Cour de Cassation concluded that the deadline to introduce a request for reversal does not start to run before the judgment by the ECtHR or an international court confirming such a violation is delivered. Moreover, it stated that a finding of a violation of the ECHR by international jurisdiction is equivalent to such a reversal. The decision shows the willingness by the Belgian Cour de Cassation to sanction the violation of the international agreement, in a previous, final judgment. Even though the judgment concerns the violation of the ECHR and not EU law, it is a good illustration of the international-friendly approach adopted by the Cour de Cassation.[358] One may wonder whether the Belgian courts also allow the establishment of a fault without a previous judgment rendered by the ECtHR or the ECJ.[359] Theoretically, the requirement of prior reversal of the contested judgment excludes such a possibility. The decision described below sheds some light on this question.

Since the judgment of the Cour constitutionnelle (Belgian Constitutional Court) delivered in 2014, the condition of prior reversal does not apply in the case of manifest violation of the applicable law by the last-instance court if no legal means are available to obtain reversal of the final judgment.[360] Moreover, the Cour constitutionnelle extended the scope of this finding, based on violation of EU law, to cover the violation of national law, in order to harmonise the requirements of judicial liability under national, EU and international regimes. This judgment by the Cour constitutionnelle is in line with the approach followed by the Cour de cassation, both courts supporting the correct application of international and EU law, and the liability of the state for judicial breaches in case of violation of these rules.

Moreover, in its judgment pronounced in 2017, the Cour constitutionnelle developed further its case-law on judicial liability.[361] The Cour constitutionnelle confirmed, first of all, that liability of the state can be engaged by reason of a violation of law committed by a last-instance court, provided

[357] (BE) Cour de Cassation, arrêt, 25/03/2010.

[358] Compare with (FR) Cour de Cassation, arrêt, 18/11/2016.

[359] Compare with (ECJ) judgments in *Brasserie du pêcheur and Factortame*, para 51; in *Hedley Lomas*, para 32.

[360] (BE) Cour constitutionnelle, arrêt, 30/06/2014.

[361] (BE) Cour constitutionnelle, arrêt, 23/02/2017.

that this violation is manifest. Then it observed that the Cour de cassation may be involved in the examination of the liability claim brought against the same court. Therefore, it examined whether the procedure that allows the Cour de cassation to take such a decision is compatible with the right to a fair hearing before an independent and impartial court. In this regard, the Cour constitutionnelle found that the impartiality of the Cour de cassation is ensured by three means. First, this court is obliged, under certain circumstances, to submit a request for a preliminary ruling to the ECJ where the interpretation of EU law is concerned. Second, the judges who rendered the contested decision are not allowed to participate in the examination of the liability action. Third, the Cour de cassation can decide, itself, to refer the case to another chamber of the court if it finds that the objectivity of the court may be endangered. This judgment confirms, once again, that a judicial liability action on the grounds of violation of law by the supreme court is accepted in the Belgian legal order. As for the merits of this decision, it is also in line with international and EU standards.[362]

Belgium appears to be particularly dynamic and efficient in the implementation of the *Köbler* principle into the national legal order. Liability of the state for breaches of EU law by national courts, including last-instance courts, is accepted in Belgian judicial practice, and actions have already been lodged on these grounds.[363] This is due to national jurisprudence which has assured the harmonisation of national rules with ECJ case-law. Despite these developments, no successful liability claim has yet been reported.

b. Bulgaria

As already mentioned, before *Köbler*, the Bulgarian legal system did not recognise liability of the state for judicial acts in general.[364] In Bulgaria, the Constitution protects a general right to compensation of damages, but this right is limited to situations enumerated in the law on state liability.[365] Concerning damages caused by a judicial act, a liability claim can be lodged only in exceptional cases, such as in the event of unlawful detention or violation of human rights.[366] However, as far as a violation of EU law is concerned, this traditional stance appears to have changed in the wake of the *Köbler* judgment. Four judicial decisions are noteworthy in this regard; one has even resulted in the allocation of damages. In should also be mentioned that in Bulgarian liability cases, the defendant is the defaulting state body itself and not the state as an entity.

[362] (ECtHR) Judgment in *Micallef v Malta*, § 99.

[363] See also (BE) Cour d'appel de Bruxelles, décision, 24/04/2015; (ECJ) judgment in *Ullens de Schooten*.

[364] See also Fartunova 2014: 163–64; Scherr 2008. See also (BG) Konstitutsiya na Republika Balgariya, Art 7; Aministrativen protsesualen kodeks, Art 203.

[365] (BG) Zakon za otgovornosta na darzhavata i obshtinite za vredi, Art 1(1).

[366] See (BG) Zakon za otgovornosta na darzhavata i obshtinite za vredi, Art 2.

In its ruling dated 2014, the Sofiyski gradski sad handed down a judgment, for the first time, in a liability case for violation of EU law by the Varhoven administrativen sad.[367] Even though Sofiyski gradski sad rejected the liability claim as it had not found a violation either of the substantive EU law or of the referral duty, the possibility of claiming damages for violation of EU law by the national supreme court has been, nevertheless, accepted as a matter of principle.

Furthermore, in a judgment of 2015, the Varhoven kasatsionen sad interpreted the national procedural rules that may provide a legal basis for a *Köbler* liability claim.[368] In fact, Bulgarian case-law had been ambiguous on the questions as to whether the law on the liability of the state, or the general rules on tort liability, should be applied in such a case.[369] The Varhoven kasatsionen sad argued that a liability claim based on violation of EU law by a supreme court should be adjudicated on the basis of the law on the liability of the state. The general rules on tort liability, therefore, do not apply. To reach such a conclusion, the Varhoven kasatsionen sad relied on the obligation of cooperation and on the principle of loyalty of the Member States under EU law. The court has also invoked ECJ case-law on state liability and the judgments in *Francovich* and in *Köbler*. Even though this order is not obligatory to the national courts, it offered guidance regarding the rules which should be applied in a liability action. Moreover, it confirmed that Bulgarian courts acknowledge and apply the principle of *Köbler* liability.

Then, in a decision rendered in 2016, the Varhoven kasatsionen sad annulled a decision of the Sofiyski apelativen sad (Sofia Appeal Court) which dismissed a liability action lodged on the basis of the *Köbler* principle invoking the principle of res judicata. The supreme court sent the case back before the first-instance court and ordered it to render a new judgment on the merits of the claim.[370] The Varhoven kasatsionen sad examined the reasons behind the EU principle of state liability and the ECJ case-law on this matter. It explained that according to the ECJ case-law, the liability action does not call into question the authority of res judicata, and that liability may incur in the event of a judicial violation. It then pointed out that the ECJ decisions are obligatory to the Bulgarian courts which are thus obliged to apply the *Köbler* principle.

In addition, as already described above, in a judgment dated 2016, the Apelativen sad – Burgas confirmed the judgment of the Okrazhen sad Yambol, which established joint and several liability of the Varhoven kasatsionen sad, as well as national administrative and legislative bodies, for the damage sustained

[367] (BG) Sofiyski gradski sad, Reshenie, 03/01/2014. For different aspects of the case, see ss 2.II.A.iv.a(4) and 2.II.B.iv.c.

[368] (BG) Varhoven kasatsionen sad, Opredelenie, 08/05/2015, reported by Todorova in Reflets no 2/2015: 24.

[369] (BG) Zakon za otgovornosta na darzhavata i obshtinite za vredi, Art 2; Zakon za zadalzheniata i dogovorite, Arts 45 and 49; see also (ECJ) judgment in *Nikolay Kantarev v Balgarska narodna banka*.

[370] (BG) Varhoven kasatsionen sad, Opredelenie, 03/02/2016.

by the claimant company due to the application of a national act contrary to EU law. Consequently, the liability court ordered the defendants to pay compensation to the claimant.[371] The particularity of this case is that the court rebuked all three branches of government for having applied a national law contrary to EU law.

Overall, Bulgarian courts apply the *Köbler* doctrine, despite the absence of national provisions providing grounds for liability for erroneous judgments. Therefore, national courts refer directly to the ECJ jurisprudence and the obligation of cooperation, enshrined in Article 4(3) TEU, as the legal basis for liability claims. As these rules are not apt to provide answers to practical questions, such as the competence of the courts and legal fees, the application of the state liability principle, in general, gave rise to several practical questions. This has not prevented, however, an appeal court from establishing the liability of the Varhoven kasatsionen sad for violation of its obligation to apply EU law and to refer a preliminary question to the ECJ.

c. Germany

Under German national rules on tort liability, liability for judicial acts can be raised on condition that the responsibility of the judge under criminal law has been previously established.[372] It is necessary that the judge be convicted of violations constituting a 'crime in office' in the terms of the criminal code.[373] Nevertheless, this rule appears to be left unapplied concerning claims of EU law violations. In this regard, two judgments deserve to be mentioned.

The first judgment was rendered by the BGH in 2004. In this decision, the BGH stated that the refusal by the Oberlandesgericht Koblenz to request a preliminary ruling was justified. It therefore dismissed the claimant's action to receive compensation for the breach of their rights under EU law in the main proceedings.[374] However, in this judgment, the BGH expressly acknowledged the possibility to hold the state liable for miscarriages of justice based on the principles developed by the ECJ in *Köbler*.

The second judgment was delivered by the BVerwG in 2009.[375] Even though this decision did not concern a liability claim, the BVerwG analysed the conditions for judicial liability actions under German and EU law. In this case, the

[371] (BG) Apelativen sad – Burgas, Reshenie, 26/04/2016; Okrazhen sad Yambol, Reshenie, 04/11/2015. For different aspects of the case, see ss 2.II.A.iv.b(1) and 2.II.B.iv.d.

[372] (DE) Grundgesetz für die Bundesrepublik Deutschland, Art 34. See especially the rule of *Richterspruchprivileg* or *Spruchrichterprivileg* in BGB, § 839, Abs 2; as well as Scherr 2008: 227; Scherr 2012:579; Terhechte 2012: 318–21, 329.

[373] (DE) Strafgesetzbuch, §§ 331–58.

[374] (DE) BHG, Beschluss, 28/10/2004, reported by Beutler 2009: 788–89; Dittert 2014: 77–78; Lock 2012: 1683–84. For more detailed information, see s 2.II.A.iv.a(4).

[375] (DE) BVerwG, Urteil, 09/06/2009, reported in Jean Monnet Database. For different aspects of the case, see s 2.II.A.iv.a(1).

BVerwG pointed out that the scope of application of the *Köbler* liability, as triggered by a breach of EU law by the German judiciary, is wider than liability for breach of official duty in terms of German law.[376] This is because state liability under EU law applies to breaches committed by the legislature and by the judiciary, whereas state liability under German law does not. Nonetheless, the BVerwG concluded that, in any case, the conditions for establishing state liability for a breach of EU law by the judiciary were not met in this situation, as the breach of law committed by the defendant was not sufficiently serious to meet the requirement of a manifest breach.

As for two additional judgments rendered by higher regional courts, the Oberlandesgericht Karlsruhe in 2006[377] and the Oberlandesgericht Frankfurt in 2008,[378] contended that state liability for miscarriages of justice could only be incurred where the infringement was attributable to a court adjudicating at last instance. These decisions did not refer to *Köbler* and *Traghetti del Mediterraneo* but to articles in German literature instead, which essentially stated that at any rate there had been no manifest infringement.[379]

Overall, it appears to be possible to hold Germany liable for a breach of EU law by its courts based on the *Köbler* principle. According to an academic writer, the *Köbler* judgment put a clear limit on the scope of applicability of the German 'judge's privilege'. This liability privilege is thus inapplicable due to the supremacy of EU law in cases of manifest infringement of EU law by a last-instance court.[380] Nevertheless, only a few cases have been rendered on such claims so far, and, according to German literature, there has been no successful claim up to 2013.[381]

d. France

According to the traditional jurisprudence of the Conseil d'État, the liability of the state for judicial acts cannot incur in cases where the contested act is a final judgment on the merits of the case.[382] However, this rule has been amended in the judicial practice regarding EU law violations. In this regard, seven decisions by the French courts will be briefly presented. Due to the distinction between administrative and civil matters and the difference of the applicable rules, the

[376] (DE) Grundgesetz für die Bundesrepublik Deutschland, Art 34; Bürgerliches Gesetzbuch, § 839, Abs 2. See also Scherr 2012: 579.

[377] (DE) Oberlandesgericht Karlsruhe, Urteil, 09/03/2006, reported by Beutler 2009: 789; Dittert 2014: 77–78; Lock 2012: 1683–84.

[378] (DE) Oberlandesgericht Frankfurt, Urteil, 13/03/2008, reported by Beutler 2009: 789, and in Juris database, para 17.

[379] Beutler 2009: 789.

[380] Terhechte 2012: 325–28.

[381] (DE) BGH, Beschluss, 28/10/2004; Dittert 2014: 77–78.

[382] (FR) Code civil, Art 1240–42; Code de l'organisation judiciaire, Art L141-1; Conseil d'État, décision, 29/12/1978. See also Scherr 2012: 581.

case-law of the administrative courts, and then that of the civil courts, will be described.

In a decision delivered in 2008 in the *Gestas* case, the Conseil d'État acknowledged for the first time that in principle it is possible to obtain damages when the content of a judgment is in manifest breach of EU law.[383] In this judgment, the Conseil d'État pointed out that the state cannot, in principle, incur liability in cases where the alleged gross negligence resulted from the content of a judicial decision that was subsequently made final.[384] Nevertheless, it ruled that liability can exceptionally occur if the content of a final judicial decision is marred by a clear violation of EU law aiming to give rights to individuals. Since the facts of the case did not give rise to any intervention of EU law, no liability was recognised. Even so, the judgment is of utmost importance as the Conseil d'État departed from its long-standing *Darmont* case-law as far as damage caused by EU law violation is concerned. According to the *Darmont* principle, the content of a judicial decision cannot be challenged by way of a liability action once it has become final.

In another decision rendered in 2013,[385] the Conseil d'État assessed whether it had committed a manifest breach of EU law in one of its previous rulings where it had decided that the state had not been liable for maintaining national rules incompatible with EU law.[386] In the second round of the liability claim, the claimants invoked the liability of the state in the exercise of its judicial functions because of the violation of the state liability principle by the Conseil d'État and because of the excessive lengths of the first liability proceedings. Without any further reasoning, the Conseil d'État ordered the state to pay €1,500 as compensation for the moral prejudice suffered because of the excessive length of the proceedings. Nevertheless, it has not analysed the claimant's motion on the violation of the principle of state liability.

In another decision delivered in 2016, the Conseil d'État pronounced on the division of competence between the French courts when adjudicating on a liability action based on violation of EU law in a final administrative judgment.[387] On this occasion, it confirmed its *Gestas* case-law and completed it with the statement that administrative courts are competent to hear the actions for damages.[388]

[383] (FR) Conseil d'État, décision, 18/06/2008, English translation in *Common Market Law Reports* (2009) 783–87, reported by Brisard in Reflets no 2008/3: 19; Dubos et al 2014: 221; Valutyté 2011: 44–45; and in database JuriFast.

[384] (FR) Code de l'organisation judiciaire, Art L141-1; Conseil d'État, décision, 29/12/1978. See also Scherr 2012: 581.

[385] (FR) Conseil d'État, décision, 27/03/2013.

[386] (FR) Conseil d'État, décision, 30/12/2009.

[387] (FR) Conseil d'État, décision, 21/09/2016.

[388] (FR) Code de justice administrative, Arts L211-1 and L311-1. For a similar conclusion, see also (FR) Tribunal de conflict, decision, 31/03/2008; (FI) Korkein hallinto-oikeus, tuomio, 28/11/2012, available in the ECLI database.

Based on that decision of the Conseil d'État regarding the allocation of competences, the case was then sent back to the Cour d'appel administrative de Nantes, which rendered its decision in 2017.[389] Based on an analysis of the *Köbler* conditions, the appeal court dismissed the liability action. Regarding the alleged violation of the substantive EU rule, the Cour d'appel administrative de Nantes analysed the ECJ case-law and concluded that the contested national decision was not necessarily incompatible with the ECJ decision. The EU provision was ambiguous at least, which excluded any manifest violation. As for the alleged failure to submit a request for a preliminary ruling, the court of appeal pointed out that French courts had already referred a question to the ECJ on the same matter of law but had not received a precise answer. In all, the appeal court concluded that in the absence of manifest infringement of EU law, the liability of the state could not be established.

As for the case law of civil courts, in a decision delivered in 2010, the Cour d'appel de Paris dismissed a claim seeking compensation for an alleged breach of EU law by the Cour de cassation.[390] In this judgment, the Cour d'appel de Paris confirmed that an error in the interpretation of law can constitute a *faute lourde* pursuant to the French rules. In fact, this court held that all acts or series of acts which prevent the system of justice to fulfil its function and to operate properly constitute a *faute lourde*. Such qualification is, nonetheless, only possible if the violation is manifest according to the criteria established in *Köbler*. Regarding the alleged breach in the case at hand, the court concluded that the contested judgment by the Cour de cassation had not fulfilled these conditions.

Afterwards, in a series of judgments handed down in 2011, the Cour constitutionnelle dealt with the question of whether the failure to make a preliminary reference can be considered a denial of justice. In this regard, it examined whether a refusal to submit a request for preliminary ruling can constitute a manifest breach entailing liability of the state for defects in the functioning of the judicial system.[391] In the case at hand, the Cour constitutionnelle found that neither substantive EU law provisions nor the obligation to submit a request had been breached, and, consequently, dismissed the claims. Scholars nevertheless note the fact that the French Constitutional Court dismissed the claim using the criterion set by the ECJ in *Köbler*, that is by evaluating the manifest character of the breach, instead of assessing it against the French *faute lourde* condition.

It is noteworthy that in a judgment pronounced in 2015, the Cour d'appel de Paris referred to the *Köbler* conditions when assessing a liability claim based on a violation of the national rules and the ECHR.[392] The Cour d'appel de

[389] (FR) Cour administrative d'appel de Nantes, décision, 25/07/2017. For different aspects of the case, see s 2.II.A.iv.a(1).

[390] (FR) Cour d'appel de Paris, arrêt, 16/03/2010. For different aspects of the case, see s 2.II.A.iv.a(3).

[391] (FR) Cour de Cassation, arrêts, 26/10/2011, all reported by Dubos et al 2014: 223–24. For a more detailed presentation of the cases, see s 2.II.A.iv.a(2).

[392] (FR) Cour d'appel de Paris, arrêt, 22/09/2015.

Paris recalled that pursuant to the French rules, the state has to compensate for the damages suffered as a result of the defects in the functioning of the judicial system. Such liability is engaged where there has been a *faute lourde*, that is a gross negligence, or a denial of justice. However, the fact that a party in the proceedings might not share the opinion of the judges is not sufficient to prove a manifest breach of the applicable law in the terms of the *Köbler* judgment, which would be necessary to establish a *faute lourde* in the case. It is noteworthy that even though the claimant alleged a violation of the French rules and the ECHR, the Cour d'appel de Paris seems to have used the *Köbler* conditions in order to assess whether the conditions of state liability were met.

Finally, in a judgment delivered in 2015, the Cour d'appel de Paris[393] found a violation of EU law by an earlier judgment of the Cour de cassation. According to academics, this was the first decision stating clearly that the Cour de cassation had erred in law.[394] Nevertheless, the Cour de cassation reversed this decision, adopting a contestable argumentation regarding the conditions of the *Köbler* liability.[395]

In conclusion, both administrative and civil courts in France have acknowledged that the state may incur liability based on the criteria established by the ECJ. Therefore, the traditional French conditions of judicial liability are to be set aside in case of EU law violations. Despite this EU-friendly attitude, there has not yet been a successful – final – *Köbler* claim before the French courts. In fact, French courts hearing the liability claims appear to be unwilling to reassess the merits of the contested decisions. Even though they recognise, theoretically, that liability of the state can occur for erroneous judicial decisions, they seem to avoid the re-examination of the case on its merits.

e. Lithuania

Under Lithuanian law, the state is liable for damages caused by unlawful judicial acts.[396] According to the jurisprudence, liability can only be raised once the unlawfulness of the contested decision has been established.[397] The Vyriausiasis administracinis teismas (Supreme Administrative Court, Lithuania) has already

[393] (FR) Cour d'appel de Paris, arrêt, 06/05/2015. For a detailed description of this case, see ss 2.II.A.iv.a(3) and 2.II.A.iv.b(4).

[394] Guiot, F-V (2016) 'La Cour de cassation et la responsabilité de l'État du fait des décisions de justice: une nouvelle illustration des faiblesses de la subsidiarité juridictionnelle', Réseau Universitaire européen dédié à l'étude du droit de l'Espace de liberté, sécurité et justice (ELSJ) www.gdr-elsj.eu/2017/01/23/informations-generales/cour-de-cassation-responsabilite-de-letat-decisions-de-justice-nouvelle-illustration-faiblesses-de-subsidiarite-juridictionnelle, referring to the rapport established by Echappé in the case.

[395] (FR) Cour de Cassation, arrêt, 18/11/2016. For other aspects of this case, see s 2.II.A.iv.a(3).

[396] (LT) Lietuvos Respublikos Konstitucija, 30 straipsnis; Lietuvos Respublikos civilinis kodeksas, 6.272 straipsnis.

[397] (LT) Lietuvos Respublikos Konstitucinis Teismas, Nutarimas, 19/08/2006, reported by Valutytė 2014: 287.

rendered a judgment on a liability claim introduced on the ground of violation of EU law.

In a judgment delivered in 2008, the Vyriausiasis administracinis teismas acknowledged liability of the state for final decisions of administrative courts contrary to EU law.[398] Acting as a second-instance court on the liability claim, the Vyriausiasis administracinis teismas held that the state is liable for damages caused by unlawful administrative court judgments, and administrative courts are competent to evaluate the illegality of the contested final decisions. To reach its conclusion, the Vyriausiasis administracinis teismas referred to the Constitutional Act of Lithuania on the EU membership of the state, to the *Köbler* judgment and to the principle of national procedural autonomy of the Member States. However, as the main proceedings had been reopened in the meantime, the Vyriausiasis administracinis teismas dismissed the claim for damages in the case at hand.

It is noteworthy that in two other cases before Lithuanian courts, the Lietuvos apeliacinis teismas (Court of Appeal) and the Vilniaus apygardos teismas (Vilnius Regional Court) have also dealt with *Köbler* liability claims. Both courts concluded, however, that neither substantive EU provisions nor the referral duty had been violated, and the claims were therefore dismissed.[399]

Lithuania follows a pro-European approach by accepting the possibility of both damages and retrial on account of violation of EU law by final judgments.[400] Nonetheless, under the Lithuanian rules, damages claims can only be satisfied if the unlawfulness of the contested decision is established.[401] Furthermore, contrary to administrative matters, neither damages claim nor retrial has yet been – even theoretically – accepted on the ground of a breach of EU law in civil cases.[402] Finally, the liability of the state has not yet been established so far, neither in administrative nor in civil cases.

f. The Netherlands

In the Netherlands, liability for erroneous judicial acts is, as a rule, excluded by judicial practice, which insists on the importance of the unquestionable nature of final judgments.[403] However, the courts seem to disregard this principle for

[398] (LT) Lietuvos vyriausiojo administracinio teismo, 10/04/2008, reported by Valutytė 2014: 288–89.

[399] (LT) Lietuvos apeliacinis teismas, 23/06/2014; Vilniaus apygardos teismas, 21/01/2015.

[400] See also Jarukaitis, 2010: 233.

[401] (LT) Lietuvos Respublikos Konstitucija, 30 straipsnis; Lietuvos Respublikos civilinis kodeksas, 6.272 straipsnis; Lietuvos Respublikos Konstitucinis Teismas, Nutarimas, 19/08/2006. See also Valutytė 2014: 286–91.

[402] (LT) Lietuvos Respublikos civilinio proceso kodekso patvirtinimo, įsigaliojimo ir įgyvendinimo įstatymas. Civilinio proceso kodeksas, 279(4) straipsnis *Sprendimo įsiteisėjimas* (binding effect of judgments). See also Valutytė 2014: 285–87, 289–91.

[403] (NL) Hoge Raad, Uitspraak, 03/12/1971; Burgerlijk Wetboek, Art 6:162; Wetboek van Burgerlijke Rechtsvordering, Art 382.

liability claims introduced on the ground of EU law violations. It is noteworthy that in the Netherlands, state liability has been developed by analogy with the legislative provision on civil liability for unlawful acts, which does not require a sufficiently serious breach, but only an unlawful act to trigger liability.[404]

In its judgment delivered in 2011, the Gerechtshof 's-Gravenhage refused compensation, relying on national procedural rules preventing the allocation of damages.[405] In this case, the claimant invoked the violation by the court of its referral duty in the underlying proceedings. They also rebuked the court for not having considered the relevant ECJ case-law in the contested judgment. The Gerechtshof 's-Gravenhage found, however, that the claimant had already received damages following an administrative procedure. Therefore, as a civil court, it did not have jurisdiction to decide again on the damages claim.[406] In another case, the appeal court refused the damages claim as the claimant had not exhausted all remedies, an appeal on points of law being still available to them.[407]

In another judgment rendered in 2015, the Gerechtshof 's-Gravenhage applied the *Köbler* conditions to decide on a liability claim lodged against a judgment of the Hoge Raad der Nederlanden (Supreme Court of the Netherlands).[408] The Gerechtshof 's-Gravenhage rejected the claim, stating that the ruling of the Hoge Raad had not violated EU law, since the supreme court based its judgment on an extensive and defensible analysis of ECJ case-law on age discrimination. In addition, the claimants made their request for a preliminary reference only at an advanced stage of the proceedings, and failed to propose detailed questions.

In general, it is theoretically possible to invoke the liability of the state for breach of EU law by the Netherlands' courts.[409] In addition to the above judgments, a report from the House of Representatives[410] and the opinion of Wattel[411] also confirm this statement. However, in individual cases, either the principle of procedural autonomy or the restrictive conditions of the *Köbler* judgment

[404] Condon and van Leeuwen 2016: 262–63.

[405] (NL) Gerechtshof 's-Gravenhage, Uitspraak, reported by Marguery and van Harten 2014: 352.

[406] Marguery and van Harten 2014: 352–53.

[407] (NL) Rechtbank' s-Gravenhage, Uitspraak, 05/03/2010, reported by Marguery and van Harten 2014: 352.

[408] (NL) Gerechtshof 's-Gravenhage, Uitspraak, 03/06/2015, reported by Loth 2017: 49. For further information on this case, see s 2.II.A.iv.a(3).

[409] (NL) Burgerlijk Wetboek, Art 6:162.

[410] (NL) Tweede Kamer (House of Representatives), 12/08/2005, 2004–05, 29279, no 28, cited in ACA Europe 2008, National report of the Netherlands, question 8. The Netherlands Parliament has asked the Government to consider amending Art 8:88 of the General Administrative Law Act in order to create the possibility of reviewing the judgment of an administrative court, if it follows from judgments of the ECtHR or the ECJ that the national judgment is contrary to ECHR or EU law. The Cabinet held that there was no reason for such a provision, in view of the right to sue the state for errors made by the highest administrative courts.

[411] (NL) Hoge Raad, Uitspraak, 07/05/2004, especially with regard to the opinion of AG Wattel, reported by Marguery and van Harten 2014: 351.

have so far hindered the effective application of this remedy.[412] Researchers have concluded that 'there could still be areas in which the *Francovich* criteria could be applied, such as in cases of erroneous interpretation of EU law by national courts.'[413]

g. Austria

The Austrian legal system recognises liability for misconduct by judicial organs.[414] However, the state cannot be held liable for acts committed by the highest courts: the VfGH, the VwGH and the Oberster Gerichtshof (OGH, Austrian Supreme Court).[415] Nevertheless, the VfGH has declared itself competent to hear actions on EU law violations, relying on a special provision of the Bundes-Verfassungsgesetz (B-VG, Federal Constitutional Law).[416] This provision provides a legal foundation for claims against the state in cases where neither civil nor administrative courts are competent to adjudicate on the matter.[417] Since 2003, when the VfGH delivered its first judgment on the issue, it has decided on a number of *Köbler* actions.

In the first case from 2003, the VfGH applied the *Köbler* conditions only two weeks after the seminal ECJ decision.[418] By this decision, the VfGH declared itself competent for the first time to hear tort actions for damage caused by a judicial decision of one of the three hightest courts allegedly in breach of EU law. The VfGH then applied the conditions set forth by the ECJ in *Köbler* to test whether the VwGH had committed a manifest breach of EU law. In the end, it ruled out a violation of EU law by the VwGH in the specific case.

In another judgment, delivered in 2004, the VfGH restated that it was not competent to review the decision of the VwGH, but could, nevertheless, examine the gravity of the violation.[419] It recalled the stricter conditions for state liability resulting from acts committed by a national judiciary, and, applying them to the case at hand, rejected the claim. The VfGH emphasised that a simple non-referral is not per se a manifest breach.[420] It argued that even though

[412] ACA Europe 2008, National report of the Netherlands, questions 14 and 13; Marguery and van Harten 2014: 354–55.

[413] Condon and van Leeuwen 2016: 264.

[414] (AT) Bundesverfassungsgesetz, Art 23. See also Potacs and Mayer 2013: 53.

[415] (AT) Amtshaftungsgesetz, § 2, Abs 3. See also Pelzl 2014: 112; Scherr 2012: 578.

[416] See also (AT) VfGH, Erkenntnis, 14/06/2004, reported by Pelzl 2014: 113; VfGH, Erkenntnis, 12/06/2008, reported by Pelzl 2014: 113; VfGH, Erkenntnis, 13/10/2004, reported by Beutler 2009: 790; Granger 2007: 167–68; Pelzl 2014: 113; and Pelzl in Reflets no 2/2005: 9.

[417] (AT) Bundesverfassungsgesetz, Art 137. See also Potacs and Mayer 2013: 54.

[418] (AT) VfGH, Erkenntnis, 10/10/2003, English summary in *European Current Law* 2 (2004) 92, and in *Jus-Extra* 226 (2003) 7, reported by Beutler 2009: 789; Granger 2007: 168; Pelzl 2014: 102; Scherr 2008.

[419] (AT) VfGH, Erkenntnis, 13/10/2004. For different aspects of the case, see s 2.II.A.iv.a(2).

[420] See also (AT) VfGH, Erkenntnis, 14/06/2004; VfGH, Erkenntnis, 12/06/2008; VfGH, Erkenntnis, 29/09/2008, reported by Pelzl 2014: 113; in the conference on *Liability of Judges in European and National Laws*, 14–15 December 2012, EUI.

the question at issue had not been specifically decided upon by the ECJ, the outcome could be easily deduced from its case-law; moreover, the VwGH had provided a very detailed statement of reasons on the issue.[421]

The approach followed by the VfGH, that is to focus on the failure to submit a request for preliminary ruling when evaluating the breach of the EU law, was reiterated in a decision in 2013.[422] Subsequently, other *Köbler* claims have also been rejected on the ground of absence of manifest infringement of the EU law in other proceedings before the VfGH.[423]

To summarise, state liability for breach of EU law by Austrian supreme courts is now accepted on theoretical grounds. As the legislator has not adopted any measures to implement the *Köbler* liability into national law, this development is due to the VfGH's jurisprudence. However, the practical use of this principle is severely restricted, as the VfGH generally considers the sole violation of the referral duty when deciding on the claim, without taking into account the potential breach of the substantive EU right. Moreover, it holds that breach of the referral duty is not in itself sufficient to trigger liability.[424]

h. Portugal

In Portugal, holding the state liable for legislative or judicial acts has been possible only after the entry into force of the new law on state liability in 2008.[425] Before that date, there had not been any legal basis for liability claims for erroneous acts by the judicature.[426] The new law now explicitly deals with questions of state liability for judicial breaches.[427] However, even after amendments to this act,[428] uncertainty remained whether it actually provides a legal basis to hold the state liable for breaches of EU law by Portuguese courts.[429] In fact, this new act establishes *expressis verbis* liability of the state for violation of its obligations under EU law; however, the two relevant provisions concern only administrative organs and the legislation.[430] Therefore, it was not obvious for

[421] See also Granger 2007: 167.

[422] (AT) VfGH, Beschluss, 19/06/2013, reported by Frodl in Reflets no 3/2013: 17. For different aspects of the case, see s 2.II.A.iv.a(2).

[423] (AT) VfGH, Erkenntnis, 12/12/2003, reported by Beutler 2009: 789; VfGH, Erkenntnis, 22/09/2009; VfGH, Beschluss, 02/05/2011; VfGH, Beschluss, 23/03/2015; VfGH, Beschluss, 21/11/2013; VfGH, Beschluss, 11/06/2015; VfGH, Beschluss, 11/05/2015; VfGH, Beschluss, 19/11/2015.

[424] According to Potacs and Mayer (2013: 57), the VfGH did not grant any damages against the OGH or VwGH for a 'sufficiently serious' breach of EU law up until they concluded their research in 2013.

[425] (PT) Lei no 67/2007, de 31 de Dezembro, Arts 12–14°.

[426] (PT) Constituição da República Portuguesa, Art 22°. See also Da Cunha Rodríguez and de Jesus Patricio 2014: 395–96; Scherr 2008: 306.

[427] (PT) Lei no 67/2007, de 31 de Dezembro, Arts 12–14°; Scherr 2012: 581.

[428] (PT) Lei no 31/2008, de 17 de Julho.

[429] See Da Cunha Rodríguez and de Jesus Patricio 2014: 398.

[430] (PT) Lei no 67/2007, de 31 de Dezembro, Arts 7° N °2 and 15° N °1. See also Da Cunha Rodríguez and de Jesus Patricio 2014: 398.

a long time, either in the case-law or legal writing, whether these modifications indeed provide a legal basis for triggering liability of the state for breach of EU law by the courts.[431] Nowadays, liability for judicial acts seems to be accepted as a principle.

Nevertheless, the practical importance of this remedy is severely restricted by the provision which requires the prior reversal of the contested judgment so that liability can be invoked.[432] This provision is highly criticised by the doctrine and has been found incompatible with the *Köbler* principle by the ECJ.[433] Moreover, in a recent judgment, the Tribunal Constitucional appears to approve the setting aside of this requirement as far as the violation of law concerns EU law.[434] From the case-law of the Portuguese courts, three judgments will be mentioned.

In the first case, the Supremo Tribunal de Justiça, sitting as an appeal court, delivered a judgment in 2009 by which it dismissed a liability claim against Portugal for breach of the EU law by the Supremo Tribunal de Justiça.[435] In this case, the Supremo Tribunal de Justiça held that there was no rule in Portuguese law under which the liability of the state for judicial breaches could be established, since the national law had not yet been in force at the time of the facts.[436]

In the second case, in a 2015 judgment the Tribunal Constitucional examined the constitutionality of the criteria requiring the prior reversal of the contested judgment as a condition for liability.[437] First, the Tribunal Constitucional stated that the legislator cannot arbitrarily and unreasonably restrict the right to compensation. The court then pointed to the conflict between judicial liability and the principles of legal certainty and res judicata. At this point, the Tribunal Constitucional made reference to the ECJ's case-law and to arguments in the judgments in *Köbler* and *Traghetti del Mediterraneo*. According to the Tribunal Constitucional, recognising judicial liability for breaches of EU law is justified because the parties do not have direct access to the ECJ, and they cannot enforce a preliminary reference being made before the ECJ. Therefore, Member State liability is important to provide effective judicial protection where violation of EU has occurred. It hence appears that, by this judgment, the Tribunal

[431] See also Da Cunha Rodríguez and de Jesus Patricio 2014: 399.

[432] (PT) Lei no 67/2007, de 31 de Dezembro, Artigo 13° N °2; Supremo Tribunal de Justiça, Acórdão 24/02/2015, reported by Cardoso in Reflets no 2/2015: 47–48. See also Da Cunha Rodríguez and de Jesus Patricio 2014: 399.

[433] (ECJ) Judgment in *Ferreira da Silva e Brito e.a.*

[434] (PT) Tribunal Constitucional, Acórdão, 09/07/2015, reported by Cardoso in Reflets no 3/2015: 44–45. See also Silveira and Fernandes 2016: 656–58.

[435] (PT) Supremo Tribunal de Justiça, Acórdão, 03/12/2009, available at Network of the presidents of the supreme judicial courts of the European Union, reported by Da Cunha Rodríguez and de Jesus Patricio 2014: 400–04. For different aspects of the case, see s 2.II.A.ii.e(2) and 2.II.A.iv.b(4).

[436] This case was brought before the ECtHR, which, however, established a violation of Art 6(1) ECHR due to the divergence in the domestic case-law as to the admissibility of state liability claims, leading to a violation of the principle of legal certainty. For different aspects of the case, see s 2.II.A.iv.b(4). See also (ECtHR) judgment in *Ferreira Santos Pardal v Portugal*.

[437] (PT) Tribunal Constitucional, Acórdão, 09/07/2015. See also Silveira and Fernandes 2016: 656.

Constitucional claimed that this restrictive condition should be set aside for claims arising from violation of EU law by Portuguese courts.

In the third case, a Portuguese court asked the ECJ whether national rules that require the reversal of the contested judicial decision as a precondition for a liability claim are compatible with the *Köbler* principle.[438] Examining this provision, the ECJ concluded in its judgment rendered in *Ferreira da Silva e Brito e.a.* that a rule of that kind may indeed make it excessively difficult to obtain reparation.[439] As such, the ECJ concluded that EU law precludes a provision of national law which, as with the Portuguese legislation, requires, as a condition for a declaration of state liability, the prior reversal of the decision that caused the loss or damage when such setting aside is, in practice, impossible.[440]

In conclusion, the main legislative barrier to the effective application of the *Köbler* principle is the condition of the prior reversal of the contested judgment.[441] Even though the doctrine has always considered this criterion to be contrary to the ECJ jurisprudence, the Supremo Tribunal de Justiça confirmed in 2015 that the prior reversal of the contested judgment is a precondition for state liability. However, the Tribunal Constitucional appears to have accepted that this condition does not apply in cases of EU law violations.

i. Finland

State liability for judicial errors is restricted under Finish law as well. In particular, liability of the state can only be invoked if either the contested decision has been reversed or the person committing the error has been found guilty of misconduct.[442] However, these rules have already been set aside in the case-law in order to harmonise Finnish rules with the EU requirements.

It is worth mentioning a judgment by the administrative court Korkein hallinto-oikeus which dealt with the implementation of the state liability principle in Finland.[443] In this judgment delivered in 2012, the Korkein hallinto-oikeus argued that the principle of state liability was to be implemented in the national legal order. It also stressed that, nevertheless, neither the ECJ nor specific national provisions determined whether a state liability claim should be assessed by a civil or an administrative court. Therefore, in order to ensure that the claimant can receive judicial relief without undue delay, the court declared that it was

[438] (ECJ) Judgment in *Ferreira da Silva e Brito e.a.*, see s 1.III.C.

[439] (ECJ) Judgment in *Ferreira da Silva e Brito e.a.*, paras 51–52.

[440] (ECJ) Judgment in *Ferreira da Silva e Brito e.a.*, para 60. The national decision rendered following the preliminary ruling of the ECJ is not available as yet.

[441] (PT) Lei no 67/2007, de 31 de Dezembro, Artigo 13° N °2.

[442] (FI) Vahingonkorvauslaki, 3 luku, 5§. As for the Constitutional basis of liability, see Suomen perustuslaki, 118§. See also Condon and van Leewen 2016: 236.

[443] (FI) Korkein hallinto-oikeus, tuomio, 28/11/2012, reported by Pedersen in Reflets no 2013/3: 22, available in the ECLI database.

appropriate to allow the damages claim be introduced before the administrative court as well.[444]

In addition, the civil court Korkein oikeus has even awarded damages in favour of the claimant based on *Köbler* liability.[445] As already described above, this judgment, rendered in 2013, has been one of the five decisions that resulted in the award of damages on the basis of the *Köbler* liability so far.

Moreover, the Korkein oikeus arrived at a similar conclusion in another case in 2016, which originated from a similar factual and legal background as the the judgment rendered in 2013.[446] In these proceedings, the first- and the second-instance courts concluded that the violation of EU law was obvious and ordered the state to pay compensation to the claimant.[447] An appeal against the second-instance court's judgment was only allowed regarding the question of the limitation period to bring proceedings. Therefore, the Korkein oikeus appreciated only whether the limitation period to bring an action for damages had already expired when the claimant lodged the proceedings and whether the claimant should have known that the contested decision was contrary to EU law. In this regard, the Korkein oikeus concluded that despite the contested decision having been delivered in 2004, the limitation period for bringing proceedings had only started in 2009, when the ECJ judgment rendered its decision in *Commission v Finland*. Before that date, the claimant could not have known that the contested decision was erroneous.

The above cases show that both Finnish supreme courts endorse the effective protection of EU law and of the rights to which individuals are entitled under EU law. The Korkein oikeus has even set aside domestic provisions contradicting the *Köbler* principle in order to align with the ECJ's requirements. Consequently, the liability regime for breaches of EU law appears to be harmonised with the ECJ case-law; moreover, it is effectively applied. In addition to the above, a research paper reports that the Finnish Ministry of Justice has also considered amending the national state liability system to align the legislative provisions with the EU requirements.[448]

j. United Kingdom

Traditionally, by law, courts had enjoyed absolute immunity from liability in the UK.[449]

[444] See also (FR) Conseil d'État, décision, 21/09/2016.
[445] (FI) Korkein oikeus, tuomio, 05/07/2013. See ss 2.II.A.iv.b(1) and 2.II.B.iv.d.
[446] (FI) Korkein oikeus, tuomio, 05/03/2016.
[447] (FI) Helsingin käräjäoikeus, tuomio, 30/09/2013; Helsingin hovioikeus, tuomio, 28/11/2014.
[448] Condon and van Leewen 2016: 236.
[449] (UK) Crown Proceedings Act 1947, s 2(5).

However, by its judgment of 2010, the Court of Appeal ruled on a case dealing with the UK courts' liability for a breach of EU law.[450] In its decision, the Court of Appeal acknowledged that a violation of EU law had been committed, as both the directive and the Treaty provision on the obligation to ask for a preliminary ruling had been breached in the main proceedings. The Court of Appeal then used the criteria established in the *Köbler* judgment to determine the gravity of the breach and concluded that both the erroneous interpretation of the substantive rule and the failure to make a preliminary reference were excusable errors. This judgment shows nevertheless that the Court of Appeal has accepted *Köbler* liability. To be able to arrive at this conclusion, it had to set aside national rules under which judicial activity is exempt from liability.[451] In fact, the UK courts seem to have created a new, specific head of tort, the 'Euro-tort', to which specific rules apply.[452] However, the application of the ECJ criterion regarding the gravity of the breach limits the practical application of the liability.

iii. Acknowledgement of the Köbler *Principle Through Legislation*

There are two Member States where *Köbler* liability was introduced via legislative changes to the national liability regime. In Italy, amendments allow the possibility to make the state liable for judicial breaches on wider grounds than previously foreseen and provide an explicit ground for liability in the event of manifest infringement of EU law.[453] In Poland, holding the supreme courts liable is possible on broader grounds in case of EU law infringements than national breaches.[454]

a. Italy

Due to the importance of res judicata and the unquestionable nature of final judicial decisions, liability for erroneous final judgments had traditionally been strictly restricted in Italy, up until 2015.[455] Liability for judicial acts was limited solely to cases of intentional fault and serious misconduct on the part of the court. Moreover, in the exercise of judicial functions, the interpretation of the provisions of law or the assessment of facts and evidence could not give

[450] (UK) Court of Appeal (England), judgment, 12/05/2010. For different aspects of the case, see s 2.II.A.iv.a(1).

[451] (UK) Crown Proceedings Act 1947, s 2(5).

[452] Clément-Wiltz 2014: 454–55.

[453] (IT) Risarcimento dei danni cagionati nell'esercizio delle funzioni giudiziarie e responsabilità civile dei magistrati, Legge, no 117, Art 2.

[454] See also (PT) Lei no 67/2007, de 31 de Dezembro, Arts 13° N °2, and (PT) Tribunal Constitucional, Acórdão, 09/07/2015; Supremo Tribunal de Justiça, Acórdão, 24/02/2015.

[455] (IT) Legge, 13/04/1988, Testo in vigore dal: 19/3/2015, Art 2. See also Costituzione della Repubblica italiana, Art 24; Regio Decreto 16/03/1942, Codice Civile; Art 2043; Gencarelli 2014: 270–71.

rise to liability.[456] As is well known, the ECJ found this so-called 'safeguarding clause'[457] contrary to EU law in its judgments in *Traghetti del Mediterraneo* and *Commission v Italy*.[458]

Following the ECJ judgment in *Traghetti del Mediterraneo*, the Tribunal di Genova, in a 2009 decision, declared the state liable for a breach of Article 267(3) TFEU by the national supreme court,[459] by setting aside the national limitations to the establishment of judicial liability. Even if the national court chose to give priority to the EU rules against the national provisions in this case, Gencarelli warned in 2014 that this might not be the general attitude of the Italian courts. He explained that since the court had given a *contra legem* interpretation to the national rules, this solution might not be followed on every occasion.[460]

Nonetheless, the *contra legem* application of national rules is no longer an issue, following the legislative modifications adopted in 2015,[461] which aimed to align national rules with the ECJ's requirements in this matter of law. Specifically, the law maintains the main rule according to which the exercise of judicial functions may not trigger, in principle, the judge's civil liability. Under the new rules, gross negligence committed by a judge may, however, give rise to liability when there is a manifest violation of national law or EU law in the form of misrepresentation of fact or evidence.[462] In addition, the new provisions specify the factors to be taken into consideration when assessing the gravity of the breach. In this regard, the elements elaborated by the ECJ in the *Köbler* judgment are borrowed, essentially. Moreover, as a different treatment of violations of EU and domestic law would have been unconstitutional, the new model of liability concerns both EU law and domestic law.[463]

b. Poland

In Poland, the general regime of state liability applies to judicial errors.[464] As such, the Polish legal system acknowledges state liability for damages caused by unlawful final judgments.[465] This is the result of a legislative reform which,

[456] Legge, 13/04/1988, Art 2.

[457] The term is borrowed from Cilento 2017: 29.

[458] (ECJ) Judgment in *Commission v Italy*, C-379/10.

[459] (IT) Tribunale di Genova, ordinanza, 31/03/2009 and (IT) Legge, 13/04/1988, Art 2. See also Scherr 2012: 581. For a more detailed presentation and for different aspects of the case, ss see 1.III.B, 2.II.A.iv.b(2) and 3.III.A.iii.

[460] Gencarelli 2014: 278–80.

[461] (IT) Legge, 13/04/1988, Art 2. This provision was modified in 2015 by Legge, 27/02/2015, Art 2, and the amendments entered into force the 19 March 2015. In a recent judgment, the Italian Constitutional Court ruled that the new provisions are not unconstitutional and do not endanger the independence of judges. See (IT) Corte Costituzionale, sentenza, 03/04/2017; Cilento 2017: 34.

[462] See also (IT) Corte di Cassazione, Prima sezione civile, sentenza, 25/05/2015, no 10749, reported by Cilento 2017: 27.

[463] See Cilento 2017: 27.

[464] (PL) Trybunał Konstytucyjny, 04/12/2001, pts IV, 3 and 5, reported by Mikłaszewicz 2014: 383.

[465] (PL) Konstytucja Rzeczypospolitej Polskiej, Art 77, § 1; Kodeks cywilny, Art 417[1], § 2. See Mikłaszewicz 2014: 383.

at the time of the accession of Poland to the EU, introduced state liability into the national legal order by amending the Civil Code and the Code of Civil Procedure.[466] This new regime was inspired by EU law. However, according to the Polish Civil Code, if the alleged damage has been inflicted by a final court ruling, it is necessary that the violation be established in appropriate proceedings.[467] The declaration of unlawfulness as a sui generis procedure is one possible way to establish such a violation of law.[468] As regards the final judgments delivered by the Naczelny Sąd Administracyjny, such a declaration of unlawfulness is only possible on the ground of flagrant breach of EU law.[469] In civil matters, contrary to the rules in administrative law, the breach of both Polish and EU law can serve as a legal basis for an action to declare a final judgment unlawful.[470] Moreover, as for judgments delivered by the Sąd Najwyższy (Supreme Court, Poland), their unlawfulness is examined directly in the liability action, without the need to be established in prior, separate proceedings.[471]

Hence, the declaration of unlawfulness of a final judgment is a procedural element of an action for damages for breach of law by Polish courts.[472] As a consequence, this remedy does not result directly in the allocation of damages, or in the annulment or revocation of the contested judgment. Instead, it helps to establish the unlawful nature of the final judgment, which is a precondition for invoking state liability for breach of law by judicial organs. As regards the strong connection between the action for liability and this special remedy, the relevant case-law on this latter procedure is summarily presented in this section.

As for administrative matters, in a judgment delivered in 2014, the Naczelny Sąd Administracyjny held that the refusal by the same court to make a preliminary reference in the previous proceedings had not breached any EU rule, as the interpretation of the EU norm was not ambiguous.[473] In particular, the Naczelny Sąd Administracyjny argued that there had not been any violation of EU law.

In another judgment, also from 2014, the Naczelny Sąd Administracyjny held that a final judgment can be declared unlawful only if its unlawfulness results

[466] (PL) Ustawa o zmianie ustawy – Kodeks cywilny oraz niektórych innych ustaw, reported by Siekierzynska and Mikłaszewicz in Reflets no 2/2005: 22. This system of liability was completed with the (PL) Ustawa o skardze na naruszenie prawa strony do rozpoznania sprawy w postępowaniu sądowym bez nieuzasadnionej zwłoki.

[467] However, if the law provides otherwise, such prior establishment of unlawfulness is not necessary. See (PL) Kodeks cywilny, Art 417^{1}, § 2; Kodeks postępowania cywilnego, Art 424^{1b}; Mikłaszewicz 2014: 379. See also Condon and van Leeuwen 2016: 265–68; Półtorak 2015: 223–41; Półtorak 2012.

[468] (PL) Prawo o postępowaniu przed sądami administracyjnymi, Art 285a; Kodeks postępowania cywilnego, Art 424^{1}.

[469] (PL) Prawo o postępowaniu przed sądami administracyjnymi, Art 285a. See Półtorak 2015: 238–39.

[470] (PL) Kodeks postępowania cywilnego, Art 424. See also Mikłaszewicz 2014: 379–80.

[471] (PL) Kodeks postępowania cywilnego, Art 424^{1a}, § 1.

[472] (PL) Prawo o postępowaniu przed sądami administracyjnymi, Art 285a; Kodeks postępowania cywilnego, Art 424.

[473] (PL) Naczelny Sąd Administracyjny, Wyrok, 11/06/2014. For various aspects of the case, see s 2.II.A.iv.a(4). See also Mikłaszewicz 2014: 382.

from a gross violation of EU law.[474] The liability claim at hand was dismissed on two main grounds. In the first place, the Naczelny Sąd Administracyjny emphasised that gross violation means that the breach is obvious and indisputable, since it clearly departs from a given rule, and therefore can be described as extraordinary. It alluded directly to the ECJ judgments in *Köbler* and *Traghetti del Mediterraneo*, and then concluded that the supreme court which had delivered the contested final judgment had not committed a gross violation of EU law. In the second place, the court emphasised that an action to declare a final judgment unlawful cannot substitute, supplement or be filed before an appeal on points of law. Therefore, as the claimant had not invoked the violation of the EU provision in the proceedings before the supreme court in the appeal procedure, it was not possible to claim a violation of EU law in an action to declare unlawful this final and legally binding judgment.

Several other judgments have also been rendered on the basis of the same provision in the Polish administrative procedural code.[475] In those cases, a few points regarding the application of this special remedy have been explained in detail. For example, in one case, the Naczelny Sąd Administracyjny dismissed the claim, as it found that the interpretation of the EU provision in the contested final decision had been correct.[476] It follows from another decision that, theoretically, both non-application and incorrect application of the substantive EU norm may give rise to the declaration of unlawfulness.[477] In a series of judgments, the Naczelny Sąd Administracyjny reiterated, however, that the interpretation and application of Polish procedural rules come under the scope of national procedural autonomy, and therefore dismissed the claims.[478] This case-law appears to suggest that the breach of the referral duty cannot serve as a ground for declaring a judgment unlawful, even if the refusal is arbitrary or provided without a statement of reasons.[479]

It is noteworthy that in a judgment rendered in 2012, the Trybunał Konstytucyjny stated that the rule allowing state liability for a court's infringement of law only in cases of a manifest breach does not violate the Polish Constitution.[480] This decision was based on an analysis of Polish constitutional law, but the Trybunał Konstytucyjny invoked the ECJ judgments about the manifest breach as the condition of the liability for courts' decisions.[481]

[474] (PL) Naczelny Sąd Administracyjny, Wyrok, 26/06/2014, reported in database JuriFast. For different aspects of the case, see s 2.II.A.ii.a(2).

[475] (PL) Prawo o postępowaniu przed sądami administracyjnymi, Art 285a; Naczelny Sąd Administracyjny, Wyrok, 28/02/2013.

[476] (PL) Naczelny Sąd Administracyjny, Wyrok, 26/08/2011, reported by Mikłaszewicz 2014: 381.

[477] (PL) Naczelny Sąd Administracyjny, Wyrok, 19/12/2013, reported by Półtorak 2015: 239.

[478] (PL) Naczelny Sąd Administracyjny, Postanowienie, 21/12/2010, reported by Mikłaszewicz 2014: 382.

[479] (PL) Naczelny Sąd Administracyjny, Wyrok, 11/06/2014. See also Mikłaszewicz 2014: 382.

[480] (PL) Trybunał Konstytucyjny, 27/09/2012, reported by Półtorak 2015: 239.

[481] See also Condon and van Leeuwen 2016: 268; Półtorak 2015: 239.

Finally, even though specific statutory provisions govern this remedy in civil matters, the gravity of the breach is evaluated according to the same standard as in administrative cases.[482] Consequently, the civil procedural rules also reflect the *Köbler* conditions. Applying these rules in a judgment handed down in 2009, the Sąd Najwyższy declared the contested final judgment unlawful. The Sąd Najwyższy arrived at this conclusion as the inconsistency of the final judgment with EU law became clear following the ECJ judgment on the same matter of law.[483] Moreover, a flagrant violation of referral duty appears in itself to suffice to declare a final civil judgment unlawful.[484]

Overall, under Polish procedural rules, final judgments contrary to EU law can only be declared unlawful if a clear, obvious and gross contravention of law is established. That leads to a result where, even though numerous final judgments have been subject to this special procedure, they have not been found unlawful in the end. In fact, Polish law seems to apply a similar condition regarding the gravity of the breach to the one that the ECJ has established as a condition of liability for judicial breaches. There is also a time limit to lodge this remedy under Polish law, which is two years after the moment the contested judgment acquired res judicata.[485] As such, there is a legal possibility to establish the liability of the state for breach of EU law by the Polish supreme courts.[486] However, this possibility is restricted due to the strict conditions attached to a previous declaration of unlawfulness of the contested final decision.[487]

iv. Member States Refusing the Application of the Köbler *Principle*

Certain Member States expressively refuse to adapt their liability regime to the requirements of the *Köbler* and *Traghetti del Mediterraneo* case-law. Such reticence characterises especially the case-law of the Hungarian Kúria, which has repeatedly held that it cannot reassess in a liability claim a final legal judgment that has already gained res judicata.[488] Nevertheless, it remains to be seen whether this court will amend its case law as a result of the changing judicial practice of the regional courts of appeal.[489] A confrontation with the *Köbler* doctrine is expressed in the recent case-law of the Czech Nejvyšší soud which, relying on national legal arrangements, declined to apply the EU doctrine on

[482] (PL) Kodeks postępowania cywilnego, Art 424. See also Mikłaszewicz 2014: 379–80.
[483] (PL) Sąd Najwyższy, Wyrok, 08/12/2009, reported by Mikłaszewicz 2014: 380–81.
[484] (PL) Sąd Najwyższy, Wyrok, 12/10/2006, reported by Mikłaszewicz 2014: 381.
[485] (PL) Kodeks cywilny, Art 417^1, § 2; Prawo o postępowaniu przed sądami administracyjnymi, Art 285a; Kodeks postępowania cywilnego, Art 424.
[486] (PL) Kodeks cywilny, Art 417^1, § 2; Sąd Najwyższy, Uchwała, 19/05/2009, reported by Mikłaszewicz 2014: 383.
[487] See also Mikłaszewicz 2014: 383–84.
[488] (HU) Kúria, ítélet, 11/12/2013; Kúria, ítélet, 28/02/2014. See also Varga 2014a, 2015a.
[489] As for such changing practice see (HU) Fővárosi Ítélőtábla, ítélet, 30/05/2017; Győri Ítélőtábla, ítélet, 29/06/2017.

state liability for judicial acts.[490] Similarly, the Irish High Court has recently insisted on the unquestionable nature of already-adjudicated cases, thereby hindering the efficient application of the *Köbler* doctrine.[491]

a. Czech Republic

Under Czech tort law, a liability claim against the state can only be introduced once the contested decision has been reversed.[492]

In a judgment issued in 2012, the Nejvyšší soud clarified the relationship between the national system for public liability and the system for state liability regarding harm caused to individuals by a breach of EU law.[493] This judgment was delivered on a liability claim against the state on account of a breach of EU law by an administrative authority; therefore, it did not concern a judicial error. Nevertheless, the Nejvyšší soud concluded that those provisions of national law which are contrary to the conditions of the state liability under EU law must be set aside. Consequently, in the terms of this judgment, a claim for damages suffered from a breach of EU law should be decided directly upon the threefold criteria established by the ECJ.

Afterwards, by its order delivered in 2015, the Nejvyšší soud rejected, in a *Köbler* liability action, an appeal on purely procedural grounds.[494] In this decision, the Nejvyšší soud did not assess the merits of the case as it found that the appeal had not fulfilled the procedural preconditions of admissibility. In particular, the claimant had not indicated whether, and if so, how, the contested judgment had departed from the case-law of the Nejvyšší soud or if it had decided on a new question of law. Therefore, the appeal introduced in a liability action was rejected based on purely national rules.

Later, in a judgment issued in 2016, the Nejvyšší soud decided on a liability claim based on an alleged breach of EU law by the Ústavní soud (Czech Constitutional Court).[495] The claimant argued that the Constitutional Court had committed maladministration when it concluded that it was not necessary to refer a question to the ECJ in the underlying case.[496] Adjudicating at last instance on the liability claim, the Nejvyšší soud pointed out that the decision of the Ústavní soud was final and binding. The Nejvyšší soud then acknowledged

[490] (CZ) Nejvyšší soud, rozsudek, 02/03/2016. Compare (FR) Cour de Cassation, Assemblée Plénière, arrêt, 18/11/2016.

[491] (IR) High Court, judgment, 17/10/2017.

[492] (CZ) Zákon o odpovědnosti za škodu způsobenou při výkonu veřejné moci rozhodnutím nebo nesprávným úředním postupem a o změně zákona České národní rady č 358/1992 Sb, § 8 (1). See also ACA Europe 2008, National report of the Republic Czech, question 14b; Petrlík 2014: 429.

[493] (CZ) Nejvyšší soud, rozsudek, 20/08/2012, reported by Kušteková in Reflets no 3/2012: 18–19 and Petrlík 2014: 427–29.

[494] (CZ) Nejvyšší soud, usnesení, 10/12/2012, available in the database ECLI.

[495] (CZ) Nejvyšší soud, rozsudek, 02/03/2016, available in the database ECLI.

[496] (CZ) Ústavní soud, usnesení ze dne 02/12/2013.

the existence of the principle of state liability for violation of EU law committed by national supreme courts. However, alluding to the ECJ decisions, the Nejvyšší soud questioned whether a simple reference by the ECJ to the common legal traditions was indeed sufficient to justify the establishment of such liability, especially in the absence of written legal norms. It then reasoned that first-instance courts are not competent to assess the legality of supreme courts' decisions unless, for example, they refer the matter to the ECJ or the ECtHR. Finally, the Nejvyšší soud concluded that in the absence of specific rules in the Czech legal system governing an action based on the *Köbler* liability of the state, it was reasonable that the national rules on state liability were used, by analogy, to determine the competent court. Then, similarly to the decision of 2015, presented above, the Nejvyšší soud dismissed the appeal on procedural grounds as it did not fulfil the preconditions of admissibility in the terms of the national rules.

In short, the Czech courts have already applied the principles established in the judgment in *Köbler*. However, in its recent judgment, the Nejvyšší soud questioned the legitimacy and the applicability of the state liability principle in the event of violation of EU law by a national supreme court. The Nejvyšší soud raised doubts, primarily, as to whether liability can be incurred on the grounds of violation of Article 267(3) TFEU. Also, the court emphasised the importance of legal stability and appeared to maintain that the Czech rules requiring the prior reversal of the contested decision aimed to ensure the legitimate purpose of legal certainty and were thus not contrary to the EU rules. Finally, this recent decision appears to negate the conclusions of the earlier decision from 2012 in so far as the new decision suggests that in the absence of national rules governing the practical terms of a state liability claim based on a breach of EU law, the national rules are applicable, by analogy, and do not need to be set aside.

b. Hungary

It is noteworthy that in Hungary the defendant in a liability action is the defaulting national court and not the Hungarian state, similarly to Bulgarian law.[497] The importance of res judicata and the unquestionable nature of final judgments are the main impediments to judicial liability in Hungary.[498] The Kúria had systematically refused to hold the state liable for the content of final judgments. This rule had been confirmed regarding EU law violations on several occasions, one judgment being particularly illustrative in this regard. Following

[497] See also (HU) Fővárosi Törvényszék, ítélet, 05/11/2013; Fővárosi Törvényszék, ítélet, 29/05/2012; Debreceni Ítélőtábla, ítélet, 01/06/2010.

[498] (HU) A bíróságok szervezetéről és igazgatásáról szóló 2011 évi CLXI. törvény, 2 § (1) bek. See also Borbás 2011; Fuglinszky 2015: 534–48; Gombos 2009; Metzinger 2014: 70–86; Pákozdi 2011, 2013; Varju 2014: 203–07.

the presentation of this judgment, three recent decisions will also be summarised which suggest changes have been made in the approach followed by several national regional courts in this respect.

The Kúria held in 2013 that a civil court adjudicating on a liability claim cannot reassess the merits of a final judgment that has already gained res judicata, notwithstanding a violation of EU law.[499] The Kúria emphasised that since the liability action is not an additional remedy, the alleged illegality of the proceedings before the administrative judge must be evaluated in the light of the national procedural rules. In this regard, the Kúria pointed out that the claimant himself had not invoked the directive in the proceedings before the administrative court. Since the court is bound by the pleas raised by the parties, the administrative court had not committed any breach when it had not considered the EU law.[500] The *Kúria* have rendered several other judgments in which it rejected the liability of the state for violation of EU law by the national courts. According to these judgments, a liability action cannot serve to review a finally adjudicated matter.[501]

It is noteworthy, however, that in a judgment pronounced in 2017, the Fővárosi Ítélőtábla (Regional Court of Appeal of Budapest) explicitly stated that the authority of res judicata cannot prevent the establishment of judicial liability where there had been a manifest violation of law in the final judgment.[502] The Fővárosi Ítélőtábla arrived at that conclusion based on the *Köbler* doctrine, and added that claims based on a violation of national law could not be assessed differently; therefore, the same standard applies to these claims as well.

Another regional court of appeal, the Győri Ítélőtábla (Regional Court of Appeal of Győr), has also rendered a decision on a *Köbler* liability claim. In this judgment, pronounced in 2017, liability was not established, but the argumentation of the court reflects a correct interpretation and application of the *Köbler* principle.[503] The Győri Ítélőtábla has not relied on the traditional argument used by the Hungarian courts, according to which there is no possibility to bring a liability action on the grounds that the content of a final judgment was contrary to EU law. Instead, the claim was dismissed on a valid and correct interpretation of the substantive EU rules on state liability.

In addition, in its request for a preliminary ruling, rendered in 2017, the Székesfehérvári Törvényszék (Székesfehérvár Regional Court) asked numerous questions aiming to clarify the scope of the *Köbler* liability, the principle of

[499] (HU) Kúria, ítélet, 11/12/2013, A Kúria Nemzetközi Kapcsolatok és Európai Jogi Irodájának Hírlevele V évfolyam 1 szám, reported by Varga in Reflets no 2/2014: 30. For different aspects of the case, see ss 2.II.A.ii.a(2) and 2.II.B.iv.c.

[500] See also (HU) Alkotmánybíróság, végzés, 19/05/2014, reported by Varga in Reflets no 2/2014: 30; (ECtHR) Judgment in *Repcevirág Szövetkezet v Hungary*.

[501] (HU) Kúria, ítélet, 28/02/2014. See also Varga 2015; Varga 2014a.

[502] (HU) Fővárosi Ítélőtábla, ítélet, 30/05/2017.

[503] (HU) Győri Ítélőtábla, ítélet, 29/07/2017.

effectiveness and the principle of res judicata in EU law.[504] Unfortunately these questions remained unanswered as the ECJ limited itself to reiterating the well-known general rules regarding the principle of state liability under EU law.

To sum up, in Hungary, the traditional approach excludes liability for final judicial acts rendered on the merits of a case.[505] Since this principle had been applied for EU law violations as well, the system was overly restrictive compared to the *Köbler* requirements up until the years 2016/2017. However, regional appeal courts have more recently started to acknowledge the possibility of bringing a liability action on the grounds that a last-instance court had infringed EU law in its final judgment. Moreover, the Fővárosi Ítélőtábla recently reasoned that once this possibility is recognised based on EU law violations, it has to be extended to violations of national rules as well. Despite these important developments, the Kúria, the court that has been attributing the greatest importance to the principle of res judicata in this context so far, has not yet validated this new judicial practice introduced by several regional courts of appeal.

c. Ireland

The liability of the state in tort is recognised under Irish law.[506] However, persons performing judicial functions enjoy absolute immunity from suit in the exercise of their judicial duties, due to their independence. In fact, as Paris points out, judges are considered not to be part of the state administration but as representatives of the people who render justice.[507] Therefore, even if Irish courts have recognised the principle of state liability arising directly from EU law,[508] this principle has only been applied thus far to breaches of law committed by public bodies other than courts. Moreover, under Irish law, the fundamental *Henderson* principle, according to which a party should not be entitled to relitigate matters or raise issues that have already been determined by a final judgment of a court, also hinders the effective application of the *Köbler* liability.[509] There has been a case where the liability of the state on account of a breach of EU law by the national court was invoked. Even though the judgment has not dealt with the

[504] (ECJ) Judgment *Hochtief Solutions AG Magyarországi Fióktelepe*, upon request for a preliminary ruling from the *Székesfehérvári Törvényszék* lodged on 02/11/2017. See also (ECJ) opinion *Hochtief Aktiengesellschaft*, upon request for a preliminary ruling from the *Székesfehérvári Törvényszék* lodged on 05/06/2018.

[505] Views urging the adaptation of domestic rules to the EU requirements were already present in the earlier literature. See Fuglinszky 2015: 542; Metzinger 2014: 85; Varju 2014: 207; Várnay 2010: 38.

[506] (IR) Supreme Court, judgment, *Kathleen Byrne v Ireland the Attorney General* [1972]; see also Binchy 2016: 203.

[507] (IR) House of Lords, judgment, 12/02/1974; Supreme Court, judgment, 30/07/1986. See also Paris 2014: 262; Scherr 2012: 576; High Court, judgment, 25/02/2009, reported by Paris 2014: 262.

[508] (IR) High Court, judgment, 03/02/1995, reported by Betlem et al 2007: 52, Granger 2007: 169; Paris 2014: 262; Circuit Court, judgment, 29/10/1990, reported by Paris 2014: 262; High Court, judgment, 07/03/2013; Supreme Court, judgment, 13/07/2017.

[509] (IR) Court of Chancery, 20/07/1943. See also Williams and Tushingham 2014.

conditions of *Köbler* liability explicitly, several interesting arguments make it worth mentioning.

In its judgment rendered in 2017, the High Court dismissed an action containing several claims, including a claim for damages, based on the principle preventing the party from raising legal points that could have been raised in the earlier proceedings.[510] The claim concerned the alleged violation by the national court to apply EU law ex officio in a case regarding consumer protection. The High Court emphasised that even if res judicata did not apply in the strict sense to the case at hand, the proceedings fall foul of the *Henderson* principle. The court then added that 'there was not any ECJ authority directly suggesting that an exception to the principle of finality should be made' because the national court had infringed its obligation to assess EU rules in its own motion in the proceedings. Despite the fact that it does not deal with the *Köbler* liability claim explicitly, this judgment is important in so far as it demonstrates the importance of the parties' arguments and complaints in the Irish proceedings. Even though the High Court acknowledged, incidentally and theoretically, the obligation of the national courts to raise EU law issues on their own motion in the context of consumer contracts, the ratio decidendi of the decision goes against that declaration.[511] Had the liability claim been assessed in the proceedings, the state should have been held liable for the breach of EU law according to the conclusions of the judgment in *Tomášová*, which addressed a very similar breach committed by a national court in relation to the same directive.

To conclude, the legal principles under Irish law as well as the recent judgment by the High Court suggest that liability of the state on account of infringement of EU law committed by last-instance national courts cannot emerge. However, there is no judgment yet available addressing this issue directly.

v. Member States Without any Sign of Accommodation or Refusal

As for Member States not mentioned above, there is no possibility to evaluate their position due to the absence of available case-law. However, the national legislative provisions do not allow, at first sight, the establishment of state liability for judicial breaches of EU law in Cyprus, Croatia, Estonia, Greece, Luxembourg, Malta, Romania, Slovakia and Slovenia.

a. Cyprus

The prior reversal of the contested judgment is a prerequisite for judicial liability in Cyprus.[512] There is no judgment available on the question of whether this condition must be set aside in the case of EU law violations.

[510] (IR) High Court, judgment, 17/10/2017. For different aspects of the case, see s 2.II.A.ii.a(2).
[511] (ECJ) Judgment in *Tomášová*, para 34.
[512] (CY) Constitution of the Republic of Cyprus, Art 146.6. See also Scherr 2008: 408; ACA Europe 2008, National report of Cyprus, question 14.

b. Croatia

In Croatia, liability of the state for judicial breaches is accepted in principle.[513] The prior reversal of the contested judgment is not a prerequisite for liability; however, in the liability procedure the court cannot reassess the contested decision. Therefore, the conditions seem to be overly restrictive compared to the *Köbler* requirements. Nevertheless, in the absence of relevant case-law, it is not possible to evaluate the courts' position on claims regarding violations of EU law.

c. Estonia

The compensation for damage caused by a public authority is governed by the state liability act in Estonia. According to this law, the criminal responsibility of the judge has to be established so that their liability can be invoked.[514] As such, the conditions of liability under Estonian law appear to be overly restrictive compared to the *Köbler* conditions. There has not yet been any sign of modification of this requirement concerning EU law violations. Nevertheless, the Riigikohus (Supreme Court, Estonia) has already declared that national provisions hindering the application of the *Francovich* doctrine, by imposing overly strict limits to the liability for breach of EU law by the legislation, must be set aside.[515]

d. Greece

Although the Greek legislation is silent on the question of whether the state can be held liable for miscarriages of justice, the jurisprudence explicitly excludes judicial acts from the scope of state liability.[516] Nevertheless, it seems possible to introduce a liability action based on infringement of the ECHR.[517] In such a case, the illegality of the national decision is established on the basis of the ECtHR judgment. However, there is no case-law available which demonstrates similar alignment of the national rules with the ECJ's requirements.

[513] (HR) Zakon o sudovima, članak 105.

[514] (EE) Riigivastutuse seadus, § 15(1). See also ACA Europe 2008, National report of Estonia, question 14. As for the constitutional basis of liability, see Eesti Vabariigi põhiseadus, § 25. See also Laffranque 2010: 203.

[515] (EE) Riigikohtu halduskolleegiumi, kohtuotsus, 28/11/2012; Riigikohtu halduskolleegiumi, kohtuotsus, 31/10/2013, para 20, reported by Evas 2016: 158. It is noteworthy that an amendment to the state liability act has already been adopted with the aim of allowing the judiciary to decide on the inactivity of the legislature. See Laffranque 2010: 198, 203, 204.

[516] (EL) Εισαγωγικός Νόμος του Αστικού Κώδικα, Art 105; Συμβούλιο της Επικρατειας 2744/2000; Άρειος Πάγος, 256/1996. See also ACA Europe 2008, National report of Greece, Rapport Hellénique, question 14; Christianos 2014: 236–37; Scherr 2012: 577; Condon and van Leeuwen 2016: 281.

[517] (EL) Άρειος Πάγος, 24/02/2012.

e. Luxembourg

Similarly to several other Member States, the importance of res judicata and the unquestionable nature of final judgments hinder the application of judicial liability in Luxembourg.[518] Nevertheless, there has already been a claim before Luxembourgish courts raised on the basis of the *Köbler* liability.

In this case from 2012, the Cour d'appel (Court of Appeal, Luxembourg) dismissed the liability action on the grounds that in the contested proceedings the action was lodged belatedly, and consequently it was time-barred.[519] Therefore, there was no causality relationship between the damages allegedly suffered and the conduct of the court regarding the allegedly erronous interpretation of EU law. It is noteworthy that the final judgment contains several paragraphs on the principle of res judicata. In this respect, the Cour d'appel explained that it could not declare inadmissible ex officio a claim because of the principle of res judicata. This argumentation suggests, however, that according to the court, had the principle of res judicata been invoked, it would have been an impediment to a liability claim. Given the fact that the defendant had not raised an objection of inadmissibility in the above case, this judgment cannot be considered a clear sign of acceptance of the *Köbler* doctrine by the Luxembourg courts. No other decisions have been identified on this matter in the available databases.

f. Malta

In Maltese law, state liability is accepted under the general regime of tort law established in the Civil Code. The articles of this code govern the liability of 'persons', which the Maltese courts interpreted as including the 'state' too, as there is no specific law on state liability. However, the cases filed to date have only dealt with the executive and legislative arms of the state, and not the judiciary.[520] Therefore, as Scherr has also pointed out, the situation under Maltese law is not entirely clear. While the legislature is silent on whether erroneous judicial acts can entail state liability, the doctrine seems to support the application of the liability regime for judicial violations of Articles 32–45 of the Maltese Constitution. Essentially, these provisions concern fundamental human rights.

g. Romania

In Romania, liability of the state for judicial errors is severely restricted as – similarly to Estonia and Germany – the establishment of criminal or disciplinary

[518] (LU) Code civil, 01.01.2004, Arts 1382, 1383; Loi du 1er septembre 1988 relative à la responsabilité civile de l'Etat et des collectivités publiques, Art 1, alinéa 1.

[519] (LU) Cour d'appel (Grand-Duché de Luxembourg), jugement, 21/03/2012. See also Ravarani 2014: 328–33.

[520] (MT) Constitution of Malta, Art 46; Civil Code, Art 1030–33. See also Scherr 2008: 168.

responsibility of the judge is a precondition for invoking such liability.[521] Since there has not yet been any sign of accommodation of this principle to the *Köbler* doctrine, conditions under the Romanian regime are overly restrictive and contrary to EU requirements.[522] It is noteworthy that there has been a legislative proposal in Romania aiming to reform judicial laws. The proposed amendments do not aim to change the rule that a claim based on judicial error must be lodged against the state, or the conditions for such liability.[523]

h. Slovakia

In Slovakia, the prior reversal of the contested judgment is a prerequisite for liability. Moreover, state liability claims presume the previous exhaustion of all available remedies.[524] This latter requirement was the subject of a reference for preliminary ruling to the ECJ in the *Tomášová* case.[525] As already discussed, in the *Tomášová* judgment the ECJ stated succinctly that the scope of compensation and the relationship between a liability action and the other actions available under national law fall within the concept of national procedural autonomy. The national decision rendered following the ECJ judgment is not yet available.[526]

i. Slovenia

In principle, state liability for judicial breaches finds its legal basis in the Constitution establishing a general right to compensation.[527] However, liability for judicial breaches can only be established if the judge has intentionally disregarded the established case-law or has ignored an entirely clear legal provision.[528] According to a judgment from 1995, liability is even restricted to cases of criminal or disciplinary offences.[529] As Trstenjak and Plaustajner point out, Slovenian

[521] (RO) Constituţia României, Art 52; Codul civil al României, Arts 1357–59; Legea nr 303/2004 privind statutul judecătorilor şi procurorilor, Art 96(4). See also Scherr 2008: 227. See also Danileţ, C and Loreley, M (n.d.) 'The Cvil Liability of Magistrates. International Standards. New Legislative Tendencies', www.cristidanilet.ro/docs/The%20civil%20liability%20of%20magistrates.doc.

[522] See also Radu, I (2009) 'Discussions on State Liability for Judicial Errors in Other Trials than the Criminal Cases', www.uab.ro/reviste_recunoscute/reviste_drept/annales_12_2009/.

[523] See Council of Europe (2018) *Group of State against Corruption, Ad Hoc Report on Romania (rule 34).*

[524] (SK) Ústava Slovenskej republiky, §§ 3, 5, 6.

[525] (ECJ) Judgment in *Tomášová*. For a more detailed presentation of the case and the judgment, see s 1.III.D.

[526] Last verified in the database DecNat on 1 February 2020.

[527] (SI) Ustava Republike Slovenije – URS, 26 člen; Obligacijski zakonik – OZ, 131 člen, 148 člen; (SI) Zakon o upravnem sporu – ZUS-1, 67(3) člen. See also Trstenjak and Plaustajner 2014: 472–73.

[528] (SI) Vrhovnega sodišča Republike Slovenije, Sodba, 12/01/2005, reported by Trstenjak and Plaustajner 2014: 472; Vrhovnega sodišča Republike Slovenije, Sodba, 13/11/2003, reported by Trstenjak and Plaustajner 2014: 472

[529] (SI) Vrhovno sodišče Republike Slovenije, VSS 2/95, reported by Scherr 2008: 227. See also ACA Europe 2008, National report of Slovenia.

legislation has not been amended in view of the ECJ case-law. Moreover, as they argue, it would appear that the domestic interpretation concerning state liability for judicial breaches is stricter than that established in *Köbler*. Consequently, Slovenian courts should still adapt their jurisprudence to the *Köbler* principles to conform to the ECJ requirements.[530]

C. Consequences of the Köbler Judgment on National Rules

i. Duplication of Liability Regimes and Spill-Over Effect

The above case-law developments show that several national courts have accepted, despite the restrictions in national laws, to hold the state liable for violation of EU law by a national supreme court based on the *Köbler* doctrine directly. Therefore, in most of those Member States, the implementation of the *Köbler* doctrine has resulted in the duplication of liability regimes.[531] It means that the conditions of state liability for judicial acts are less strict with regard to damages caused by violation of EU law rather than violation of national law in nine Member States (Bulgaria, Germany, France, Lithuania, the Netherlands, Austria, Portugal, Finland and the UK).[532]

The exception is Belgium, where the jurisprudential changes have general application. Due to the judgment of 2014 by the Cour constitutionnelle, the overly strict condition regarding the prior reversal of the contested decision no longer applies to manifest violation of the applicable law by a court adjudicating at last instance under certain circumstances.[533] In order to reach this conclusion, the Cour constitutionnelle argued that state liability for violation of EU law arises when a Member State court adjudicating at last instance manifestly disregards the ECJ case-law. The court then extended the scope of this finding to cover the violation of national law, in order to harmonise the requirements of judicial liability under national, EU and international regimes.

Similarly, the Spanish Tribunal Supremo and the Hungarian Fővárosi Ítélőtábla have also extended the application of the more favourable rules regarding EU law to purely national situations in certain cases. In this respect, several authors argue that the Tribunal Supremo, by relying partially on the *Köbler* principle, extended the reach of ECJ case-law on state liability to purely domestic situations in its 2004 judgment.[534] As for the Fővárosi Ítélőtábla, in

[530] Trstenjak and Plaustajner 2014: 472–73.

[531] See also Giliker 2017: 454.

[532] This phenomenon is not special to the conditions of state liability. See eg Gordon and Moffatt 2014: 97.

[533] (BE) Cour constitutionnelle, arrêt, 30/06/2014. For a more detailed presentation of this case, see s 2.III.B.ii.a.

[534] (ES) Tribunal Supremo, Sentencia, 23/01/2004, reported in Reflets no 1/2004: 8, and by Granger 2007: 168. For different aspects of the case, see s 2.III.B.i.c.

a judgment pronounced in 2017, the second most prominent Hungarian court explicitly stated that the authority of res judicata cannot prevent the establishment of judicial liability where there had been a manifest violation of law in the final judgment.[535] The Fővárosi Ítélőtábla arrived at that conclusion based on the *Köbler* doctrine, and added that claims based on a violation of national law could not be assessed differently; therefore, the same standard applies to these claims as well. However, these latter cases appear to be isolated and there is no sign that Hungarian and Spanish courts follow a coherent approach in this respect.

It should also be noted that in the two Member States where the implementation of the *Köbler* judgment had been made through legislative amendments (Italy, Poland),[536] these latter concern liability claims based on both EU and national law, with the exception of Polish administrative law.

ii. Conclusion on National Restrictions

Two main conclusions can be drawn from the national case-law on *Köbler* claims. On the one hand, several Member States have implemented the *Köbler* liability into their legal framework, despite the limitations in the domestic statutory provisions. Even though legal provisions have not been changed in most of these states, some courts have adjudicated liability claims directly based on the *Köbler* judgment. On the other hand, even in these Member States, compensation has been allocated only in the rarest of circumstances. This is despite indications that Member State supreme courts have indeed rendered judgments contrary to EU law.[537]

Therefore, even in Member States where liability for breaches of EU law by courts is recognised, there have been very few successful claims based on the *Köbler* doctrine. Why is this enforcement deficit of the *Köbler* doctrine observed? In this regard, it is common to raise questions about the adequate nature of the 'manifest breach' criterion; and objections emanating from the principle of res judicata arise regularly. These hindrances have already been studied and analysed in the previous sections of this book. However, one should not neglect other important issues either, such as the legal environment in which the *Köbler* doctrine operates. In order to understand the whole context of the *Köbler* doctrine, it is necessary to examine the system of remedies in which the principle applies, and, especially, the existence of other remedies available under national laws in case of violation of EU law by a national supreme court.

[535] (HU) Fővárosi Ítélőtábla, ítélet, 30/05/2017. For different aspects of the case, see s 2.III.B.iv.b.

[536] See ss 2.III.B.iii.a and 2.III.B.iii.b.

[537] See (DE) BVerfG, Beschluß, 08/04/1987 and, for a recent example, (DN) Højesteret, Judgment, 06/12/2016. For an annotation to this judgment, see Holdgaard et al 2018; Šadl and Mair 2017. For a reference to other cases, see Anagnostaras 2001c: 295, nn 45 and 46; Komárek 2005b: 26, n 75; Prete and Smulders 2010; Timmermans 2004: 161–62; Taborowski 2012: 1902–06; Várnay et al 2006: 69–74; Prete 2017.

IV. ALTERNATIVE REMEDIES IN USE IN THE MEMBER STATES

However, before criticising the Member States for not offering effective judicial protection to the individuals and before considering the need to impose more stringent conditions on the Member States, it seems appropriate to examine whether there exist other remedies available to individuals. If these other methods are in use and provide at least equivalent protection of individual rights and effectiveness as EU law, this may necessitate a reassessment of the role of the *Köbler* liability doctrine in the system of EU rights protection.

This section focuses on remedies other than *Köbler* liability that are available for individuals against supreme court judgments infringing rights conferred by EU law. Two main methods are presented and examined in detail. The first is retrial, which can bring substantial remedy for the aggrieved individual through a new legal procedure that leads to a new judgment of the court. The second is constitutional complaint for alleged violation of the right to a lawful judge, introduced on the ground that the supreme court breached its obligation to make a preliminary reference to the ECJ. This section analyses both alternative remedies from a doctrinal and a practical point of view, and includes an overview of the case-law of the ECJ and of the Member State courts.

Certainly, lodging an application against the state before the ECtHR for violation of the right to a fair trial enshrined under Article 6(1) ECHR is also a remedy in the event of breach of EU law by a Member State court. However, since the focus of this book is the presentation of national remedies, the relevant ECtHR jurisprudence will not be systematically analysed. The case-law of the ECtHR will only be mentioned as far as it is relevant to the subject at issue.[538]

A. Retrial on the Ground of Violation of EU Law

i. Theory on Retrial

In several Member States, there is a possibility for an individual whose rights have been infringed by a final judgment to invoke the violation of EU law as a ground for retrial.[539] It is usually a subsequent ECJ judgment on the same

[538] See also Lacchi 2015: 114–16.

[539] To ensure clarity and mutual understanding, a unification of terminology has been made when referring to these principles, procedures or remedies in English. Therefore, the following terminology will be used in the main text of the analysis: The term 'retrial' covers procedural means that allow for a case already decided by the court of final instance to be 'reopened' (see ECHR Art 4, Protocol 7; ECJ judgment in *Lucchini*, para 59) and for a final judicial decision that has acquired res judicata to be 'revised' (see ECJ judgments in *Târşia*, paras 16, 19; in *Impresa Pizzarotti*). The term 'revocation' refers to public authorities' powers to revoke their own acts, whether confirmed or not by the administrative court (see ECJ judgment in *Lucchini*, para 36). The term 'reversal' is used when referring to the precondition of state liability, which requires any form of prior annulment, overturning, quashing, removal, revocation, setting aside or withdrawal of the contested judgment (see ECJ judgment in *Ferreira da Silva e Brito e.a.*).

question of law which reveals the inconsistency of the national judgment with the EU norm.[540]

Several authors favour retrial, which they find a more effective remedy than the *Köbler* action. Their main arguments are that, first of all, it allows a high standard of culpability (namely the application of the criterion of 'manifest infringement' or 'serious breach' as set out in *Köbler*) to be avoided.[541] Furthermore, the principle of legality is served optimally by giving precedence to judicial actions that award substantive protection, as opposed to mere economic compensation.[542] Moreover, in situations where non-pecuniary damage is at stake, suing the state for damages can even be insufficient.[543] Therefore, as Wattel and Anagnostaras point out, pecuniary reinstatement may help to ease the injustice suffered, but it remains only the second-best solution compared to alternative forms of substantive relief.[544] Kornezov even arrives at the conclusion that there is a genuine need under certain circumstances to allow cases to be reopened if the final judgment has proved to contrary to EU law.[545]

In my view, retrial is a more generous tool than liability to protect individual rights for another reason as well. In fact, not only does the gravity of the breach not need to be manifest, but there is no need to prove a 'tort' on the side of the court either. In fact, the violation of the substantive EU norm may in itself be a sufficient ground for retrial, while liability requires the violation by the court of one of its procedural obligations regarding the application of the substantive norm.

Considering all arguments above, retrial appears to be more suitable to remedy infringed rights, while liability is more of a preventive tool, useful to deter supreme courts from infringements.[546]

ii. ECJ Case-Law on Retrial

It must be emphasised that EU law does not require the mandatory reopening of domestic procedures following ECJ judgments. According to the ECJ, such a general possibility would endanger the corollary principles of res judicata and legal certainty. Hence, under EU law, retrial is exceptional and conditional upon the special circumstances of the case. It holds true, even for cases where reopening would make it possible to remedy an infringement of EU law by the judgment in question.[547]

[540] The results of the research conducted on the subject-matter of this chapter were first published in Varga 2017c.

[541] Anagnostaras 2007: 737; Wattel 2004: 189; Sowery 2016: 1720–21.

[542] Anagnostaras 2007: 736–37.

[543] Kornezov 2014a: 810, 838.

[544] As Anagnostaras (2007: 737) points out, that is also one of the reasons behind the operation of the mitigation principle in the field of liability suits.

[545] Kornezov 2014a: 838.

[546] For further discussion on this topic, see s 3.I.

[547] See (ECJ) judgments in *Kapferer*, paras 20–22; in *Fallimento Olimpiclub*, paras 22–23; in *Commission v Slovakia*, paras 59–60; in *Impresa Pizzarotti*, paras 54, 59, 62, 64; in *Târşia*, paras 28–29;

Referring to Kornezov, res judicata and retrial are considered as two sides of the same coin for the purposes of the present analysis.[548] The main connection between them is that if a previously adjudged issue is contrary to EU law and comes within the scope of res judicata, it can be remedied only through retrial.[549] Therefore, retrial is an exceptional measure, with the result of setting aside the effects of res judicata of final judgments under special circumstances. Due to this connection between the two concepts, ECJ case-law regarding res judicata is briefly presented here.[550]

The judgment in *Kühne & Heitz*[551] concerned the infringement of EU law by an administrative decision, which was confirmed by the administrative court with the result of attaching res judicata to the matter under dispute.[552] The ECJ declared that the revocation of such a decision by the administrative authority is required only if several conditions are fulfilled. First of all, the national court of last instance reached the wrong decision without having submitted a request for preliminary ruling to the ECJ. Moreover, the national administrative authority had the power, under national law, to revoke its own decisions. Furthermore, a subsequent ECJ judgment revealed the inconsistency of the decision with EU law. Finally, the aggrieved party complained to the administrative authority immediately after becoming aware of that decision of the ECJ.[553] This principle has been confirmed in the order in *i-21 Germany and Arcor*.[554] It is noteworthy that the above two cases concerned the revocation by the administrative authority of a previous administrative decision, confirmed by the administrative court. As such, these judgments concerned erroneous final judicial decisions only indirectly. However, several ECJ judgments have directly dealt with the issue of reopening judicial proceedings by the court.

In the judgment in *Lucchini*[555] the ECJ concluded, albeit in a highly specific situation, that the principle of res judicata had to be set aside, ensuring that the case would be reopened by the court itself. The judgment concerned the recovery of state aid granted in breach of EU law. The national court that handed down the final judgment manifestly lacked jurisdiction as to the substance of the case, as the Commission has exclusive competence to assess the compatibility of a national state aid measure with EU law. According to some legal commentators,

in *Klausner Holz Niedersachsen*, paras 38–39, in *XC e.a.*, para 52. See on this question Groussot and Minssen 2007; Lenaerts et al 2014: 148–50; Maisto 2014; Sowery 2016: 1714–20; Tridimas 2006: 164–71, 423–27; Varga 2019.

[548] See also Turmo 2017.

[549] See also Kornezov 2014a: 812–14.

[550] In the case (ECJ) *Fernand Ullens de Schooten*, the referring court asked several questions regarding the application of the principle of res judicata in relation to the obligation of national courts in the context of liability proceedings. However, for procedural reasons, the ECJ did not answer these questions.

[551] (ECJ) Judgment in *Kühne & Heitz*.

[552] See also Hofstötter 2005: 179–80.

[553] (ECJ) Judgment in *Kühne & Heitz*, para 28.

[554] (ECJ) Order in *i-21 Germany and Arcor*.

[555] (ECJ) Judgment in *Lucchini*, see the case note by Biondi 2008.

due to this circumstance, the national judgment should have been considered null and therefore lacking the authority of res judicata.[556]

The *Klausner Holz Niedersachsen* case concerned the application of EU rules on state aid as well. The national rules on res judicata did not allow the national court to draw all consequences of a breach of EU rules on state aid because of a previous, final judicial decision. Specifically, this previous decision had been given in a dispute that did not have the same subject-matter and did not concern, either principally or incidentally, the state aid characteristics of the contracts at issue. The ECJ found these domestic rules incompatible with the principle of effectiveness; and emphasised that a principle as fundamental as that of the control of state aid cannot be justified either by the principle of res judicata or by the principle of legal certainty.[557]

In the judgment in *Fallimento Olimpiclub*, the ECJ once again found the application of the principle of res judicata incompatible with the effectiveness of EU law because of the scope and effect at issue in the specific case. As the ECJ pointed out, the way in which res judicata was construed under Italian law not only prevented a final judicial decision from being reopened, but also prevented judicial scrutiny in the context of a different tax year of any finding on a fundamental issue contained in a final judicial decision. This resulted in a recurring violation of EU law, without the possibility of remedying the breach.

As Kornezov concludes, the ECJ favours a narrow concept of res judicata, which, on the one hand, requires the identity of the subject-matter, and, on the other hand, only extends to the matters of fact or law actually or necessarily settled by the judicial decision in question.[558] National rules on res judicata appear to infringe EU law only where they have a wider scope of application.

The judgment in *Kapferer* is sometimes cited as an example of leaving the authority of a final judgment's res judicata unfettered, despite its alleged inconsistency with EU law.[559] The ECJ held in this judgment that the principle of cooperation does not require a national court to set aside its internal rules of procedure in order to review and set aside a final judicial decision if that decision should be contrary to EU law.[560] The same principle was confirmed by the ECJ in its judgment in *Commission v Slovakia*.[561]

In *Impresa Pizzarotti*, concerning rules on a public works contract, the ECJ confirmed this principle once again;[562] and supplemented it with a new point.

[556] See also Kornezov 2014a: 821–22; and the ECJ's own interpretation of *Lucchini* in (ECJ) judgments in *Fallimento Olimpiclub*, para 25; in *Impresa Pizzarotti*, para 61.

[557] (ECJ) Judgment in *Klausner Holz Niedersachsen*, paras 45–46.

[558] Kornezov 2014a: 823–24. For further decisions regarding the concept of res judicata under EU law, see (ECJ) judgments in *Gothaer Allgemeine Versicherung and Others*; in *P&O European Ferries (Vizcaya) and Diputación Foral de Vizcaya v Commission*, para 44; in *Commission v Luxembourg*, para 26; in *ThyssenKrupp Nirosta v Commission*, para 123; in *XC e.a.*, paras 52–54.

[559] (ECJ) Judgment in *Kapferer*. See Kornezov 2014a: 833.

[560] (ECJ) Judgment in *Kapferer*, para 20. See also Kornezov 2014a: 833.

[561] (ECJ) Judgment in *Commission v Slovakia*, paras 59–60. See Taborowski 2012: 1893–94.

[562] (ECJ) Judgment in *Impresa Pizzarotti*, para 60.

As a result, if the applicable domestic rules provide the possibility for a national court to go back on its decision in order to render the situation compatible with national law, there must also be the possibility for the situation at issue to be brought back into line with EU legislation.[563] Accordingly, to the extent that it is authorised to do so, a national court which has given a ruling at last instance, without a reference having first been made to the ECJ under Article 267 TFEU, must either supplement or go back on that definitive ruling to take into account any interpretation of that legislation provided by the ECJ subsequently.[564] This duty is the result of the principles of equivalence and effectiveness.

In short, the ECJ accepts the procedural limitations to reopening a finally adjudicated case in national laws, notwithstanding its violation of EU law. However, it requires reopening if such a possibility exists in national laws, or if the scope of application of res judicata under the national legal order is wider than the meaning of res judicata under EU law.

One may wonder whether denying retrial in cases of breach of EU law is compatible with the principle of equivalence, if the same remedy is offered against breaches of the ECHR or the national constitution.[565] The ECJ has recently addressed this issue regarding the ECHR in quite a specific setting due to the ECJ's attitude towards the ECHR and the protection of human rights, on the one hand, and to the characteristics of the Austrian legal order, on the other hand.[566]

In *XC e.a.*, the ECJ arrived at the conclusion that EU law, in particular the principles of equivalence and effectiveness, do not require a national court to extend retrial, available in event of infringement of the ECHR, to violations of the Charter. Regarding this topic, it is important to recall that retrial following judgments by the ECtHR or constitutional courts is, generally, only possible in the particular case about which the earlier judgment was concerned. This means that the parties in the cases before the ECtHR or the constitutional court and before the national courts need to be identical, contrary to what is usually the situation in the event of violations of EU law. This is because of the different role and position of the ECtHR, the constitutional courts and the ECJ in the legal order. Consequently, allowing retrial based on violation of the ECHR and the national constitution, while denying it in cases of violation of the EU law, does not seem to be, in general, contrary to the principle of equivalence.[567]

[563] (ECJ) Judgment in *Impresa Pizzarotti*, para 62.

[564] (ECJ) Judgment in *Impresa Pizzarotti*, para 64.

[565] Kornezov 2014a: 835. See also (ECJ) judgment in *Târşia* and the annotation to this case by Sowery 2016: 1722–25.

[566] (ECJ) Judgment in *XC e.a.* See also, by analogy (ECJ) judgment in *Transportes Urbanos y Servicios Generales*; and Plaza 2010: 35, 45.

[567] See (ECJ) Opinion of AG Bobek in *Commission v Zagoriou*, para 40; opinion of AG Bobek in *Oana Mădălina Călin*, paras 76–77; Varga 2019: 1690–92 and compare with Kornezov 2014: 835, 836.

However, it is an important question for the purposes of the present analysis whether retrial is applied in the Member States to remedy a violation of EU law and, if this is the case, to what extent. In the words of Hofstötter, what position does the approach of 'try again' hold in the Member States in comparison to the *Köbler* liability doctrine?[568]

iii. Judgment of the ECtHR in the Dangeville *Case*

It is noteworthy that the ECtHR found in its judgment from 2002, rendered in the case of *Dangeville SA*, that the principle of res judicata cannot jeopardise the right to the recovery of unduly paid taxes.[569]

This case concerned a company which, after having paid VAT under French law, invoked an exemption granted in the VAT directive. Relying on its rights conferred by EU law, the company sought reimbursement of the overpaid VAT. However, the French authorities, including the Conseil d'État, denied such exemption. They argued that the directive, having not yet been implemented into national law, could not be relied on before the national courts.[570] At that time, the Conseil d'État had not yet recognised the direct effect of EU directives. After the refusal, the company made a further claim, seeking compensation on the ground that the French state was liable for VAT unduly paid.[571] Although by then the Conseil d'État had recognised the principle of direct effect, it refused to revise its original judgment because of the principle of res judicata. The Conseil d'État argued that the matter constituted a res judicata, since the recovery claim had already been rejected at last instance.[572] Having been refused the recovery of the overpaid tax by the French courts, the company brought a case before ECtHR, claiming that it had been deprived of its possessions within the meaning of Article 1 of Protocol I of the ECHR. The company argued that it was a creditor of the state but had been definitively deprived of the possibility of enforcing its debt because of the decisions of the Conseil d'État dismissing its claims.

In its judgment, the ECtHR qualified the right to restitution of the unduly paid tax as a possession within the meaning of the ECHR. Hence, it concluded unanimously that the refusal of such restitution constituted an infringement of the property right, despite the principle of res judicata. The applicant was therefore awarded the pecuniary damage claimed. This judgment is a good illustration of a situation where the recovery of unduly paid tax and the compensation of damage suffered lead to the same result.

[568] Hofstötter 2005: 179–81.

[569] (ECtHR) Judgment in *SA Dangeville v France*, § 71.

[570] (FR) Conseil d'État, décision, 19/03/1986.

[571] See (FR) Cour administrative d'appel de Paris, arrêt, 01/07/1992. See also Anagnostaras 2001b: 148.

[572] (FR) Conseil d'État, arrêt, 30/10/1996.

iv. Member States' Positions

a. Overview of the Legislative Provisions

On the one hand, in several Member States it is possible to reopen final judgments by reason of their incompatibility with EU law.[573] Three groups of states can be distinguished in this regard. First, finally adjudicated matters can be reopened by reason of a manifest breach of law in six Member States (Denmark, Malta, Finland, Sweden, the UK and, in administrative matters, Lithuania). In these Member States, retrial can theoretically be granted regardless of whether the violation concerns EU or national law – however, the breach must be qualified. This latter requirement sets a similar condition to the 'manifest breach' in the terms of the *Köbler* judgment. Second, retrial is possible in three Member States (Latvia, Portugal and, in administrative matters, Poland)[574] on the ground that an international agreement or the inconsistency of the national judgment with the decision of an international court requires it. It is not obvious, however, whether retrial is restricted to cases in which the international jurisdiction has delivered its judgment, or whether it can also be applied to other national judgments concerned with the same matter of law. Third, legislative provisions have been introduced to procedural codes in order to recognise the violation of EU law as a specific ground for retrial in three Member States (Croatia, Romania and Slovakia). However, in Croatia, such a revision is not possible concerning final judgments rendered by the supreme court. On the contrary, in Romanian administrative and Slovakian civil procedural law, a single violation of law is sufficient to reopen finally adjudicated cases, and the identity of the parties is not required either. Therefore, even if the scope of application of these two latter provisions is narrow, they provide generous protection.

However, there is no clear position on the issue at hand in two Member States (Bulgaria and Cyprus). In Bulgarian law, both procedural codes and case-law have to date remained silent on whether an ECJ judgment may offer a ground for retrial. The legal scholarship, however, does not exclude the possibility that new ECJ case-law could eventually be considered as a new fact, and could serve as a ground for retrial. In Cyprus, the Supreme Constitutional Court holds the right to adjudicate finally on a recourse made to it on a complaint that a decision of an organ of the state is contrary to law. There is no case-law available on how to interpret this rule in the context of a violation of EU law.

In addition, administrative authorities in two Member States (Estonia and Poland) hold the right to revoke their own decisions if contrary to EU law. In Poland, this possibility is granted regardless of whether the administrative

[573] For the terminology used, see n 539 above.

[574] In fact, there is a similar provision in Czech law, which provides for the possibility to ask for the case to be reopened before the Constitutional Court on the ground of a judgment of an international court delivered in the same case. However, this remedy seems to apply primarily to ECtHR judgments. See (CZ) Zákon o Ústavním soudu, § 119.

decision has become final following the approval of the administrative court. This possibility appears to be given to Estonian administrative authorities under the general rules, even if there is no available case-law from the field of EU law.

On the other hand, in five Member States, available case-law has explicitly excluded retrial on the ground of inconsistency between the final decision and a prior or later ECJ judgment (Italy, Hungary, the Netherlands and Austria, as well as in civil matters in Poland). According to these decisions, a subsequent ECJ judgment on the interpretation of the EU norm is not a reason under national laws to reopen finally adjudicated cases. Similarly, the inconsistency of the final judgment with EU law is not a basis for reopening the case under the legislation of ten Member States (Belgium, Czech Republic, Germany, Ireland, Greece, Spain, France, Luxembourg, Slovenia, as well as in civil cases in Lithuania). Under the above last 15 regimes, retrial is considered as an extraordinary remedy, the use of which is exhaustively listed in national legislations. According to Kornezov, the conditions for retrial may vary between civil, administrative and criminal law, but could be loosely fitted into four main groups: discovery of fresh evidence or of the fact that the evidence had been falsified or involved fraud; default judgments; contradictory judgments; or grave legal errors.[575] Erroneous interpretation of the law is therefore not a reason to make use of this extraordinary remedy.

Nevertheless, as already mentioned, in several Member States a judgment by the ECtHR is a ground in its own right to reopen cases.[576] In this regard, the Council of Europe has even published a recommendation on the re-examination or reopening of certain cases at domestic level following judgments by the ECtHR.[577] In this document, the panel invites the Contracting Parties to ensure that there exist, at national level, adequate possibilities to achieve, as far as possible, *restitutio in integrum*, for example by way of reopening cases. Such provisions can be found in the criminal procedural code of most EU Member States,[578] and also in the civil or administrative procedure in Bulgaria, Germany, Estonia, Hungary, Lithuania, Netherlands, Spain and Romania, for example.[579] The possibility of retrial on the basis of a breach of the ECHR is, however,

[575] Kornezov 2014a: 829.

[576] It is noteworthy that in the event of reopening of the final judgment on the ground of breach of the ECHR, the breach must usually be established by the ECtHR in the same case, and the reopening concerns only the main proceedings at issue.

[577] (ECHR) Recommendation No R (2000) 2 of the Committee of Ministers to Member States on the re-examination or reopening of certain cases at domestic level following judgments of the European Court of Human Rights (Adopted by the Committee of Ministers on 19 January 2000 at the 694th meeting of the Ministers' Deputies).

[578] (LV) Kriminālprocesa likums, 655 pants (2) 5); (EE) Kriminaalmenetluse seadustik, § 366 (7); (EL) Κώδικας Ποινικής Δικονομίας, Αρθρο: 525(1).

[579] (BG) Grazhdanski protsesualen kodeks, Art 303, § 1, 7); Aministrativen protsesualen kodeks, Art 239, § 6); (DE) Zivilprozessordnung, § 580, nr 8; Bundestag-Drucksache, 13/3594, 29/01/1996; (EE) Halduskohtumenetluse seadustik, § 240(2) 8); Tsiviilkohtumenetluse seadustik, § 702(2) 8). See also ACA Europe 2008, National report of Estonia, question 14; (HU) A polgári perrendtartásról szóló 2016. évi CXXX. törvény, 393. § c); (LT) Civilinio proceso kodeksas, XVIII Skyrius, 366 straipsnis 1.1); Lietuvos Respublikos administracinių bylų teisenos įstatymas, 156 straipsnis 2.1);

usually limited to specific cases in which the ECtHR has rendered its judgment; this is therefore a system different to the ECJ enforcement system.[580]

b. Retrial Available in Extraordinary Situations

(1) **Denmark**

In Denmark, cases can be reopened in extraordinary situations.[581] Due to the general scope of application of this provision, it appears suitable for providing remedy for violation of EU law as well. However, there is no case-law available to confirm this assumption.

(2) **Cyprus**

In Cyprus, the Supreme Constitutional Court has the final decision on a complaint that a decision of a state body is contrary to the law. There is, however, no case-law available on the application of this rule to violations of EU law.[582]

(3) **Lithuania**

Under Lithuanian law, cases before administrative courts can be reopened on condition that the applicant submits clear evidence showing a fundamental violation of a substantive provision of law that led to the illegality of the judgment.[583] According to the case-law of the Vyriausiasis administracinis teismas, the infringement is considered to be obvious when there is no reasonable doubt regarding the erroneous interpretation of the norms.[584] These rules have general application, and both breach of substantive law connected to EU legal rules and infringement of national law fall into this category. Administrative proceedings can therefore be reopened where the administrative court of last instance has committed a manifest infringement of substantive EU law.[585] However, as for civil matters, retrial by reason of violation of law is possible on more limited grounds. As such, only judgments of inferior courts, which became final in the absence of appeal against them, can be revised for this reason in retrial proceedings.[586] Reopening of cases where the judgments have been rendered by superior courts is not provided on the ground of erroneous

(NL) Wetboek van Burgerlijke Rechtsvordering, Art 382; (ES) Ley 29/1998, de 13 de julio, reguladora de la Jurisdicción Contencioso-administrativa, Art 102.2; (RO) Codul de procedură civilă, Art 509(1) 10; Legea nr 554/2004 contenciosului administrative, Art 21, § 1. See also (HR) Zakon o parničnom postupku, članak 382(2)(3).

[580] See also (ECJ) judgment in *XC e.a.*; Varga 2019: 1690–92.

[581] (DN) Bekendtgørelse af lov om rettens pleje (Retsplejeloven), § 399, and §§ 975–78. See also ACA Europe 2008, National report of Denmark, question 8b.

[582] (CY) ACA Europe 2008, National report of Cyprus, question 14.

[583] (LT) Lietuvos Respublikos administracinių bylų teisenos įstatymas, 156. straipsnis. See also ACA Europe 2008, National report of Lithuania, questions 1–4, 11; Valutytė 2014: 301.

[584] Valutytė 2014: 301–02.

[585] Valutytė 2014: 301. See also ACA Europe 2008, National report of Lithuania, question 3.

[586] (LT) Civilinio proceso kodeksas, XVIII Skyrius, 366 straipsnis 1.9).

interpretation of law. Moreover, both civil and administrative procedure codes provide explicit grounds for retrial where a judgment by the ECtHR establishes the violation of the fundamental rights by a final national decision. However, these provisions only make reference to the ECtHR judgments, and not to ECJ decisions.[587] As for the judicial practice, the Vyriausiasis administracinis teismas has already applied the domestic rules on retrial in EU-related cases. Two judgments are worth mentioning in this regard.

In the first case from 2008, the Vyriausiasis administracinis teismas, deciding on the motion for retrial, came to the conclusion that the EU provisions should have been applied in the underlying proceedings and could have had an impact on the outcome of the case.[588] It therefore decided that there were sufficient grounds to establish a fundamental infringement of substantive legal provisions in the main proceedings, suitable to justify the reopeining of the case.

In the second judgment from 2009, the Vyriausiasis administracinis teismas even established the infringement of EU law by the Konstitucinis Teismas (Constitutional Court, Lithuania).[589] Discussing the obligations of the Konstitucinis Teismas as a body of public administration, the Vyriausiasis administracinis teismas stressed that the latter has to interpret the Constitution in the light of EU law. Moreover, the Konstitucinis Teismas also has the obligation to submit a preliminary question if the interpretation of EU law arises before it.[590] However, the claim was finally rejected, as the applicant had not asked for a review of the decision or compensation for damages but for the case to be reopened, which the Vyriausiasis administracinis teismas could not satisfy.

In conclusion, retrial on the ground of manifest breach of EU law has been accepted and applied by the Vyriausiasis administracinis teismas in administrative cases. On the basis of the above information, we can draw two conclusions. First, due to the objective condition regarding the infringement, situations where the violation became apparent, either due to a prior or subsequent judgment of the ECJ, can provide sufficient grounds to reopen and re-examine a final judgment. However, as the violation of EU law must be manifest, a final judgment based on the misinterpretation of EU law can only be reopened in the event of a serious breach of substantive law.[591] Second, in Lithuanian administrative law, the conditions for retrial and liability appear to be similar. Moreover, it seems that the two types of proceedings can be undertaken concurrently, as there is no formal link between these two remedies. In this regard, on the one hand, the modification or the overturning of the decision in the retrial procedure can

[587] (LT) Civilinio proceso kodeksas, XVIII Skyrius, 366 straipsnis 1.1); Lietuvos Respublikos administracinių bylų teisenos įstatymas, 156 straipsnis 2.1).

[588] (LT) Lietuvos vyriausiojo administracinio teismo, 10/04/2008.

[589] (LT) Lietuvos vyriausiojo administracinio teismo, 31/07/2009, reported by Valutytė 2014: 293–95.

[590] Valutytė 2014: 293–95.

[591] ACA Europe 2008, National report of Lithuania, question 3.

give rise to posterior liability proceedings instituted by the party having suffered damages caused by the illegal final judgment. On the other hand, the retrial procedure is not a precondition for a liability claim. Apparently, it is for the applicant to decide which remedy to seek and the Vyriausiasis administracinis teismas will decide accordingly.[592]

(4) **Malta**

In Malta, cases can be reopened by reason of a wrong application of the law.[593] Even if there is no case-law on the application of this rule for violation of EU law, it seems plausible to initiate retrial proceedings on these grounds.

It may be interesting to mention in this context the judgment by the ECtHR in the case of *San Leonard Band Club v Malta* from 2004 which concerned this particular ground for retrial relating to a 'wrong application of the law'. In fact, the ECtHR stated that this was similar to an appeal on points of law before a court of cassation, and, therefore, Article 6(1) ECHR had been held to be applicable to it. As, under Maltese rules, retrial proceedings are filed before the same judge who decided the contested case,[594] courts are in fact called upon to decide whether or not they themselves have committed an error of legal interpretation or application in their previous decision. For that reason, the ECtHR concluded that there had been a violation of the right to fair trial.[595]

(5) **Finland**

In Finland, reopening a case – in the terms of the Finnish law, the 'annulment' of a final judgment – is possible on the ground of a manifest breach of law.[596] Specifically, in the terms of the civil and administrative procedure codes, a case can be reopened 'if the final judgment is based on manifestly erroneous application of the law or on an error which may have had an essential effect on the decision'. This exceptional remedy is therefore available for both national and EU law violations, but the breach must be qualified, and the reopening must be justified by reasons of individual or general interest. The jurisprudence has already provided some examples for the application of these rules in cases regarding EU law violations. Mention will therefore be made of six judgments, four rendered by the Korkein hallinto-oikeus, and two delivered by the Korkein oikeus.

In a judgment from 2009, the Korkein hallinto-oikeus declared that an administrative case can be reopened by the court on the ground of manifestly

[592] See also (LT) Lietuvos vyriausiojo administracinio teismo, 31/07/2009; ACA Europe 2008, National report of Lithuania, question 14.

[593] (MT) Code of Organization and Civil Procedure, Art 811(e). See also ACA Europe 2008, National report of Malta, question 8.

[594] (MT) Constitutional Court, judgment, 10/10/1991.

[595] (ECtHR) Judgment in *San Leonard Band Club v Malta*, §§ 43 and 64.

[596] (FI) Hallintolainkäyttölaki, 11 luku, 63 § (1)(2); Oikeudenkäymiskaari, 31 luku, 7–10 §.

erroneous application of EU law by the administrative authority.[597] However, the Korkein hallinto-oikeus dismissed the motion for retrial, since it concluded that no individual or general interest justified the reopening in the case.[598] In subsequent cases from 2010 and 2013, the Korkein hallinto-oikeus reached the same conclusion.[599] As for the decision of 2013, the dismissal was also based on the fact that the applicant had already been given compensation for the damages suffered in a liability action.

Then, in a judgment delivered in 2011, the Korkein hallinto-oikeus reopened a case and annulled, for the first time, one of its former final judgments on the ground of infringement of EU law.[600] The applicant requested the reopening of the final judgment, relying on an ECJ decision which made it clear that the interpretation of the EU law by the national court in the main proceedings was incorrect. Examining the motion for retrial, the Korkein hallinto-oikeus stated that the breach of the referral duty justified the reopening of the case. In fact, the ECJ case-law had not been sufficiently clear at the time of the main proceedings, which means that a request for preliminary ruling should have been submitted by the court.

As for civil matters, in a judgment rendered in 2007, the Korkein oikeus reopened the case and annulled a final judgment of a first-instance court, due to the manifestly erroneous application of EU law.[601] In this case, after the first-instance court's decision was pronounced, the ECJ handed down a judgment which interpreted the relevant provisions of the EU directive. Following this judgment, the Korkein oikeus itself changed its case-law concerning the interpretation of the EU provision at issue. Relying on the new case-law, the Korkein oikeus found in the retrial proceedings that the final judgment had applied the EU provisions erroneously. Hence, it declared the applicant's claim well founded. Finally, in another judgment, also pronounced in 2007, the Korkein oikeus declared inadmissible a motion for retrial because of the expiry of the time limit to submit such a request.[602]

In summary, reopening a case – in the terms of the Finnish rules, the 'annulment' of the final judgment – by reason of violation of EU law is possible and subject to the assessment of a case's specific circumstances under Finnish administrative and civil law.[603] As such, the necessity to set aside the res judicata is evaluated on a case-by-case basis. The time limit to submit a motion for retrial differs in administrative and civil matters. As for the former, they must

[597] (FI) Korkein hallinto-oikeus, 07/12/2009, reported by Kanninen 2014: 195–96.
[598] (FI) Hallintolainkäyttölaki, 11 luku, 63 § (1)(2). See also Kanninen 2014: 195.
[599] (FI) Korkein hallinto-oikeus, 30/06/2010, reported by Kanninen 2014: 196–97; Korkein hallinto-oikeus, 27/12/2013, reported in database JuriFast.
[600] (FI) Korkein hallinto-oikeus, 11/04/2011, reported by Kanninen 2014: 197.
[601] (FI) Korkein oikeus, 02/04/2007, reported Kanninen 2014: 193–94.
[602] (FI) Korkein oikeus, 02/04/2007, reported by Kanninen 2014: 194.
[603] (FI) Hallintolainkäyttölaki, 11 luku, 63 § (1)(2); Oikeudenkäymiskaari, 31 luku, 7–10 §.

be presented within five years following the judgment acquired res judicata;[604] as for the latter, the time limit is only one year.[605] Finnish law does not seem to attribute importance to the distinction whether the ECJ judgment was rendered before or after the national decision. In fact, under Finnish rules, the mere breach of law may be sufficient to justify retrial.[606] The question whether the violation became apparent due to an ECJ judgment delivered before or after the decision seems thus to be irrelevant.

(6) Sweden

Swedish procedural laws provide a general possibility for the courts to remedy a substantive defect in the final judgment.[607] This remedy may eventually be applied to misinterpretation of EU law by a final judgment.[608] However, there is no available case-law regarding the application of this remedy to violations of EU law.

c. Retrial Available Based on Violation of EU Law under Certain Circumstances

(1) Bulgaria

In Bulgarian law, procedural codes and case-law have both remained silent on whether an ECJ judgment may offer a ground for retrial.[609] Retrial is granted, inter alia, where a subsequent judgment by the ECtHR makes it necessary,[610] and also where new facts that could have had an influence on the final decision have been discovered.[611] The legal literature does not exclude, however, the possibility that new ECJ case-law could eventually be considered as a new fact, and could serve as a ground for retrial. In particular, Fartunova relies on two decisions of the Bulgarian highest courts to conclude that such reopening might eventually be possible in the event of violation of EU law, under certain conditions.

In the first decision, rendered in 2012, the Varhoven kasatsionen sad refused the motion for retrial as it had not found any connection between the underlying case and EU law.[612] According to Fartunova's interpretation of this judgment,

[604] (FI) Hallintolainkäyttölaki, 11 luku, 64 § (2).

[605] (FI) Oikeudenkäymiskaari, 31 luku, 10 §.

[606] Under the Finnish rules, both damages claim and application for retrial can be lodged where a final judgment proves to be contrary to EU law. See also Condon and van Leewen 2016: 239.

[607] (SE) Förvaltningsprocesslag, 37b §; Rättegångsbalk, 58 kap, § 1.

[608] ACA Europe 2008, National report of Sweden, questions 1, 4. See also Göransson 2014: 495. (SE) Skattebetalningslag, 21 kap, § 3, Göransson 2014: 493. See also (ECJ) judgment in *Åkerberg Fransson*.

[609] (BG) Grazhdanski protsesualen kodeks, Art 303; Aministrativen protsesualen kodeks, Art 239.

[610] (BG) Grazhdanski protsesualen kodeks, Art 303, § 1, 7); Aministrativen protsesualen kodeks, Art 99, § 1, 7) and 239, § 6).

[611] (BG) Grazhdanski protsesualen kodeks, Art 303, § 1, 1); Aministrativen protsesualen kodeks, Art 239, § 1.

[612] (BG) Varhoven kasatsionen sad, Reshenie, 09/02/2012, reported by Fartunova 2004: 159–60, rendered on the basis of Grazhdanski protsesualen kodeks, Art 303.

the situation would have been different had the case concerned EU law. In such a hypothetical situation, the infringement of the obligation to refer a question to the ECJ would have had the result of preventing the discovery of new facts having a potential influence on the final judgment.

In the second case, the Varhoven administrativen sad pronounced on the relationship between a violation of EU law and national rules on retrial concerning an administrative dispute. In its decision from 2012, it found that the conditions for retrial had not been met in the case.[613] According to Fartunova, a judgment of the ECJ can, however, constitute a new fact or circumstance justifying the reopening of the case if the applicant had only received knowledge of it after the contested decision was made.[614]

In short, even if the opinion of legal literature is in favour of an interpretation of national rules allowing retrial on the ground of infringement of EU law in Bulgaria, it remains to be seen whether the courts will follow this reasoning.

(2) **Poland**

Misinterpretation of law is not a ground for retrial in the Polish procedural codes.[615] The Sąd Najwyższy already decided, in a civil judgment rendered in 2009, that the inconsistency of a final judgment with EU law is not a reason for reopening cases.[616] As for administrative matters, retrial can be granted whenever an obligation under an international agreement requires it.[617] According to the legal literature, this rule can eventually serve as a legal basis for retrial on account of a subsequent ECJ judgment.[618] However, it is not possible to know how this rule is applied in practice, in the absence of relevant case-law.

Nevertheless, in Poland, fiscal authorities hold the right to revoke their previous decisions which prove to be inconsistent with EU law in the light of a subsequent ECJ judgment.[619] Authorities have this competence even if the final decision has already been confirmed by the administrative court.[620] As such, this procedure can be considered as a method for remedying a violation of EU law by the administrative court, which confirmed an erroneous administrative decision. However, this *Kühne & Heitz* remedy is only accepted in fiscal matters, as the possibility for the administrative authority to revoke its final decision by reason of a subsequent ECJ judgment that revealed the inconsistency of national

[613] Varhoven administrativen sad, Reshenie, 03/07/2012, reported by Fartunova 2004: 161, rendered on the basis of Aministrativen protsesualen kodeks, Art 239.

[614] Fartunova 2004: 161.

[615] (PL) Kodeks postępowania cywilnego, Art 403.

[616] (PL) Sąd Najwyższy, Postanowienie, 22/10/2009, reported by Mikłaszewicz 2014: 377, on the interpretation of the ground for reopening a final civil judgment.

[617] (PL) Prawo o postępowaniu przed sądami administracyjnymi, Art 273, § 3. See also Mikłaszewicz 2014: 376.

[618] Mikłaszewicz 2014: 376–78.

[619] (PL) Ordynacja podatkowa, Art 240, § 1, pts 9 and 11. See also ACA Europe 2008, National report of Poland, questions 1 and 4; Mikłaszewicz 2014: 374; Półtorak 2015: 231.

[620] (PL) Naczelny Sąd Administracyjny, Wyrok, 04/12/2008, reported by Mikłaszewicz 2014: 374.

judgments with EU law in administrative matters in general is subject to doctrinal debates.[621] Through several judgments, the Naczelny Sąd Administracyjny has clarified a few points regarding the application of this special remedy. First, the identity of the parties before the national court and the ECJ is not a condition for revoking the decision confirmed by the court.[622] However, appellants are required to specify the ECJ decision on which they rely in their action.[623] Moreover, the ECJ case-law must be new, in the sense that it should differ from previous case-law on the same question.[624] Finally, the time limit for a motion to declare a final judgment unlawful is one month after the publication of the ECJ judgment in the *Official Journal*.[625]

As a conclusion, the most suitable method for remedying a violation of EU law by national administrative bodies is the revocation of the contested decision by the administrative authority in Poland. As this remedy is available where the administrative court has already confirmed the decision, it may be suitable to remedy erroneous application of EU law by the national courts as well. Moreover, this remedy seems to be an effectively used technique to provide substantive relief for violation of EU law – however, it can only be applied in fiscal matters.

(3) **Romania**

In Romania, legislative provisions have been introduced to the administrative procedural code in order to recognise the violation of EU law as a specific ground for retrial.[626] Apparently, the sole violation of law is sufficient to reopen final judgments, and the identity of the parties is not required either. Therefore, even if the scope of application *ratione materiae* of this remedy is narrow, it provides generous protection in administrative cases. Moreover, this rule has already been applied on several occasions by the courts.

In one such judgment, dated 2012, the Curtea de Apel Timişoara (Court of Appeal, Timişoara) reopened the case and overturned its previous final judgment. The court held that the final judgment infringed the primacy of EU law, since it had not applied the directly effective provisions of the applicable EU directive.[627] In its judgment, the Curtea de Apel Timişoara pointed out that final

[621] See ACA Europe 2008, National report of Poland and Mikłaszewicz 2014: 373, 375.

[622] (PL) Wojewódzki Sąd Administracyjny w Olsztynie, Wyrok, 19/09/2013; Wojewódzki Sąd Administracyjny w Łodzi, Wyrok z 13/02/2014; Wojewódzki Sąd Administracyjny w Łodzi, Wyrok z 05/03/2014; Wojewódzki Sąd Administracyjny w Łodzi, Wyrok z 05/03/2014; Naczelny Sąd Administracyjny, Wyrok, 05/08/2010.

[623] (PL) Naczelny Sąd Administracyjny, Wyrok, 18/03/2011.

[624] (PL) Naczelny Sąd Administracyjny, Wyrok, 24/03/2010, reported by Mikłaszewicz 2014: 375. See also Ordynacja podatkowa, Art 247, § 1, pt. 3.

[625] (PL) Wojewódzki Sąd Administracyjny w Rzeszowie, Wyrok, 03/12/2009, reported by Mikłaszewicz 2014: 375.

[626] (RO) Legea nr 554/2004 contenciosului administrative, Art 21(2).

[627] (RO) Curtea de Apel Timişoara, 06/10/2012. In terms of the contested judgment, the applicant company was liable to pay VAT.

judgments contradicting EU law can be revised because of the non-observance of the primacy of EU law.[628] Several final judgments, mainly in fiscal matters, have also been reopened and overturned because of their inconsistency with EU law.[629]

Considering the ECJ case-law on state liability and on the principle of res judicata, it appears that Romanian retrial rules grant broader protection of EU rights than is required under EU law. Finally adjudicated administrative cases can be reopened by relying on ECJ judgments and there is no condition on the gravity of the breach. The mere violation of the principle of primacy of EU law, such as the non- or misapplication of EU rules, is sufficient to overturn a final administrative judgment. Moreover, there is no time limit for a motion for retrial and the identity of the parties in the national proceedings and in the proceedings before the ECJ is not a precondition for relying on the ECJ's subsequent judgment. As for the ECJ judgment providing a legal basis for retrial, it seems irrelevant whether it had been rendered before or after the contested national judgment is made. The procedural rules on retrial for violation of EU law do not exclude the possibility of relying on a previous ECJ judgment. Moreover, Romanian law accepts retrial because of the principle of primacy of EU law.[630] This may suggest that the violation of the EU norm is considered to be have been made with the delivery of the judgment. Subsequent ECJ case-law only makes the violation apparent. However, retrial on ground of EU law violation is limited to administrative matters – it cannot be used to reopen civil cases.[631]

(4) Slovakia

Under Slovakian rules, retrial on the ground of infringement of EU law is possible only in civil matters. According to the civil procedure code, if a final civil judgment proves contrary to ECJ case-law, this inconsistency is a special ground for retrial.[632] This provision was introduced into Slovakian law in 2008 in order to ensure coherence between ECJ and national case-law in EU law matters.[633] The identity of the parties in the national procedure and before the ECJ is not relevant. It is only the subject-matter of the two cases that needs to concern the same question of law. As there is no condition regarding the gravity of the infringement, the mere inconsistency with ECJ case-law is sufficient for a review of the final judgment. In that regard, national law has a wide scope of application.

[628] (RO) Legea nr 554/2004 contenciosului administrative, Art 21(2).

[629] (RO) Tribunalul Suceava, 19/05/2011, confirmed in appeal by Curtea de Apel Suceava, 10/11/2011; Tribunalul Suceava, 19/05/2011, confirmed in appeal by Curtea de Apel Suceava, 13/10/2011.

[630] (RO) Constituţia României, Arts 20(2), 148(2).

[631] See also (ECJ) opinion of AG Jääskinen in *Târşia*, paras 49–51; judgment in *Târşia*, para 34.

[632] (SK) Občiansky súdny poriadok, § 228(1) e). The amendments entered into force on 15 October 2008 and were introduced by Zákon č 384/2008 Z z, Čl I 127–28. The new Slovak civil procedures code has the same content, see Civilný sporový poriadok, § 397 e).

[633] The project of the law refers to the (ECJ) judgment in *Lucchini*.

However, the time limit set out by national law restricts the practical use of this remedy. Theoretically, no problem arises if the ECJ renders a judgment on the interpretation of the EU norm in question after the national judgment is delivered. In such a scenario, the applicant can ask for the reopening of the case for 20 days after the date on which they have official knowledge of the new ECJ case-law. However, if the applicant alludes to an ECJ judgment that was rendered prior to the contested national decision, the date from which the time limit starts to run is not obvious, since national case-law is divergent in this regard.

This remedy has already been applied in several cases by various courts, mainly in consumer law matters. For example, in a decision from 2013, the Krajský súd v Banskej Bystrici (Regional Court in Banská Bystrica) dismissed a motion for retrial introduced on the grounds that the final judgment was inconsistent with the ECJ case-law.[634] The regional court stated that the applicant has only 20 days after becoming aware of an ECJ decision to introduce a request for retrial. Since the ECJ judgment had already been published before the contested national decision was delivered, the time limit had already expired. Contrary to the above decision, the motion for retrial was accepted by several Slovakian courts, notwithstanding the fact that the ECJ judgment preceded the national decision.[635]

In summary, the mere violation of EU law is sufficient to reopen a civil case in Slovakia, and the identity of the parties is not required either. Therefore, even if the scope of application of this provision is narrow, it provides generous protection. Moreover, considering the exceptional nature of retrial under EU law, the conditions under Slovakian civil law even exceed the requirements established by the ECJ. This holds true even with regard to the seemingly strict time limits, according to which the deadline starts to run on the day when the ECJ judgment is published.

(5) United Kingdom

In the UK, cases can be reopened on discretionary grounds, on condition that the party has suffered substantive injustice as a result of unfair proceedings.[636] Two judgments delivered in cases based on an alleged violation of EU law are noteworthy in this regard.

In the first judgment, rendered in the *Edwards* case in 2010, the Supreme Court of England admitted the theoretical possibility of reopening cases due to the inconsistency of the final judgment with ECJ case-law. However, it denied

[634] (SK) Krajský súd Banská Bystrica, Uznesenie, 18/12/2012; Krajský súd Banská Bystrica, Uznesenie, 27/06/2013 and Krajský súd Trnava, Uznesenie, 09/07/2013.

[635] (SK) Okresný súd Prešov, Rozsudok, 08/10/2013; Okresný súd Rožňava, Uznesenie, 20/12/2013.

[636] (UK) Civil Procedure Rules, Rule 52.30. See also ACA Europe 2008, National report of the United Kingdom, questions 8 and 14; Kornezov 2014a: 830.

retrial in the case at hand, since it found that the applicant had not suffered injustice as a result of unfair proceedings.[637]

In the second judgment, delivered in 2010, the Court of Appeal concluded that the principle of effectiveness does not require setting aside national rules on retrial.[638] In this regard, the Court of Appeal specifically held that the principle of effectiveness did not require reopening adjudicated matters, by reason of violation of EU law. The position would have been different only if the conduct of the national authorities would have had the effect of depriving the appellants of any opportunity of enforcing their EU law rights.[639] It is noteworthy that the Court of Appeal arrived at this conclusion on the basis of EU law, and its argumentation is in line with the requirements set by the ECJ.

In conclusion, under UK law, retrial is possible but subject to the condition that the applicant suffered injustice as a result of unfair proceedings. This conclusion is in line with Kornezov's statement, according to which in England and Wales, while the bar created by cause of action estoppel is, in principle, absolute, issues previously decided may be reopened where 'special circumstances' justify this measure.[640] In UK law, the discretionary nature of judicial review is an important factor. According to the procedural rules, the reopening of a final decision must be necessary to avoid real injustice, and there must be no alternative effective remedy.[641] Moreover, an applicant in judicial review proceedings must obtain the permission of the court for the case to proceed to a full hearing, and permission will only be granted if the claim is arguable, in the sense that it has a real prospect of success. However, the process of judicial review is less formalised and is intended to provide a speedy remedy.[642]

(d) Retrial not Available Based on Violation of EU Law

(1) Belgium

Under Belgian procedural laws, misinterpretation of law in a final judgment cannot serve as a ground for retrial, regardless of whether the breach concerns national or EU rules.[643]

(2) Czech Republic

The Czech civil and administrative procedure codes do not allow for the reopening of cases on the ground of breach of national or EU rules, because of the

[637] (UK) Supreme Court, judgment, 15/12/2010, paras 34–36.

[638] (UK) Court of Appeal, judgment, 29/06/2010, paras 58–72, reported by Clément-Wiltz 2014: 450–51.

[639] Auburn, Moffett and Sharland 2013: § 4.82. See also Ormerod and Laird 2014: 6–7.

[640] Kornezov 2014a: 830.

[641] (UK) Civil Procedure Rules, Rule 52.30. See also ACA Europe 2008, National report of the United Kingdom, questions 8 and 14.

[642] ACA Europe 2008, National report of the United Kingdom, question 14.

[643] (BE) Arrêté du Régent déterminant la procédure devant la section du contentieux administratif du Conseil d'État, Arts 40–50, 50bis–50sexies; Code judiciaire, Arts 23–28 and 1113–14; Loi spéciale sur la Cour constitutionnelle Loi spéciale sur la Cour constitutionnelle. See also Houyet 2014: 123, 126–27.

principle of res judicata.[644] It is nevertheless possible to ask for the reopening of the case before the Ústavní soud if an international court has subsequently delivered a judgment in the same case that contradicts the national decision. However, this remedy appears to apply to ECtHR judgments, and not to ECJ decisions. Moreover, such an application for retrial is inadmissible if the consequences of the violation of human rights have been sufficiently remedied, for instance by providing just satisfaction via compensation.[645]

In addition, in the terms of a judgment of the Nejvyšší správní soud from 2010, a subsequent ECJ judgment on the interpretation of the EU norm is not a reason to revoke administrative decisions already confirmed by the administrative court.[646] This judgment concerned, therefore, a *Kühne & Heitz* situation, namely a review of an administrative decision which acquired res judicata. The Nejvyšší správní soud found that as this extraordinary remedy serves to correct factual mistakes and not the erroneous interpretation of law.[647]

(3) **Germany**

Similarly to most Member States, the inconsistency of a final judgment with national or EU law is not a ground for retrial according to the German procedural rules.[648]

(4) **Estonia**

Concerning the remedial system of Estonia, legislative provisions stating the grounds for retrial only make reference to ECtHR judgments, and not to ECJ decisions.[649] As such, there appears to be no provision applicable for EU law violations. Moreover, Estonian courts held that reopening cases is only possible if compensation for damages is not available, since Estonian laws give priority to liability claim over retrial.[650] However, as for the revocation of a final administrative decision, the authority has the right to revoke its decision, contrary to EU law, even if it has become final following the approval of the administrative court. This possibility appears to be given to Estonian administrative authorities under the general rules,[651] even if there is no specific case-law available in the field of EU law.[652]

[644] Petrlík 2014: 427. See also (CZ) Občanský soudní řád, § 159a(4), §§ 228–29; Zákon soudní řád správní, § 111.

[645] (CZ) Zákon o Ústavním soudu, § 119.

[646] (CZ) Nejvyšší správní soud, rozsudek, 27/10/2010, reported by Petrlík 2014: 420, 425.

[647] (CZ) Zákon správní řád, §§ 100–02; Zákon daňový řád, §§ 117–20. See also (CZ) Zákon správní řád, §§ 94–99; (CZ) Zákon daňový řád, §§ 121–24a; as well as Petrlík 2014: 421–24.

[648] (DE) Verwaltungsgerichtsordnung, § 153; Zivilprozessordnung, § 580. See also Dittert 2014: 66; Oberlandesgericht Köln, Urteil, 31/03/2004; Verwaltungsverfahrensgesetz (VwVfG), § 51.

[649] (EE) Halduskohtumenetluse seadustik, § 240(2) 8); Tsiviilkohtumenetluse seadustik, § 702(2) 8). See also ACA Europe 2008, National report of Estonia, question 14.

[650] (EE) Riigivastutuse seadus, § 15(1).

[651] (EE) Haldusmenetluse seadus, §§ 64–70 and §§ 71–74.

[652] ACA Europe 2008, National report of Estonia, questions 1–4, 8.

(5) Ireland

The reopening of cases in which the High Court or the Supreme Court has delivered a final judgment is not possible in Ireland either.[653] Moreover, in Ireland the principle of finality of judgments is interpreted and applied widely as the *Henderson* principle prevents any abuse of process in the sense that it does not allow a party advancing matters that should have been addressed in earlier proceedings. In its judgment rendered in 2017, the High Court dismissed an action based on violation of EU law, containing several claims, relying on the principle that prevents a party from raising legal points which could have been raised in earlier proceedings.[654]

(6) Greece

Greek law likewise does not provide a ground for retrial in cases of violation of national or EU rules by the final judgment.[655] Even so, the Areios Pagos (Greek Supreme Court of Cassation) has ruled that an ECtHR judgment can serve as a reason for reopening final judgments only in criminal cases.[656] As for civil or administrative disputes, an ECtHR judgment can only give rise to compensation, but cannot provide ground for reopening a final judgment.[657]

(7) Spain

In Spain, misinterpretation of law is not a ground for reopening finally adjudicated matters. The inconsistency of a final judgment with EU law is, therefore, not a reason for retrial either.[658] Nevertheless, since the modifications entered into force in 2015, inconsistency with an ECtHR judgment may serve as grounds to reopen a case.[659] However, the Spanish legislator has not provided for this

[653] (IR) *Blackhall v Grehan* [1995] 3 IR 208 and *LP v MP* [2002] 1 IR 219, reported by Paris 2014: 260.

[654] (IR) High Court, judgment, 17/10/2017. For a more complete presentation of this case, see s 2.III.B.iv.c.

[655] Retrial is not possible in civil matters and administrative matters. See (EL) Κώδικας Πολιτικής Δικονομίας, Αρθρο: 538–51, 544; Κώδικας Διοικητικής Δικονομίας, Αρθρο: 197; Άρειος Πάγος, 16/03/2011. See also Christianos 2014: 235–36. As for the possibility for the administrative bodies to revoke their own decisions, see Κώδικας Διοικητικής Διαδικασίας, Ο παρών Κώδικας κυρώθηκε με το πρώτο άρθρο του N 2690/1999, Αρθρο: 25.

[656] (EL) Κώδικας Ποινικής Δικονομίας, Αρθρο: 525(1). See also Christianos 2014: 235–36.

[657] (EL) Άρειος Πάγος, 14/12/2004; Άρειος Πάγος, 24/02/2012.

[658] (ES) Ley 29/1998 reguladora de la Jurisdicción Contencioso-administrativa, Art 102; Ley 1/2000 Enjuiciamiento Civil, Art 509–10; Ley de Enjuiciamiento Criminal, Art 954. The only exception comes from the field of state aid, where violation of EU rules is a ground for reimbursement of the illegal aide. See Ley 38/2003, de 17 de noviembre, General de Subvenciones, Arts 36–42; as well as ACA Europe 2008, National report of Spain; Sarmiento 2014: 175. In addition, illegal administrative decisions can be revoked or annulled by a superior administrative authority and may also be a ground for compensation. See, respectively, Ley 39/2015, de 1 de octubre, del Procedimiento Administrativo Común de las Administraciones Públicas, Arts 47, 106; Ley 40/2015 de Régimen Jurídico del Sector Público, Art 32.

[659] (ES) Ley 29/1998 reguladora de la Jurisdicción Contencioso-administrativa, Art 102.2. The amendment was introduced by Ley Orgánica 7/2015, de 21 de julio, por la que se modifica la Ley Orgánica 6/1985, de 1 de julio, del Poder Judicial, Art único 3. See also (ES) Ley 1/2000, de 7 de enero, de Enjuiciamiento Civil, Art 510.2, amended by the same Ley Orgánica 7/2015.

possibility in case of inconsistency with an ECJ judgment.[660] Two decisions are presented where a motion for retrial based on ECJ judgments were rejected by the Spanish supreme court.

In its judgment rendered in 2016, the Tribunal Supremo decided on the question whether a final judgment can be reopened following an ECJ decision interpreting the legal provision applicable to the case.[661] The Tribunal Supremo explained that retrial is only possible in cases when the newly discovered evidence or document had already existed at the time when the contested decision was made. In the case at hand, retrial could not be granted, as the ECJ judgment was not a document or evidence, but a judicial decision regarding the interpretation of legal norms. Moreover, the ECJ judgment was rendered after the contested judicial decision was made. Finally, the claimant has not presented any fact qualifying force majeure which would have prevented it from using the evidence in the main proceedings. Afterwards, the Tribunal Supremo made it clear that under Spanish law there is no possibility to reopen a case following an ECJ decision. Then, in another judgment delivered in 2016, the Tribunal Supremo reiterated its case-law set forth in the above-presented decision.[662]

(8) France

Under French law, it is not possible to compromise the res judicata of a final judgment by invoking an erroneous interpretation of law. Retrial is therefore not possible on grounds of misinterpretation of national or EU law, in either administrative or civil matters.[663]

(9) Croatia

In Croatia, although the civil procedure act provides for a revision against a second-instance decision when necessary in the light of the jurisprudence of the ECJ,[664] revision is excluded against the second-instance decisions of the national supreme court.[665]

(10) Italy

In the Italian legal system, the principle of res judicata is of paramount importance;[666] hence, retrial is not an accepted method for remedying

[660] (ES) Nonetheless, the same act modificatif introduced a new provision (Art 4bis) into the Ley Orgánica 6/1985 which states that the national judges shall apply EU law in accordance with the case-law of the ECJ. See (ES) Ley Orgánica 7/2015, de 21 de julio, por la que se modifica la Ley Orgánica 6/1985, Art único 2

[661] (ES) Tribunal Supremo, Sentencia, 18/02/2016.

[662] (ES) Tribunal Supremo, Sentencia, 19/12/2016.

[663] See Dubos et al 2014: 210–17. See also (FR) Code de justice administrative, Art R421-1; Conseil d'État, décision, 26/10/2001; Conseil d'État, décision, 29/03/2006, reported by Dubos et al 2014: 200–10.

[664] (HR) Zakon o parničnom postupku, članak 382(2)(3).

[665] (HR) Zakon o parničnom postupku, članak 382.a(1).

[666] (IT) Codice Civile, Art 2909; Codice di procedura civile, Art 395. See also Legge sul procedimento amministrativo, Art 21-nonies; Gencarelli 2014: 275–78.

misinterpretations of law. In the national follow-up of the *Lucchini* judgment,[667] the Tribunale di Roma denied retrial, even following the ECJ decision rendered in the same case.[668] According to the court, the principle of res judicata does not allow the reopening of the case, despite the preliminary ruling by the ECJ. On the other hand, in a judgment from 2008, the Corte Suprema di Cassazione accepted, as a consequence of the *Lucchini* judgment, that res judicata can be set aside in very exceptional circumstances.[669] As in Italy retrial can be granted in very exceptional, state aid-related cases only, it cannot be considered as a generally available remedy for violation of EU law.

(11) **Latvia**

In Latvia, the judgment of the ECtHR or other international or supranational courts can serve as a ground for retrial – in the terms of the Latvian rules, 'adjudication of matters de novo' – in connection with newly discovered facts.[670] The ECJ is considered to be one such international court. However, for the application of this provision, the jurisprudence appears to require that the judgment of the international court be made in the same case as is concerned by the motion for retrial.[671]

(12) **Luxembourg**

Under the Luxembourgish procedural rules, the misinterpretation of national or EU law by a final judgment is not a reason for retrial either.[672]

(13) **Hungary**

Hungarian courts have repeatedly held that a breach of law in a final judgment is not a ground for retrial according to the procedural rules.[673] It is noteworthy that, during the codification of the new Hungarian Code of Civil Procedure,[674] the idea emerged whether retrial should be granted on the ground of violation of EU law by a final judgment.[675] In the end, the idea was rejected; and this possibility does not appear in the new act which entered into force in 2018. Hence, the new code did not amend the provisions of the previous act, and does not grant retrial based on violation of EU law by a final judgment. However, the new code

[667] (IT) Tribunale di Roma, Sentenza, 23/03/2011, reported by Gencarelli 2014: 273.

[668] See (ECJ) judgment in *Lucchini*.

[669] (IT) Corte di Cassazione, sentenza, 19/05/2008, reported by Gencarelli 2014: 273.

[670] (LV) Administratīvā procesa likums, 353 pants 6); Civilprocesa likums, 479 pants 6).

[671] (LV) Latvijas Republikas Augstākās tiesas, Senāta Administratīvo lietu departamenta, spriedums, 14/11/2011.

[672] (LU) Nouveau Code de Procédure Civile, Art 617. See also (LU) Règlement grand-ducal du 8 juin 1979 relatif à la procédure à suivre par les administrations relevant de l'Etat et des communes, Art 8.

[673] (HU) A polgári perrendtartásról szóló 1952 évi III törvény, 260 §.

[674] The Concept of the new Hungarian Civil Procedure Act (approved by the Government on 14 January 2015).

[675] The Concept of the new Hungarian Civil Procedure Act, annex VI, point VII.

provides for the possiblity to reopen a finally adjudicated civil judgment based on an ECtHR judgment.[676]

In particular, the judgment by the Fővárosi Törvényszék (Budapest Municipal Court, Hungary) applying the above principle in an EU-related case[677] was confirmed by the Alkotmánybíróság (Constitutional Court) in 2014.[678] In this regard, the Fővárosi Törvényszék explained that a subsequent judgment by the ECJ, rendered in a distinct procedure, cannot be considered as a new fact, and therefore cannot justify reopening of the case. The Alkotmánybíróság emphasised in this regard that the ECJ judgment has only ex nunc effect.

In addition, in a request for a preliminary ruling submitted in 2017, the Székesfehérvári Törvényszék asked several questions on the scope of the obligation to reopen finally adjudicated matters in the event of a violation of EU law.[679] At the origin of this referral was an earlier decision rendered in a matter of public procurement by a Hungarian court which denied retrial, as it found that there was no ground for the application of this extraordinary remedy.[680]

(14) The Netherlands

The Dutch procedural rules do not provide a legal basis for retrial on the ground of misinterpretation of law.[681] National case-law has also confirmed that, in the application of Dutch procedural rules, a subsequent ECJ judgment on the interpretation of the EU norm is not a reason for reopening cases.[682]

One such judgment was delivered by the Hoge Raad in 2011.[683] In that decision, the court concluded that a subsequent ECJ judgment cannot be considered as a fact or circumstance which occurred before, and was unknown at the time the contested judgment was made. Moreover, the Hoge Raad emphasised the importance of legal certainty and res judicata, making reference to ECJ judgments on this matter.[684]

[676] (HU) A polgári perrendtartásról szóló 2016 évi CXXX törvény, 393 §.

[677] (HU) Fővárosi Törvényszék, végzés, 3.Kf.650.165/2013/3.

[678] (HU) Alkotmánybíróság, végzés, 07/07/2014 reported by Varga in Reflets no 3/2014: 27. See also A polgári perrendtartásról szóló 1952 évi III törvény, XIII fejezet, 260 §; A polgári perrendtartásról szóló 2016 évi CXXX törvény, 393 §.

[679] (ECJ) Judgment *Hochtief Solutions AG Magyarországi Fióktelepe*. For more detailed information about the case, see s 2.III.B.iv.b

[680] (HU) Fővárosi Törvényszék, végzés, 18/11/2015.

[681] (NL) Algemene wet bestuursrecht, Art 8:119; Wetboek van Burgerlijke Rechtsvordering, Artikel 382. See also ACA Europe 2008, National report of the Netherlands, introduction. See also Algemene wet bestuursrecht, Art 4:48, 4:49.

[682] (NL) Centrale Raad van Beroep, 17/11/2006, reported in ACA Europe 2008, National report of the Netherlands, question 8; Afdeling bestuursrechtspraak van de Raad van State, 27/10/2004, reported in ACA Europe 2008, National report of the Netherlands, question 8.

[683] (NL) Hoge Raad, Uitspraak, 24/06/2011, reported by Marguery and van Harten 2014: 348; Centrale Raad van Beroep, 17/11/2006. Algemene wet bestuursrecht, Art 8:119; Wetboek van Burgerlijke Rechtsvordering, Art 382.

[684] (ECJ) Judgments in *Köbler*, para 38; in *Kühne & Heitz*, para 24; in *Kapferer*, para 24.

There is no legal basis for retrial in the event of violation of EU law by a final judgment in the Netherlands. Consequently, Dutch courts reject motions for retrial submitted on these grounds. Moreover, the Tweede Camer (Lower House) argued that there was no reason to adopt legislative amendments allowing the reopening of cases following ECJ and ECtHR judgments. In this regard, the panel pointed out that state liability for judicial errors has already been recognised and it was sufficient to remedy these violations.[685]

(15) **Austria**

There are two judgments reported from Austria confirming that, under this regime, a subsequent ECJ judgment on the interpretation of the EU norm is not a reason for reopening proceedings.

In this regard, according to the judgment of the VwGH rendered in 2009, there is no provision in the General Administrative Procedure Act to allow retrial on this ground.[686] As for civil matters, the OGH rendered a similar decision regarding the interpretation of the Code of Civil Procedure in 2012.[687] Moreover, the same rule applies equally to fiscal matters.[688]

(16) **Portugal**

Since 2008, Portuguese legal provisions provide a ground for reopening a case where the final judgment is contrary to a decision of an international court. The international court must have jurisdiction vis-à-vis Portugal[689] – the ECJ qualifies as one such court. However, it is not obvious whether the judgment of the international court must be made in the same case, or only regarding the same matter of law. In the absence of relevant case-law, the position of Portuguese courts is not yet known.

(17) **Slovenia**

In Slovenia, the reopening of a case is possible on limited grounds – linked, for example, to the existence of new facts or a false statement by a witness – once a final judgment has been given in the dispute. As such, the inconsistency with EU law of a final judgment is not a reason for retrial under Slovenian procedural rules.[690] As for the revocation of a final administrative decision, no act provides

[685] (NL) Tweede Kamer, 12/08/2005. See also ACA Europe 2008, National report of the Netherlands, question 8, and Algemene wet bestursrecht, Art 8:88.

[686] See also (AT) Verwaltungsgerichtshof, Erkenntnis, 21/09/2009, reported by Pelzl 2014: 97; Allgemeines Verwaltungsverfahrensgesetz, §§ 68 and 69; Bundesabgabenordnung, §§ 299 and 303; Pelzl 2014: 98–104.

[687] (AT) OGH, Beschluss, 12/06/2012, reported by Pelzl 2014:100, rendered on the basis of Zivilprozessordnung, Arts 530–31.

[688] (AT) Bundesabgabenordnung, § 303; Pelzl 2014: 98–104.

[689] (PT) Código de Processo Civil, Art 696º f); Código de Processo nos Tribunais Administrativos, Artigo 154º. See ACA Europe 2008, National report of Portugal, questions 1, 9.

[690] (SI) Zakon o upravnem sporu, 96 člen. See also Trstenjak and Plaustajner 2014: 463, 473.

a legal basis for a review of a final administrative decision based on a misinterpretation of EU law. However, a judgment by the Upravno sodišče (Slovenian Administrative Court) of 2008 deals with this possibility.

This judgment seems to suggest that administrative authorities can revoke a final administrative decision which acquired res judicata as a result of a judgment based on a misinterpretation of EU law.[691] However, as Trstenjak and Plaustajner warn, this conclusion must be treated with caution. In fact, as these authors point out, the Upravno sodišče did not refer to a particular national legal provision in this regard, but to the ECJ judgment alone. In this regard, neither the legislation applicable within the administrative procedure, nor the legislation applicable within the administrative dispute, provides an obvious legal basis for a review of a final administrative decision based on a misinterpretation of EU law.[692]

In conclusion, Slovenian rules do not provide a ground for retrial in the event of violation of EU law by a final judgment.

e. Conclusion on the Remedy of Retrial

(1) Comparative Analysis of National Rules

The above points demonstrate that retrial on the ground of breach of EU law appears to be an effectively used remedy in Finland, in Romania (in administrative matters) and in Slovakia (in civil matters). It has also been accepted in Lithuania (in administrative cases), and under special circumstances in the UK. In Lithuania, Finland, Romania and Slovakia, cases have actually been reopened due to violation of EU law in the final judgment.[693]

In two national laws, legislative provisions had been introduced into the procedural codes in 2008 in order to recognise the violation of EU law as a specific ground for retrial. It has been the case in Romania, where amendments concerned the administrative procedural code, and in Slovakia, where the civil procedural code was amended.

In Lithuania, Finland and the UK, the application of retrial to breaches of EU law is possible due to the broad scope of application of this remedy. In these legal systems, retrial is granted in the event of manifest, substantive or extraordinary breach of law. In this regard, legal rules in Denmark, Malta and Sweden

[691] (SI) Upravno sodišče Republike Slovenije, Odločba, 17/06/2008, reported by Trstenjak and Plaustajner 2014: 470–80.

[692] See (SI) Zakon o splošnem upravnem postopku – ZUP, 260 člen and 274–77 člen; Trstenjak and Plaustajner 2014: 463, 472.

[693] ACA Europe 2008, National report of Finland; (RO) Curtea de Apel Timişoara, Secţia contencios administrativ şi fiscal, 06/10/2012; (SK) Civilný sporový poriadok, § 397 e), see also Občiansky súdny poriadok, § 228(1) e); (LT) Lietuvos vyriausiojo administracinio teismo, 10/04/2008, nutartis administracinėje byloje Nr P444-129/2008; Lietuvos Respublikos administracinių bylų teisenos įstatymas, 156 straipsnis. See also ACA Europe 2008, National report of Lithuania, questions 1–4, 11; Valutytė 2014: 301.

are similar, and therefore also seem capable of offering adequate protection. Moreover, in Poland, fiscal authorities hold and exercise the right to revoke their previous decisions on the ground of infringement of EU law.[694]

The Romanian and Slovak solutions appear particularly favourable regarding the application of EU law. This is mainly because the identity of parties in the national procedure and before the ECJ is not relevant, and the only criterion is that the subject-matter of the two cases concern the same matter of law. Moreover, a violation of EU law alone is sufficient to reopen a final judgment, and the gravity of the infringement need not be considered. This solution may probably be attributed to the willingness of the national legislator to apply EU law correctly before the national courts – taking into account the reality that, for multiple reasons, judges of the new Member States are often not specialists in this matter of law. In fact, this new ground for retrial might be assimilated to the widely used criterion of 'discovery of new facts'. In addition, the fact that this new ground for retrial is applicable only in civil matters in Slovakia, and only in administrative matters in Romania, led us to believe that the legislative amendments aimed to address specific issues that had been discovered, and were not part of a strategic vision regarding national remedies in the event of a violation of EU law. Consequently, the specific scope of application of this remedy may cause discrepancies within the same national legal order regarding the remedies provided in different matters of law (administrative and civil), or with regard to violating rules that have a different origin (national, EU, international).

The other group of Member States allowing retrial based on violation of EU law appear to use a more coherent framework. In these Member States, retrial is possible in cases of manifest, substantive or extraordinary breach of law. These criteria seem particularly suitable to embrace violations of EU law in situations where it is necessary, because of, for example, the gravity of violation or the extent of the prejudice suffered. It also gives magistrates the necessary flexibility to assess the particularities and circumstances of the case at hand. However, the use of such a general criterion is governed by the legal traditions of the Member States.

In the above-mentioned Member States, the remedies of reopening or revocation seem to offer an at least equivalent protection to individuals' rights as *Köbler* liability. Retrial even appears to be more efficient in practice than a liability claim. This is partly due to the fact that while retrial is of an objective nature, liability is a subjective remedy, where the gravity of the breach is also evaluated. Consequently, even the tort on the part of the court is not necessary for retrial – as opposed to a liability claim.[695]

[694] In Poland, the reopening of the administrative procedure on the ground of breach of an international agreement does also exist. See (PL) Prawo o postępowaniu przed sądami administracyjnymi; as well as ACA Europe 2008, National report of Poland, questions 1, 4; Mikłaszewicz 2014: 373–75.

[695] Retrial has a wider scope of application than liability, also because the infringement of the substantive EU norm is sufficient to reopen the case, and the violation by the court of a procedural obligation is not a condition. However, Sowery (2016: 1721) points out that the ECJ judgments

Nevertheless, the conclusion remains that in most Member States retrial is not possible based on a violation of EU law.

(2) **Relationship between State Liability and Retrial**

It is also interesting to note that the relationship between the remedies of state liability and retrial varies from state to state. However, the conclusion that the cumulative use of them is not necessary seems to be uniform throughout the legal systems.

In this respect, there have been national decisions in which the liability claim was dismissed on the grounds that the contested national decision had already been reopened, and, consequently, compensation was not necessary to remedy the damages suffered. In this regard, in a judgment delivered in 2008, the Lithuanian Vyriausiasis administracinis teismas acknowledged liability of the state for final decisions of administrative courts contrary to EU law, but nevertheless dismissed the claimant's request for compensation in the case at hand.[696] The reason for the dismissal of the liability action was that the case in which the alleged infringement of EU law had occurred had been reopened in the meantime and it was thus not able to give rise to damages. Similarly, in a judgment delivered in 2013, the Finnish Korkein hallinto-oikeus dismissed a motion for retrial concerning a case in which it had delivered a final judgment.[697] It reached this decision after having concluded that there had been no specific reasons justifying the reopening of the case, and also because the applicant had already been given compensation in a liability action for the damages suffered.

In the six Member States where retrial is available on the general grounds of 'manifest infringement of substantive rules' (Denmark, Malta, Finland, Sweden, the UK and Lithuania in administrative cases), national provisions appear to be sufficiently wide to embrace violations of EU law. The case-law of the Finnish, Lithuanian and UK courts has already confirmed this statement. Since most of these Member States accept, at least theoretically, the application of the *Köbler* principle as well, there is a possibility of double remedies. Moreover, no hierarchy appears to exist between the two courses of action in these Member States. Consequently, it is for the claimant to decide which remedy to seek; and there is no sign of a clear preference for the use of one or another in this regard. This can be explained by the fact that the criteria to evaluate the gravity of the breach are very similar for the two types of remedies.

setting an obligation to grant retrial on the basis of violation of EU law generally involved a manifestly inappropriate behaviour (judgment in *Lucchini*), and/or a possible continuous disregard of EU rules (judgments in *Klausner Holz Niedersachsen*, *Fallimento Olimpiclub* and *Commission v Slovakia*). In other words, the intervention was only warranted where there was a problem of sufficient gravity.

[696] (LT) Lietuvos vyriausiojo administracinio teismo, 24/04/2008. For a more detailed presentation of the case, see s 2.III.B.ii.e.

[697] (FI) Korkein hallinto-oikeus, 27/12/2013. For a more detailed presentation of the case, see s 2.IV.A.iv.b(5).

This duplication of remedies is also a theoretical possibility in the three Member States where retrial is guaranteed on the ground of inconsistency with judgments of international courts (Latvia, Poland and Portugal). However, if these rules imply requiring the identity of parties in the national procedure and before the international court, retrial will have a much narrower and quite different scope of application than *Köbler* liability. As for the two states where specific rules have been introduced to allow retrial on the ground of infringement of EU law (Romania, Slovakia), the duplication of remedies is not excluded either.

To conclude, the cumulative use of the two remedies seems unnecessary. As the Romanian government in the *Târşia*[698] case has suggested: it is irrelevant in terms of EU law which possibility is granted in the Member State so long as the rights of the individual are effectively protected.[699] Therefore, where a retrial can be used to remedy a violation of the EU rights by a final judgment, a liability claim may be superfluous and unnecessary. Moreover, in cases where there is no need to prove a qualified breach of law to allow a retrial (Romanian administrative and Slovakian civil law), this remedy offers a higher standard of judicial protection than the *Köbler* liability.

However, in most legal systems retrial is more exceptional than a liability claim. Even the case-law of the ECJ reflects this position.[700] What is interesting for the present analysis is that several legal systems establish *expressis verbis* a hierarchy between retrial and state liability. Such explicit statements have been found in six Member States, although not necessarily in the context of EU law (Bulgaria, Czech Republic, Estonia, Greece, Spain and the Netherlands). Under Bulgarian legislative rules, retrial is only possible if it is necessary to remedy an injustice suffered.[701] In the Czech Republic, a motion for retrial on the ground of breach of fundamental rights is inadmissible if the consequences of the violation have already been remedied, for instance by providing just satisfaction.[702] Similarly, Estonian law gives priority to a liability claim over retrial.[703] The Riigikohus (Supreme Court) stated, concerning ECHR violations, that reopening cases is only possible if compensation by damages is not available.[704] In Greece, the Areios Pagos pointed out that a judgment of the ECtHR can only give rise to compensation, but not to retrial.[705] In the Netherlands, the Tweede Camer reasoned that there was no reason to adopt legislative amendments allowing cases to be reopened on the ground of their inconsistency with ECJ

[698] (ECJ) Opinion of AG Jääskinen in *Târşia*, para 29.

[699] The subsidiary nature of the liability claim to the retrial seems to be accepted by the ECJ as well. See (ECJ) Judgment in *Târşia*, para 40.

[700] (ECJ) Judgments in *Kapferer*, paras 20–21; in *Fallimento Olimpiclub*, paras 22–23; in *Impresa Pizzarotti*, paras 54, 59, 62, 64; in *Commission v Slovakia*, paras 59–60. See also Kornezov 2014a: 839–40.

[701] (BG) Grazhdanski protsesualen kodeks, Art 303; Aministrativen protsesualen kodeks, Art 239.

[702] (CZ) Zákon o Ústavním soudu, § 119.

[703] (EE) Riigivastutuse seadus, § 7(1), (2^1) on § 7.

[704] (EE) Riigikohtu halduskolleegiumi, 22/02/2010; Riigikohtu üldkogu, 10/03/2008.

[705] (EL) Άρειος Πάγος, 24/02/2012; Άρειος Πάγος, 14/12/2004.

and ECtHR judgments. To arrive at that conclusion, the Tweede Camer emphasised that the state is already obliged to compensate for the damages suffered.[706] The Spanish Tribunal Supremo pronounced on 1 September 1991 that even if retrial was not possible, a liability claim could be lodged.[707]

On the other hand, in several legal systems, liability claims are considered as offering only subsidiary, secondary relief in cases where primary actions have not succeeded. For example, the case-law of the German BGH reflects this position.[708] Similarly, in Poland, the declaration of unlawfulness of a final judgment – which is a procedural element of a liability claim – can only be introduced if the claimant has used all remedies available to them before lodging the liability claim. State responsibility is therefore secondary to all other remedies.[709]

(3) Prior or Subsequent Judgment

As for the date of the delivery of the ECJ judgment, Slovakian rules reveal an interesting question, concerning the extent to which it is relevant whether the ECJ rendered its judgment on which the applicant relies before or after the delivery of the national decision.[710] As regards the gravity of the breach, violation of established case-law is more serious than a breach that became clear only after the national decision was made. It can therefore be wondered whether it does make any difference if the ECJ judgment was delivered before or after the erroneous national decision. This issue can be examined from several points of view.

From the point of view of EU law, two remarks can be made. On the one hand, in *Kühne & Heitz*, the ECJ made specific reference to a *subsequent* ECJ judgment as a ground for revocation. This conclusion appears logical, since, in comparative law, the theory of retrial is strongly associated with the concepts of *new* facts or new law. However, and on the other hand, the ECJ interprets an EU norm with retroactive effect in a preliminary procedure.[711] The legal doctrine and the case-law seem to agree on the conclusion that an ECJ judgment giving interpretation of an EU provision is neither a new law nor a new fact. On this basis, there is no underlying legal foundation to grant retrial by reason of inconsistency of a national judgment with a subsequent ECJ judgment. The ECJ case-law – which is especially restrictive in this regard and requires retrial only in exceptional circumstances – does not seem to contradict this main, theoretical rule.

Considering the above two issues from the Member States' point of view, the following conclusions can be reached. On the one hand, the date of the ECJ

706 (NL) Tweede Kamer, 12/08/2005.

707 (ES) Tribunal Supremo, Sentencia, 01/09/1991. See also Sarmiento 2014: 170–74.

708 (DE) BGH, Urteil, 09/10/2003, reported by Dittert 2014: 77.

709 (PL) Kodeks postępowania cywilnego, Art 424^1, § 1. See also Mikłaszewicz 2014: 379.

710 See also Sowery 2016: 1715–20.

711 (ECJ) Judgments in *Denkavit italiana*, para 16; in *Kühne & Heitz*, para 21; in *Kempter*, para 35; in *Manea*, para 53; as well as order in *Commission v Ireland*, C-455/08, para 39.

judgment is often irrelevant in Member States where retrial is provided due to inconsistency with the EU law of a final judgment. The exception is Slovakian law. However, neither Finnish nor Romanian or Polish rules distinguish according to the date of the delivery of the ECJ judgment.[712] Considering the above statement on the role of the preliminary ruling of the ECJ – ie to give a general explanation for the correct application of the existing EU rule – this latter standpoint cannot be questioned. On the other hand, the main reason why most Member States refuse to allow reopening cases on the ground of infringement of EU law in a final judgment that only became clear in hindsight is the absence of any *new* law or new fact.

B. Constitutional Complaint on the Ground of Infringement of the Lawful Judge Principle

i. Right to One's Lawful Judge and the Obligation to Make a Preliminary Reference to the ECJ

There is another, constitutional path in several Member States to annul a final judgment that is contrary to EU law, in particular by reason of the violation of the obligation to request a preliminary ruling. This remedy is the constitutional complaint on the ground of breach of the right to a lawful judge[713] or a fair trial,[714] expressly protected under most constitutional regimes.[715] Should the constitutional court conclude that such a violation had taken place during the procedure before the national court, the usual consequence of that finding is the annulment of the judgment concerned.[716] Via this constitutional path,

[712] If a time limit is applied by national laws, it seems to start running at the earliest on the day of the delivery of the national judgment. If there is a subsequent ECJ judgment, it starts running when the ECJ decision is pronounced.

[713] In several Member States the English equivalents of the original term would be 'the right to one's statutory judge', or 'the right to a judge assigned by the law' or 'the right of access to the court appointed by law'. In this book, only the term 'right to a lawful judge' will be used.

[714] The violation of the referral duty can equally be construed more generally as disregard of the right to judicial protection or a right to a fair trial. This is the solution adopted by the Spanish and Polish Constitutional Courts. See Navrátilová, M (n.d.) 'The Preliminary Ruling before the Constitutional Courts' www.law.muni.cz/sborniky/dp08/files/pdf/mezinaro/navratilova.pdf; as well as (PL) Trybunał Konstytucyjny, Wyrok, Kp 3/08, reported by Mikłaszewicz 2014: 363; Konstytucja Rzeczypospolitej Polskiej, Art 45, § 1.

[715] (CZ) Listina základních práv a svobod, Čl 38 odst 1; (DE) Grundgesetz für die Bundesrepublik Deutschland, Art 101, Abs 1, S 2; (EE) Eesti Vabariigi põhiseadus, § 24; (ES) Constitución Española, Art 24; (AT) Bundesverfassungsgesetz, Art 83(2); (SK) Ústava Slovenskej republiky, Čl 46 ods 1, Čl 48 ods 1; (SI) Ustava Republike Slovenije, 23 člen. It is noteworthy that there is no explicit reference in the French legislative rules to the right to a lawful judge; however, the principle is applied by the judges on the basis of several fundamental rights. See Code de l'organisation judiciaire, Art L111-5; Jeuland 2008: 33–42.

[716] To ensure clarity and mutual understanding, a unification of terminology has been made when referring to these principles, procedures or remedies in English. The term 'annulment' is used in the context of appeals on points of law or constitutional complaints, where the constitutional or

constitutional courts contribute, on the one hand, to secure citizens' access to the ECJ, and, on the other, to remedy any violation of the obligation by the national court to consult the ECJ in the case.[717]

The application of this remedy is strongly related to the method of cooperation between national courts and the ECJ, provided under the EU Treaty. Therefore, considering the connection between constitutional remedy and the procedure for preliminary ruling, the main characteristics of the latter will be briefly discussed here. The role of this procedure is to provide a possibility for national courts to ask for – and for the ECJ to give – an authentic interpretation of the EU rule relevant to the case. Due to the direct effect of EU law, EU provisions are applied by national courts within the national proceedings, without the necessary involvement of the ECJ. However, national courts can turn for help to the more competent judicial organ regarding the correct interpretation of EU norms, through the procedure for preliminary ruling. Moreover, the preliminary proceedings allow the ECJ to retain the final word on the interpretation of EU rules. This authority of interpretation is guaranteed by the rule declaring that – with regard to national courts adjudicating at last instance – the option of submitting a request for preliminary ruling turns into an obligation under certain circumstances. This is the element where the right of the party to have a question referred to the ECJ in their case emerges.[718]

However, several important limitations must be set before examining whether, and to what extent, a constitutional complaint can be compared with *Köbler* liability. On the one hand, this remedy internalises the breach, in the sense that a constitutional complaint is offered against a breach of a national fundamental provision and not on the basis of a violation of EU law.[719] Consequently, the use of this remedy is not required under EU law but remains entirely at the discretion of the Member States. Accordingly, there is no ECJ case-law on this matter either. On the other hand, this remedy can only be provided if two preconditions are fulfilled in the Member State's constitutional law. As the violation of the constitutional right usually consists of the violation of the right to a lawful judge,[720] the ECJ must be recognised as such a judge in the Member State. Consequently, if the ECJ, as lawful judge of the case at hand, has been unlawfully excluded from the procedure, this could amount to a breach of the party's constitutional right. However, only five Member States have so far qualified

supreme court annuls, overturns or reverses a judgment. However, when it offers clarity and simplicity without compromising precision, the judicial decision rendered on appeal is described with regard to its outcome vis-à-vis the original claim (eg 'dismissed the claim'), and not with regard to its outcome vis-à-vis the appealed decision ('annulled or confirmed the contested decision').

[717] Lacchi 2015b: 1663–1700; Lacchi 2016: 692–98; Valutytė 2012a: 1173–74.

[718] See also Lacchi 2015a: 97–99.

[719] Lenaerts 2003: 881; Lacchi 2016: 696–98.

[720] The violation of the obligation to make a preliminary reference can equally be construed more generally as disrespect towards the right to judicial protection or a right to a fair trial.

the ECJ as a legal judge within the meaning of their fundamental laws (Czech Republic, Germany, Austria, Slovakia and Slovenia).[721]

The other condition is the existence of the possibility for individuals to raise constitutional complaints in the national legal order.[722] This remedy, which provides infringed individuals with the right to bring their case before their country's constitutional court, is recognised in 11 Member States (Belgium, Czech Republic, Germany, Spain, Croatia, Cyprus, Latvia, Hungary, Austria, Slovenia and Slovakia).[723] However, not all of these regimes allow individuals to contest a judicial act before the constitutional court (Belgium and Latvia).

It is equally important that there are several rules under EU law determining the conditions under which a request for a preliminary ruling must be submitted to the ECJ. Article 267 TFEU establishes the primary rule in this regard. Under this provision, if a question on the interpretation of the EU law is raised before a court against whose decisions there is no judicial remedy, this court is bound to bring the matter before the ECJ. However, the ECJ has set a threefold limit to the obligation to make a reference in its judgment in *Cilfit*.[724] According to the *Cilfit* exceptions, the national supreme court is exempted from the obligation to refer a question in the following situations: first, if the question is not relevant; second, if the question raised has already been answered by the ECJ decision in other proceedings; and third, if the correct application of the EU law is so obvious as to leave no scope for any reasonable doubt. The second and third *Cilfit* criteria – known respectively as *acte éclairé* and *acte clair* doctrines – link

[721] (CZ) Listina základních práv a svobod, Čl 38 odst 1; (DE) Grundgesetz für die Bundesrepublik Deutschland, Art 101, Abs 1, S 2; (AT) Bundesverfassungsgesetz, Art 83(2); (SK) Ústava Slovenskej republiky, Čl 46 ods 1, Čl 48 ods 1; (SI) Ustava Republike Slovenije, 23 člen.

[722] In most Member States, the constitutional court's competence is to examine the constitutionality of legal provisions in abstracto, but not their application in a specific case. See Cour de justice de l'Union européenne 2009: 32, 67, 103, 127, 151, 195, 228, 266, 284, 367, 396, 417, 432, 447, 478, 505, 532, 534, 548, 565, 589, 660 and 685; as well as Venice Commission 2011: 16, 23–24, 49–50, 61–63. However, in Member States where the constitutional relevance of the right of the parties to be referred before the ECJ is recognised, but where the individual constitutional complaint does not exist, this right might be invoked before and defended by the courts of general jurisdiction in appeal proceedings. See Valutytė 2012a: 1183; as well as the case-law of the OGH on this matter.

[723] Only the following Member States seem to acknowledge the individual constitutional complaint: Belgium, Czech Republic (*ústavní stížnost*), Germany (*Verfassungsbeschwerde*), Spain (*recurso de amparo*), Croatia (*ustavna tužba*), Cyprus, Latvia (*konstitucionālā sūdzība*), Hungary (*alkotmányjogi panasz*), Austria (*Entscheidungsbeschwerde*), Slovenia (*ustavna pritožba*) and Slovakia (*sťažnosti*). See (CZ) Ústava České republiky, Čl 87, d); Zákon o Ústavním soudu, §§ 64 and 72; (DE) Grundgesetz für die Bundesrepublik Deutschland, Art 93, Abs 1, Nr 4a; Bundesverfassungsgerichtsgesetz, § 13, Abs 8bis, § 90, Abs 1, and § 95, Abs 2; (ES) Constitución Española, Arts 53, 161–62, 161.1.b); Ley Orgánica 2/1979, Arts 41–44; (HR) Ustav Republike Hrvatske, članak 129; Ustavni zakon o Ustavnom sudu Republike Hrvatske, članak 62–64; (CY) Constitution of the Republic of Cyprus, Art 146.1; (LV) Satversmes tiesas likums, 17 pants; (HU) Az Alkotmánybíróságról szóló 2011 évi CLI törvény, 27 § (1); (AT) Bundesverfassungsgesetz, Art 144; Verfassungsgerichtshofgesetz, Art 82; (SI) Ustava Republike Slovenije, 160 člen; Zakon o ustavnem sodišče – ZUstS, 24 člen and 50 člen; (SK) Ústava Slovenskej republiky, čl 127, 130; Zákon Národnej rady Slovenskej republiky o organizácii Ústavného súdu Slovenskej republiky, o konaní pred ním a o postavení jeho sudcov, § 18 h), and § 49; as well as Venice Commission 2011: 16, 23–24, 49–50, 61–63.

[724] (ECJ) Judgment in *Cilfit and Others*.

the referral obligation to the substantive EU norm that needs to be interpreted. Consequently, the characteristics of this substantive norm will also determine whether the request for preliminary ruling is necessary. The above different EU rules hence determine overall the scope of the obligation to refer a question to the ECJ. Due to the subjective nature of these conditions, considerable discretion remains with the national court on whether to make a preliminary reference. This margin of discretion makes it difficult to evaluate whether the violation of referral duty, or a breach of the right to a lawful judge, has indeed taken place.

Moreover, it is still an unresolved issue of *Köbler* liability whether the misapplication of a substantive EU norm or the violation of the referral duty determines the gravity of the breach of EU law by the national court.[725] Similarly, it has not yet been decided whether the sole violation of the obligation to have a question referred to the ECJ is sufficient for the *Köbler* liability to be incurred.[726]

All things considered, despite uncertainties on the judicial error that can trigger the annulment of the final judgment in a constitutional complaint, on the one hand, and the *Köbler* liability, on the other hand, there is certainly common ground in the application of these two remedies. In addition, a successful constitutional complaint may result not only in the annulment of the concerned judgment, but also in the allocation of damages in several Member States.[727]

In the following sections, the case-law of Member State courts applying the lawful judge doctrine to the ECJ will be briefly presented. The presentation will cover the jurisprudence of Member States that have acknowledged applying this doctrine to violation of EU law, namely the Czech Republic, Germany, Austria, Slovenia, Slovakia and Spain. In addition, ECtHR and Hungarian case-law will also briefly be mentioned, as they raise interesting issues.

ii. ECtHR Case-Law on the Obligation to Make a Preliminary Reference

The question of whether the violation of the referral duty constitutes a violation of the right to a fair trial enshrined under the ECHR has also been dealt with by the ECtHR.[728]

The European Commission of Human Rights stated, in a judgment delivered in 1993 in the *Divagsa Company* case, that the ECHR does not guarantee the absolute right to have an issue of EU law discussed before the ECJ. However,

[725] Anagnostaras 2006; Classen 2004: 821; Jans 2004: 172; Tridimas 2007: 156–57; Rodríguez 2004–05: 619.

[726] Anagnostaras 2006: 745–57; Cabral and Chavez 2006: 122; Classen 2004: 816–17; Dougan 2000: 606–08; Nassimpian 2007: 824; Rodríguez 2004–05: 618.

[727] (HR) Ustavni zakon o Ustavnom sudu Republike Hrvatske, članak 63(3); Venice Commission 2011: 110; (CY) Constitution of the Republic of Cyprus, Art 146.6; ACA Europe 2008, National report of Cyprus, question 14; (MT) Constitution of Malta, Art 46; Scherr 2008: 168.

[728] See Wattel 2014: 200–01, referring to the (ECtHR) judgment in *Hornsby v Greece*. See also Broberg 2016; Broberg and Fenger 2016; Krommendijk 2017; Lacchi 2015a: 95–125; Lacchi 2016: 698–700; Laffranque 2018; Neamt 2016.

this right is protected indirectly by securing the right to a fair trial laid down in Article 6(1) ECHR.[729] In particular, the right to a fair trial may be infringed when the refusal by a national court to submit a request for a preliminary ruling to the ECJ appears to be arbitrary.[730] According to the European Commission of Human Rights, this was not the case in the main proceedings in *Divagsa*. This jurisprudence has been confirmed on several occasions, also by the ECtHR, with the conclusion that the decision of the national court had not been arbitrary.[731] Initially, the ECtHR used the criterion of arbitrariness, but did not specify what was required from national courts in terms of the level of stating reasons.[732]

In the judgment in *Ullens de Schooten and Rezabek*, rendered in 2011, the ECtHR went one step further and concluded that the national courts have to state reasons for any decision in which they refuse to submit a request for preliminary ruling.[733] In this case, it found no violation of the applicants' right to a fair hearing under Article 6(1) ECHR. The ECtHR recalled that the obligation to submit a referral to the ECJ is not absolute, as is clear from the *Cilfit* judgment. National courts are not required to refer a question where they established that it was irrelevant or that the EU provision in question had already been interpreted by the ECJ, or where the correct application of EU law was so obvious as to leave no scope for any reasonable doubt. In the case at hand, the national supreme courts had given reasons for their refusal, citing the exceptions under the *Cilfit* case-law. In the light of the reasons given by the national courts and having regard to the proceedings as a whole, the ECtHR held that there had been no violation of the applicants' right to a fair hearing under Article 6(1) ECHR in the case at hand. In further decisions, several applications had been rejected on the grounds that either the applicants had not explicitly requested the national jurisdictions to refer questions to the ECJ,[734] the request to obtain a preliminary ruling was insufficiently pleaded,[735] or the questions that the applicants requested to refer to the ECJ were not pertinent.[736]

By a judgment rendered in 2014 in the *Dhahbi* case, the ECtHR concluded for the first time that a refusal to request a preliminary ruling was arbitrary to such an extent that it amounted to a violation of the right to a fair trial under the ECHR.[737] According to the ECtHR, national courts whose decisions are not open to appeal under domestic law are required to give reasons for their refusal

[729] (ECtHR) Decision in *Divagsa Company v Spain*.
[730] See also Coutron 2014: 19–20; Valutytė 2012b.
[731] (ECtHR) Judgments in *Bosphorus Hava Yolları Turizm ve Ticaret Anonim Şirketi v Ireland*, § 143; *Harisch v Germany*, § 43; *Somorjai v Hungary*, §§ 52–62; decisions in *Desmots v France*, § 2; *Dotta v Italy*, § 13; *Herma v Austria*, § 2; *Stichting Mothers of Srebrenica v The Netherlands; Schweighofer and Others v Austria*; *Peter Moosbrugger v Austria*, § 2.
[732] Krommendijk 2017: 48–50.
[733] (ECtHR) Judgment in *Ullens de Schooten and Rezabek v Belgium*, § 54.
[734] (ECtHR) Judgment in *Ryon and Others v France*; decision in *Greneche and Others v France*.
[735] (ECtHR) Judgment in *John v Germany*; in *Wallishauser v Austria*.
[736] (ECtHR) Decision in *Sindicatul pro Asistenţă Socială v Romania*.
[737] (ECtHR) Judgment in *Dhahbi v Italy*, §§ 33–34.

to refer a preliminary question to the ECJ on the interpretation of EU law. This statement of reasons should be based on the interpretation of the applicable law, and the exceptions laid down in ECJ case-law. In other words, Member State courts should set out reasons for considering that the question is not relevant, that the provisions had already been interpreted by the ECJ, or that the correct application of EU law is so obvious as to leave no scope for reasonable doubt. The ECtHR pointed out in particular that, in the case at hand, it was not possible to evaluate whether the national court even considered the request of the complainant to submit a referral for preliminary ruling. In fact, the national judgment contained neither reference to ECJ case-law nor a statement of reasons for such a refusal. Consequently, if a national court of last instance refuses to make a reference to the ECJ, without any reason, such refusal amounts to a breach of Article 6(1) ECHR.

Moreover, in the *Schipani* judgment delivered in 2015, the ECtHR went even further as it found a violation of Article 6(1) ECHR on the ground of a non-referral in a case where the national court had considered the arguments of EU law, but omitted all reference to the reasons why referral was unnecessary.[738] According to the ECtHR, it was not clear from the reasoning of the impugned judgment whether the question was considered not to be relevant or to relate to a provision which was clear or had already been interpreted by the ECJ, or whether it was simply ignored. Therefore, the ECtHR concluded that the refusal by the national court to submit a referral constituted a breach of Article 6(1) ECHR. An analogous conclusion was reached under similar circumstances in the *Sanofi Pasteur* case in 2020.[739] In this judgment as well, the ECtHR found a violation of the Convention, this time by the French Cour de cassation, as the national court had not referred to any of the *Cilfit* conditions but limited itself to stating that the applicant's claim should be rejected without any need to refer a preliminary question to the ECJ.

In the judgment in *Ferreira Santos Pardal* from 2015 the ECtHR found a violation of Article 6(1) ECHR due to an internal jurisprudential divergence regarding the admissibility of liability actions brought against the state for damages caused in the exercise of the judicial function.[740] The application was introduced subsequent to the decision of the Portuguese Supremo Tribunal de Justiça denying such a claim.[741] The national supreme court concluded in this decision that the domestic rules on judicial liability were not applicable, *ratione temporis*, to the case at hand, and therefore, there had not been any ground to establish state liability based on a judicial error. The particularity of this case

[738] (ECtHR) Judgment in *Schipani v Italy*, §§ 71–73. See the analysis of the case and of the development of the ECtHR case-law in Lacchi 2015a: 99–106 and Krommendijk 2017.

[739] (ECtHR) Judgment in *Sanofi Pasteur v France*, § 78.

[740] (ECtHR) Judgment in *Ferreira Santos Pardal v Portugal*.

[741] (PT) Supremo Tribunal de Justiça, Acórdão, 03/12/2009. For further analysis on this case, see ss 2.II.A.ii.e(2) and 2.II.A.iv.b(4).

is that the national courts had not submitted a request for a preliminary ruling to the ECJ at any stage of the national proceedings, even though the applicant claimed that a violation of EU law had occurred. Therefore, the ECJ was denied the possibility to assess whether the interpretation of the applicable EU rules was correct, the request for preliminary ruling was necessary or the *Köbler* conditions were established. Following the contestation of the national decision before the ECtHR by the applicant, the ECtHR found a violation of Article 6(1) ECHR. The violation consisted in the breach of the principle of legal certainty, as the Portuguese judicial practice was divergent on the question as to whether judicial liability could be established. Even though the ECtHR could not evaluate, for lack of jurisdiction, whether there had been a violation of EU law,[742] the breach that was established indicates a more serious violation if one considers EU case-law on this matter: the decision of the Supremo Tribunal de Justiça clearly departed from established ECJ case-law on judicial liability.[743]

Then, in the *Arlewin* judgment delivered in 2016, the ECtHR found that the Swedish courts' decision to decline jurisdiction in defamation proceedings lodged by the applicant regarding allegations made against him in a television programme broadcast in Sweden constituted a violation of Article 6(1) ECHR.[744] The refusal to exercise jurisdiction deprived the applicant of an effective access to court. An interesting aspect of these proceedings is that, had the Swedish courts introduced a request for preliminary ruling, the ECJ would have probably affirmed that the referring courts were competent to hear the case. However, the national courts applied EU law in a manner inconsistent with ECJ case-law, and relied, erroneously, on the *acte clair* doctrine instead. Even though the ECtHR decision has not dealt with the obligations of the national courts under Article 267 TFEU in this case, it sanctioned, nevertheless, an incorrect application of EU law by the Member State courts.

However, in its judgment rendered in 2018 in the *Baydar* case, the ECtHR found no violation of the ECHR by the Hoge Raad because the court had refused to submit a request for preliminary ruling to the ECJ.[745] The national court dismissed the applicant's request and stated that its decision required no further reasoning as the appeal in cassation had not constituted grounds for overturning the impugned judgment. The reasoning had not contained, therefore, any reference to the conditions under which a referral is obligatory, or any reference to the material rules of EU law. Nevertheless, the ECtHR found that the summary reasoning was sufficient as it was clear from the circumstances that the decision was not arbitrary or otherwise manifestly unreasonable. Therefore,

[742] (ECtHR) Judgments in *Ullens de Schooten and Rezabek v Belgium*, § 66; *Bosphorus Hava Yolları Turizm ve Ticaret Anonim Şirketi v Ireland*, § 143; *Dhahbi v Italy*, § 31; from the perspective of the ECJ, see (ECJ) opinion 2/13, para 246.

[743] For a more comprehensive analysis of this case, see Silveira and Fernandes 2016.

[744] (ECtHR) Judgment in *Arlewin v Sweden*.

[745] (ECtHR) Judgment in *Baydar v the Netherlands*.

the ECtHR accepted that the absence of any reference to EU procedural or substantial rules may not necessarily entail a violation of Article 6(1) ECHR if it is obvious under national rules that the request or appeal were to be dismissed. By this judgment, the ECtHR has therefore departed from its previous line of cases which appeared to introduce gradually more stringent conditions for the national courts to justify their refusal to submit a request for preliminary ruling.

Finally, the judgment rendered in 2019 in the *Repcevirág* case is noteworthy.[746] These proceedings concern a Hungarian case, in which the Kúria and the Alkotmánybíróság rendered judgments, after having refused to refer questions to the ECJ.[747] The particularity of this case is that by the impugned decision, the Kúria decided on a *Köbler* liability claim. In its judgment delivered in this case, the ECtHR explained that the obligation under Article 6(1) ECHR for domestic courts to provide reasons for their judgments and decisions cannot be understood to mean that a detailed answer to every argument is required. The extent to which the duty to provide reasons applies may therefore vary according to the nature of the decision. Applying these principles to the case at hand, the ECtHR concluded that there had been no violation of Article 6(1) ECHR in this case.[748] Based on similar arguments, the Strasbourg court reached the same conclusion in the *Harisch* case.[749]

Overall, according to the ECtHR, a refusal to grant a referral may be deemed arbitrary in cases where the applicable rules allow no exception to the granting of a referral, where the referral is based on reasons other than those provided for by the rules, or where the refusal was not duly explained.[750]

Three conclusions are particularly interesting regarding the ECtHR case-law.

First, the ECtHR insists, in particular in its recent judgments in *Baydar*, *Harisch* and *Repcevirág*, on the importance of the particuliarities of the case and of the request for a referral introduced by the applicant itself before the national court.[751] In short, the more the request is substantiated and justified, the more detailed and targeted reasoning is necessary to dismiss the request.[752] By contrast, if the request is insufficiently pleaded or if it is formulated only in broad terms, the refusal by the national court can be more succinct.[753] Therefore, the violation of Article 6(1) ECHR depends on the quality of the request to submit a referral, which is a logical conclusion of the fact that Article 6(1) ECHR protects the right of the applicant, in the specific case, to a fair trial. In this respect, the right to a fair trial may be compromised if the national court fails to properly respond to the request of the applicant for referral. Had the ECtHR

[746] (ECtHR) Judgment in *Repcevirág Szövetkezet v Hungary*.

[747] (HU) Kúria, ítélet, 11/12/2013; Alkotmánybíróság, végzés, 19/05/2014.

[748] (ECtHR) Judgment in *Repcevirág Szövetkezet v Hungary*, §§ 52–62.

[749] (ECtHR) Judgment in *Harisch v Germany*, § 34.

[750] (ECtHR) Judgment in *Baydar v The Netherlands*, § 39.

[751] (ECtHR) Judgment in *Baydar v The Netherlands*, §§ 40–44; in *Harisch v Germany*, § 34; in *Repcevirág Szövetkezet v Hungary*, §§ 49–51. See also judgment in *Sanofi Pasteur v France*, §§ 71–72.

[752] (ECtHR) Judgment in *Repcevirág Szövetkezet v Hungary*, § 50.

[753] (ECtHR) Judgment in *Repcevirág Szövetkezet v Hungary*, § 51.

not connected violation of fundamental rights to the request of the applicant, it would have risked interpreting EU law itself.

Secondly, the ECtHR considers, in abstracto, the *Cilfit* exceptions when evaluating the breach of fair trial on the ground of an arbitrary decision by a national court not to make a referral to the ECJ. The judgments mentioned above suggest a development in the ECtHR case-law. Earlier, the ECtHR appears to have accepted that the national court simply refers to one of the *Cilfit* criteria or states the reason that the request was not relevant. Lately, it has started to require that the national courts explain the concrete reasons why they think that the referral is not necessary.[754] The question nevertheless remains whether the ECtHR will ever set more stringent conditions in this regard and will ever consider in substance whether the reference to the *Cilfit* exceptions was justified.

Thirdly, the ECtHR does not take into account the gravity of the interference of the contested decision with the right of the applicant. In other words, it seems to be irrelevant for the ECtHR whether the failure to give reasons and the absence of a preliminary reference have entailed a loss for the applicant.[755] In the context of *Köbler* liability, this is an issue that gives rise to problems in relation to the causal link between the damages suffered and the breach of EU law concerning damages claims for a simple failure to refer.

iii. Lawful Judge Cases Before the Member State Courts

a. Czech Republic

The right of the parties to introduce a constitutional complaint (*ústavní stížnost*) before the Ústavní soud is enshrined in the Czech Constitution.[756] Moreover, the Czech Charter of Fundamental Rights protects the right of the parties to their lawful judge (*pravo na zákon ného sudce*).[757] These conditions made it possible for the Ústavní soud to declare – following its German and Austrian counterparts – that the violation of the referral obligation may amount to the violation of the national fundamental laws as well. Three judgments are illustrative in this regard.

By the first judgment rendered in 2009 in the *Pfizer* case, the Ústavní soud concluded that the arbitrary decision by the Nejvyšší správní soud on the refusal to make a preliminary reference had amounted to a violation of the constitutional right to a lawful judge.[758] In the view of the Constitutional Court, the Nejvyšší správní soud had committed a breach of the complainant's fundamental rights as it had shed no light at all on the ECJ's jurisprudence while interpreting

[754] (ECtHR) Judgments in *Schipani v Italy*, §§ 71–73; in *Sanofi Pasteur v France*, § 78.
[755] See (ECtHR) Judge Wojtyczek's dissenting opinion to the *Schipani* judgment.
[756] (CZ) Ústava České republiky, Čl 87, d); Zákon o Ústavním soudu, §§ 64, 72.
[757] (CZ) Listina základních práv a svobod, čl 38 odst 1.
[758] (CZ) Ústavní soud, nález ze dne 08/01/2009, reported by Škvařilová in Reflets no 1/2009: 27, Petrlík 2014: 416, Valutyté 2012a: 1179, and in the database JuriFast.

EU law. In fact, neither had it referred to the exceptions to the obligation to refer preliminary questions, nor had it taken the arguments of the complainant into consideration. Moreover, the court had not dealt with the interpretation of the aims pursued by the directive appropriately. The Ústavní soud confirmed the above jurisprudence in a judgment in 2011.[759]

Finally, in a judgment rendered in 2015, the Ústavní soud annulled a judgment of Obvodní soud pro Prahu 6 (6th District Court of Prague) for failure to request a preliminary ruling from the ECJ on the interpretation of EU law.[760] The Constitutional Court found that the Obvodní soud should have consulted the ECJ on the correct interpretation of the EU regulation applicable to the case, as there had not been any previous case-law on the legal question at issue. Therefore, the rights of the parties to effective judicial protection had been breached in the main proceedings.

In all, the Ústavní soud has recognised that the violation of the right to one's lawful judge may emerge where a Czech court has failed to refer a preliminary question to the ECJ. In particular, the breach of right occurs when a court of last instance applies EU law but fails – in an arbitrary manner[761] – to make a request for preliminary ruling.[762] The Ústavní soud has determined its own standard regarding the arbitrary violation of the obligation to refer. In this regard, it defines arbitrary conduct by a court of last instance, first, where the court has entirely omitted to consider whether it should refer a preliminary question to the ECJ; and second, where the court has not complied with its obligation to state reasons for its refusal to refer, including an assessment of the exceptions that the ECJ has elaborated in its case-law.[763] In the Ústavní soud's view, the bare opinion of a court, that it considers the interpretation of the given problem to be obvious, cannot be considered as adequate reasoning. The reasoning is also insufficient where it fails to explain how and why the solution chosen is in line with the purpose of a relevant EU legal norm.[764]

b. Germany

With the remedy of individual constitutional complaint (*Verfassungsbeschwerde*) provided in the Grundgesetz (GG, German Fundamental Law),[765] and the right to a lawful judge (*Recht auf den gesetzlichen Richter*) recognised as a fundamental right,[766] the preconditions for the development of this principle have

[759] (CZ) Ústavní soud, nález ze dne 29/11/2011, reported by Petrlík 2014: 416.

[760] (CZ) Ústavní soud, rozsudek ze dne 19/05/2015, reported by Kušteková in Reflets no 1/2016: 37.

[761] (CZ) Ústava České republiky, Čl 1(1).

[762] Lacchi 2015b: 1682–83; Valutyté 2012a: 1178.

[763] Valutyté 2012a: 1178, and Valutyté 2014: 297.

[764] Valutyté 2012a: 1178–79.

[765] (DE) Grundgesetz für die Bundesrepublik Deutschland, Art 93, Abs 1, Nr 4a; BVerfGG, § 13, Abs 8bis, § 90, Abs 1, and § 95, Abs 2. See also Dittert 2014: 61.

[766] (DE) Grundgesetz für die Bundesrepublik Deutschland, Art 101, Abs 1, S 2.

been secured under German law. Moreover, the Bundesverfassungsgericht (BVerfG, Federal Constitutional Court, Germany) was the first court to recognise, in 1986, that the breach of the referral duty might amount to a breach of the party's constitutional rights. Since then, numerous decisions followed; several were successful, others not.

According to the BVerfG's position, if doubts arise regarding the application or interpretation of EU law, German courts must, first of all, refer the relevant questions to the ECJ in accordance with Article 267(3) TFEU. The ECJ is the lawful judge in these cases. Nevertheless, failure to comply with the duty of referral under EU law does not always amount to a violation of Article 101(1) GG. The BVerfG limits its review to whether the allocation of jurisdiction set out in the Treaty is interpreted and applied in a manner that is not considered manifestly untenable.

The following account of the BVerfG's case-law is not exhaustive but aims to provide a general overview of the reasoning followed by the court on this matter. In this context, several cases will be briefly presented, starting with the unsuccessful, then continuing with the successful constitutional complaints.

The first case that must be mentioned is the *Solange II* decision rendered in 1986.[767] By this judgment, the BVerfG recognised, for the first time, that since the ECJ enjoys a monopoly regarding the interpretation and the validity of EU law, it represents a lawful judge in this sphere. According to the BVerfG's reasoning, if there is a need for the ECJ to participate in the proceedings and the national court infringes its obligation to bring the case before the ECJ, a violation of the right to a lawful judge is present. However, a mere procedural defect is not sufficient; the violation of the obligation must be considered arbitrary and non-justifiable. The BVerfG concluded that no violation of the lawful judge principle occurred in this case, since the decision by the court not to refer a preliminary question to the ECJ was neither arbitrary nor non-justifiable. In the subsequent case-law of the BVerfG, constitutional complaints were dismissed on several occasions, basically for the same reason.[768]

In the *Zusatstoff* decision rendered in 1987, the BVerfG clarified the conditions under which it is possible for a national court to rely on the *acte clair* doctrine.[769] The BVerfG stated that the *acte clair* principle could only be employed if the interpretative question had only one answer, according to the reasonable opinion of experienced lawyers. Therefore, the national court has to

[767] (DE) BVerfG, Beschluß, 22/10/1986.

[768] (DE) BVerfG, Beschluß, 05/08/1998, reported in the XVIth Annual Report on monitoring the application of Community law (1998), Annex VI, 184; BVerfG, Beschluss, 10/05/2001, reported by Arndt 2001; BVerfG, Beschluss, 30/01/2002, 1 BvR 1542/00, reported by Derlén 2009: 90–92, and in the XXth Annual Report on monitoring the application of Community law (2002), Annex VI, 10; BVerfG, Beschluss, 14/07/2006, reported in the XXIVth Annual Report monitoring the application of EU law (2006), Annex VI, I-7; BVerfG, Beschluss, 06/07/2010, reported by Valutytė 2012a: 1176–77; (DE) BVerfG, Beschluss, 10/11/2010, reported in the ECLI database; BVerfG, Beschluss, 15/12/2011, 2 BvR 148/11, reported by Geppert in Reflets no 2/2012: 41.

[769] (DE) BVerfG, Beschluß, 09/11/1987, reported by Derlén 2009: 87–89.

evaluate whether the EU provision in question could reasonably allow more than one interpretation according to the above objective criterion.

In another decision, delivered in 1998, the BVerfG dismissed the constitutional complaint as it found that the Bundesarbeitsgericht (Federal Labour Court) had provided adequate grounds for declining to refer the question to the ECJ; therefore, the view taken by the Bundesarbeitsgericht was not in excess of its discretionary powers.[770] Also, in a decision delivered in 2001, the BVerfG dismissed the constitutional complaint on the grounds that it had not been demonstrated that legal opinions contrary to the opinion taken by the Oberverwaltungsgericht (Higher Administrative Court) were clearly preferable.[771] Then, the BVerfG found unfounded a constitutional complaint in the *Biobronch* case as well, in a judgment rendered in 2002.[772] This judgment illustrates the limited review conducted by the BVerfG, as the BVerfG admitted that the interpretation performed by the Oberlandesgericht was, in all likelihood, flawed, but emphasised that only arbitrariness could be subject to review.[773] In another decision, dated 2006, the BVerfG concluded that the failure to submit a reference for preliminary ruling had not infringed the right of the complainant to a lawful judge, as the BGH examined in detail the relevant ECJ case-law, and explained why the reference had not been necessary in the case at hand.[774] In another decision rendered in 2008, the BVerfG rejected the constitutional complaint as it found that the complainants had not substantiated an infringement of their right to a lawful judge according to the constitutional requirements.[775]

The *Honeywell* decision from 2010 dealt, amongst other things, with the scope of the obligation to submit a request for a preliminary ruling to the ECJ.[776] As for the violation of the complainant's right to their lawful judge, the BVerfG held that the Bundesarbeitsgericht had reasonably presumed that it was not under the obligation to refer a question to the ECJ in the contested proceedings. It reiterated that not every breach of Article 267 TFEU constitutes a violation of the constitutional right, and that it is not obliged to fully review the decision made by the Bundesarbeitsgericht in this respect.

Then, in a decision rendered in 2010, the BVerfG dismissed another constitutional complaint on the grounds that in the case at hand the interpretation of the directive was not necessary as it was irrelevant to deciding on the liability claim.[777] Furthermore, in a decision rendered in 2011, the BVerfG dismissed a constitutional complaint which was lodged on the ground that the BGH had

[770] (DE) BVerfG, Beschluß, 05/08/1998.
[771] (DE) BVerfG, Beschluss, 10/05/2001.
[772] (DE) BVerfG, Beschluss, 30/01/2002.
[773] Derlén 2009: 92.
[774] (DE) BVerfG, Beschluss, 14/07/2006.
[775] (DE) BVerfG, Beschluss, 06/05/2008.
[776] (DE) BVerfG, Beschluss, 06/07/2010.
[777] (DE) BVerfG, Beschluss, 10/11/2010.

deviated from the ECJ case-law on state liability without submitting a request for preliminary ruling.[778] In its judgment, the BVerfG concluded that the BGH had not manifestly disregarded its obligation to submit a request and had not deviated from the established ECJ case-law either. In this regard, the Constitutional Court emphasised that a referral is obligatory only if the national court has doubts on the correct interpretation of EU law. Also, by its decision delivered in 2011, the BVerfG dismissed a complaint as, in the view of the BVerfG, the BGH did not go beyond the limits of this discretion in the case at issue.[779]

On the other hand, constitutional complaints have been successful on several occasions before the BVerfG. In this respect, in the *Kloppenburg* decision delivered in 1987, the BVerfG found that the refusal by the national court to make a referral was 'arbitrary and non-justifiable'.[780] According to the BVerfG, if the Bundesfinanzhof did not intend to comply with the opinion expressed by the ECJ in a prior preliminary ruling, it was compelled to refer the matter again to the ECJ and set forth new argumentation in its favour. The disregard of a binding opinion of the ECJ was deemed as an arbitrary violation of the duty to make a referral.

Similarly, in the *Rinke* decision, delivered in 2001, the BVerfG found that the BVerwG had answered the question on the conflict between directives in a manner that was not acceptable under EU law, as it had justified its ruling on the national law alone.[781] The BVerwG had not referred to a single decision of the ECJ regarding the problem of conflicts between directives, even though there were many of them. The BVerfG stated that as BVerwG had not investigated EU law properly, it had been in breach of the conditions under which a reference for a preliminary ruling was mandatory.

Afterwards, in a decision rendered in 2004, the BVerfG held a constitutional complaint well founded and annulled the judgment of the Oberlandesgericht Frankfurt am Main (Higher Regional Court, Frankfurt am Main).[782] The BVerfG pointed out that the simple referral by the Oberlandesgericht to the fact that the ECJ case-law had not applied to the case was insufficient and therefore constituted a violation of the right to a lawful judge. The Oberlandesgericht should have analysed, in a detailed manner, the circumstances that led it to this conclusion, and should have presented the ECJ case-law in this matter as well.

[778] (DE) BVerfG, Beschluss, 21/11/2011.

[779] (DE) BVerfG, Beschluss, 15/12/2011. The dispute at the origin of the complaint concerned the *ne bis in idem* principle, enshrined in Art 50 of the Charter.

[780] (DE) BVerfG, Beschluß, 08/04/1987, English translation in *The Relationship Between European Community Law and National Law: The Cases* (1994) 496–519, reported by Navrátilová, M (n.d.) 'The Preliminary Ruling before the Constitutional Courts' www.law.muni.cz/sborniky/dp08/files/pdf/mezinaro/navratilova.pdf.

[781] (DE) BVerfG, Beschluss, 09/01/2001, reported in Reflets no 1/2001: 4; in the XIXth Annual Report on monitoring the application of Community law (2001), Annex VI, 39–41.

[782] (DE) BVerfG, Beschluss, 29/07/2004, reported in the XXIIIth Annual Report on monitoring the application of EU law (2005), Annex VI, I-5.

Then, in a decision rendered in 2005, the BVerfG annulled a judgment of the Bayerischer Verwaltungsgerichtshof (Administrative Appeal Court of Bavaria), as this latter court could not have rendered its decision without submitting a request for preliminary ruling to the ECJ.[783] The referral to the ECJ would have been necessary to evaluate the compatibility of the German legal provision with EU law in the main proceedings. Without such a referral, the right of the complainant to effective judicial protection had been infringed.

In another decision from 2010, the BVerfG established again the infringement of the complainant's right to a lawful judge, and annulled the contested judgment of the BGH.[784] The BVerfG pointed out that, in this case, there was no indication that the BGH had considered the relevant EU law and the ECJ case-law at all. Moreover, there were strong arguments in favour of an obligation to refer because, at the very least, defensible opinions different from those held by the BGH did not appear impossible.

The last decision summarised in this section was pronounced in 2017.[785] In this decision, the BVerfG concluded, again, that the right of the complainant to their lawful judge was infringed as the ECJ was not consulted, via the preliminary procedure, in the underlying proceedings before the Hanseatische Oberlandesgericht (Higher Regional Court). The BVerfG emphasised that the case-law of the ECJ had not yet fully resolved the decisive issue in the matter at hand and the Hanseatische Oberlandesgericht exceeded its margin of assessment in a manner untenable under constitutional law by refraining from requesting a preliminary ruling.

Overall, the most elaborate case-law related to the obligation under national constitutional laws to submit a request for preliminary ruling has definitively been developed by the BVerfG, which has been the first court to apply the lawful judge principle to the ECJ. The BVerfG does not use the criteria given in the *Cilfit* judgment but has created its own standards.[786] As shown, not all violations of the obligation to make a preliminary reference constitute a breach of the German constitutional right to a lawful judge.[787] The review conducted by the BVerfG does not protect against misapplications of law due to mistakes or misinterpretation, but only against arbitrariness.[788] According to the BVerfG, the obligation to make a referral is dealt with in a *manifestly untenable manner*,

[783] (DE) BVerfG, Beschluss, 27/04/2005, reported in the XXIIIth Annual Report monitoring the application of EU law (2005), Annex VI, I-5.

[784] (DE) BVerfG, Beschluss, 30/08/2010, reported by Geppert in Reflets no 3/2010: 9, and Valutytė 2012a: 1176–77.

[785] (DE) BVerfG, Beschluss, 19/12/2017.

[786] (DE) BVerfG, Beschluss, 25/02/2010, reported by Dittert 2014: 62–63. See also Navrátilová, M (n.d.) 'The Preliminary Ruling before the Constitutional Courts' www.law.muni.cz/sborniky/dp08/files/pdf/mezinaro/navratilova.pdf.

[787] EU law does not require the Member State's constitutional court to make a full review of the violation of the obligation to make a submission under EU law and to take the case-law on Art 267(3) TFEU of the ECJ as an orientation. See Lacchi 2015b: 1679–81; Valutytė 2012a: 1174–75.

[788] Valutytė 2012a: 1174–75.

particularly if an action of a national court – or its failure to act – falls into one of the three following categories:[789] first, fundamental disregard of the obligation to refer;[790] second, deliberate deviation from the ECJ case-law;[791] and third, unjustifiable application of the *acte clair* approach.[792] The first two situations are clear violations of the duty to request a preliminary ruling. However, the third situation only amounts to a violation of the referral duty – and of the right to a lawful judge – if the violation is obvious.[793]

Therefore, in this respect, while deciding whether or not to make a reference, German courts of last instance have to evaluate all circumstances of the case, the goal and content of a relevant EU legal act, the existing practice of the ECJ and its possible development, and besides that, the practice of other states and possible counterviews.[794] In particular, where the case-law of the ECJ applies to the case at hand, it must be analysed and reflected in the decision rendered by the German court. On this basis, the court must reach the reasonable conclusion that the applicable legal standards are either clear from the outset (*acte clair*) or clarified beyond reasonable doubt in the case-law of the ECJ (*acte éclairé*). In conclusion, the German Constitutional Court protects the interpretative authority of the ECJ on EU law matters and prohibits the German courts from developing their own interpretation on matters that have not yet been clearly clarified by the ECJ.

c. Austria

Under Austrian law, the right to a lawful judge is protected under the Constitution (B-VG),[795] and an individual constitutional complaint (*Entscheidungsbeschwerde*) is recognised in administrative matters.[796] In these proceedings, the VfGH exercises its jurisdiction as a special administrative court (*Sonderverwaltungsgerichtsbarkeit*). The legal consequence of a successful constitutional complaint is the annulment of the unconstitutional decision of the administrative body by the VfGH. In this way, the underlying constitutional conditions for the recognition of the lawful judge doctrine have been united in

[789] Valutytė 2012a: 1175.

[790] This situation can be labelled as the ignorance approach, since a national court does not even discuss the possibility of a preliminary ruling despite admitting the absence of *acte clair*.

[791] This category can be called a rebellious approach, since a national court intentionally departs from the case-law of the ECJ. For examples from judicial practice, see eg (FR) Cour de Cassation, arrêt, 25/10/2016. Even more rebellious is when the national court submitting the request for preliminary ruling expressly refuses to accept the ECJ's decison. See (DE) BVerfG, Beschluß, 08/04/1987, and, for a recent example, (DN) Højesteret, Judgment, 06/12/2016.

[792] In this situation, the decisive factor is not primarily the justifiability of the non-constitutional courts' interpretation of substantive EU law relevant to the case in question, but the justifiability of the courts' treatment of the obligation to refer under Art 267(3) TFEU.

[793] Valutytė 2012a: 1175–76.

[794] Valutytė 2012a: 1177.

[795] (AT) Bundesverfassungsgesetz, Art 83(2).

[796] (AT) Bundesverfassungsgesetz, Art 144; Verfassungsgerichtshofgesetz, Art 88.

Austrian law. Under these circumstances, the VfGH concluded that the violation of the referral duty may constitute a violation of the B-VG. However, an important limitation *ratione materiae* of the use of this remedy is that the VfGH can only review rulings by administrative courts of first instance. Therefore, the right of the party to have his case referred to the ECJ cannot be protected via the constitutional complaint if the court adjudicating in the main proceedings is a civil court or the VwGH.[797]

In a judgment rendered in 1995, the VfGH acknowledged the ECJ as lawful judge within the meaning of the Constitution, with regard to the application of the right to a lawful judge.[798] The VfGH pointed out that a national authority violating its duty to refer a question to the ECJ deprives the parties of their lawful judge, since the ECJ is prevented from deciding on a question that is reserved to its exclusive jurisdiction. The national body, when deciding in the case before it, is bound by the preliminary ruling of the ECJ.[799] However, it results from the *acte clair* doctrine that a national body only infringes its duty under the Treaty to make a preliminary reference if it has doubts about the compatibility of its interpretation of the national law with the applicable EU law.

In contrast to the above judgment, the VfGH saw a violation of the right to a lawful judge caused by the BVA in failing to make a preliminary reference in several cases. In a judgment handed down in 1996,[800] the VfGH declared that all violations – and not only gross violations – of the referral duty lead to a breach of the right to a lawful judge. The application of this principle led to the annulment of two decisions of the Bundesvergabeamt (BVA, Federal Procurement Office), by judgments delivered in 1997 and in 2001.[801]

Similarly, by a judgment pronounced in 2003, the VfGH annulled a decision of the Oberste Berufungs- und Disziplinarkommission (OBDK, Supreme Appeal and Disciplinary Committee), for violating the complainant's right to his lawful judge.[802] The VfGH pointed out that the OBDK had erroneously applied the *acte clair* principle in the case because the facts at the origin of the dispute before the OBDK (on which there had been no relevant jurisprudence) and at the origin of the judgment on the ECJ had been different. Hence, the OBDK was in breach of its duty to make a referral to the ECJ for a preliminary ruling.

[797] The violation in a civil proceeding of a constitutional right can, however, be invoked in an appeal proceeding before the OGH. See (AT) OGH, Beschluß, 27/05/1997, reported by Pelzl 2014: 95; OGH, Beschluß, 25/06/2002, reported by Pelzl 2014: 95–96; OGH, Urteil, 26/11/2002, reported by Pelzl 2014: 95–96; OGH, Urteil, 22/10/2007, reported by Pelzl 2014: 95–96.

[798] (AT) VfGH, Erkenntnis, 11/12/1995, English summaries in *Public Procurement Law Review* (1996) 164 and *European Current Law* no 42 (1997) part 3, reported by Pelzl 2014: 96.

[799] This principle has been confirmed at several occasions. See eg (AT) VfGH, Erkenntnis, 30/11/1999, reported by Pelzl 2014: 93.

[800] (AT) VfGH, Erkenntnis, 30/09/1996, reported by Pelzl 2014: 93 and Marktler 2008: 300.

[801] (AT) VfGH, Erkenntnis, 26/06/1997, reported by Pelzl 2014: 94 and Marktler 2008: 300; VfGH, Erkenntnis, 08/03/2001, reported by Pelzl 2014: 94 and Marktler 2008: 300.

[802] (AT) VfGH, Erkenntnis, 30/09/2003, reported in Reflets no 2/2004: 6 and by Pelzl 2014: 93.

It results from the case-law of the VfGH that a violation of the duty to make a preliminary reference under Article 267 TFEU may induce a violation of the right to a lawful judge under the B-VG. In this regard, the VfGH has explicitly stated that all violations – not just gross violations – of the duty to make a preliminary reference lead to a breach of the right to a lawful judge.[803] Moreover, the VfGH has elaborated no rules specifying the arbitrariness in the failure to refer the matter to the ECJ but applies the *Cilfit* criteria in a rather modified way. According to the case-law of the VfGH, the application of the EU law must not be in the evident conflict with the consistent interpretation provided by the ECJ.[804]

d. Slovenia

The Slovenian Constitution assures the right of parties to their lawful judge,[805] and enables them to introduce a constitutional complaint (*ustavna pritožbah*) on the ground of breach of their human rights or fundamental freedoms by an individual act.[806] This legal background made it possible for the Ustavno sodišče (Constitutional Court) to declare the violation of the referral duty as a violation of the parties' fundamental procedural rights. Two judgments are noteworthy in this context.

In the first judgment, rendered in 2009, the Ustavno sodišče accepted that an unexplained departure from settled ECJ case-law might constitute a violation of the Constitution, which entails a prohibition of arbitrary judgments.[807] However, the court did not satisfy the constitutional complaint on its merits, due to the absence of *ratione temporis* applicability of EU law in the case.[808]

By the second judgment, dated 2013, the Ustavno annulled the judgment of the Vrhovno sodišče (Supreme Court) because of the violation of the referral duty.[809] In its decision, Ustavno sodišče stressed that the ECJ is the sole body entitled to give a preliminary ruling on questions relating to the interpretation and validity of EU law. As the ECJ is to be regarded as a court within the meaning of the Slovenian Constitution, the constitutional right to access to justice includes the obligation of a national court to make a reference for a preliminary ruling to the ECJ, unless the *Cilfit* conditions are fulfilled. In this regard, any

[803] Valutytė 2014: 297.

[804] Navrátilová, M (n.d.) 'The Preliminary Ruling before the Constitutional Courts' www.law.muni.cz/sborniky/dp08/files/pdf/mezinaro/navratilova.pdf; see also Lacchi 2015b: 1681–82; Pelzl 2014: 91–94.

[805] (SI) Ustava Republike Slovenije, 23 člen.

[806] (SI) Ustava Republike Slovenije, 160 člen; Zakon o ustavnem sodišču, 24 člen, 50 člen.

[807] (SI) Ustavno sodišče Republike Slovenije, Sklep, 24/11/2009, reported by Trstenjak and Plaustajner 2014: 475–76.

[808] See also Trstenjak and Plaustajner 2014: 476–78.

[809] (SI) Ustavno sodišče Republike Slovenije, Odločba, 21/11/2013, reported by Sever in Reflets no 1/2014: 42–44, and Trstenjak and Plaustajner 2014: 477–78.

refusal must be justified adequately so that the Ustavno sodišče can verify the compatibility of the decision with the Constitution.

In summary, the Ustavno sodišče has acknowledged the constitutional relevance of the referral duty. The conditions applied by the Ustavno sodišče are strict, obliging the supreme court to explain in detail the reasons that led it to refrain from making a referral.

e. Slovakia

As individual constitutional complaint (*sťažnosti*) exists in the Slovakian legal order, individuals have the possibility to invoke the violation of their constitutional rights before the Ústavný súd (Constitutional Court).[810] Moreover, both the right to an effective judicial protection, and right to a lawful judge are enshrined under the Constitution of the Slovak Republic.[811] Given this legal framework, the Ústavný súd has developed its own case-law regarding the lawful judge principle. Two judgments deserve attention in this context.

In the first decision, delivered in 2007, the Ústavný súd held that a violation of the constitutional right to effective judicial protection may occur when the Najvyšší súd (Supreme Court) unlawfully refuses to submit a question for preliminary ruling to the ECJ.[812] However, the Ústavný súd pointed out that the ECJ had no jurisdiction to answer preliminary questions when the facts of the main proceedings predated the accession of the Member State to the EU. In the case at hand, the administrative authority had delivered its decision before the accession of Slovakia to the ECJ. Therefore, if the Najvyšší súd had approached the ECJ, the latter would only have stated its lack of competence without addressing the substance of the questions. As a result, the lawful judge principle had not been infringed in that case.

In the second decision, rendered in 2008, the Ústavný súd ruled explicitly for the first time that the violation of the obligation to refer a question to the ECJ constitutes a violation of the right to a lawful judge within the meaning of the Constitution.[813] It concluded that, if the ECJ is excluded from the procedure where the interpretation of EU norms is a relevant question, it means that the court has not been legally composed.[814] However, as the contested judgment had been delivered by the Krajský súd v Bratislave (Regional Court of Bratislava), the

[810] (SK) Ústava Slovenskej republiky, čl 127, 130; Zákon Národnej rady Slovenskej republiky o organizácii Ústavného súdu Slovenskej republiky, o konaní pred ním a o postavení jeho sudcov, Art 18 f), 49; Ústava Slovenskej republiky, čl 127, 130.

[811] (SK) Ústava Slovenskej republiky, Čl 46 ods 1, Čl 48 ods 1.

[812] (SK) Ústavný súd Slovenskej republiky, uznesenie zo dňa 29/05/2007, reported by Škvařilová in Reflets no 2/2008: 28 and Procházka 2013: 351–52.

[813] (SK) Ústavný súd Slovenskej republiky, uznesenie zo dňa 03/07/2008, reported by Škvařilová in Reflets no 2/2009: 23 and Procházka 2013: 352.

[814] (SK) Najvyšší súd Slovenskej republiky, uznesenie zo dňa 20/01/2011, reported by Procházka 2013: 352.

Ústavný súd stated that the Najvyšší súd had competence to rule on the violation of the fundamental right in the case at hand.

In short, the Ústavný súd thus referred to the right to an effective judicial protection, as well as to the right to a lawful judge to sanction the unlawful refusal by the supreme courts to make a preliminary reference. However, as Procházka points out, there is an important limitation to a possible finding of a breach of constitutional rights on these grounds. In fact, the Ústavný súd insists that it is only where the national judge 'did not recognise' their referral duty (in the sense of being aware of it) that its breach makes an extraordinary appeal available. A mere *error in procedendo* does not entitle the complainant to pursue any such claim.[815]

f. Spain

In Spain, a constitutional complaint (*recurso de amparo*) can be lodged by the parties in the event of violation of their constitutional rights during the main proceedings.[816] However, the Tribunal Constitucional (Constitutional Court) has for a long time refused to interpret a failure to make a preliminary reference as a breach of due process.[817] It has revised its consolidated doctrine on the constitutional relevance of the reference for preliminary ruling only in the 2000s.[818] Even so, the Tribunal Constitucional has only used this path to guarantee the application of national law, and not that of individual rights enshrined under EU law, until 2015. Four judgments are noteworthy in this regard.

In the first judgment, rendered in 2004, the Tribunal Constitucional declared a *recurso de amparo* well founded on the ground, inter alia, that the lower court had not submitted a request for preliminary ruling to the ECJ before deciding to disapply national law because of its incompatibility with EU law.[819] In this regard, the Tribunal Constitucional stated that a decision not to apply domestic law because it is supposedly incompatible with EU rules might imply a violation of the guarantees that constitute due process. This is especially true if the court of last instance renders such a decision without having previously requested a preliminary ruling, and if the decision constitutes a deviance from the national judicial doctrine.[820] The principle was confirmed by the Tribunal Constitucional in the second judgment, dated 2006.[821]

[815] Procházka 2013: 352–54.

[816] (ES) Constitución Española, Arts 53, 161–62; Ley Orgánica 2/1979 del Tribunal Constitucional, Arts 41–44.

[817] (ES) Constitución Española, Art 24.

[818] Lacchi 2015b: 1684–86; Navrátilová, M (n.a.) 'The Preliminary Ruling before the Constitutional Courts' www.law.muni.cz/sborniky/dp08/files/pdf/mezinaro/navratilova.pdf; Valutyté 2012a: 1180.

[819] (ES) Tribunal Constitucional de España, Sentencia 58/2004, English translation in *CMLR* (2005) 535–48, reported by Sarmiento 2014: 168–69 and Valutyté 2012a: 1180–81. For a detailed analysis of the case, see Alonso García 2005.

[820] See Valutyté 2012a: 1180–81.

[821] (ES) Tribunal Constitucional de España, Sentencia, 19/06/2006, reported by Azcárraga in Reflets no 1/2007: 11, Sarmiento 2014: 168; Valutyté 2012a: 1180.

In the third judgment, delivered in 2010, the Tribunal Constitucional clarified its jurisprudence by stating that the breach of a fair trial can only be established under the above circumstances if the question of EU law had not previously been answered by the ECJ.[822] This adjustment of jurisprudence was necessary especially with regard to ECJ case-law, which clearly states that the national court is not obliged to submit a request for preliminary ruling before leaving the domestic rule contrary to EU law unapplied.[823] Consequently, the Tribunal Constitucional confirmed that Spanish courts are obliged to make a reference to the ECJ before leaving a national rule unapplied only where the *acte éclairé* doctrine cannot be applied.[824]

Finally, by its judgment rendered in 2015, the Tribunal Constitucional declared for the first time that the disregard of ECJ case-law by a Spanish court amounted to a violation of the right to an effective judicial protection enshrined under the Article 24 of the Spanish Constitution.[825] The Tribunal Constitucional pointed out that the ECJ had already declared the Spanish rules, which had been applied in the main proceedings, contrary to EU law. Moreover, the facts at the origin of one of the ECJ judgments and of the actual claim were identical. Also, the Tribunal Superior de Justicia de Madrid ignored the ECJ case-law despite the fact the party expressly invoked the relevant judgments during the trial. In all, the contested judgment infringed not only the principle of supremacy of the EU law but also the right to an effective judicial protection in the sense of the national Constitution.

As a conclusion, it was in 2015 when the Tribunal Constitucional declared for the first time that disregarding ECJ case-law might amount to the constitutional right to effective judicial protection.

iv. Member States Reluctant to Apply the Lawful Judge Principle to the ECJ

In addition to the above five Member States with the possibility of constitutional complaint in their legal system, Belgium, Croatia, Cyprus, Latvia and Hungary also acknowledge this type of remedy. However, these is no available case-law as yet from Belgium, Croatia, Cyprus and Latvia regarding the use this constitutional protection to assert individuals' rights under EU law. Nevertheless, interesting developments can be observed in the Hungarian constitutional case-law on this matter.

[822] (ES) Tribunal Constitucional de España, Sentencia, 20/10/2010, reported by Sarmiento 2014: 169.

[823] (ECJ) Judgment in *Kücükdeveci*.

[824] Sarmiento 2014: 169.

[825] (ES) Tribunal Constitucional de España, Sentencia, 05/11/2015, reported by Oró Martinez in Reflets no 1/2016: 15.

a. Hungary

In Hungary, individuals have the right to introduce a constitutional complaint (*alkotmányjogi panasz*) before the Alkotmánybíróság (Constitutional Court), invoking the violation of their constitutional rights during judicial proceedings.[826] Despite the conditions being present for the application of this constitutional protection, the Alkotmánybíróság has declined to apply it to EU law violations so far.

In particular, by its order handed down in 2014, the Alkotmánybíróság dismissed a complaint lodged due to the alleged violation of the complainant's right to a lawful judge.[827] First of all, the Alkotmánybíróság refused to recognise the ECJ as a lawful judge within the meaning of the Hungarian Fundamental Law. Moreover, it also denied that the refusal by the national court to submit a request for preliminary ruling had any relevance under the fundamental law at all. In its subsequent case-law, the Alkotmánybíróság has confirmed the above jurisprudence and refused constitutional complaints on the same grounds on several occasions.[828]

A decision of the Alkotmánybíróság from 2015 also concerns the obligation of the Hungarian courts to make a referral, albeit from a slightly different point of view.[829] In this judgment, similarly to the precedent decisions, the Alkotmánybíróság refused the constitutional complaint, as it found that the interpretation of the EU law was not necessary in the main case. Nevertheless, the Alkotmánybíróság decided to examine, on its own initiative, the constitutionality of the national procedural rules with regard to the referral obligation. In this context, it explained that the civil procedure code does not contain any obligation for the Hungarian courts to duly explain their decisions concerning the refusal of the party's request to make a preliminary reference to the ECJ. According to the Alkotmánybíróság, this absence infringes the right of the parties to a fair trial. Consequently, it ordered the legislation to adopt the necessary amendments by the end of 2015.[830]

Finally, a decision dated 2016 from the same court confirms the judicial practice of the Alkotmánybíróság regarding the constitutional irrelevance of the refusal to submit a request for preliminary ruling.[831] As a minor development in its case-law, the Constitutional Court pointed out that in the case at

[826] (HU) Az Alkotmánybíróságról szóló 2011 évi CLI. törvény, 27 § (1). Individual constitutional complaint has been part of Hungarian constitutional law since 2012.

[827] (HU) Alkotmánybíróság, végzés, 19/05/2014. The right to one's lawful judge in enshrined under (HU) Magyarország Alaptörvénye, XXVIII cikk. See the annotations to the case by Naszladi 2014; Naszladi 2015; Varga 2014b.

[828] See (HU) Alkotmánybíróság, végzés, 16/12/2014; Alkotmánybíróság, végzés, 15/12/2014; Alkotmánybíróság, végzés, 09/02/2015; Alkotmánybíróság, végzés, 09/02/2015.

[829] (HU) Alkotmánybíróság, határozat, 14/07/2015, reported by Varga in Reflets no 3/2015: 33.

[830] These amendments have been adopted and entered into force 4 December 2015.

[831] (HU) Alkotmánybíróság, végzés, 4/12/2016.

hand, the Kúria had sufficiently justified its decision on not to proceed with a request. This means that the Alkotmánybíróság went a step further in the appreciation of the violation of the right to a fair trial than in the previous cases, in so far it considered, in accordance with its decision of 2015, whether the refusal was substantiated by the court. Despite these arguments, the complaint was, however, declared non-admissible.

To summarise, the Hungarian Alkotmánybíróság is consistently refusing to satisfy constitutional complaints lodged on the ground of infringement of the obligation to make a preliminary reference. The only achievement in this regard is that the Alkotmánybíróság has, nevertheless, acknowledged the importance of a due statement of reasons for such a refusal.

v. Conclusion on the Remedy of Constitutional Complaint

Certainly, national constitutions do not explicitly guarantee the right of the parties to have a question referred to the ECJ. In several legal orders, this right is, however, considered as a constituent part of the right to a fair trial or the right to a lawful judge, which is guaranteed at constitutional level. This is where the connection between constitutional rights and EU rights can be established.[832]

However, the function of constitutional courts is to observe constitutionality – and not to guarantee the application of EU law. Therefore, the determination of the criteria concerning the violation of constitutional rights lies within the competence of constitutional courts. These courts are free to decide whether they follow the standard set by the ECJ or establish their own criteria. In fact, constitutional courts usually assert a violation of constitutional rights if the decision on the refusal by the national court is arbitrary. This seems to be the situation in the case of fundamental disregard of the applicable EU law or of the obligation to refer, as well as in the event of deliberate deviation from ECJ case-law. However, for less evident situations, the level of substantiation required from a national court differs from court to court. This is especially the situation concerning the application of the *Cilfit* exceptions.[833]

In this regard, the Czech Ústavní soud created its own rules to safeguard the right to one's lawful judge.[834] The Ústavní soud demands a comprehensive report on the decision to opt for *acte clair* or *acte éclairé* arguments. Therefore, a national court cannot justify its refusal by simply stating that the interpretation of a given problem is obvious in the ECJ case-law. In this regard, mentioning the *Cilfit* criteria is not in itself sufficient to remove the referral duty. On the contrary, Czech courts are obliged to include the assessment of the ECJ jurisprudence and

[832] Lacchi 2016: 692–98; Lacchi 2015b: 1686–87.
[833] Lacchi 2015b: 1689.
[834] Valutyté 2012a: 1178.

to duly explain how and why the solution chosen comports with the purpose of a relevant EU legal norm.[835]

The German BVerfG has also developed its own criteria; and the *Cilfit* exceptions only serve as the first filter to evaluate the infringement of constitutional rights. While deciding whether or not to make a reference, German courts have to evaluate all circumstances of the case: the goal and content of a relevant EU legal act, the existing practice of the ECJ and its possible development, and, besides that, the practice of other states and even the possible counterviews.[836] Moreover, there are concurrent views on whether the unjustifiable application of the *acte clair* approach might in itself constitute a violation, regardless of the breach of a substantive EU right. According to the more pro-European view, the constitutional complaint should only be evaluated against the procedural rule regarding the obligation to refer, and, therefore, a breach can occur even if the substantive EU norm had been correctly applied.[837] If accepted, this latter stance might even guarantee protection beyond the *Köbler* requirements. On the other hand, it is also true that the German constitutional complaint does not protect against misapplications of law due to mistakes or misinterpretation in general.[838]

In this regard, the Austrian VfGH has not devised specific rules concerning the arbitrariness in the failure to refer a matter to the ECJ but applies the *Cilfit* criteria in a modified way. According to the VfGH, the application of EU law must not be in apparent conflict with the stable interpretation provided by the ECJ.[839]

As there are very few decisions from the Slovenian Ustavno sodišče, and the Slovakian Ústavný súd, it is difficult to draw any conclusion from their jurisprudence. It seems, however, that the Slovenian Constitutional Court requires national courts to explain to a clear and sufficient degree why they did not follow the proposal of a party to make such a preliminary reference. As for the Slovakian Constitutional Court, it recognises violation of the constitutional rights only where the national supreme court has not shown any awareness of being subject to the referral duty. Therefore, it dismisses actions in cases where the court has recognised that it was subject to a referral duty but has decided not to comply with it – whether because of the *acte clair* doctrine or by reference to *rationae temporis* arguments.[840]

[835] See also Valutytė 2012a: 1178–79; Valutytė 2014: 297.

[836] Valutytė 2012a: 1177.

[837] This is the view the first Senat of the BVerfG seems to follow. However, the second Senat continues to take into consideration the violation of the substantive norm as well. See eg (DE) BVerfG, Beschluss, 25/02/2010. For further information, see Dittert 2014: 64–65; Lacchi 2016: 693, 697.

[838] See also Valutytė 2012a: 1174–76.

[839] Navrátilová, M (n.d.) 'The Preliminary Ruling before the Constitutional Courts' www.law.muni.cz/sborniky/dp08/files/pdf/mezinaro/navratilova.pdf; and Valutytė 2014: 297. See also Pelzl 2014: 91–94.

[840] Procházka 2013: 352–53.

The application of the Spanish *recurso de amparo* in relation to referral duty has, for a long time, been very specific. In fact, even though it has been used to oblige the national courts to refer to the ECJ, the final aim was not to protect the substantive rights conferred by EU law. On the contrary, the Tribunal Constitucional referred to the duty under Article 267 TFEU to hinder the direct application of EU rules. This stance changed in 2015. As for the case-law of the Spanish Tribunal Constitucional, a *recurso de amparo* is available not against a breach of the obligation to request a preliminary ruling, but against arbitrary or patently erroneous grounds used in deciding on the merits of the case. This court declared in 2015 for the first time that the disregard of ECJ case-law amounted to a violation of the claimant's constitutional right to an effective judicial protection.

Given these points, the constitutional complaint may provide – under several laws and certain circumstances – an effective judicial protection for individuals regarding their rights to have their case referred to the ECJ. Through the protection of constitutional rights to a fair trial and to a lawful judge, this remedy can ensure that a case concerning the interpretation of EU law is referred to the ECJ. Therefore, this can indirectly lead to the protection of their substantive rights conferred by EU rules. As for EU law, the ECJ has also linked the *Köbler* liability to the violation of Article 267 TFEU; furthermore, the scope of the referral obligation is not obvious under EU law either. Therefore, it is not excluded that the remedy of constitutional complaint might provide – as applied under certain national regimes – at the least an equivalent protection to the *Köbler* doctrine, especially with regard to the fact that it sets a less stringent condition than *Köbler* liability in relation to the loss or damages sustained by the complainant.

C. Special Remedies

Moreover, there are other special remedies that can prevent the occurrence or make good damages already incurred in the event of violation of the EU law in a final judicial decision. Some examples are provided, without being exhaustive, with the aim of reflecting the variety of possibilities in this regard.

i. Amtshaftungsanspruch *under Austrian Law*

For example, under Austrian law, *Amtshaftungsanspruch* (state responsibility) can be used to claim damages from the state on the ground of breach of law by the courts.[841] The law excludes, however, responsibility for acts of the supreme courts – the VfGH, the VwGH and the OGH.[842] The courts of general

[841] (AT) Amtshaftungsgesetz. See also Pelzl 2014: 69.
[842] (AT) Amtshaftungsgesetz Art 2 § 3.

jurisdiction have competence to adjudicate on such claims, with the OGH deciding as court of last resort. In fact, the OGH has already decided on several appeals raised in state liability actions on the ground of infringement of the right to a lawful judge, due to the refusal to submit a preliminary question to the ECJ. Inspired by the case-law of the VfGH, the OGH stressed that such a refusal has to be carefully reasoned.[843] However, it has not yet found such an appeal well founded.[844]

ii. Anhörungsrüge *under German Law*

Under German law, there is a special remedy against the violation of the constitutionally guaranteed right to be heard.[845] The remedy of *Anhörungsrüge* (violation of the right to be heard) is intended to ensure that decisions made by the courts are free of substantive or procedural errors due to the submissions of the parties not being considered or taken into account in the decision-making process. If the court fails to address the essential substance of a party's factual submission on a question of particular importance for the proceedings, this indicates that the submission was not taken into account, unless it was insignificant or obviously unsubstantiated, according to the legal position of the court.

iii. Domvilla *under Swedish Law*

In Sweden, the remedy of *domvilla* (miscarriage of justice) appears to correspond to the needs of EU law.[846] A judgment can be set aside as a result of a miscarriage of justice even if the stipulated appeal period has expired. It could, for example, be so if the case is taken up despite the fact that there are impediments to a hearing (eg if the case should be dealt with by another type of court), the judgment is written in such a way that it is not clear what the court has adjudicated, or another serious procedural error has emerged which can be assumed to have had an impact on the outcome of the case.

iv. Vollstreckungsabwehrklage *and* Drittwiderspruchsklage *under German Law*

Furthermore, under German law, *Vollstreckungsabwehrklage* (action raising an objection to the claim being enforced)[847] or *Drittwiderspruchsklage* (action to

[843] The OGH made especially reference to the following judgment: (AT) VfGH, Erkenntnis, 11/12/1995.
[844] (AT) OGH, Beschluß, 27/05/1997; OGH, Beschluß, 25/06/2002; OGH, Urteil, 26/11/2002; OGH, Urteil, 22/10/2007.
[845] (DE) Verwaltungsgerichtsordnung (VwGO), Art 152a.
[846] (SE) Rättegångsbalk, 59 kap.
[847] (DE) Zivilprozessordnung, § 767.

prevent the enforcement of a judgment)[848] can serve to prevent the enforcement of a final, albeit unlawful, judgment. These remedies have already been used in cases with EU law relevance, by the Landgericht Wiesbaden (Regional Court, Wiesbaden) and the BVerwG, respectively.

In a decision of 2011, the Landgericht Wiesbaden did not impose a fine on an individual for having accepted and having collected sports bets without holding the required licence. Even though an enforceable decision had already prohibited the individual from pursuing such activity, the Landgericht Wiesbaden arrived at the conclusion that it was contrary to EU law, and therefore refused to give effect to the decision.[849] Similarly, the BVerwG suspended, by a judgment of 2009, the execution of a final decision ordering the expulsion of a foreign national to his country of origin, invoking his rights under EU law.[850]

The German courts rendered the above judgments despite the fact that national rules do not provide a legal basis to oppose the enforcement of a final judgment on the ground of violation of EU law.[851]

v. Recours dans l'intérêt de la loi *under French Law*

According to commentators, the French *recours dans l'intérêt de la loi* (remedy in the interest of justice) is an extraordinary remedy that is suitable for the needs of EU law. This is a jurisprudential remedy, which does not concern the unlawful decision itself but prevents making a precedent of it.[852]

vi. Wytyk *under Polish Law*

Under Polish law, an appeal court has the possibility to issue a *wytyk* (reproach) against a judge sitting in an inferior court where it finds that the latter has committed a manifest breach of law. Furthermore, the disciplinary liability of the judge can also be invoked in case of obvious and flagrant violation of law.[853]

vii. Recovery of Tax Declared Incompatible with EU Law

In its case-law, the ECJ has stated that the recovery of sums levied by a Member State in breach of EU law is a remedy under EU law. Member States are therefore in principle required to repay these charges.[854]

848 (DE) Zivilprozessordnung, § 771.
849 (DE) Landgericht Wiesbaden, Urteil, 07/02/2011, reported by Dittert 2014: 69.
850 (DE) BVerwG, Urteil, 22/10/2009, reported by Dittert 2014: 69–70.
851 See also Pelzl 2014: 69.
852 Dubos et al 2014: 216–17.
853 Mikłaszewicz 2014: 384.
854 (ECJ) Judgments in *Târşia*, paras 24–25; in *San Giorgio*, para 12; in *Comateb and Others*, para 20; in *Fantask and Others*, para 38. See also the analysis by Lenaerts et al 2014: 121–27; Maisto 2014: 177–80; Van Gerven 2000: 516–21.

Even if this section has not dealt with this remedy, it is not excluded that it can also be relied on where the breach of EU law was committed by national courts of last instance. In fact, a lot of cases for breach of EU law by Member State bodies originate from the violation of the VAT directives by one or more arms of government. If the use of this remedy is possible, the recovery action is more favourable to the applicant, as only the unlawfulness of the contested decision must be established, and it must not be qualified or serious.[855] However, as practice shows, restitution claims are mainly used as an alternative to the *Francovich* liability and not instead of the *Köbler* doctrine. In fact, it primarily serves as a method of making good the damages caused by an administrative breach.

D. Conclusion on Alternative Remedies

The choice between judicial remedies is generally conditioned by the national legal system. There are several Member States where it is possible to identify a clear preference for one or other means of remedy.[856] As we have seen, Member States may have other methods than *Köbler* liability to protect individual rights and to make good damages caused by final judicial decisions contrary to the EU law.

These remedies may eventually offer a real alternative to *Köbler* claims in making good damages suffered as a result of the violation of EU law by the national supreme courts. Moreover, the reliance upon them may even ensure, depending on the conditions attached to them, a higher standard of protection of individual rights than a judicial liability claim.[857]

As for retrial, in four Member States, cases have actually been reopened due to violation of EU law in a final judgment (Lithuania, Romania, Slovakia and Finland). In two of them, legislative provisions had been introduced into the procedural codes in order to recognise the violation of EU law as specific ground for retrial in 2008. It has been the case in Romania, where amendments concerned the administrative procedural code, and in Slovakia, where the civil procedural code was amended. In the other two Member States (Lithuania and Finland), the application of retrial to breaches of EU law was possible due to the broad scope of application of this remedy. In these legal systems, retrial is granted in the event of a manifest, substantive or extraordinary breach of law. In this regard, legal rules in Denmark, Malta, Sweden and the UK are similar, and therefore also seem capable to offer adequate protection.

[855] On the controversial relationship between the recovery action and the *Francovich* liability, see the following publications: Anagnostaras 2001a: 356–61; Anagnostaras 2007: 727–39; Van Gerven 2000: 506–20; Wattel 2008: 109–32.

[856] While liability claims are preferred in Bulgaria, Czech Republic, Estonia, Greece, Spain and Netherlands, in Germany and Poland they can only be subsidiary to other forms of remedies.

[857] See also Beutler 2009: 792; Golecki and Wojciechowski 2009: 195–97; Komárek 2005b: 17; Rodríguez 2004-2005: 614–15; Valutytė 2011: 37, 47.

As for constitutional complaint, in five Member States, individuals can indirectly invoke the violation of their rights under EU law before the constitutional court (Austria, Germany, and recently in the Czech Republic, Slovakia, Slovenia and Spain). Through the protection of constitutional rights to a fair trial and to a lawful judge, this remedy can ensure that a case concerning the interpretation of EU law is referred to the ECJ. Therefore, this can indirectly lead to the protection of their substantive rights conferred by EU rules. It should also not be forgetten that the ECJ has also linked the *Köbler* liability to the violation of Article 267(3) TFEU. Furthermore, the scope of the referral obligation is not obvious under EU law either. Therefore, it is not excluded that the remedy of constitutional complaint might provide – as applied under certain national regimes – at the very least an equivalent protection to the *Köbler* doctrine.

With regard to the strict conditions attached to a liability claim, these remedies might not be considered, in general, less favourable for an individual than to invoke the *Köbler* principle. Therefore, even if Member States happen to set overly restrictive conditions regarding a *Köbler* claim, it does not necessarily mean that an effective judicial protection is not accessible under these laws for breach of EU law by the national supreme court.[858] The question arises, however, whether the ECJ accepts these alternative forms of remedies to substitute *Köbler* liability actions.[859] This topic will be addressed on the chapter of the book focusing on the eventual future developments of the *Köbler* principle.[860]

V. CONCLUSIONS ON THE HISTORY OF THE KÖBLER LIABILITY

The ECJ has established the principle of Member State liability in order to provide a way to obtain individual compensation and, at the same time, to help ensure the full effectiveness of EU law.[861]

The analysis of the national practice of *Köbler* liability confirms academic opinions that *Köbler* liability has not proved to be an effective tool to achieve this dual aim.[862] Concerning impediments to the effectiveness of the Köbler doctrine, it is common to raise questions about the adequate nature of the 'sufficiently serious breach' criterion and to point to domestic legislative limitations.

As for the criterion of 'manifest breach of the applicable law', research reveals two main concerns regarding the high standard of liability. The first one relates to inconsistencies between the conditions of liability for legislative and executive state bodies, on the one hand, and for the judiciary, on the other. The

[858] See the summary table in the Annex to this book.

[859] See Anagnostaras 2001a: 355–83; Anagnostaras 2007: 727–39; Arnull 2011: 51–70; Eeckhout 1998: 66–70, 72; Van Gerven 2000: 506–20; Kornezov 2014a; Leczykiewicz 2015; Wattel 2008: 109–32.

[860] See s 3.II.

[861] (ECJ) Judgment in *Francovich and Others*, para 33.

[862] See Beutler 2009: 790; Nassimpian 2007: 834; Lock 2012: 1685.

second problem is that, given the national courts' obligation to request a preliminary ruling, the possible establishing of a manifest breach is restricted to very limited situations.[863] In particular, it seems that the criteria linked to the manifest infringement of the applicable law is fulfilled, in general, when a national supreme court takes the deliberate decision to depart from the established ECJ case-law on a given matter.

National restrictions on judicial liability and the resistance by national courts to apply the principle, however, have not proven to be major obstacles for liability claims. Even though on several occasion actions have been refused by reason of the absence of legal basis to such claims,[864] the stance of the courts in the Member States appears to be changing. It appears that national supreme courts are gradually accepting the *Köbler* principle and are ready to adjudicate liability claims directly on the basis of a judgment of the ECJ, by setting aside the overly strict legislative provisions in their national laws.[865]

Furthermore, there is another factor that affects the application of the Köbler doctrine. In fact, on several occasions, liability claims have been refused as the injured individual had already received relief by alternative means of remedy.[866] Given the existence of alternative courses of action in national laws in the event of violation of EU law by Member State courts, individuals rely on these alternatives instead of invoking liability, if the conditions are less strict and they have a better prospect of success.

Therefore, several questions arise. First, is the standard of liability adequate or should it be lowered? What is the relationship between *Köbler* liability and other remedies available in case of violation of EU law before national courts? Should *Köbler* liability be substituted by other means of remedies? Moreover, can liability be raised on the ground of violation of the referral duty alone? Or can liability be incurred by a violation of fundamental procedural rights by national courts?

These issues are addressed in the following chapter, which focuses on future developments of the principle.

[863] (BG) Sofiyski gradski sad, Reshenie, 03/01/2014; (DE) BGH, Beschluss, 28/10/2004; (FR) Cour de cassation, Arrêt, 26/10/2011.

[864] (FR) Tribunal de grande instance de Paris, 07/05/2008; (HU) Kúria, ítélet, 11/12/2013; (PT) Supremo Tribunal de Justiça, Acórdão, 03/12/2009.

[865] (AT) VfGH, Erkenntnis, 10/10/2003; (BE) Cour de cassation, arrêt, 19/12/1991; Cour constitutionnelle, arrêt, 30/06/2014; (BG) Varhoven kasatsionen sad, Opredelenie, 08/05/2015; (FI) Korkein oikeus, tuomio, 05/07/2013; (FR) Conseil d'État, décision, 18/06/2008; (DE) BHG, Beschluss, 28/10/2004; BVerwG, Urteil, 09/06/2009; (LT) Lietuvos vyriausiojo administracinio teismo 2008 m balandžio 24; (LU) Cour d'appel (Grand-Duché de Luxembourg), jugement, 13/01/2010; (NL) Gerechtshof 's-Gravenhage, Uitspraak, 15/02/2011; (PL) Naczelny Sąd Administracyjny, Wyrok, 11/06/2014; Sąd Najwyższy, Wyrok, 08/12/2009; (PT) Tribunal Constitucional, Acórdão, 09/07/2015; (SK) Okresný súd Prešov, Uznesenie, 12/03/2015; (SE) Justitiekanslern, beslut, 06/04/2009; (UK) Court of Appeal (England), judgment, 12/05/2010.

[866] (LT) Lietuvos vyriausiojo administracinio teismo 2008 m balandžio 24; (NL) Gerechtshof 's-Gravenhage, Uitspraak, 15/02/2011.

3

Perspectives for the Future

As Sarmiento has written recently, commenting on the *Commission v France* case:[1]

> One of the fascinating features of EU law is that no matter how well established its classics may be, they are revisited over and over again. If you thought you had seen it all about preliminary references, think twice. Always think twice, because you can never be fully sure until the [ECJ]'s next judgement.[2]

In the spirit of this statement, this chapter explores future developments regarding the application of the *Köbler* doctrine. Four of these developments will be addressed and analysed: (i) the establishment of a more adequate liability standard; (ii) the reassessment of the role of *Köbler* liability and its relationship with other means of national remedies; (iii) the recognition of state liability on the grounds of the violation of the referral duty; and (iv) acknowledgement of liability based on the violation of the Charter by Member State courts.

I. ADEQUATE LIABILITY STANDARD INSTEAD OF MANIFEST INFRINGEMENT

As experience shows, even in Member States where the *Köbler* liability is accepted theoretically, it is not a frequently used method of making good the damages caused to individuals by a final judgment of a national supreme court.[3] Moreover, even on the rare occasions when it has been relied on, compensation has almost never been awarded.

This problem is related to the conditions for liability as set by the ECJ, and to the question whether they – especially the seriousness of the breach – are adequate and not overly strict. Doubts have emerged whether it is at all possible to fulfil the required conditions.[4]

[1] (ECJ) Judgment in *Commission v France*, C-416/17.

[2] Sarmiento, D (2018) 'Judicial Infringements at the Court of Justice: A Brief Comment on the Phenomenal Commission/France (C-416/17)' Blog Despite our Differences, despiteourdifferencesblog.wordpress.com/2018/10/09/judicial-infringements-at-the-court-of-justice-a-brief-comment-on-the-phenomenal-commission-france-c-416-17/.

[3] See also Granger 2017: 110; Wilman 2016: 905–06.

[4] On this topic, see s 2.II.A.v.

Therefore, as Nassimpian puts it:

> Even though there is undeniable value in confirming and building upon the available avenues leading to effective judicial protection of individuals' rights, it is equally hard to refute arguments contending that this may be doomed to remain largely theoretical in effect.[5]

She is not the only one to claim that the *Köbler* liability is not an effective remedy for infringed individual rights.[6] However, one should not forget that it serves as an incentive for Member State courts to fulfil their obligations in applying EU law, and therefore can prevent the occurrence of damage. Hence, as a preventive or deterrent tool, it can contribute to the effective application of EU law.[7]

In this regard, it is noteworthy that academics have already pointed out that the state liability concept is not coherent enough, and it should be determined whether its primary function is to remedy infringed rights or to deter non-compliant supreme courts.[8] Doing so would be essential, also because the two concepts relate to different theories of the general liability doctrine. In fact, a compensation-focused regime is characterised by the following features: firstly, the existence of loss is a necessary condition for an award; secondly, the award reflects the value of losses which have been proved; and finally, the award may be conditional on proving that the defendant acted negligently (was at fault), but the gravity of the defendant's misconduct nevertheless does not affect the measure of damages. An enforcement-focused regime has, in contrast, the following features: firstly, the existence of loss is not a necessary condition of liability; secondly, the necessary condition of liability is a breach of a regulatory standard; thirdly, the award may exceed the value of losses which have been proved; fourthly, the gravity of the defendant's misconduct affects the measure of damages (directly or at least indirectly), and therefore a slight violation of a norm may be left unsanctioned; and finally, punitive damages are not excluded.[9]

The choice between the two systems affects the appropriate liability standard, the amount of compensation, and the consequences of the contribution of a third party or the claimant in the damage being incurred. For example, the gravity of the defendant's misconduct affects, directly or at least indirectly, the extent of damages, and a slight violation of a norm may be left unsanctioned under an enforcement-focused regime. However, in a compensation-focused regime the gravity of the defendant's misconduct does not affect the extent of damages. Moreover, the principle of full compensation cannot be departed from in a system whose primary function is providing compensation, but it can be

[5] Nassimpian 2007: 834.

[6] See also Beuter 2009: 790; Bobek 2013: 201, 209; Broberg 2016: 250; Condon and van Leeuwen, 2016; Lock 2012: 1685.

[7] See also Giliker 2017: 452; Granger 2017: 94; Lock 2012: 1676, 1700, 1701.

[8] Dougan 2017; Giliker 2017: 450; Leczykiewicz 2012: 1–3; Leczykiewicz 2017: 63–64; Reich 2017: 114–15, 122–23; Rodríguez 2004–05: 611, 614–15; Turmo 2019: 348, 356, 388.

[9] Leczykiewicz 2012: 1–2.

modified in a system which focuses on enforcement, where effective deterrence is more important than restoration. Finally, the claimant's misconduct affects the extent of damages in a compensation-focused regime; however, in an enforcement focused regime it does not.[10] If one assumes, like Leczykiewicz, that a defendant-focused regime, based on the idea of enforcement, is a more suitable approach in the area of EU law, the conditions of *Köbler* liability should reflect this objective.[11]

As already mentioned, according to academics, *Köbler* liability can hardly work, in its current form, as an effective deterrent for national courts. Considering the specific obligations of national courts in respect of the application of EU law and the *acte clair* doctrine, this means that the liability standard should be lowered. The research confirms that in order for the criteria of 'manifest infringment' to be established, it is necessary, in practical terms, that the national supreme court deliberately go against an established and clear ECJ case-law.[12] Economic analysis of the adequate judicial liability standard within the multicentric legal system reinforces this conclusion.[13]

In addition, the research has also revealed that applying different liability standards for breaches committed by the legislative, the executive and the judicial branches of government might cause incoherence in cases where several organs of the state contributed to the violation of EU law.[14] To remedy such problems arising from the inconsistencies between *Francovich* and *Köbler* liability, considering the liability of the state as a whole can be, at least theoretically, a solution. This is, however, more a theoretical than a practical solution, because in order to be able to apply such a stance, it is necessary that the national law foresee the liability of the state and not that of the state bodies. Otherwise, it is the responsibility of the claimant to be vigilant and sue all branches of government that contributed to the breach.

II. EFFECTIVE REMEDIAL SYSTEM INSTEAD OF EFFECTIVE REMEDIES

It has also been demonstrated that Member States have other methods than *Köbler* liability to protect individual rights and to make good damages caused by final judicial decisions contrary to the EU law.

These remedies can offer a real alternative to *Köbler* claims in making good damages suffered as a result of a violation of EU law by the national supreme courts. Moreover, the reliance upon them may even ensure, depending on the

[10] Leczykiewicz 2012: 1–3, 17.

[11] See also Granger 2017: 96; Haba 2015; Lock 2012: 1701–02; Loth 2017: 49–50; Reich 2017: 114–15, 122–23, 127.

[12] See s 2.II.A.v.

[13] Golecki and Wojciechowski 2009: 195–97. For another economic analyses, see Dyèvre 2016; Loth 2017: 52–53.

[14] For the discussion on this topic, see s 2.II.B.

conditions attached to them, a higher standard of protection of individual rights than a judicial liability claim.[15]

Therefore, even if a Member State happens to set overly restrictive conditions regarding a *Köbler* claim, it does not necessarily mean that an effective remedy is not accessible under these laws for breach of EU law by the national supreme court.[16] The question arises, however, whether the ECJ accepts these alternative forms of remedies to substitute *Köbler* liability actions.[17]

A. Foundations of the State Liability Principle

Before analysing the available ECJ case-law and the doctrinal opinions, it is necessary to recall the two underlying principles of EU law that may have an influence on the recognition of alternative national remedies: the principle of effectiveness and the right to effective judicial protection.[18]

These were precisely the two principles that led the ECJ to develop the doctrine of state liability in the beginning of the 1990s.[19] In fact, liability of the Member States for violation of EU law was, at the first time, established in order to complete the system of enforcement of EU rights,[20] which had not provided any means to protect individual rights and ensure their full effect where the national legislature had infringed its obligation to implement into the national legal order dispositions of EU law lacking direct effect.[21] Afterward, this principle 'inherent in the system of the Treaty' was interpreted as having general scope of application, and applying regardless of the nature of the infringed EU norm[22] and the Member State body responsible for the breach.[23] Nevertheless, it does not mean that liability must be provided in every situation and regardless of whether there are other available means to remedy the infringements.[24] In fact, state liability was construed on the general principles common to the laws of the Member States and the liability of the EU based on Article 340 TFEU (ex 288 EC).[25] Neither of these systems foresees the absolute availability of compensation.

[15] Beutler 2009: 792; Golecki and Wojciechowski 2009: 195–97; Komárek 2005b: 17; Rodríguez 2004–05: 614–15; Valutytė 2011: 37, 47.

[16] See the summary table in the Annex to this book.

[17] Anagnostaras 2001a: 355–83; Anagnostaras 2007: 727–39; Arnull 2011: 51–70; Eeckhout 1998: 66–70, 72; Van Gerven 2000: 506–20; Kornezov 2014a; Leczykiewicz 2015; Wattel 2008: 109–32.

[18] According to Wallerman (2016a: 341–43), it is appropriate to take into account the principle of sincere cooperation as well in this regard.

[19] Jans and Duijkersloot 2015: 437–85.

[20] Biondi and Farley 2009: 3–10.

[21] (ECJ) Judgment in *Francovich and Others*.

[22] Steiner 1993: 3.

[23] (ECJ) Judgment in *Brasserie du pêcheur and Factortame*, paras 21–22, 29, 32, 34; see also Biondi and Farley 2009: 17–18.

[24] See ss 3.II.C, 3.II.D, and Anagnostaras 2001a: 356–61; Anagnostaras 2007: 727–39; Van Gerven 2000: 506–20; Wattel 2008: 109–32.

[25] (ECJ) Judgment in *Brasserie du pêcheur and Factortame*, paras 27, 42.

B. Effectiveness and Effective Judicial Protection

As is well known, pursuant to the effectiveness principle, the enforcement of EU rights at national level must not be 'virtually impossible or excessively difficult'.[26] This principle, together with the principle of equivalence, operates as a framework limiting the procedural or remedial autonomy of the Member States. These principles aim primarily to guarantee an effective application of substantive EU law.

Since the entry into force of the Lisbon treaty, the principle of effective judicial protection has acquired written primary law status, and is now enshrined in Article 47 of the Charter.[27] Prechal and Widdershoven argue that national procedural and remedial provisions should therefore be tested not only against the principle of effectiveness but also against the right to effective judicial protection. They point out that while there is a connection between the two principles, there are also a number of differences. In particular, the right to effective judicial protection imposes a positive obligation on the Member States to create new remedies at national level.[28] Therefore, effective judicial protection can be regarded as a more robust manifestation of the principle of effectiveness.[29]

According to Lenaerts, the partial overlap between the two principles is the aspect of the principle of effectiveness which focuses on the need for judicial supervision. Thus, where Member States are implementing EU law, the rights that EU law confers on individuals must be accompanied by effective judicial remedies (*ubi ius ibi remedium*). Where EU rights are violated, the national court must be empowered to grant remedy.[30] Thus, although it is for the Member States to establish a system of legal remedies and procedures, EU law requires them to do so in a way that ensures respect for the right to effective judicial protection. This judge-made principle is now codified in the second paragraph of Article 19(1) TEU.[31]

Also, in my opinion, the principle of effective judicial protection sets more stringent conditions than the principle of effectiveness, due to the fact that the latter can be justified using the procedural right of reason test, while the former

[26] (ECJ) Judgments in *Rewe-Handelsgesellschaft Nord and Rewe-Markt Steffen*; in *Comet*, paras 13 and 15; in *Agrokonsulting-04*, para 35; in *Križan and Others*, para 85. See also Accetto and Zleptnig 2005; Flynn 2008; Krommendijk 2016; Galetta 2010: 34–38; Lenaerts et al 2014: 118–19; Maisto 2014: 163–82; Šadl 2016: 82–87, 99–101; Tridimas 2006: 423–27; Wallerman 2016a: 351–54.

[27] See also Dougan 2004: 62–65; Gutman 2019; Paunio 2014: points 47.94–47.112; Pernice 2013: 381–95; Prechal and Widdershoven 2011; Wilman 2015: 14–19; Wilman 2016.

[28] Prechal and Widdershoven 2011: 39–42, 50; and, in the same line Gordon and Moffatt 2014: 79, as well as Van Cleynenbreugel 2012a: 93. See also (ECJ) judgment in *DEB*, paras 36, 45–47, 49–51; the annotations to the case by Engström 2011; Oliver 2011.

[29] Prechal and Widdershoven 2011: 39–42. See also Lacchi 2016: 689–90; Safjan 2014: ch B; Varga 2019: 1685; Wattel 2014: 198–99 and (ECJ) judgment in *Orizzonte Salute*, para 49. Compare with (ECJ) judgment in *XC e.a.*

[30] See also Lenaerts et al 2014: 110–13.

[31] See also (ECJ) judgment in *Johnston*; as well as Barents 2010: 715; Dougan 2004: 4–7; Safjan 2014.

cannot. The principle of effective judicial protection can only be limited if the necessary conditions under Article 52(1) of the Charter are fulfilled.[32]

In any case, the principle of effective judicial protection has primary importance in the context of national remedies.[33]

C. ECJ Case-Law on Alternative Remedies

As for the relationship between effectiveness and effective judicial protection, there is no clear rule in the ECJ's case-law.[34] In *Unibet* and *Impact*, the ECJ considered effectiveness as part of the more encompassing effective judicial protection principle; in *Alassini*, the two principles had their specific focus on their own. In *Mono Car Styling*, the two principles were placed in juxtaposition; while in *DEB*, they were considered interchangeable.[35]

Therefore, as Prechal and Widdershoven point out, both principles are relevant to examine the compatibility of national remedial rules with the requirements under EU law.[36]

As for the question whether it is possible to remedy breaches of EU law by national supreme courts through means other than the *Köbler* liability, there is no explicit guidance from the ECJ.[37] Nonetheless, there are some indications with regard to the autonomous nature of the *Francovich* liability that can be useful to address this issue.[38] Moreover, in several cases the ECJ has dealt with the question of whether the individual was entitled to insist on a particular remedy when the national system offered alternative means that might have used to protect their rights under EU law.

In *Bonfaci* and *Maso*, the question emerged whether a Member State is entitled to apply retroactively the adopted implementing measures in making good the damage sustained by employees because of the belated transposition of the directive. The ECJ concluded that retroactive and proper application in full of these measures suffices to ensure reparation. However, the ECJ pointed out that Member States must also make good any eventual complementary

[32] See also Gutman 2019: 895–96.

[33] Adinolfi 2012: 298; Varga 2019: 1685.

[34] Prechal and Widdershoven 2011; Safjan 2014: ch B.

[35] (ECJ) Judgments in *Unibet*, paras 40–41; in *Impact*, para 51; in *Alassini and Others*; in *Mono Car Styling*, para 49; in *DEB*, paras 36, 45–47, 49–51; see also Prechal and Widdershoven 2011: 44–46; Lacchi 2016: 689–90.

[36] Prechal and Widdershoven 2011: 52.

[37] Ortlep and Widdershoven 2015: 333–434; Safjan 2014: ch II, point A.

[38] On the exceptional and complementary nature of the liability claim, see (ECJ) opinions of AG Mischo in Joint Cases *Francovich and Others*, para 42; of AG Tesauro in Joined Cases *Brasserie du pêcheur and Factortame*, paras 100–04; of AG Léger in *Hedley Lomas*, paras 193–201; of AG Jacobs in *Denkavit Internationaal and Others*, para 80; as well as the commentary on the case by Anagnostaras 2001a: 371–72. On the contrary stance, see the (ECJ) opinion of AG Jacobs in *Fantask and Others*, paras 83–84; as well as judgments in *Sutton*; in *Comateb and Others*.

loss sustained.[39] Nevertheless, the ECJ appears to have accepted the retroactive application of the belatedly transposed directive in place of the damages claim against the state for non-implementation of the directive in time.

The *Stockholm Lindöpark* case concerned whether the violation of the VAT directive constituted a serious breach of EU law that entails liability of the state. Examining the circumstances of the case, the ECJ deemed the infringement sufficiently serious to render the state liable for damages. However, the ECJ also mentioned that such a liability action did not seem necessary at first sight. In this regard, the ECJ pointed out that the claimant might properly pursue the debts directly on the provisions of the directive which are in its favour.[40] The ECJ appears to have admitted that a liability claim against the state is not necessary if the recovery of unlawfully paid taxes is possible through other means of remedy.

The judgment in *TWD Textilwerke Deggendorf* concerned the relationship between the action for annulment and preliminary rulings on validity. It provided a rule to prevent the evasion of time limits when an applicant had a clear possibility of bringing an action for annulment.[41] Essentially, if a claimant would clearly have had standing to bring a direct action for annulment under Article 263 TFEU but did not do so within the time limit, the ECJ will not entertain a reference on validity if the claimant subsequently brings proceedings before the national court. It means, however, that the action for annulment of an EU act and a preliminary reference on validity, introduced via the national court, are considered to be alternative remedies which complete each other in order to provide – a complete system of – legal remedies for the individuals. The reasoning of the General Court in *Iberdrola* confirms this point of view.[42] Moreover, in *Sina Bank*, the General Court argued that the remedy of the plea of illegality is open only in the absence of any other available remedy.[43]

In *Levez*, the question emerged whether the right to equal pay under EU law precluded the application of a national limitation period to bring proceedings before the employment tribunal. Under national law, the claimant also had the possibility to bring proceedings before the courts of general jurisdiction, where the time limit would not have applied. Therefore, the national time limit – that was eventually found to be contrary to the effectiveness principle – applied only to one type of remedy, and not to another type of action. Grounding its judgment on the principle of equivalence, the ECJ held that the existence of this

[39] (ECJ) Judgment in *Bonifaci and Others et Berto and Others*, para 53 in *Maso and Others*. See also Dougan 2000a: 111; Tridimas 2006: 541–42.

[40] (ECJ) Judgment in *Stockholm Lindöpark*, para 35.

[41] (ECJ) Judgment in *TWD Textilwerke Deggendorf*, para 17. See also Albors-Llorens 2017: 295–97; Wyatt 1997.

[42] (ECJ) Judgment in *Iberdrola*, para 43. See also Bogojević 2015: III, B.

[43] (ECJ) Judgment in *Sina Bank*, para 43; see also judgments in *Nachi Europe*, para 36; in *Roquette Frères*, para 40.

alternative remedy makes no difference if it is likely to entail procedural rules or other conditions that were less favourable than those applicable to claims brought before employment tribunals under domestic employment law.[44]

In *Impact*, the issue of availability of alternative remedies was addressed again. In this case, the national legislature had conferred jurisdiction to hear actions based on the national measure implementing the framework agreement on fixed-term work on specialised courts. Since the EU directive was belatedly implemented, the claimants were obliged to split their actions into separate claims – the specialised courts having jurisdiction only for claims concerning the period after the entry into force of the national implementation measure. Nonetheless, as the jurisdiction of the specialised courts was only optional, individuals could also pursue a single action before the courts of general jurisdiction. In this regard, they had the possibility to bring proceedings either against their employer for failure to apply the directive directly, or against the state for failure to transpose it on time. However, the ECJ found that, in so far as dividing the action would result in procedural disadvantages for individuals seeking to rely directly on EU law, the principle of effectiveness mandates specialised national courts to extend their jurisdiction accordingly, in order to remedy that discrepancy.[45]

In *Pontin*, the essential question raised was whether national law could restrict the remedies available to a dismissed pregnant worker to nullity and reinstatement, to the exclusion of all other remedies under employment law, such as an action for damages. The ECJ concluded that national legislation laying down a specific remedy with its own procedural rules, where pregnant workers were dismissed, was legitimate as long as the principles of equivalence and effectiveness were satisfied. However, if this specific remedy does not comply with the principle of effectiveness, this would infringe the requirement of effective judicial protection.[46]

In *Gavieiro*, the ECJ suggested that an action for damages is not necessary if the individuals can rely directly on the unconditional and sufficiently precise EU norm in order to enforce their rights under EU law. In this respect, the ECJ clearly explained that the temporary teachers employed by an autonomous Spanish community could rely directly on the framework agreement before a national court in order to obtain recognition of their entitlement to three-year length-of-service increments in respect of the period starting with the date by which the Member States should have transposed directive and ending with the entry into force of the national law transposing that directive into the domestic law of the Member State concerned. Therefore, as the ECJ put it ‘an action for

[44] (ECJ) Judgment in *Levez*, para 53. See also the commentary on the case by Arnull 2011: 56–57; Tridimas 2000: 473.

[45] (ECJ) Judgment in *Impact*, para 55. See also Arnull 2011: 57–58.

[46] (ECJ) Judgment in *Pontin*, para 69. See also Arnull 2011: 60–61.

damages founded on … liability of the Member States for breaches of EU law does not seem necessary'.[47]

In *Unibet*, the ECJ was asked whether national law had to permit a free-standing action for review of a national provision's compatibility with the EU law where there were other legal remedies available to a claimant that would allow the issue to be examined. The answer of the ECJ to this question was essentially negative. The ECJ held that EU law does not interfere with national remedies unless it is apparent from the overall scheme of the national legal system that no legal remedy exists to ensure, even indirectly, the respect of individual's right under EU law.[48] Therefore, it is up to the Member States to guarantee the effective judicial protection of EU rights. When laying down the respective rules, Member States must ensure that the principles of equivalence and effectiveness are respected.[49] The legal arrangements on national remedies remain intact, so long as they suffice to guarantee effectiveness. Only where these would be infringed does EU law require the creation of new remedies within the national legal system.

The *Samba Diouf* case concerned the implementation of the directive on granting and withdrawing refugee status, which lays down the right to effective remedy. The question arose whether the Luxemburgish remedy system complied with this right and Article 47 of the Charter. The ECJ found that the absence of a remedy against the decision to examine the asylum application under an accelerated procedure does not infringe the right to an effective remedy if the legality of the final decision adopted in that procedure may be thoroughly reviewed within the framework of an action against the decision rejecting the application. This notably concerns the reasons for applying the accelerated procedure.[50]

The *Târşia* case concerned the compatibility with EU law of a national remedial system which allows for cases to be reopened where the final judgment is contrary to EU law exclusively in administrative proceedings but excludes such reopening in civil or administrative proceedings. The ECJ stated that EU law, in particular the principles of equivalence and effectiveness, does not preclude such legal arrangements. It also mentioned that, according to settled case-law, individuals are entitled to bring a liability claim against the state in order to obtain legal protection of their rights in such situations.[51]

In the *Tomášová* case the national court asked the ECJ whether the Member State could be held liable on the grounds of the *Köbler* doctrine even if the

[47] (ECJ) Judgment in *Gavieiro and Torres*, para 87.

[48] (ECJ) Judgment in *Unibet*, paras 40–41. See also the commentary on the case by Anagnostaras 2007: 734.

[49] Prechal and Widdershoven 2011: 45.

[50] (ECJ) Judgment in *Samba Diouf*. See also Safjan 2014.

[51] The subsidiary nature of the liability claim to the retrial seems to be accepted by the ECJ. See (ECJ) judgment in *Târşia*, para 40; as well as opinion of AG Jääskinen in *Târşia*, paras 27–33, and, for a thorough analysis of the case, Sowery 2016.

claimant had not used all ordinary legal remedies available under the applicable national law before bringing a liability action. The referring court also asked whether an action for recovery of a sum unduly paid, as a legal remedy, has priority over compensation for damages. The ECJ stated, succinctly, that the relationship between a liability claim and the other actions available under national law is determined by the national laws, subject to observance of the principles of equivalence and effectiveness.[52]

Even if *Jégo-Quéré* and *Inuit* did not concern national remedies but the remedial system of the EU, several considerations by the ECJ may be interesting for the purposes of the present analysis. Both cases concerned the locus standi of individuals in direct actions for annulment of EU legislative acts.[53] In *Jégo-Quéré*, the General Court stated that the applicant could not be regarded as individually concerned by the contested legislative measure, even if the provisions of general application had directly affected their legal situation. It then went on to examine whether, in such a case, the inadmissibility of the action for annulment would deprive the applicant of the right to an effective remedy. In this regard, it pointed out that there exist two further procedural routes through which the applicant might bring the case before the ECJ. However, neither proceedings before national courts giving rise to a reference for a preliminary ruling, nor an action for damages based on the non-contractual liability of the EU were found to provide a satisfactory solution to protect the interest of the individual.[54] The General Court therefore concluded that the strict interpretation of the notion of a 'person individually concerned', as applied until then, must be reconsidered.[55]

In *Inuit*, the ECJ concluded that the applicants did not satisfy the conditions of admissibility.[56] In its reasoning, the ECJ highlighted the principle of procedural autonomy of the Member States. It then held that neither the TFEU nor Article 19 TEU intended to create new remedies before national courts to ensure the observance of EU law other than those already laid down by national law. This would be otherwise only if the structure of the domestic legal system concerned were such that there was no remedy making it possible, even indirectly, to ensure the observance of the rights which individuals derive from EU law.[57] Afterward, on several occasions, the ECJ confirmed that even though an

[52] (ECJ) Judgment in *Tomášová*, para 40. This judgment is interesting in the light of the earlier case-law concerning the duty to mitigate one own's losses, which appeared to be an integral part of the state liability doctrine. See also Anagnostaras 2001a: 363, 374–75.

[53] (EU) Art 263 TFEU. See also (ECJ) judgment in *Plaumann v Commission*; Albors-Llorens 2014: 265–80.

[54] (ECJ) Judgment in *Jégo-Quéré v Commission*, paras 44–46. See also the annotation to the case by Brown and Morijn 2004.

[55] (ECJ) Judgment in *Jégo-Quéré v Commission*, paras 49–51.

[56] (ECJ) Judgment in *Inuit Tapiriit Kanatami and Others v Parliament and Council*. See the analysis by Arnull 2015: 391–98; and the annotation to the case by Kornezov 2014b: 251–63; as well as Lenaerts et al 2014: 113–18.

[57] (ECJ) Judgment in *Inuit Tapiriit Kanatami and Others v Parliament and Council*, paras 100–04.

action for annulment of an EU legislative act was not available for the individual, the judicial protection of the applicant was ensured by alternative means of remedy (such as via the possibility for the national court to make a request to the ECJ for a preliminary ruling on the validity of the legislative act,[58] an action for non-contractual liability under Article 268 TFEU and the second paragraph of Article 340, or availability of other action before national courts).[59]

Finally, in *XC e.a.*, when comparing the enforcement system of the ECHR and EU law, the ECJ suggested that invocation mechanisms (such as direct effect, primacy, indirect effect, preliminary ruling procedure), which distinguish the EU legal system from that of the ECHR, ensure the correct application of EU law even before the national decision acquires res judicata and therefore they make the use of the remedy of retrial unnecessary under EU law. In fact, in this judgment, the ECJ relied on the availability of invocation entitlements to reject the idea that the remedy of retrial should be made available for violation of the Charter rights based on the principle of equivalence, given that such remedy was available under Austrian law for the violation of the ECHR. Therefore, the ECJ considered the system of enforcement of EU law as a whole with all possible mechanisms available when it made its decision.[60]

The common point in the above judgments is that the ECJ appears to have considered the structure of the remedial system when evaluating whether it fulfils the requirements of effectiveness and effective judicial protection.[61] Therefore, one may conclude that state liability claims are unnecessary when the *effet utile* of EU rules can be ensured by alternative means.[62] Conversely, the introduction of a new remedy into the national legal order in the form of a liability action is not required if it is unnecessary in order to protect individuals' rights.[63] Moreover, we can observe that both *Francovich* and *Köbler* liability have been recognised as a matter of EU law to ensure individual rights in cases where this protection could not have been provided by other means.[64]

Nonetheless, because ECJ judgments are formulated in a general way, the rulings in *Köbler* and *Traghetti del Mediterraneo* merely state a general principle, without making reference to the wider context of remedies and the interrelationship between national remedies. Moreover, it is widely accepted that remedies and procedures are two distinct legal concepts. Since remedies are governed by the *ubi ius, ibi remedium* principle, they are determined by EU

[58] See also Broberg 2015: 33–35; Broberg 2017:108–09; Krommendijk 2017: 53–58; Lacchi 2016: 687–91.

[59] (ECJ) Order in *Verein Deutsche Sprache v Council*, paras 30–31; judgments in *Reynolds Tobacco and Others v Commission*, paras 82–83; in *Unión de Pequeños Agricultores v Council*, paras 39–41; see also Gutman 2011: 704–08.

[60] (ECJ) Judgment in *XC e.a.*, paras 39–48; Varga 2019: 1684–1685; 1690–96.

[61] Considering the judgments in *Metallgesellschaft* and *Fuß*, in their context, they do not seem to contradict the above conclusion either. See also Sowery 2016: 1722; Lacchi 2016: 686.

[62] Dougan 2000a: 110.

[63] Anagnostaras 2007: 736.

[64] Jacobs 1993: 980.

law.[65] In this regard, *Francovich* and *Köbler* claims are considered to be autonomous and independent from other existing remedies in national laws.

D. Doctrinal Views on Alternative Remedies

Scholars have dissenting opinions on whether a claimant has the right to a particular remedy when the national system offers alternative means that might have been used to protect its rights under EU law.

Leczykiewicz expressly states that national courts are, in certain situations, obliged to make a state liability action available to individuals, even if other enforcement mechanisms could ensure effective judicial protection of EU rights.[66] However, this position is highly criticised by, among others, Wattel and Harlow, who oppose the overly intrusive measures taken by the ECJ in national remedial competence.[67] Adinolfi points out that remedial provisions are tightly linked to national legal traditions, and are usually embodied in long-standing codes or deeply rooted case-law. Therefore, whenever the ECJ declares that national rules cannot provide adequate judicial protection, the ruling is likely to produce a critical response in the Member State concerned.[68] Reich also suggests, albeit in the context of EU private law, that it is for the national law to provide adequate remedy for violation of EU rights in the first place. Only when the remedy provided does not ensure the effectiveness of EU law must the national remedy be 'upgraded'.[69]

As Anagnostaras points out, EU law does not interfere with the nature of the action that claimants bring in their national courts, so long as the principle of effectiveness is satisfied. In this regard, the very existence of liability proceedings is demanded by EU law, because this is considered necessary to satisfy the effectiveness requirements.[70] Moreover, according to Eilmansberger, neither the loyalty principle, nor the principle of uniform application of EU law, nor the principle of *effet utile*, can explain why a particular remedy must be provided.[71] Hofmann argues that a global assessment of the Member State's legal system needs to be made before the last-resort measure of crafting a new remedy is taken.[72] Dougan even suggests that state liability does not create a right specifically to damages against the state for its breach of EU law, but has instead introduced a general right to reparation in whatever form the Member State finds it most convenient to provide.[73]

[65] Van Gerven 2000: 522.
[66] Leczykiewicz 2012: 2.
[67] Wattel 2008: 125–28; Harlow 2010: 7, 77–78; see also Drake 2010: 77; Tomkins 2003: 287.
[68] Adinolfi 2012: 287.
[69] Reich 2013.
[70] Anagnostaras 2001a: 377; Anagnostaras 2007: 734; see also Dougan 2000a: 109.
[71] Eilmansberger 2004: 1232.
[72] Hofmann 2014: point 47.57.
[73] Dougan 2000a: 109, 119, 127; see also Lacchi 2016: 686.

E. ECtHR Case-Law on Effective Judicial Protection

Given that Article 47(1) of the Charter corresponds, substantially, to Article 13 ECHR, it seems useful to briefly recall the relevant ECtHR case-law as well.[74] It is further justified by the fact that the ECJ has often referred to the ECtHR's case-law when interpreting Article 47 of the Charter.[75] Furthermore, in the terms of the Charter, the level of protection guaranteed by Article 47 may never be lower than the level of protection guaranteed by the ECHR.[76]

The *Kudła* case concerned the right to an effective remedy in respect of a complaint about the length of court proceedings. In its judgment, the ECtHR reiterated that Article 13 of the ECHR guarantees the availability at national level of a remedy to enforce the substance of the Convention rights in whatever form they may happen to be secured in the domestic legal order. In this regard, even if a single remedy does not by itself entirely satisfy the requirements of Article 13, the aggregate of remedies provided for under domestic law may do so. However, the required remedy must meet the standard of 'effectiveness', which means that it must be effective both in law and in practice.[77]

These same principles were enounced in the *İlhan* case, with regard to a claim of ill-treatment in criminal proceedings. In *Cocchiarella*, the ECtHR reiterated that the Contracting States are afforded some discretion as to the manner in which they provide individuals with the relief required by Article 13 in the event of violation of Article 6(1) ECHR.[78]

In the *Lukenda* case the ECtHR held that Article 13 requires that the parties not only have the general obligation to solve the problem that led the ECtHR to find a violation of a right under the ECHR, but they must also provide the procedures within their respective legal system for the effective redress of violation of the ECHR's rights.[79]

Therefore, according to the established case-law of the ECtHR, Contracting States are afforded some discretion as to the manner in which they conform to their Convention obligations under Article 13 ECHR.

F. Conclusion on the Effective Remedial System

As already emphasised, the question of whether an individual possesses a specific remedy or standing in a given situation is not decided. As such, the division of competences between EU law and national law needs to be clarified

[74] See also Safjan 2014: ch 4, A; Van Cleynenbreugel 2012a: 98.

[75] (ECJ) Judgments in *Heylens and Others*, para 14; in *Johnston*, paras 18–19; in *Unibet*, para 67; in *DEB*, paras 36, 45–47, 49–51; *in Agrokonsulting-04*, para 61.

[76] (EU) Charter, Art 53; see also Hofmann 2014: points 47.42–47.46; Wattel 2014: 199–202.

[77] (ECtHR) Judgment in *Kudła v Poland*, § 157.

[78] (ECtHR) Judgments in *Kaya v Turkey*, § 106; in *İlhan v Turkey*, § 97; in *Cocchiarella v Italy*, § 79.

[79] (ECtHR) Judgment in *Lukenda v Slovenia*, §§ 94–95; see also Lacchi 2015a: 122–23.

and it needs to be determined why and what remedies must be available by national law.[80]

Several academics are in favour of a unified system of judicial protection, and of a harmonisation of national remedial and procedural rules. They argue that the absence of such harmonisation jeopardises the uniformity and effectiveness of EU law.[81] However, other scholars insist that national procedural autonomy must be respected. More reasons may justify this autonomy, such as legitimate national interests, local cultural choices and the integrity of national law.[82] Furthermore, several commentators argue in favour of a sectoral approach. They support that the EU's remedial competence should be selectively matched to the degree of EU substantive competence exercised over any given policy.[83]

In my view, there is no reason for not accepting the use of alternative remedies. As for the ECJ, it can easily accommodate its case-law to that position. In fact, if the ECJ confirms clearly that Member States have the right to set a hierarchy between *Köbler* actions and other remedies, that means that *Köbler* will offer only a standard of protection and not necessarily a new remedy.[84]

After all, legal writing has observed that, in its recent case-law, the ECJ leaves the assessment to national courts more frequently, and is more selective with regard to the national rules with which it takes issue.[85] The underlying rationale behind this selective deference seems to be that, since the general principles of the law governing remedies have now been established, the ECJ can entrust national courts to apply those principles.[86]

As a consequence, overly restrictive conditions concerning *Köbler* claims may cause problems with regard to the right to effective judicial protection only in Member States where the remedial structure does not provide other effective remedy either.[87]

Therefore, and making reference to Dougan, it is argued that the appropriate interpretation of the state liability principle should be the following: *Köbler* does not create a right specifically to damages against the Member State for its breach of EU law, but has instead introduced a general right to remedy in whatever form the Member State finds it most convenient to provide.[88] This apparently new stance leads us back to the traditional principle regarding the division of competence: it is within the power of national law to determine remedies and

[80] Anagnostaras 2001a: 372; Eilmansberger 2004: 1236, 1245, 1246.

[81] Himsworth 1997; Storme 1994; Van den Bossche 2014. See also Drake 2010: 78; Dougan 2004: 94–105; Faure 2017: 428–29, 434, 436, 437, 440; Van Boom 2009: 437–39.

[82] Dougan 2004: 105–12.

[83] Dougan 2004: 67, 171–226.

[84] See (ECJ) judgment in *Tomášová*, paras 40–41.

[85] Adinolfi 2012: 301; Wallerman 2016a: 354–55, making reference to the (ECJ) judgments in *Van Schijndel*, in *Kraaijeveld*, in *Kühne & Heitz* and in *Uniplex*.

[86] Tridimas 2000: 466.

[87] This seems to be the situation in the following Member States: Estonia, Ireland, Greece, Cyrus, Luxembourg and Hungary.

[88] Dougan 2004: 109, 119, 127.

procedures, except that they provide an effective protection of rights conferred by EU law. The only modification is that from now on, the effective protection, that is the standard of adequate protection, is going to be evaluated against the *Köbler* criteria.[89]

III. VIOLATION OF THE REFERRAL DUTY AS A SEPARATE GROUND FOR LIABILITY

The topic of the two following sections is whether *Köbler* liability can be incurred in case of the violation of two obligations imposed on Member State courts under EU law. The first is the violation of the referral duty, that is the arbitrary or unexplained decision not to make a preliminary reference. The second one is the violation of the right to have someone's case heard within reasonable time.

A. ECJ Case-Law and the Doctrine

The next topic to be addressed is the possibility to bring a liability suit for the mere infringement of the obligation to make a reference to the ECJ, without connecting it with the *mistaken application or interpretation of a substantive EU norm.*

i. ECJ Case-Law on the Violation of the Referral Duty

There has already been a request for preliminary ruling before the ECJ on this question. In *Consiglio Nazionale dei Geologi*, the referring court asked the ECJ about the factual and legal circumstances under which the failure to comply with Article 267(3) TFEU constitutes a 'clear breach of EU law' in the sense of the *Köbler* judgment. Unfortunately, the ECJ has not answered this question, which was considered manifestly irrelevant and hypothetical in the context of the main proceedings.[90]

Another occasion to shed some light on this matter could not be seized in the *Aquino* case either. The national court submitted a request for preliminary ruling in the context of national proceedings aimed at the establishment of the *Köbler* liability of the state for violation of Article 267(3) TFEU. The referring court asked three questions, of which one concerned the notion of a last-instance court and two the obligation to refer a question for a preliminary ruling to the ECJ. In its judgment, the ECJ reiterated the well-known principles regarding to

[89] See (ECJ) judgment in *Tomášová*, paras 40–41.

[90] (ECJ) Judgment in *Consiglio Nazionale dei Geologi and Autorità garante della concorrenza e del mercato*, paras 20 and 35.

the notion of a last-instance court and national procedural autonomy, without further clarifying the conditions of *Köbler* liability.[91]

Nevertheless, in *Diageo Brands*, the ECJ argued that an unjustified failure on the part of the court to make a referral would have resulted in rendering the Member State liable in accordance with the rules established in this respect by the ECJ case-law and, especially, in *Köbler*.[92] This statement seems to suggest that violation of Article 267(3) TFEU is in itself capable of triggering state liability. Nevertheless, it appears that one should not make far-reaching conclusions from this sentence, which referred to a purely hypothetical situation in the case. Moreover, the ECJ has also added that such liability would have only emerged 'in accordance with the rules established in this respect'. In fact, there has not yet been clear indication on the part of the ECJ regarding the question whether the violation of the referral obligation can be a separate ground for liability.

Even though there are views that the judgment in *Ferreira da Silva* might be an example for the establishment of state liability due to a violation of the referral duty,[93] this does not result from the ECJ decision in my view. It is true that the ECJ stated, for the first time, that a national supreme court had breached its duty to submit a request for preliminary ruling, finding that the *acte clair* doctrine could not be applied. Moreover, the ECJ has also concluded, answering the referring court's question, that the conditions of state liability for judicial errors were contrary to the *Köbler* requirements under Portuguese law.[94] Nevertheless, the judgment does not connect these two issues together, and the ECJ has not assessed whether liability may arise due to the violation of the referral duty.

It is noteworthy that in infringement proceedings in *Commission v France*, the ECJ has condemned a national supreme court for the breach of its obligation to refer to the ECJ for a preliminary ruling.[95] Given that this judgment was rendered in infringement proceedings, the seriousness of the violation was not assessed. Nonetheless, this was the first time in history that a national supreme court was 'convicted' by the ECJ because of the violation of the referral duty. As Sarmiento comments, the complex repercussions of this judgment are still too early to envisage, but it is clear that the decision is a tremendous step forward in the development of a coherent system of remedies in Europe.[96]

[91] (ECJ) Judgment in *Aquino*, paras 38, 56. For different aspects of the case, ss see 2.II.B.v.b and 2.III.B.ii.a.

[92] (ECJ) Judgment in *Diageo Brands*, para 66.

[93] Silveira and Fernandes 2016: 651. For a summary of the judgment in *Ferreira sa Silva e Brito e.a.* this case, see s 1.III.C.

[94] (ECJ) Judgment in *Ferreira sa Silva e Brito e.a.*, paras 45, 60.

[95] (ECJ) Opinion of AG Wathelet in *Commission v France*, C-416/17; judgment in *Commission v France*, C-416/17. For different aspects of the case, see s 2.II.A.ii.g(4).

[96] Sarmiento, D (2018) 'Judicial Infringements at the Court of Justice: A Brief Comment on the Phenomenal Commission/France (C-416/17)' Blog Despite our Differences, despiteourdifferencesblog.wordpress.com/2018/10/09/judicial-infringements-at-the-court-of-justice-a-brief-comment-on-the-phenomenal-commission-france-c-416-17/.

In the *Hochtief Solutions AG* case, the referring court asked several questions regarding the remedies to be provided in case of violation of EU law by a national supreme court, and, in particular, regarding retrial and *Köbler* liability.[97] One of these questions was whether the violation by a national supreme court, which had refused to submit a request for preliminary ruling but had given reasons for this decision in the terms of the *Cilfit* judgment, can incur liability for the state, if this justification provided is in violation of the ECJ case-law. Unfortunately the ECJ has not answered this question explicitly as it limited itself to reiterating the already well-known general principles regarding the establishement of liability and regarding the assessment of the gravity of the violation.[98] Nevertheless, Advocate General Bobek has made it clear in his opinion that the standard by which any such potential matter of state liability is to be assessed is that of the *Köbler* criteria and not the *Cilfit* standard. Therefore, the element to assess is whether the failure of the national court to refer a preliminary question was a 'manifest breach of the case-law of the Court in the matter'.[99] It appears that under the expression 'case-law of the Court' Bobek refers both to the jurisprudence interpreting the substantive EU norm at stake in the case, and to decisions interpreting the conditions of the referral duty.

ii. Doctrinal Views

Based on traditional ECJ case-law, earlier legal scholarship seems to be unanimous in the conclusion that the mere infringement of the referral duty is not sufficient to entail liability for the state.[100] This is mainly for two reasons.

First of all, the violation of the referral duty does not cause material damage to the individuals.

Secondly, the possibility to receive compensation exists only when the infringed provision intends to confer rights upon individuals. However, the obligation to make a reference serves the uniform application of the law and the interests of effective judicial protection. According to the traditional approach, it does not create any enforceable rights, separate from the ones that arise from the substantive provisions. Nevertheless, it is important to mention that, lately, it has been increasingly argued in the doctrine that the preliminary ruling procedure does intend to create individual rights as well. Broberg, Krommendijk and Lacchi have recently contended that such approach has been widely adopted by national courts, the ECtHR and, on several occasions, by the ECJ as well.[101]

[97] (ECJ) Judgment in *Hochtief Solutions AG Magyarországi Fióktelepe*. For different aspects of this case, see ss 2.III.B.iv.b and 2.IV.A.iv.d(13).

[98] (ECJ) Judgment in *Hochtief Solutions AG Magyarországi Fióktelepe*, para 48.

[99] (ECJ) Opinion of AG Bobek in *Hochtief Solutions AG Magyarországi Fióktelepe*, paras 127–35.

[100] (ECJ) Opinion of AG Léger in *Köbler*, paras 147–52; Anagnostaras 2006: 745–46; Classen 2004: 820; Hofstötter 2005: 132–36; Rodríguez 2004-2005: 617–18; Wattel 2004: 178–82.

[101] Broberg 2016: 244–55; Krommendijk 2017: 53–62; Lacchi 2016: 687–707.

iii. National Case-Law

As for judicial practice, it is noteworthy that in its decision from 2009, the Italian Tribunale di Genova, the court which made the preliminary reference in *Traghetti del Mediterraneo*, declared the state liable for a breach of Article 267(3) TFEU by the national supreme court.[102] In this regard, the Tribunal di Genova found that the violation of EU law consisted of the refusal, by the Corte Suprema di Cassazione, to introduce a request for a preliminary ruling to the ECJ. The court argued that the request for a preliminary ruling would have been necessary in the underlying case, as the compatibility of the national rules with the EU requirements had not been obvious at the time of those proceedings.[103] Had the Corte Suprema di Cassazione submitted a request for a preliminary ruling during the main proceedings, the outcome of the case could have been different. Consequently, the Tribunal di Genova found that the conditions of state liability were fulfilled according to the *Köbler* criteria. Regarding the claim for compensation, the Tribunal di Genova decided that it had to be assessed in separate proceedings.[104]

Moreover, in several unsuccessful liability actions, the claims have been dismissed solely on the ground that there had not been any violation of the referral duty, without an assessment on the substantial violation having been conducted.[105] It is nevertheless true that the fact that a national court dismisses a liability claim on the grounds that there had not been a violation of the referral duty does not necessarily allow the conclusion that a violation of such duty may in itself constitute a ground for liability. The judgments of the VfGH show, nevertheless, that this court focuses on the referral duty while assessing a liability claim.

For example, in a judgment delivered in 2004, the Austrian VfGH confirmed the limits of state liability for damages allegedly resulting from a decision of a national court which failed to refer a question to the ECJ. The VfGH considered that a simple non-referral is not per se a manifest breach. It argued that even though the question at issue had not been specifically decided upon by the ECJ, the outcome could be easily deduced from its case-law. Hence, the VwGH could reasonably conclude that the correct application of EU law left no doubt as to the solution to be adopted. Moreover, the VwGH had provided a very detailed statement of reasons on the issue.[106] The approach followed by the VfGH to

[102] (IT) Tribunale di Genova, ordinanza, 31/03/2009 and (IT) Legge, 13/04/1988, Art 2. See also Scherr 2012: 581. For different aspects of the case, see ss 1.III.B, 2.II.A.iv.b(2) and 2.III.B.iii.a. In addition, in several Member States constitutional claims have already been successful on such basis. On this respect, see s 2.IV.B.

[103] See also (ECJ) judgment in *Fallimento Traghetti del Mediterraneo SpA v Presidenza del Consiglio dei Ministri*.

[104] Unfortunately, it was not possible to identify the decision rendered in these proceedings. All information provided originates from the order of 31 March 2009 of the Tribunale di Genova, which was published in the journal *Il Diritto Marittimo* no 3–4 (2010) 665–70.

[105] See s 2.II.A.iv.a(2).

[106] (AT) VfGH, Erkenntnis, 13/10/2004.

focus on the failure to submit a request for preliminary ruling when evaluating the breach of the EU law was reiterated in a later judgment. In a decision 2013, the VfGH confirmed that the infringement of the duty to make a reference for a preliminary ruling to the ECJ does not as such trigger Austria's liability.[107]

B. Analysis

In the following analysis, I will explore whether it is reasonable to argue that *Köbler* liability should be accepted on the grounds of violation of the referral duty alone. As has been demonstrated, state liability occurs where a national court has infringed its procedural obligation to apply a substantive EU norm, which results in a breach of individual rights of a party to the proceedings. According to ECJ case-law and after a theoretical analysis of the rules on state liability, both the violation of a substantive norm conferring individual rights and an infringement by the national court of its procedural obligation are necessary in order for liability to be invoked.[108]

Therefore, to conduct that analysis it is important to distinguish the hypotheses where Article 267(3) TFEU is to be considered a *procedural* obligation of the national court merely supporting the correct application and interpretation of a substantive norm, on the one hand, or whether it is to be considered as a *substantive* norm infringed in itself, on the other hand.[109]

The confusion regarding the *procedural* or *substantial* nature of Article 267(3) TFEU is understandable. In fact, the procedural obligations of national courts – as well as of other national bodies – are often strictly linked to, and even inseparable from, the substantive norm whose application they protect. This is the case with the obligations to apply *the* directly effective substantive norm or to leave unapplied *the* national provision that is contrary to the EU provision. With regard to these, the connection between the substantive norm and the procedural obligation to apply it is obvious. Moreover, these obligations are often not codified under the Treaty, but they have been developed in the case-law of the ECJ. The obligation to make a preliminary reference is different from this point of view, as it has a double value: on the one hand, it is a procedural obligation supporting the application and the correct interpretation of the substantive EU norm; on the other hand, it is autonomous obligation imposed on the Member State court by the Treaty. This is why there may be doubt regarding its relationship with the infringed substantive EU norm and it has even been suggested that it is the infringed substantive norm itself which should be applied.

[107] (AT) VfGH, Beschluss, 19/06/2013. For different aspects of this topic, ss see 2.II.A.iv.a(2) and 2.III.B.ii.g.

[108] This stance is criticised by Kornezov (2016: 1335–36, 1339–41).

[109] In addition to the above, it also emerged in the legal doctrine that the referral duty may come under the scope of application of several procedural fundamental rights of the parties, protected under the Charter. On this matter, see s 3.IV.A.

i. Referral Duty as a Procedural Obligation Imposed on the National Courts

The qualification of the referral duty as a procedural obligation imposed on the national courts by the Treaty is in line with traditional ECJ case-law, according to which the preliminary procedure serves as the dialogue between judges with the aim of ensuring the uniform application of EU law.[110]

Therefore, in the dichotomy of procedural obligations and substantive norms the referral duty qualifies as a procedural obligation, similar to the obligation to apply a directly effective norm or to interpret it correctly. If it is the case, the discussion whether it confers rights on individuals is unimportant. In fact, this latter criterion is to be evaluated with regard to the substantive norm whose correct application or interpretation is a procedural duty is to support.

This can be demonstrated through the example of the violation of Article 288 TFEU. The procedural obligation of the national legislation to transpose a directive into the domestic legal order is an express provision laid down in the Treaty, similarly to Article 267(3) TFEU. These two articles are, therefore, likely to trigger similar confusion.[111] Regarding Article 288 TFEU, it is established ECJ case-law that the violation by the Member State legislative body of its obligation to transpose a directive into the national legal order is a sufficient ground to establish state liability. Nevertheless, Article 288 TFEU does not confer any substantive right on individuals. In fact, concerning the violation of Article 288 TFEU, the examination of the violation of substantive rights has always been carried out regarding the specific directive provision that was infringed because the directive had not been implemented.[112] Transposing this solution to breaches of the referral duty means that it is not Article 267(3) TFEU but the substantive norm (the correct interpretation or application of which the reference should support) that needs to confer rights on individuals.

The above considerations do not change the fact that it is the violation of the *procedural* obligation – Articles 288 or 267(3) TFEU – that triggers liability.[113] Nevertheless, this violation must be coupled with the infringement of a *substantive* norm conferring rights on individuals.[114] As Reich has argued, the condition regarding the conferral of individual rights must be understood as the principle of *ubi ius ibi remedium* turned upside down: if the individual does not have a

[110] (ECJ) Judgments in *Welmory*, para 33; in *Danske Svineproducenter*, para 32; in *Hochtief and Linde-Kca-Dresden*, paras 20, 21.

[111] See also Dougan 2000b: 606–08.

[112] See also Anagnostaras 2001a: 358–60; Bobek 2017: 147; Dougan 2017; Eilmansberger 2004: 1226; Hilson and Downes 1999: 123–24, 130; Prechal 2006a: 305–06; Ruiz-Jarabo Colomer 2010: 407–09; Van Gerven 2000: 507.

[113] See (ECJ) judgments in *Francovich and Others*; in *Faccini Dori*; in *El Corte Inglés*; in *Dillenkofer and Others*; in *Dorsch Consult*; in *Brinkmann*; in *EvoBus Austria*; in *Iaia and Others*; and Anagnostaras 2001a: 359.

[114] It could be also the violation by the national court of its obligation to apply the principle of direct effect or indirect effect.

right under EU law, then they cannot claim compensation: 'Where there is no right there is no remedy!'[115] It means that the criterion regarding the conferral of individual rights is important in order to identify the 'protective scope' of the EU norm, or the person entitled to compensation.[116]

That means in practice that if the violation of the referral duty does not result in a simultaneous violation of individual rights conferred by a substantive EU norm, such a breach is not capable of triggering state liability. This conclusion is in line with the conventional findings: the infringement of the referral duty must be coupled with the infringement of the substantive EU provision to trigger state liability.

As a conclusion, if one qualifies the referral duty (only) as a procedural obligation imposed on national courts (and not as a substantive norm itself), the reason why its violation does not result in state liability is the absence of the violation of a substantive norm conferring such rights – and not the fact that Article 267(3) TFEU itself does not confer any individual rights.[117]

ii. Referral Duty as a Substantive Norm of the Treaty

The second possibility is to consider Article 267(3) TFEU as a substantive norm in the view of this analysis. The procedural obligation regarding this substantive norm would be to apply it. In this scenario, it is indeed relevant whether or not Article 267(3) TFEU confers rights on individuals. As already mentioned, there are ongoing discussions on this topic, also in the view of the evolving case-law.[118]

In order to conduct a proper analysis as to whether Article 267(3) confers rights to individuals in the sense that its violation may result in triggering state liability for a violation of EU law by a Member State supreme court, it seems appropriate to distinguish different elements of the referral duty. As has been already extensively discussed above, the referral obligation – as a substantive norm – has also several components.[119] The first one, which was referred to above as the *material element* of the referral duty, is the obligation to submit a request for a preliminary ruling under the conditions established in Article 267(3) TFEU and in the *Cilfit* judgment. This obligation includes the duty to properly interpret and apply the EU rules regarding the referral duty, and it is violated if the national court does not correctly apply Article 267(3) TFEU or misuses the

[115] Reich 2007: 719–21. See also Dougan 2017; Lacchi 2016: 687–91; Prechal 2006a: 305–06.

[116] See also Eilmansberger 2004: 1245; Prechal 2006a: 310; Ruiz-Jarabo Colomer 2010: 407–09; Vehovec 2012: 876.

[117] This distinction is tiny and without any practical importance. However, I think that from the systemic point of view it is worthwhile to make this distinction and emphasise that Art 267(3) TFEU is parallel – regarding the concept of state liability – to Art 288 TFEU or to the other procedural obligations of national courts or state bodies with regard to the application of EU law.

[118] Broberg 2015: 33; Kornezov 2016: 1339–42; Krommendijk 2017: 53–58; Lacchi 2016: 687–91, as well as s 3.III.A.ii.

[119] See s 2.II.A.ii.g(2) and Brogerg and Fenger 2016: 599–601.

Ciflit criteria. In this respect, the question that arises is whether the individual has the right under EU law to oblige the national judge to submit a request for a preliminary ruling to the ECJ in a case where the conditions under Article 267(3) TFEU are met and where the *Ciflit* exceptions do not apply. The second component, that is the *procedural element* of this duty, is the obligation to state reasons for a decision on not to make a referral. This procedural element of the referral duty is therefore connected to the procedural fundamental right to a good administration or to a fair trial. The questions that we need to analyse in this respect are whether the individual has the right under EU law to have its request to submit a referral for a preliminary ruling duly substantiated, and whether the national court refusing such a request must provide adequate written explanation for this decision.

Moreover, for the sake of the present analysis, we can identify an eventual additional element of the referral duty, which derives from its material element and which manifests as another procedural fundamental right: the right to an effective judicial protection. In fact, if one accepts that individuals have a right to require their national supreme court to submit a request for a preliminary ruling to the ECJ in their case under the conditions specified in Article 267(3) TFUE and in the *Cilfit* judgment, this right, by its very nature and content, will be the manifestation of their fundamental right to an effective judicial protection or to an effective remedy, or, as understood under several national laws, to one's lawful judge.

Therefore, in the following analysis, I will examine whether any of these elements of the referral duty may confer rights on individuals in the sense that their eventual violation should be compensated in a *Köbler* liability action. The first, material element will be explored in this section, then, the second, procedural element will be dealt with in the next section consacred to state liability based on the violation of Charter rights. This is because the fundamental rights to a good administration, including to the statement of reasons for a decision, are enshrined in EU law as Charter rights.

a. Right to Have a Request for a Preliminary Ruling Submitted to the ECJ

Before analysing the question as to whether there is – or should be – a right under EU law to have someone's case referred to the ECJ when the applicable conditions are met, it appears noteworthy to explore this question from the point of view of the ECHR and national constitutional rights.

(1) ECtHR Case-Law

It is clear from the ECtHR case-law that the Strasbourg court does not guarantee, as such, the right to have a case referred to another national court for a preliminary ruling. As the ECtHR explains, it is for the national courts to interpret and apply domestic law and to decide on whether it is necessary to seek a preliminary ruling from the ECJ to enable them to give judgment. Therefore, the

ECtHR does not examine whether the decision on not to make a referral was correct or incorrect on the substance.[120]

(2) **National Case-Law**

As has also been discussed already,[121] the decision not to submit a referral for a preliminary ruling to the ECJ might amount to a violation of fundamental constitutional rights under several national legal systems. In particular, Member States that acknowledge that a refusal may amount to a violation of the right to one's lawful judge tend to sanction the violation of the material element of the procedural duty.[122]

This is clearly the case in Austria, where the VfGH assesses on the substance whether a violation of the referral duty had taken place. It considers that, if a national authority violates its duty to refer, this failure deprives the parties of their lawful judge. In this respect, the VfGH itself verifies whether the application and interpretation of the EU law by the national court was in conflict with the consistent ECJ case-law and whether the national court applied correctly the *Cilfit* exceptions.[123]

Similarly, in Germany, in the BVerfG's view, if doubts arise regarding the interpretation or application of EU law, the German courts must refer a preliminary question to the ECJ as this latter court is the competent judicial forum to hear this issue. This means that the BVerfG cleary sanctions the violation of the material element of the referral duty. This is true even though only a serious, arbitrary or non-justifiable failure will amount to a violation of the fundamental right. This means that the BVerfG takes into account the specific nature of the judicial role – which consists in the interpretation of abstract rules to concrete cases – and to which a certain margin of appreciation is inherent. Therefore, only a serious violation (of the material element) of the referral duty amounts to a violation of the constitutional rights.[124] Nevertheless, it does not change the fact that the BVerfG does not limit itself to the verification whether the national court has stated reasons for its decision on not to submit a referral, but examines as well, using their own criteria, whether the merits of this decision were tenable or justifiable on the substance.

Due to the scarcity of judgments available, it is difficult to make far-reaching conclusions regarding Czech, Slovak and Slovenian constitutional

[120] (ECtHR) Judgments in *Baydar v The Netherlands*, § 39; in *Bosphorus Hava Yolları Turizm ve Ticaret Anonim Şirketi v Ireland*, § 143; in *Harisch*, § 33; in *Repcevirág Szövetkezet v Hungary*, § 48; in *Schipani v Italy*, § 69; in *Ullens de Schooten and Rezabek v Belgium*, § 54. See also Laffranque 2018: 20.

[121] See s 2.IV.B.iii.

[122] Even though the national constitutional courts use their own constitutional standards to assess whether a violation had been committed, and do not rely directly on Art 267(3) TFUE, it is safe to say that they rely on the material element of the referral duty in these cases and not only on the aspect that requires the statement of reasons of the decision rendered.

[123] See s 2.IV.B.iii.a.

[124] See s 2.IV.B.iii.b.

case-law. However, in the Czech Republic, the Ústavní soud held that the violation of the right to a lawful judge may consist in the arbitrary or erroneous failure to submit a preliminary question to the ECJ.[125] The Slovenian Ustavno sodišče seems to have confirmed as well that the national last-instance court is obliged to make a reference unless the *Cilfit* conditions are fulfilled, in order to respect the right of the complainant to its lawful judge.[126] These judgments suggest that these constitutional courts consider the rules of Article 267(3) TFEU and of the *Cilfit* criteria when adjudicating on a constitutional complaint, and, therefore sanction the violation of the material element of the referral duty.

As for the question of the damages to be compensated, even if the consequence of a successful constitutional complaint is generally the annulment of the contested judgment, it may also give rise to damages in several states. For example, such right to compensation is enshrined under Slovenian and Slovakian acts.[127]

(3) ECJ Case-Law Developments

As for the ECJ case-law, the preliminary referral proceedings are considered as a method of cooperation between the national courts and the ECJ. It is therefore seen as a tool of interjudicial cooperation, with no rights conferred on the parties in this respect. As researchers point out, there are a few decisions from the 2000s and 2010s which suggested that the preliminary proceedings might have an aspect aiming to protect individual rights as well.

In particular, in its Opinion 1/09 the ECJ declared that

> [T]he system set up by Article 267 TFEU … establishes between the [ECJ] and the national courts direct cooperation as part of which the latter are closely involved in the correct application and uniform interpretation of [EU] law and also in the *protection of individual rights conferred by that legal order.*[128]

Moreover, in the judgments *Inuit* and *Jégo-Quéré*, the ECJ considered the effective legal protection in the context of the complex system of remedies available under EU law, including the preliminary ruling proceedings.[129] These formulations gave some indication that the preliminary ruling proceedings may be considered as conferring rights on individuals.

However, these considerations have not been reiterated since. On the contrary, in its Opinion 2/13, even though the ECJ insisted on the primordial

[125] (CZ) Ústavní soud, nález ze dne 08/01/2009; Ústavní soud, nález ze dne 29/11/2011; (CZ) Ústavní soud, rozsudek ze dne 19/05/2015. See especially s 2.IV.B.iii.a.

[126] (SI) Ustavno sodišče Republike Slovenije, Odločba, 21/11/2013. See s 2.IV.B.iii.d.

[127] (SI) Zakon o ustavnem sodišču, 46 člen; as well as Venice Commission 2011: 110; (SK) Ústava Slovenskej republiky, čl 127(3); as well as Venice Commission 2011: 110.

[128] (ECJ) Opinion 1/09, para 84, emphasis added. This statement was reiterated in the judgment in *Georgsmarienhütte and Others*, para 21.

[129] (ECJ) Judgments in *Inuit Tapiriit Kanatami and Others v Parliament and Council*, para 93; in *Commission v Jégo-Quéré*, paras 30–32. See also s 3.II.C.

importance of the preliminary proceedings, seen as a keystone of the judicial system of EU law,[130] it explained that it serves to set up a dialogue between one court and another, and therefore has the object of securing uniform interpretation of EU law; without mentioning the element of judicial protection.[131] The same observation can be made regarding the judgment *XC e.a.*, which reiterates the above statement.[132]

It seems, therefore, that the ECJ does not wish – at least for now – to recognise that the preliminary ruling procedure aims to confer rights on individuals. Therefore, it does not seem likely that the violation of the material element of the referral duty may be sanctioned using *Köbler* liability, despite the fact that it is now clearly capable of triggering condemnation of the state in infringement proceedings.[133] Nevertheless, it is not excluded that different considerations apply to the procedural element of the referral duty.

IV. DAMAGES LIABILITY ON THE GROUNDS OF VIOLATION OF THE CHARTER

The first subsection of this chapter will be devoted to the analysis of the violation of the procedural element of the referral duty, that is the obligation to state reasons for the refusal, as an eventual ground for state liability. Similarly to the previous section, this hypothesis will be explored following a comparative overview on how the ECtHR and national constitutional courts approach this issue. Then, when dealing with this question from the EU law perspective, it will be examined whether the two main obstacles to the acknowledgement of state liability – regarding the absence of individual rights and of material damages – can be overcome. Then, the second subsection will analyse whether the violation of other rights enshrined under the Charter, such as the violation of the right to an effective remedy or to a timely decision, may entail state liability.

A. Referral Duty and the Charter

Under the Charter, the right to an effective remedy and to a fair trial, including the right to one's lawful judge, is enshrined under Article 47 and the obligation of the administration to give reasons for its decisions is enshrined under Article 41, 'Right to Good Administration'. The question arises whether a decision by a national supreme court regarding a referral for a preliminary ruling, and, in

[130] (ECJ) Opinion 3/12, point 198.
[131] (ECJ) Opinion 3/12, point 176.
[132] (ECJ) Judgment in *XC e.a.*, para 41.
[133] (ECJ) Judgment in *Commission v France*, C-416/17.

particular, whether the rejection by such a court of a request from a party to submit a referral, comes under the scope of application of the Charter.

According to Article 51(1) of the Charter, its rules apply to the Member States only when they are implementing Union law. This provision confirms the ECJ's settled case-law, which states that the fundamental rights guaranteed in the legal order of the EU are applicable in all situations governed by EU law, but not outside such situations. Even though the notion of 'implementing' is not unambiguous in every situation, a judicial decision on not to submit a referral to the ECJ is, in my view, clearly an implementation of EU law, as there is an obvious connection between the national situation and EU law.[134]

In particular, in *Åkerberg Fransson*, the ECJ concluded that the Charter was applicable to a situation where national administrative and criminal sanctions were imposed cumulatively, as the national proceedings before the referring court concerned sanctions inflicted because of the violation of the obligations to pay VAT. As VAT is a tax regulated – at least partially – by EU law, the case at hand fell within the scope of application of the Charter.[135]

Then, in *DEB*, the ECJ acknowledged that the national rules of German civil procedure imposing excessively strict conditions for granting legal aid to moral persons came under the scope of the Charter, as in the main proceedings the applicant sought to establish the liability of the state for violation of EU law. Therefore, the ECJ analysed this question from the perspective of Art. 47 of the Charter, which applied to the case as there had been a connection between the main proceedings and EU law.[136]

Later, in *Toma*, under similar conditions, the ECJ reached the same conclusion regarding Romanian procedural rules. In this case, the ECJ assessed the compatibility of national procedural rules on judicial stamping fees with Article 47 of the Charter as the purpose of the main proceedings was the enforcement of a judicial decision ordering the repayment of a pollution tax for motor vehicles levied in breach of EU law.[137]

In the view of the above case-law it appears clear that a national supreme court decision rendered on the question whether to submit a referral for a preliminary ruling to the ECJ concerns EU law and falls within the scope of the Charter. Also, the Charter rights seem to apply, in general, to national judicial proceedings concerning actions founded on EU law.

Before examining the requirements enshrined in the Charter regarding the statement of reasons, fair trial and the right to have one's case heard within a

[134] See also Aalto 2014: points 47.113–47.139; Lacchi 2015a: 116–21; Lacchi 2016: 688–89, 704–06; Ward 2011.

[135] (ECJ) Judgment in *Åkerberg Fransson*, paras 17–27.

[136] (ECJ) Judgment in *DEB*, paras 30, 59.

[137] (ECJ) Judgment in *Toma and Biroul Executorului Judecătoresc Horaţiu-Vasile Cruduleci*, paras 22–28.

reasonable time, the corresponding ECtHR and national constitutional case-law will be summarised.

i. Right to Statements of Reasons for a Refusal to Submit a Referral to Preliminary Ruling

a. ECtHR Case-Law

As was examined in detail above,[138] according to the ECtHR, even if the Convention does not guarantee, as such, the right to have a case referred to another court for a preliminary ruling, this matter is, however, not unconnected to Article 6(1) ECHR since a domestic court's refusal to grant a referral may, in certain circumstances, infringe the fairness of proceedings where the refusal is arbitrary.[139] It is, therefore, through the right to a fair trial and to a statement of reasons that the refusal to submit a request for a preliminary ruling may infringe Article 6(1) ECHR. In this respect, the ECtHR does not verify the merits of the decision regarding the refusal or the legality of the interpretation and the application of the relevant law. On the contrary, the verification by the ECtHR consists in ensuring that the impugned decision was accompagnied by an adequate reasoning, taking into account the *Cilfit* criteria as well.[140]

Moreover, the level of explanation required depends on the particularities of the case and of the request for a preliminary ruling.[141] As the ECtHR has clearly explained recently, in situations where an explicit request was made for a referral for a preliminary ruling and where the request was accompanied by due argumentation, the national supreme court has to provide reasons, in the light of the applicable law, for any decision refusing to refer a question for a preliminary ruling to the ECJ. In such a case, the ECtHR will verify whether the decision indicated the reasons why the national court found that the question was irrelevant, an *acte clair* or an *acte éclairé*.[142] However, if the request was insufficiently pleaded or formulated in broad or general terms, or where the applicant had failed to explicitly ask for a preliminary ruling, the ECtHR found it acceptable to dismiss the complaint by mere reference to the

[138] See s 2.IV.B.ii.

[139] (ECtHR) Judgments in *Baydar v The Netherlands*, § 39; in *Bosphorus Hava Yolları Turizm ve Ticaret Anonim Şirketi v Ireland*, § 143; in *Harisch*, §§ 33; in *Repcevirág Szövetkezet v Hungary*, § 48; in *Schipani v Italy*, § 69; in *Ullens de Schooten and Rezabek v Belgium*, § 54.

[140] (ECtHR) Judgments in *Baydar v The Netherlands*, § 44; in *Dhahbi v Italy*, § 31; in *Harisch v Germany*, § 46; in *Repcevirág Szövetkezet v Hungary*, § 50; in *Schipani v Italy*, § 69; in *Ullens de Schooten and Rezabek v Belgium*, §§ 59–62.

[141] (ECtHR) Judgments in *Baydar v The Netherlands*, § 40; in *Harisch v Germany*, § 34; in *Repcevirág Szövetkezet v Hungary*, § 49.

[142] (ECtHR) Judgments in *Dhahbi v Italy*, §§ 31–33; in *Repcevirág Szövetkezet v Hungary*, § 50; in *Schipani v Italy*, § 42.

relevant legal provisions governing such complaints. It must however, also in this context, ascertain that decisions of national courts are not flawed by arbitrariness or otherwise manifestly unreasonable.[143] Therefore, the ECtHR may verify whether the refusal was based on reasons linked to the *Ciflit* criteria but will not examine the merits of the decision.

Under the ECHR, the applicant has therefore the right to know the reasons of a refusal of its request to submit a referral for a preliminary ruling. In all, according to the ECtHR, a refusal to grant a referral may be deemed arbitrary in cases where the applicable rules allow no exception to the granting of a referral, where the referral is based on reasons other than those provided for by the rules, or where the refusal was not duly explained.[144]

Moreover, as for the question of the damages, the ECtHR regularly orders Contracting States to pay compensation to the individual for breaches of Article 6(1) ECHR. In this regard, the ECtHR does not allow a claim for reparation of material damage, since it holds that is not possible to speculate on what would have been the outcome of proceedings in conformity with Article 6(1) ECHR. By contrast, taking account of the seriousness of the non-material damage sustained, the ECtHR accepts that the breach of the procedural right to a fair hearing justifies the award of a certain sum by way of reparation.[145]

b. National Case-Law

In all Member States where the violation of the referral duty comes under the scope of national constitutional rights, the violation of the obligation to state reasons for the refusal of a request for a preliminary ruling is likely to compromise the right to a fair trial.[146]

This is the case in Austria and in Germany, where the constitutional courts apply even more stringent standards than the obligation to state reasons because they assess the merits of the reasons given as well. Therefore, the violation of the obligation to state reasons will necessarily be sanctioned by these courts, if the applicable conditions are met. In this respect, in Austria, all violations of the referral duty are considered to infringe the constitutional right to a lawful judge. In Germany, fundamental disregard of the obligation to make a reference, deliberate deviation from ECJ case-law without the willingness to make a submission, and even unjustifiable error in the interpretation

[143] (ECtHR) Decision in *John v Germany*; and judgment in *Repcevirág Szövetkezet v Hungary*, § 51.

[144] (ECtHR) Judgment in *Baydar v The Netherlands*, § 39.

[145] (ECtHR) Judgment in *Coëme and Others v Belgium*; decision in *Živulinskas v Lithuania*; (ECJ) opinion of AG Léger in *Köbler*.

[146] As for the relationship between national Constitutions and the Charter, see eg Kokott and Sobotta 2010: 7–8, 11–12; Komárek 2014. For further details, see s 2.IV.B.iii.

of the obligation to refer are considered faults amounting to the violation of constitutional rights.

Similarily, in the Czech Republic, a national court that failed to explain why its interpretation of the pertinent EU norm was clear and obvious in the light of EU law committed, according to the Ústavní soud, a violation of constitutional rights.[147] In Slovenia, the Ustavno sodišče requires that national courts adequately justify their decision on not to make a referral,[148] and in Slovakia, the Ústavný súd seems to sanction where national supreme courts do not recognise at all their referral duty.[149]

As already explained, the consequence of a successful constitutional complaint is generally the annulment of the contested judgment. However, such a violation may also result in the allocation of damages.

c. Case-Law and Doctrine

As also already explained above, a national judicial decision that concerns EU law and which, in particular, deals with a request to submit a referral to the ECJ is an implementation of EU law within the meaning of Article 51(1) of the Charter. Therefore, the Charter is applicable to such a decision. As for the particular right that might be affected by a decision which lacks adequate reasoning, in the ECJ case-law, the violation of the obligation to give reasons for a decision comes under the scope of application of Article 47 protecting the 'right to an effective remedy and to a fair trial'.[150]

In this respect, in *ZZ*, which concerned the freedom of movement of persons, the ECJ explained that national courts, when denying entry to a citizen of another Member State on grounds of state security, must inform precisely and in full the citizen concerned on the essence of the grouds on which the decision is based. Such requirement derives from the fundamental right to effective judicial protection enshrined under Article 47 of the Charter.[151] Similarly, in *flyLAL-Lithuanian Airlines AS* and *Trade Agency*, when interpreting the rules regarding the recognition and enforcement of judgments rendered in other Member States, the ECJ explicitly held that the observance of the right to a fair trial referred to in Article 47 of the Charter requires that all judgments be reasoned in order to enable the defendant to see why the judgment has been propounded and to bring appropriate and effective appeal against it.[152]

[147] (CZ) Ústavní soud, nález ze dne 08/01/2009; Ústavní soud, nález ze dne 29/11/2011; (CZ) Ústavní soud, rozsudek ze dne 19/05/2015. See especially s 2.IV.B.iii.a.

[148] (SI) Ustavno sodišče Republike Slovenije, Odločba, 21/11/2013. See s 2.IV.B.iii.d.

[149] (SK) *Ústavný súd Slovenskej republiky*, uznesenie zo dňa 29/05/2007; *Ústavný súd Slovenskej republiky*, uznesenie zo dňa 03/07/2008. See s 2.IV.B.iii.d

[150] (ECJ) Judgments in *ZZ*, para 65; in *Trade Agency*, paras 52–53; in *Gaydarov*, para 41; in *flyLAL-Lithuanian Airlines AS*, paras 51–52.

[151] (ECJ) Judgment in *ZZ*, paras 65, 69. See also judgment in *Gaydarov*, para 41.

[152] (ECJ) Judgment in *flyLAL-Lithuanian Airlines AS*, para 51; *in Trade Agency*, paras 52–53.

It is noteworthy that, since the obligation to state reasons for the refusal to submit a request for preliminary ruling falls within the scope of application of Article 47 of the Charter, there is no need to examine whether Article 267(3) TFEU confers rights to individuals as the Charter right certainly does.

As for the specific requirements resulting from Article 47 of the Charter, it is interesting to observe that codified EU law imposes explicitly the obligation on national courts to state reasons for a decision to submit a referral for preliminary ruling, but does not set such explicit obligation regarding a refusal to make a referral.[153] However, the ECJ has an elaborate case-law on the requirements concerning the statement of reasons that had been elaborated with regards to decisions rendered by EU institutions.[154] This case-law should be applicable for Member State court decisions falling within the scope of application of the Charter as well.

Also, there have been some cases where the ECJ pronounced precisely about the level of substantiation required from national courts with respect to decisions rendered in cases concerning EU law. In this respect, in *flyLAL-Lithuanian Airlines AS* and *Trade Agency*, the ECJ held that the extent of the obligation to give reasons may vary according to the nature of the decision and must be examined, in the light of the proceedings taken as a whole and all the relevant circumstances, taking account of the procedural guarantees surrounding that decision, in order to ascertain whether the latter ensure that the persons concerned have the possibility to bring an appropriate and effective appeal against that decision.[155]

Also, according to the ECJ case-law established in *MM* and *Mukarubega*, concerning asylum seekers, the right to be heard encompasses the right that the authorities sufficiently address the parties's submissions and give a statement of reasons that is sufficiently specific and concrete to allow the person to understand why their application is being rejected.[156] Similarly, the judicial duty to provide reasons for court decisions is recognised as part of the right to a fair trial. Reasons are required to ensure that court decisions are comprehensible and acceptable for the parties. Without sufficient reasons, a party cannot challenge the decision and the appellate court cannot conduct a meaningful review of the decision give by the lower court.[157]

Moreover, it must be emphasised that the ECtHR considers arbitrary a refusal to grant a referral in cases where the applicable rules allow no exception to the granting of a referral, where the referral is based on reasons other than

[153] (EU) Recommendations to national courts and tribunals in relation to the initiation of preliminary ruling proceedings, point 15.
[154] See the point 3.08.08.01 of the Répertoire de la jurisprudence de la Cour.
[155] (ECJ) Judgment in *flyLAL-Lithuanian Airlines AS*, para 52; in *Trade Agency*, para 60.
[156] (ECJ) Judgments in *MM*, para 88; in *Mukarubega*, para 48.
[157] Verbruggen and Kryla-Cudna 2020: 209.

those provided for by the rules, or where the refusal was not duly explained.[158] In this respect it must be emphasised that, according to Article 52(3) of the Charter, the level of protection provided for by the Charter should be at least equivalent to the level of protection provided for by the ECHR. In its case-law the ECJ emphasised that the right to a fair trial results from the constitutional traditions common to the Member States and was reaffirmed in Article 47(2) of the Charter, 'which corresponds, as is clear from the explanations relating to that article, to Article 6(1) of the ECHR'.[159] In *DEB* and *Toma*, which concerned precisely this article of the Charter, the Court explained that, in so far as the Charter contains rights which correspond to those guaranteed by the ECHR, their meaning and scope are to be the same as those laid down not only by the ECHR but also by the case-law of the ECtHR.[160] Moreover, regarding the statement of reasons, in *ASML*, the ECJ referred explicitly to the ECtHR case-law according to which the defendant's lack of awareness of the grounds of a judgment constituted an infringement of the Article 6(1) ECHR because the person concerned had been unable to bring an appropriate and effective appeal.[161]

Therefore, it seems appropriate that the ECJ consider also the requirements resulting from Article 6(1) ECHR when interpreting the duty to refer a preliminary ruling request provided by Article 267(3) TFEU. This means that, at the very least, the national judicial decisions rejecting a request of one of the parties to submit a referral to the ECJ must state adequate reasons for this decision. This is a requirement resulting directly from EU law and in particular from Articles 47 and 53(2) of the Charter and Article 19(1) TEU.[162]

Finally, as for the question of the damages to compensate, it should be noted that even if the mere violation of the right to a fair trial or the right to adequate written explainations do not necessarily cause material damage to the individual, the compensation of non-material damage should be compensated.[163] In fact, the ECJ has already awarded compensation for non-pecuniary loss resulting from the violation of fundamental procedural rights by the EU institutions. In particular, the *Staelen v Ombudsman* case concerned the violation by the European Ombudsman of the duty to act diligently and of the right of the applicant to have her requests dealt with in a reasonable time. The ECJ concluded that the failure to respect that time, as well as the maladministration of the case, constituted a sufficiently serious

[158] (ECtHR) Judgment in *Baydar v The Netherlands*, § 39.

[159] (ECJ) Judgment in *Trade Agency*, para 52.

[160] (ECJ) Judgments in *DEB*, para 35; in *Eurofood IFSC Ltd*, para 65; in *McB*, para 53; in *Toma and Biroul Executorului Judecătoresc Horațiu-Vasile Cruduleci*, para 41.

[161] (ECJ) Judgment in *ASML Netherlands BV*, para 28.

[162] See also Krommendijk 2017: 48; Spaventa 2018.

[163] See also Lacchi 2015b: 1693–95; Lacchi 2016: 705–06.

breach of a rule of law intended to confer rights on individuals which is capable of establishing the liability of the EU.[164] Moreover, the undue delay in proceedings by the General Court has given rise to compensation of the non-material damages suffered in several cases.[165]

In the light of the *Brasserie du Pêcheur* and *Bergaderm* case-law, the conditions under which the state may incur liability for damage caused to individuals by a breach of EU cannot, in the absence of particular justification, differ from those governing the liability of the EU in like circumstances. This is because the protection of the rights which individuals derive from EU law cannot vary depending on whether a national authority or a EU authority is responsible for the damage.[166] Therefore, the non-material damages suffered because of the infringement of the Charter rights by national supreme courts should be compensated in just the same way that non-material damages are compensated in the event of violation of Charter rights by EU courts.

ii. Right to an Effective Judicial Protection

a. Case-Law and Doctrine

For the sake of completeness, it should be noted that if it is accepted that the referral obligation confers rights on individuals and can be seen as a 'remedy', this may lead to the consequence that the violation of the material element of the referral duty (that the violation of the rule enshrined under Article 267(3) TFEU or the misapplication of the *Cilfit* criteria) entails the violation of the 'right to an effective remedy and to a fair trial', enshrined under Article 47 of the Charter as well.[167]

In the doctrine, Lacchi argues that given the inherently strong connection between the principles of effectiveness of EU law and of effective judicial protection of the rights conferred by EU law on individuals, the preliminary ruling proceedings – which clearly aim to ensure the former principle – serve the interest of protection of individual rights as well.

B. Undue Delay in Proceedings

The very last question is whether the undue delay in proceedings before national courts can trigger liability of the state in the terms of the *Köbler* doctrine. It is

[164] (ECJ) Judgments in *Staelen v European Ombudsman*, paras 269, 293; in *Claire Staelen v European Ombudsman*, C-337/15 P, paras 127–31.

[165] See s 3.IV.B.

[166] (ECJ) Judgments in *Laboratoires Pharmaceutiques Bergaderm SA*, para 41; in *Brasserie du Pêcheur and Factortame*, para 42.

[167] Hofstötter 2005: 13; Lacchi 2016: 703–07.

generally accepted, also by the ECJ, that the infringement of the right of the parties to have their case heard within a reasonable time amounts to a breach of the right to a fair trial.[168]

As for the ECHR, the ECtHR requires that Contracting States organise their legal systems in such a way that their courts can guarantee the right of everyone to obtain a final decision on disputes relating to civil rights and obligations within a reasonable time. The breach of this obligation amounts to a violation of Article 6(1) ECHR, and results in the liability for damages of the Contracting State.[169] Moreover, according to Article 13 ECHR, the states are required to introduce effective domestic remedies for complaints about the length of civil proceedings before their courts.[170]

Compensation for the moral damage caused by the undue delay of proceedings is accepted under most national laws as well. This is also due to the ECtHR case-law, which obliges Contracting States, under Article 13 ECHR, to provide an effective remedy for violation of Article 6(1) ECHR. Violations of Articles 6 and 13 ECHR on account of the length of the domestic proceedings and the lack of an effective domestic remedy in that regard have given rise to the condemnation of Contracting States for the payment of non-pecuniary damages.[171] In several Member States, rules on compensation are found in the constitutional rules, while in others these rules are in the civil or criminal codes or procedural codes[172] or in separate legal acts.[173]

In this regard, the Austrian VfGH has rendered an interesting judgment.[174] In this case, the VfGH stated that the national law on state liability must be interpreted as ensuring compensation for the undue delay in proceedings before the Asylgerichtshof (Asylum Court). According to the VfGH, this obligation arises not only from the ECHR but also from Article 47 of the Charter. The

[168] See eg Tesauro 2013: 325–26; Verbruggen and Kryla-Cudna 2020: 209, 222–25.

[169] (ECtHR) Judgments in *Scordino v Italy*, § 183; in *Sürmeli v Germany*, § 129; in *Vocaturo v Italy*, § 17; *Cappello v Italy*, § 17.

[170] In certain cases, the ECtHR has considered that it was not necessary to examine a complaint under Art 13 when a violation of Art 6 had been found, there being no legal interest in re-examining the same subject-matter under the less strict requirements of the former provision. However, there is no overlap when, as in this case, the violation of Art 6 concerns the length of proceedings, this being a separate issue from the question of the availability of an effective remedy to complain about such length. See (ECtHR) judgment in *Kudła v Poland*, § 146.

[171] (ECtHR) Judgments in *İlhan v Turkey*, § 97; *Kaya v Turkey*, § 106; *Kudła v Poland*, §§ 156, 157; *Sürmeli v Germany*; *Vilho Eskelinen and Others v Finland*; *McFarlane v Ireland*; *Rutkowski v Poland*; *Gazsó v Hungary*; *Valada Matos das Neves v Portugal*; *Cipolletta v Italy*; *Negrea and Others v Romania*.

[172] (HU) A polgári perrendtartásról szóló 1952 évi III törvény, 2 § (1) bekezdés; Kúria, ítélet, 28/01/2015; Fővárosi Ítélőtábla, ítélet, 31/10/2013. See also Borbás 2014: 201–08.

[173] (IT) Legge, 24/03/2001, no 89, Art 2; Corte di Cassazione, sentenza, 26/07/2002, reported in Reflets no 2/2003: 22.

[174] (AT) VfGH, Urteil, 09/10/2012, reported by Windisch in Reflets no 1/2013: 35. See also VfGH, Beschluss, 19/06/2013.

VfGH has pointed out that provisions of the Charter are applicable, within its scope of application, for national proceedings.[175]

The *Magiera* decision of the French Conseil d'État rendered in 2002 is also noteworthy in this context, as it concerned an action for damages for violation of Article 6(1) ECHR because of an excessive delay in the judicial proceedings.[176] In this decision the Conseil d'État confirmed that its *Darmont* case-law[177] applies to damages claims resulting from the breach of international conventions as well. Then it went on to withdraw, referring to the ECHR, the restrictive requirement of *faute lourde* for state liability claims for excessive length of proceedings. It is, however, true that in the terms of the judgment, the *faute simple* is sufficient to engage state liability only when it comes to the daily administration of justice. If the activity touches at 'the heart of the judicial activity', state liability can be engaged only for a *faute lourde*.[178]

As for EU law, the liability of the EU for the infringement of the right of the parties to have their case heard within a reasonable time has already been confirmed by the ECJ. In particular, the ECJ has admitted that the General Court can be indicted for infringing its obligation to adjudicate on cases within a reasonable time, although the consequences of this breach were not clearly defined at the beginning.[179] Subsequent case-law has evolved towards admitting that the appropriate sanction for a breach by a Court of the EU of its obligation under Article 47 of the Charter is an action for damages brought before the General Court.[180] The ECJ has concluded that such action constitutes, therefore, an effective remedy.[181] Then, in *Gascogne Sack Deutschland* and *Kendrion*, the General Court ordered, for the first time, the EU to pay *ex aequo et bono* €5,000 or €6,000 to each of the applicant companies for the damage they suffered as a result of the prolonged state of uncertainty in which they each found themselves during the proceedings.[182] As far as the allocation of compensation for

[175] (EU) Charter, Art 51.

[176] (FR) Conseil d'État, 28/06/2002, reported by Granger 2007: 167, 181, Betlem et al 2007: 48–49, and in Reflets no 1/2003: 9.

[177] In its *Darmont* decision, the Conseil d'État held that the content of a judicial decision could not be challenged by way of a state liability action once it had become final. See (FR) Conseil d'État, décision, 29/12/1978.

[178] (FR) Cour d'appel de Paris, arrêt, 31/10/2017.

[179] See (ECJ) judgments in *Baustahlgewebe v Commission*; in *Limburgse Vinyl Maatschappij and Others v Commission*; in *Der Grüne Punkt – Duales System Deutschland v. Commission*, paras 183–85, 194; Safjan 2014: ch 3, B.

[180] Arts 256(1) and 340 TFEU.

[181] (ECJ) Judgments in *Der Grüne Punkt – Duales System Deutschland v Commission*, para 195; in *Gascogne Sack Deutschland v Commission*, C-40/12 P, paras 89–90; in *Kendrion v Commission*, C-50/12 P, paras 93–94; in *Groupe Gascogne v Commission*, C-58/12 P, paras 82–83; in *FLSmidth v Commission*, para 116; in *Deltafina v Commission*, paras 86–89; in *FLS Plast v Commission*, para 135; in *ICF v Commission*, C-467/13 P, paras 57–58; as well as opinion of AG Wahl in Case *EU v Gascogne Sack Deutschland and Gascogne*. See also Gutman 2017: 49–54; Jenkins and Bushell 2015; Verbruggen and Kryla-Cudna 2020: 209, 222–25.

[182] (ECJ) Judgments in *Gascogne Sack Deutschland and Gascogne v EU*, T-577/14, paras 78–81, 151–165; in *Kendrion v EU*, T-479/14, paras 121–35.

the non-material damages suffered as a result of a breach of the obligation to adjudicate within a reasonable time was concerned, these decisions were upheld on appeal before the Court.[183]

Therefore, taking into account the *Bergaderm* case-law, the breach of the right of the parties to have their case heard within a reasonable time should be acknowledged as a ground for a *Köbler* liability action if the case concerns rights conferred by EU law.

C. Conclusion on Liability for Violation of the Referral Duty and of the Charter

Traditionally, two issues are mentioned as being the main obstacles preventing the application of the *Köbler* principle to breaches of Article 267(3) TFEU. First, the preliminary proceedings are not regarded as a remedy conferring rights on individuals. Second, the establishment of such liability necessitates the recognition of state liability for moral damages.

However, (at least) the violation of the obligation to state reasons for a decision on not making a referral should be regarded as a breach of the Charter as well. Moreover, it could also be argued that the violation of the referral duty itself affects the right of individuals to effective judicial protection. Therefore, the violation of the material and/or the procedural elements of the referral duty should be analysed as a violation of Article 47 of the Charter. The question arises whether Member States should be held liable in the terms of the *Köbler* judgment for the violation of their rights enshrined in the Charter by national supreme courts.

In the past, academics have expressed concerns about establishing liability for violation of the Charter. The central issue regarding the extension of the scope of liability was whether the stringent state liability principle in EU law is appropriate to protect fundamental rights. According to Rodríguez, the ECJ case-law suggests that it certainly is not the case.[184] Wattel emphasised the main differences between the ECtHR and the ECJ in this regard. First, the primary aim of the ECHR is to protect fundamental rights; and second, the Contracting States have expressively accepted their liability for breaches of these rights.[185]

Nevertheless, state liability for breaches of EU law – including infringements committed by the national courts – has been increasingly accepted by the Member States. Also, there is a clear tendency in the ECJ case-law towards the

[183] (ECJ) Judgments in *EU v Gascogne Sack Deutschland and Gascogne*, C-138/17 P, paras 61–62; in *EU v Kendrion*, C-150/17 P, paras 106–13.

[184] Rodríguez 2004–05: 618–19.

[185] Wattel 2004: 187.

recognition of non-pecuniary damages awarded to individuals on the account of the infringement of procedural rights on the basis of the EU law.

Moreover, as far as the protection of its own competencies regarding the protection of fundamental rights is concerned, the ECJ has been quite active lately.[186] In the view of its Opinions 1/09 and 2/13 as well as of the *XC e.a.* judgment, it seems that the ECJ is keen on emphasising its own jurisdiction vis-à-vis other international courts, in particular when it comes to the protection of its competencies regarding the protection of fundamental rights.[187] In particular, this desire to distinguish the fundamental rights protection system of the EU from other national and international sources of fundamental rights, may – and should – lead to the enforcement of the protection offered in the EU. This means that the ECJ needs to define the conditions and the consequences of the breach of the Charter by national courts. This is even more important as in the absence of clear guidance by the ECJ the national courts might be tempted to focus solely on the ECtHR case-law.[188]

In the view of this, the ECJ should make it clear that a violation of Charter rights, at least a breach of the obligation to state reasons for a national judgment concerning rights conferred by EU law on individuals, might give rise to *Köbler* liability claims, if the necessary conditions are fulfilled.

[186] (ECJ) Opinion 2/13; judgments in *A v B*, and in *XC e.a.*

[187] (ECJ) Opinion 1/09, para 68; Opinion 2/13, para 175; judgment in *XC e.a.*, paras 40, 45. See also Varga 2019: 1694–96.

[188] Krommendijk 2017: 55–56.

4

Findings

THE OPERATION OF every legal system rests essentially on the existence of a scheme of procedures and remedies, which serve to safeguard and enforce the application of its substantive provisions. This remedial system specifies the courses of action accessible to individuals and the exact circumstances under which they may seek judicial protection. It also describes the type of remedy that is available in the case of a successful claim and the conditions that need to be satisfied to this end by the claimant. Nevertheless, EU law is characterised by the absence of such a procedural and remedial organisation, save only in cases where some degree of legislative harmonisation has already taken place. This obliges it to rely extensively on the respective national legal arrangements, borrowing in essence the solutions that have been adopted in the area with regard to similar domestic claims.[1] However, where national rules do not provide adequate protection of substantive rights conferred by EU law, the ECJ intervenes.

The aim of this book was to provide an example of such an intrusion of EU law into the field and competence of national remedies, specifically in cases where violation of EU law by Member State supreme courts has taken place. On the basis of research and the partial conclusions already presented, the following conclusions can be drawn.

I. CONCLUSIONS FROM THE PAST

A. Genuine Life of *Köbler* Doctrine Before National Courts

Contrary to what might have been previously expected, the *Köbler* liability has found a certain acceptance in several national regimes. In particular, 13 Member States have accepted, at least theoretically, to hold the state liable for breaches of EU law by their supreme courts (Belgium, Bulgaria, Germany, France, Italy, Lithuania, the Netherlands, Austria, Poland, Portugal, Finland, Sweden and the UK). Moreover, recent requests for a preliminary ruling submitted by Hungarian and Slovak courts suggest that certain courts of these states are also inclined to accept state liability.

[1] Anagnostaras 2007: 727–28.

In most of these Member States, the *Köbler* principle has been transposed into the national legal order through jurisprudence. In nine Member States, courts have relied directly on the *Köbler* principle to adjudicate on claims regarding violation of EU law by national courts. To do so, they had to set aside domestic rules restricting state liability for judicial breaches. Therefore, in these Member States, the implementation of the *Köbler* doctrine has resulted in the duplication of liability regimes. It means that the conditions of state liability for judicial acts are less strict with regard to damages caused by violation of EU law rather than violation of national law in nine Member States (Bulgaria, Germany, France, Lithuania, the Netherlands, Austria, Portugal, Finland and the UK). The exception is Belgium, where the judicature has made general adjustments, altering the liability regime for violation of law by national supreme courts in general. A Hungarian regional court adopted a similar approach as the Belgian Constitutional Court; however, the supreme court has not yet validated this case-law. Moreover, the duplication of liability regimes is due to legislative amendments in two Member States (Italy and Poland).

In Sweden, as an informal way to receive damages before the Justitiekanslern already existed, it was possible to apply the *Köbler* doctrine under this procedure without any legislative amendment or judicial intervention. Moreover, national provisions do not appear to exclude the theoretical possibility of holding the state liable for breach of EU law by supreme courts in two Member States (Denmark and Latvia). Therefore, even if there has not yet been an available judgment on a *Köbler* claim from these Member States, the application of the doctrine should not, in principle, face major difficulties.

There are, however, Member States that still refuse to adapt their liability regime to the requirements of the *Köbler* case law (Hungary, Czech Republic, Ireland). As for the ten Member States not mentioned above, there has not been any evidence of accommodation of the restrictive national conditions on state liability to the *Köbler* doctrine.

Nevertheless, as experience shows, even in Member States where *Köbler* liability is accepted theoretically, it is not a frequently used method for making good the damages caused to individuals by a final judgment of a national supreme court. In fact, even on the rare occasions when it has been relied on, compensation has almost never been awarded. Research and theoretical reflection confirm that only in rare circumstances is it possible to find a manifest breach of EU law committed by a national supreme court. In practical terms, the criterion of manifest infringement is probably fulfilled in cases where a national supreme court has taken a deliberate decision to deviate from established ECJ case-law on the specific matter relevant to the case. As experience shows, such a situation can happen, but it would probably be a delicate issue to condemn a national supreme court for such a deliberate decision, either by a national inferior court, or, via a preliminary ruling, by the ECJ in a subsequent liability action.

B. Impact and Importance of the *Köbler* Principle

The ECJ jurisprudence on remedies, including the *Köbler* judgment, has certainly had an impact on national regimes. It has especially contributed to raising the level of protection of individual rights in general. This follows not only from the adaptation of liability regimes to the *Köbler* principle (see the answer to the first question), but also from the introduction of new alternative remedies into the national remedial systems (see the answer to the third question). On a few occasions, these new remedies even exceed the level of protection required under EU law.

As for the question whether *Köbler* liability has proved specifically to be an effective remedy in individual cases, we need to answer in the negative. In fact, pecuniary compensation has been awarded on very few (according to the research, only on five) occasions.[2] This shows that *Köbler* liability is more a deterrent tool to prevent violation than a remedy for infringed individual rights. Therefore, its primary function appears to be an incentive for Member States to fulfil their obligations regarding the application of EU law.[3]

C. Other Means of Remedies in Use

From the empirical point of view, besides *Köbler* liability, Member States have other methods to protect individual rights and to make good any damages caused by final judicial decisions contrary to EU law. The two most important such national alternative methods are retrial and constitutional complaint. These remedies may eventually offer a real alternative to *Köbler* claims. Moreover, the reliance upon them even ensures, depending on the conditions attached to them, a higher standard of protection of individual rights than a liability claim.

As for retrial, in five Member States, cases have actually been reopened due to violation of EU law in the final judgment (Lithuania, Romania, Slovakia, Finland and the UK). In two of these, legislative provisions had been introduced into the procedural codes in 2008 in order to recognise the violation of EU law as specific ground for retrial. That has been the case in Romania, where amendments concerned the administrative procedural code, and in Slovakia, where the civil procedural code was amended. In the other three Member States (Lithuania, Finland and the UK), the application of retrial to breaches of EU law was possible due to the broad scope of application of this remedy. In these legal systems, retrial is granted in the event of manifest, substantive or extraordinary breach of law. In this regard, legal rules in another three Member States

[2] See (IT) Tribunale di Genova, ordinanza, 31/03/2009; (SE) Justitiekanslern, Beslut, 06/04/2009; (FI) Korkein oikeus, tuomio, 05/07/2013 and Korkein oikeus, tuomio, 05/03/2016; (BG) Apelativen sad – Burgas, Reshenie, 26/04/2016.

[3] See also Lock 2012: 1676, 1700, 1701; Leczykiewicz 2012: 1–3; Rodríguez 2004–05: 611, 614–15.

(Denmark, Malta and Sweden) are also similar, and therefore also seem capable of offering adequate protection.

Concerning constitutional complaint, individuals can indirectly invoke the violation of their rights under EU law before constitutional courts in six Member States: Czech Republic, Germany, Austria, Slovenia, Slovakia and Spain. Through the protection of constitutional rights to a fair trial and to a lawful judge, this remedy can ensure that a case concerning the interpretation of EU law is referred to the ECJ. Therefore, this can indirectly lead to the protection of substantive rights conferred by EU rules. As for EU law, the ECJ has also linked the *Köbler* liability to the violation of Article 267(3) TFEU; furthermore, the scope of the referral obligation is not obvious under EU law either. Therefore, it is not excluded that the remedy of constitutional complaint might provide – as applied under certain national regimes – at the least an equivalent protection to the *Köbler* doctrine.

With regard to the strict conditions attached to a liability claim, these alternative remedies might not be considered, in general, less favourable for an individual than to invoke the *Köbler* principle.[4]

II. PERSPECTIVES FOR THE FUTURE

A. Harmonisation of National Remedies at EU Level

I support the view that harmonisation of national remedies, and, in particular, of the conditions on state liability, is not absolutely necessary. I think that Member State remedial or procedural rules which are in violation of the *Köbler* principle must not be necessarily considered incompatible with EU law. Therefore, even if claiming damages for breach of EU law by national supreme courts is excessively difficult, the principles of effectiveness and effective judicial protections are not infringed as long as other alternative means exist to protect individual rights and the application of EU law. This means that the appropriate interpretation of the state liability principle should be the following: *Köbler* does not create a right specifically to damages against the Member State for its breach of EU law, but has instead introduced a general right to remedy in whatever form the Member State finds it most convenient to provide.[5]

Accepting this stance means extending the application of the effectiveness principle to the system of national remedies, instead of considering it within the framework of the principle of judicial liability. Adopting this solution presents the advantage of leaving unfettered the main principles of EU law, such as procedural autonomy, effectiveness and effective judicial protection of

[4] See the summary table in the Annex to this book.
[5] Dougan 2004: 109, 119, 127.

individual rights. It is also easily concealable with the procedural rule of reason, and leaves the universality of remedies also untouched.[6] Moreover, by giving national courts more leeway to decide on how EU rights should be enforced in the national environment, the complications arising from the problem of reverse discrimination can also be avoided.[7]

It is, however, true that practical application of this approach may have difficulties, as the compatibility of national regimes with EU law is normally evaluated in the framework of the preliminary procedures. In this regard, the information provided by the national courts does not always enable the ECJ to carry out such a complex analysis as to examine and understand the interrelationship between diverse national remedies.[8] Moreover, the ECJ judgments are formulated in a general way, which can inevitably cause misunderstandings and lead to confusion. In addition, as Dougan has already pointed out, to accept a degree of reparative flexibility would also imply a reappraisal of the basic nature of state liability case-law and in particular of the traditional assumption that it creates Union remedies in the form of damages.[9]

Finding the optimal solution means finding the appropriate balance between national procedural – for that matter 'remedial' – autonomy and the uniform and effective application of EU law. This aim has always guided the ECJ throughout the development in its case-law on national remedies. Moreover, the ECJ has always found a way to adapt its stance on national remedies to the ever-changing exigencies of time and ever-developing EU law.

B. Effective Judicial Protection in the Event of Violation of EU law by Member State Courts

The main function of the *Köbler* judgment lies in that it has determined an adequate standard of protection of individual rights, which must be granted in national laws in the event of violation of EU law by supreme courts.

In general, this standard is observed where manifest or deliberate violations of EU law are sanctioned, and if there is an objective possibility to re-examine a final decision on the grounds that it is contrary to EU law. However, for non-deliberate breaches, Member States appear to be free to set the subjective standard, namely the criteria regarding the gravity of the breach.

Moreover, an acceptance that state liability can be substituted by equally efficient domestic remedies means that Member States are only required to offer any kind of remedy in the event of manifest or deliberate violation of EU law by national supreme courts.

[6] Tridimas 2000: 466.
[7] Adinolfi 2012: 289; Wallerman 2016a: 356–57.
[8] See also Adinolfi 2012: 289; Nassimpian 2007: 826; Plaza 2010: 38; Rodríguez 2004–05: 620.
[9] Dougan 2000a: 110.

However, research shows that even this relatively low standard of protection is not provided in each Member State (see the examples of Estonia, Ireland, Greece, Spain, Cyprus, Luxembourg and Hungary). In this regard the question arises whether measures should not be taken against Member States not offering any remedy against manifest or deliberate violations of EU law by their national supreme courts. One possibility is to apply to the ECJ on the basis of Articles 258 or 260 TFEU for a declaration of an infringement on the part of the Member State for not providing adequate judicial protection. Given that a consistent and general violation in the application of law by national courts, as well as a national legislation non-compliant with EU requirements, are sufficient for such a declaration of infringement on the part of the state, such action would probably be successful. The other possibility would be to lodge an application to the ECtHR invoking the violation of the right to an effective remedy, enshrined under Article 13 ECHR.

C. Violation of the Duty to Refer a Preliminary Question to the ECJ as a Ground for a Liability Claim

State liability occurs where a national court has infringed its procedural obligation to apply a substantive EU norm, and this has resulted in a breach of individual rights of a party to the proceedings. According to the present ECJ case-law and after theoretical analysis of the rules on state liability, both violation of individual rights and infringement by the national court of its procedural obligation are necessary so that liability can be invoked.

In order for the mere breach of the referral duty to result in state liability, it is necessary to acknowledge, first, that preliminary ruling proceedings confer substantive rights upon individuals, and, second, that liability may arise in case of non-material damages suffered. As for the first point, at the very least, the procedural element of the referral duty, that is the obligation to state clear reasons for a refusal to submit a preliminary question, which comes under the scope of application of Article 47 of the Charter, can be considered as conferring rights on individuals. As for the second point, the liability of the EU for non-material damages caused by violation of fundamental procedural rights has already been acknowledged in the ECJ case-law.

Moreover, taking into account the ECtHR case-law, it seems appropriate that the ECJ consider also the requirements resulting from the ECHR when interpreting the duty to refer a preliminary ruling request to the ECJ. This means that, at the very least, the national judicial decisions rejecting a request of one of the parties to submit a referral to the ECJ must state adequate reasons for this decision. This is a requirement resulting directly from EU law.

Finally, one must not forget that in recent years the ECJ has put a particular emphasis on the importance of the preliminary ruling proceedings and of the autonomous nature of the constitutional legal order of the ECJ. The explicit extension of *Köbler* liability for violation of the referral duty and for violation of the Charter would perfectly fit into this jurisprudence. Such developments would probably go together with the lowering of the liability standard as well.

Annex

Remedies under national laws offering a comparable level of protection of individual rights to that provided by the *Köbler* principle in the event of breach of EU law by Member State courts.[1]

	State liability	**Retrial**	**Constitutional complaint**
Belgium			
Bulgaria			
Czech Republic			
Denmark			
Germany			
Estonia			
Ireland			
Greece			
Spain			
France			
Croatia			theoretical possibility
Italy			
Cyprus			
Latvia			
Lithuania	in administrative law	in administrative law	
Luxembourg			
Hungary	recognised only by regional appeal court		
Malta			

[1] The summary table provides an indicative overview of all theoretical possibilities acknowledged in the Member States to remedy the violation of EU law by Member State supreme courts in 2018. Light grey shading indicates that Member State courts have already expressively used the remedy for violation of EU law. Dark grey shading indicates that despite the existence of such a remedy in the domestic legal order, it has not yet been successfully used for EU law violations; or it has only been accepted in one matter of law.

	State liability	Retrial	Constitutional complaint
Netherlands			
Austria			in administrative law
Poland		in fiscal law	
Portugal			
Romania		in administrative law	
Slovenia			
Slovakia		in civil law	
Finland			
Sweden			
United Kingdom			

Bibliography[1]

Aalto, P (2014) 'Art 47 – Right to an Effective Remedy: V. Damages for Breach of the Charter' in S Peers, T Hervey, J Kenner, J and A Ward (eds) *The EU Charter of Fundamental Rights: A Commentary* (Oxford, Hart Publishing) 1235–41.

ACA Europe (2008) *National Reports: Consequences of Incompatibility with EC Law for Final Administrative Decisions and Final Judgments of Administrative Courts in the Member States*, 21st colloquium, Warsaw, 15 June 2008.

Accetto, M and Zleptnig, S (2005) 'The Principle of Effectiveness: Rethinking its Role in Community Law' 11 *European Public Law* 375–403.

Adams, M, de Waele, HCFJ, Meeusen, J and Straetmans, G (eds) (2013) *Judging Europe's Judges: The Legitimacy of the Case Law of the European Court of Justice Examined* (Oxford, Hart Publishing).

Adinolfi, A (2012) 'The "Procedural Autonomy" of Member States and the Constraints Stemming from the ECJ's Case-Law: Is Judicial Activism Still Necessary?' in H-W Micklitz and BEFM de Witte (eds) *The European Court of Justice and the Autonomy of the Member States* (Cambridge, Intersentia) 281–303.

Albors-Llorens, A (2017) 'Judicial Protection Before the Court of Justice of the European Union' in C Barnard and S Peers (eds) *European Union Law*, 2nd edn (Oxford, Oxford University Press) 262–309.

Alonso García, R (2005) 'Spanish Constitutional Court: Tax on the Use of Gambling Machines' 42 *Common Market Law Review* 535–48.

Anagnostaras, G (2000) 'State Liability v Retroactive Application of Belated Implementing Measures: Seeking the Optimum Means in Terms of Effectiveness of EC Law' 1 *Journal of Current Legal Issues*, www.bailii.org/uk/other/journals/WebJCLI/2000/issue1/anagnostaras1.html.

—— (2001a) 'State Liability and Alternative Courses of Action: How Independent Can an Autonomous Remedy Be?' 21 *Yearbook of European Law* 355–83.

—— (2001b) 'The Allocation of Responsibility in State Liability Actions for Breach of Community Law: A Modern Gordian Knot?' 26 *European Law Review* 139–58.

—— (2001c) 'The Principle of State Liability for Judicial Breaches: The Impact of European Community Law' 7 *European Public Law* 281–305.

—— (2002) 'Not as Unproblematic as You Might Think: The Establishment of Causation in Governmental Liability Actions' 27 *European Law Review* 663–76.

—— (2006) 'Erroneous Judgments and the Prospect of Damages: The Scope of the Principle of Governmental Liability for Judicial Breaches' 31 *European Law Review* 735–47.

—— (2007) 'The Quest for an Effective Remedy and the Measure of Judicial Protection Afforded to Putative Community Law Rights' 32 *European Law Review* 727–39.

Arndt, F (2001) 'The German Federal Constitutional Court at the Intersection of National and European Law: Two Recent Decisions' 2 *German Law Journal*, doi:10.1017/S2071832200003655.

Arnull, A (2011) 'The Principle of Effective Judicial Protection in EU Law: An Unruly Horse?' 36 *European Law Review* 51–70.

—— (2015) 'Judicial Review the European Union' in A Arnull and D Chalmers (eds) *The Oxford Handbook of European Union Law* (Oxford, Oxford University Press) 377–402.

[1] The literature on the subject is vast and, therefore, it is impossible to provide a comprehensive guide on the studies that have dealt with the issues addressed here. This list is therefore limited to the literature that were specific points of reference for this book.

Arnull, A and Chalmers, D (eds) (2015) *The Oxford Handbook of European Union Law* (Oxford, Oxford University Press).

Auburn, J, Moffett, J, and Sharland, A (2013) *Judicial Review: Principles and Procedure* (Oxford, Oxford University Press).

Barents, R (2010) 'The Court of Justice after the Treaty of Lisbon' 47 *Common Market Law Review* 709–28.

Barnard, C and Peers, S (eds) (2017) *European Union Law*, 2nd edn (Oxford, Oxford University Press).

Beatson, J and Tridimas, T (eds) (1998) *New Directions in European Public Law* (Oxford, Hart Publishing).

Becker, F (2007) 'Application of Community Law by Member States' Public Authorities: Between Autonomy and Effectiveness' 44 *Common Market Law Review* 1035–56.

Bernitz, U, Groussot, X and Schulyok, F (eds) (2013) *General Principles of EU Law and European Private Law*, European Monographs 84 (Alphen aan den Rijn, Kluwer Law International).

Besselink, L, Penning, F and Prechal, S (eds) (2011) *The Eclipse of the Legality Principle in the European Union*, European Monographs 75 (Alphen aan den Rijn, Kluwer Law International).

Betlem, G (1995) 'The Principle of Indirect Effect of Community Law' 3 *European Review of Private Law* 1–19.

—— (2002) 'The Doctrine of Consistent Interpretation: Managing Legal Uncertainty' 22 *Oxford Journal of Legal Studies* 397–418.

Betlem, G, González, CP, Granger, M-P and Schoißwohl, B (2007) 'Francovich Follow-Up: Cases on State Liability for Breach of European Community Law' (The Hague, TMC Asser Institute), www.asser.nl/upload/eel-webroot/www/documents/Dossiers/FrancovichFollowUp.pdf.

Beutler, B (2009) 'State Liability for Breaches of Community Law by National Courts: Is the Requirement of a Manifest Infringement of the Applicable Law an Insurmountable Obstacle?' 46 *Common Market Law Review* 773–804.

Binchy, W (2016) 'Tort Law in Ireland: A Half-Century Review' 56 *Irish Jurist* 199–218.

Biondi, A (2008) 'Case C-119/05, Ministero dell'Industria, del Commercio e dell'Artigianato v Lucchini SpA, formerly Lucchini Siderurgica SpA, Judgment of the Court of Justice (Grand Chamber) of 18 July 2007, 2007 [ECR] I–6199' 45 *Common Market Law Review* 1459–67.

Biondi, A and Farley, M (2009) *The Right to Damages in European Law*, Kluwer European Law Collection 5 (Alphen aan den Rijn, Kluwer Law International).

Blutman, L (2003) 'A tagállami bíróságok általános kötelezettségei a közösségi jog alapján' 13 *Bírák Lapja* 27–48.

—— (2004) 'A közösségi jogon alapuló igények érvényesítése a belső jogban' 4 *Európai Jog* 12–18.

—— (2015) 'Az Alkotmánybíróság és az előzetes döntéshozatali eljárás' 8 *Közjogi Szemle* 1–8.

Bobek, M (2008) 'Thou Shalt Have Two Masters; The Application of European Law by Administrative Authorities in the New Member States' 1 *Review of European Administrative Law* 51–63.

—— (2010) 'The New European Judges and the Limits of the Possible' in A Łazowski (ed), *The Application of EU Law in the New Member States* (The Hague, TMC Asser Press) 127–53.

—— (2012) 'Why There Is No Principle of "Procedural Autonomy" of Member States' in H-W Micklitz and BEFM de Witte (eds) *The European Court of Justice and the Autonomy of the Member States* (Cambridge, Intersentia) 305–23.

—— (2013) 'Of Feasibility and Silent Elephants: The Legitimacy of the Court of Justice through the Eyes of National Courts' in M Adams, H de Waele, J Meeusen and G Straetmans (eds) *Judging Europe's Judges: The Legitimacy of the Case Law of the European Court of Justice Examined* (Oxford, Hart Publishing) 197–234.

—— (ed) (2015) *EU Law in the Member States: Central European Judges Under the European Influence. The Transformative Power of the EU Revisited* (Oxford, Hart Publishing).

—— (2017) 'The Effects of EU Law in the National Legal Systems' in C Barnard and S Peers (eds), *European Union Law*, 2nd edn (Oxford, Oxford University Press) 140–73.

Bogojević, S (2015) 'Judicial Protection of Individual Applicants Revisited: Access to Justice through the Prism of Judicial Subsidiarity' 34 *Yearbook of European Law* 5–25.

Boom, WHV (2009) 'Harmonising Tort Law: A Comparative Law and Economics Analysis' in MG Faure (ed), *Encyclopedia of Law and Economics*, 1: *Tort Law and Economics*, 2nd edn (Cheltenham, Elgar) 437–439.

Borbás, B (2011) 'Fejezetek a bírósági kárfelelősség köréből a magyar és az európai szabályozás tükrében – különös tekintettel a tisztességes eljárás követelményére' PhD thesis (Pécs, Pécsi Tudományegyetem).

—— (2014) *A bírói hatalom kárfelelőssége* (Budapest, HVG-Orac).

Breuer, M (2004) 'State Liability for Judicial Wrongs and Community Law: The Case of Gerhard Köbler v Austria' 29 *European Law Review* 243–54.

Broberg, MP (2008) 'Acte Clair Revisited: Adapting the Acte Clair Criteria to the Demands of the Times' 45 *Common Market Law Review* 1383–97.

—— (2011) 'Finding Light in the Darkness: On the Actual Application of the Acte Clair Doctrine' 30 *Yearbook of European Law* 180–212.

—— (2015) 'Judicial Coherence and the Preliminary Reference Procedure' 8 *Review of European Administrative Law* 9–37.

—— (2016) 'National Courts of Last Instance Failing to Make a Preliminary Reference: The (Possible) Consequences Flowing Therefrom' 22 *European Public Law* 243–56.

—— (2017) 'Preliminary References as a Means for Enforcing EU Law' in A Jakab and D Kochenov (eds), *The Enforcement of EU Law and Values: Ensuring Member States' Compliance* (Oxford, Oxford University Press) 99–111.

Broberg, MP and Fenger, N (2016) 'Preliminary References to the Court of Justice of the EU and the Right to a Fair Trial under Article 6 ECHR' 41 *European Law Review* 599–607.

Brokelind, C (ed) (2014) *Principles of Law: Function, Status and Impact in EU Tax Law* (Amsterdam, IBDF).

Brown, C and Morijn, J (2004) 'Case C-263/02 P, Commission v Jego-Quere & Cie SA' 41 *Common Market Law Review* 1639–59.

Brown, N (1997) 'National Protection of Community Rights: Reconciling Autonomy and Effectiveness' in J Lonbay and A Biondi (eds), *Remedies for Breach of EC Law* (Chichester, John Wiley) 67–71.

Buksinski, T and Juchacz, PW (eds) (2009) *Multicentrism as an Emerging Paradigm in Legal Theory* (Frankfurt am Main, Peter Lang).

Burgorgue-Larsen L (ed) (2017) *La Charte des droits fondamentaux saisie par les juges en Europe – The Charter of Fundamental Rights as Apprehended by Judges in Europe*, Cahiers européens/ IREDIES 10 (Paris, Pedone).

Cabral, P and Chaves, MC (2006) 'Member State Liability for Decisions of National Courts Adjudicating at Last Instance' 13 *Maastricht Journal of European and Comparative Law* 109–26.

Caranta, R (1995) 'Judicial Protection against Member States: A New Jus Commune Takes Shape' 32 *Common Market Law Review* 703–26.

Christianos, V (2014) 'Rapport hellénique' in L Coutron (ed), *L'obligation de renvoi préjudiciel à la Cour de justice une obligation sanctionnée?* Droit de l'Union européenne: Monographies 6 (Bruxelles, Bruylant) 227–37.

Cilento, A (2017) 'The Civil Responsibility of the Italian Judiciary: A Double Speed System' 3 *Italian Law Journal* 19–36.

Claes, MLHK (2006) *The National Courts' Mandate in the European Constitution*, Modern Studies in European Law 5 (Oxford, Hart Publishing).

—— (2015) 'The Primacy of EU Law in European and National Law' in A Arnull and D Chalmers (eds), *The Oxford Handbook of European Union Law* (Oxford, Oxford University Press) 178–211.

Classen, CD (2004) 'Case C-224/01, Gerhard Köbler v Republik Österreich' 41 *Common Market Law Review* 813–24.

Clément-Wiltz, L (2014) 'Rapport britannique' in L Coutron (ed), *L'obligation de renvoi préjudiciel à la Cour de justice une obligation sanctionnée?* Droit de l'Union européenne: Monographies 6 (Bruxelles, Bruylant) 433–57.

Colgan, D (2002) 'Triangular Situations: The Coup de Grace for the Denial of Horizontal Direct Effect of Community Directives' 8 *European Public Law* 545–68.

Condon, R and Van Leeuwen, BJ (2016) 'Bottom Up or Rock Bottom Harmonization? Francovich State Liability in National Courts' 35 *Yearbook of European Law* 229–90.

Council of Europe (2018) *Group of State against Corruption, Ad Hoc Report on Romania (rule 34)*, adopted by GRECO at its 79th plenary meeting (Strasbourg, 19–23 March 2018).

Cour de justice de l'Union européenne (2009) *Les juridictions des États membre de l'Union européenne. Structure et organisation* (Luxembourg, Office des publications officielles des Communautés européennes).

Coutron, L (2014) 'L'irénisme des cours européennes. Rapport introductif' in L Coutron (ed), *L'obligation de renvoi préjudiciel à la Cour de justice une obligation sanctionnée?* Droit de l'Union européenne: Monographies 6 (Bruxelles, Bruylant) 13–58.

—— (ed) (2014) *L'obligation de renvoi préjudiciel à la Cour de justice une obligation sanctionnée?* Droit de l'Union européenne: Monographies 6 (Bruxelles, Bruylant).

Craig, P (1997) 'Directives: Direct Effect, Indirect Effect and the Construction of National Legislation' 22 *European Law Review* 519–38.

Craig, PP and Rawlings, R (eds) (2003) *Law and Administration in Europe: Essays in Honour of Carol Harlow* (Oxford, Oxford University Press).

Cremona, M, de Witte, BEFM and Francioni, F (eds) (2012) *Compliance and the Enforcement of EU Law*, Collected Courses of the Academy of European Law 20/2 (Oxford, Oxford University Press).

Curtin, D and Heukels, T (eds) (1994) *Institutional Dynamics of European Integration: Essays in Honour of Henry G Schermers*, vol II. (Dordrecht, Nijhoff).

Cygan, AJ and Spadacini, L (eds) (2010) *Constitutional Implications of the Traghetti Judgment* (Gussago, Bibliofabbrica).

Czoboly, GI (2012) 'A kereseti kérelemhez kötöttség az uniós joggal érintett közigazgatási perekben' in Á Fuglinszky and A Klára (eds), *Európai jogi kultúra: Megújulás és hagyomány a magyar civilisztikában* (Budapest, ELTE Eötvös) 351–67.

Da Cruz Vilaça, JL (2013) 'Le principe de l'effet utile du droit de l'Union dans la jurisprudence de la Cour' in A Rosas, E Levits and Y Bot (eds), *The Court of Justice and the Construction of Europe: Analyses and Perspectives on Sixty Years of Case-Law = La Cour de Justice et La Construction de l'Europe: Analyses et Perspectives de Soixante Ans de Jurisprudence* (Berlin, Springer, The Hague, TMC Asser Press) 279–306.

Da Cunha Rodríguez, JN and de Jesus Patricio, HM (2014) 'Rapport portugais' in L Coutron (ed), *L'obligation de renvoi préjudiciel à la Cour de justice une obligation sanctionnée?* Droit de l'Union européenne: Monographies 6 (Bruxelles, Bruylant) 389–407.

De Búrca, G (1997) 'National Procedural Rules and Remedies: The Changing Approach of the Court of Justice' in J Lonbay and A Biondi (eds), *Remedies for Breach of EC Law* (Chichester, John Wiley) 37–46.

De Visser, M (2004) 'The Concept of Concurrent Liability and its Relationship with the Principle of Effectiveness: A One-Way Ticket into Oblivion' 11 *Maastricht Journal of European and Comparative Law* 47–71.

De Witte, BEFM, Mayoral Díaz-Asensio, JA, Jaremba, U, Wind, M and Podstawa, K (eds) (2016) *National Courts and EU Law: New Issues, Theories and Methods* (Cheltenham, Edward Elgar).

De Zwaan, JW, Jans, JH, Nelissen, FA and Blockmans, S (eds) (2004) *The European Union: An Ongoing Process of Integration: Liber Amicorum Alfred E Kellermann* (The Hague, TMC Asser Press).

Demaret, P, Govaere, I and Hanf, D (eds) (2007) *European Legal Dynamics: Revised and Update Edition of 30 Years of European Legal Studies at the College of Europe? = Dynamiques juridiques européennes: Édition revue et mise à jour de 30 ans d'études juridiques européennes au Collegue d'Europe*, College of Europe Studies 2 = Cahiers du Collège d'Europe no 2 (Bruxelles, PIE Peter Lang).

Derlén, M (2009) *Multilingual Interpretation of European Union Law* (Alphen aan den Rijn, Kluwer Law International).

Díez de Velasco Vallejo, M and Pérez González, M (eds) (1993) *Hacia un Nuevo Orden Internacional y Europeo: Estudios en Homenaje al Profesor Don Manuel Díez de Velasco* (Madrid, Tecnos).

Dittert, D (2014) 'Rapport allemande' in L Coutron (ed) *L'obligation de renvoi préjudiciel à la Cour de justice une obligation sanctionnée?* Droit de l'Union européenne: Monographies 6 (Bruxelles, Bruylant) 59–82.

Do, TU (2010) 'Droit Fiscal: Arrêt "Commission Européenne c Royaume d'Espagne" Arrêt du 12 Novembre 2009, Aff C-154/08' *Revue du droit de l'Union européenne* no 1, 146–48.

Dougan, M (2000a) 'The "Disguised" Vertical Direct Effect of Directives?' 59 *Cambridge Law Journal* 586–12.

—— (2000b) 'The Francovich Right to Reparation: Reshaping the Contours of Community Remedial Competence' 6 *European Public Law* 103–28.

—— (2001) 'Case C-443/98, Unilever Italia v Central Food, Judgment of the Court of Justice of 26 September 2000, [2000] ECR I-7535. Full Court' 38 *Common Market Law Review* 1503–17.

—— (2004) *National Remedies Before the Court of Justice: Issues of Harmonisation and Differentiation*, Modern Studies in European Law 4 (Oxford, Hart Publishing).

—— (2007) 'When Worlds Collide! Competing Visions of the Relationship between Direct Effect and Supremacy' 44 *Common Market Law Review* 931–63.

—— (2017) 'Addressing Issues of Protective Scope within the Francovich Right of Reparation' 13 *European Constitutional Law Review* 124–65.

—— (2019) 'Primacy and the Remedy of Disapplication' 56 *Common Market Law Review* 1459–1508.

Douglas-Scott, S (2002) *Constitutional Law of the European Union* (Harlow, Pearson Longman).

Drake, S (2005) 'Twenty Years after Von Colson: The Impact of 'Indirect Effect' on the Protection of the Individual's Community Rights' 30 *European Law Review* 329–49.

—— (2010) 'State Liability for Judicial Error: All Bark and No Bite? The Consequences of National Courts' Failure to Refer' in AJ Cygan and L Spadacini (eds), *Constitutional Implications of the Traghetti Judgment* (Gussago, Bibliofabbrica) 49–80.

Dubos, O, Katz, D and Mollard, P (2014) 'Rapport français' in L Coutron (ed), *L'obligation de renvoi préjudiciel à la Cour de justice une obligation sanctionnée?* Droit de l'Union européenne: Monographies 6 (Bruxelles, Bruylant) 201–26.

Dyèvre, A (2016) 'Domestic Judicial Defiance in the European Union: A Systemic Threat to the Authority of EU Law?' 35 *Yearbook of European Law* 106–44.

Ebers, M (2010) 'From Océano to Asturcom: Mandatory Costumer Law, Ex Officio Application of European Union Law and Res Judicata' 18 *European Review of Private Law* 823–46.

Eeckhout, P (1998) 'Liability of Member States in Damages and the Community System of Remedies' in J Beatson and T Tridimas (eds), *New Directions in European Public Law* (Oxford, Hart Publishing) 63–75.

Eilmansberger, T (2004) 'The Relationship between Rights and Remedies in EC Law: In Search of the Missing Link' 41 *Common Market Law Review* 1199–1246.

Engström, J (2008) 'National Courts' Obligation to Apply Community Law Ex Officio: The Court Showing New Respect for Party Autonomy and National Procedural Autonomy?' 1 *Review of European Administrative Law* 67–89.

—— (2011) 'The Principle of Effective Judicial Protection after the Lisbon Treaty' 4 *Review of European Administrative Law* 53–68.

Escudero, ML (2011) 'Case C-154/08, Commission v Spain, Judgment of the Court (Third Chamber) of 12 November 2009, Not Yet Reported' 48 *Common Market Law Review* 227–42.

European Commission, *Annual Reports to the European Parliament on Monitoring the Application of EU Law* (Annex VI: Application of Community law by national courts: a survey).

European Current Law Year Book 1996–2014 (London, Sweet & Maxwell).

Evas, T (2016) 'Judicial Reception of EU Law in Estonia' in BEFM De Witte et al (eds), *National Courts and EU Law: New Issues, Theories and Methods* (Cheltenham, Edward Elgar) 146–67.

Fartunova, M (2014) 'Rapport bulgare' in L Coutron (ed) *L'obligation de renvoi préjudiciel à la Cour de justice une obligation sanctionnée?* Droit de l'Union européenne: Monographies 6 (Bruxelles, Bruylant) 145–164.

Faure, MG (2017) 'The Harmonization of EU Tort Law: A Law and Economic Analysis' in P Giliker (ed), *Research Handbook on EU Tort Law*, Research Handbooks in European Law (Cheltenham, Edward Elgar) 415–42.

—— (ed) (2009) *Encyclopedia of Law and Economics*, 1: *Tort Law and Economics*, 2nd edn (Cheltenham, Edward Elgar).

Fazekas, J (2015) 'Az EU jogrendszere' in A Osztovits (ed), *EU-jog* (Budapest, HVG-Orac) 165–256.

Fekete, B and Mancaleoni, AM (2017) 'Application of Primary and Secondary EU Law on the National Courts' Own Motion' in CH Sieburgh and W Devroe (eds), *Cases, Materials and Text on European Law and Private Law*, Ius Commune Casebooks for the Common Law of Europe (Oxford, Hart Publishing) 421–61.

Fennelly, N (2013) 'The National Judge as Judge of the European Union' in A Rosas, E Levits and Y Bot (eds), *The Court of Justice and the Construction of Europe: Analyses and Perspectives on Sixty Years of Case-Law = La Cour de Justice et La Construction de l'Europe: Analyses et Perspectives de Soixante Ans de Jurisprudence* (Berlin, Springer, The Hague, TMC Asser Press) 61–79.

Flynn, L (2008) 'When National Procedural Autonomy Meets the Effectiveness of Community Law, Can it Survive the Impact?' 9 *ERA Forum* (Trier, Springer) 245–58.

Franklin, CNK (ed) (2018) *The Effectiveness and Application of EU and EEA Law in National Courts: Principles of Consistent Interpretation* (Cambridge, Intersentia).

Fuglinszky, Á (2008) 'Felróható károsulti közrehatás és kárenyhítési kötelezettség a magyar polgári jogban' 10 *Polgári Jogi Kodifikáció* 3–23.

—— (2015) *Kártérítési jog* (Budapest, HVG-Orac).

Fuglinszky, Á and Klára, A (eds) (2012) *Európai jogi kultúra: Megújulás és hagyomány a magyar civilisztikában* (Budapest, ELTE Eötvös).

Galetta, D-U (2010) *Procedural Autonomy of EU Member States: Paradise Lost? A Study on the 'Functionalized Procedural Competence' of EU Member States* (Heidelberg, Springer).

Gencarelli, B (2014) 'Rapport italien' in L Coutron (ed), *L'obligation de renvoi préjudiciel à la Cour de justice une obligation sanctionnée?* Droit de l'Union européenne: Monographies 6 (Bruxelles, Bruylant) 267–282.

Giliker, P (2017) 'The Future of EU Tort Law' in P Giliker (ed), *Research Handbook on EU Tort Law* (Cheltenham, Edward Elgar) 445–67.

—— (ed) (2017) *Research Handbook on EU Tort Law* (Cheltenham, Edward Elgar).

Golecki, MJ and Wojciechowski, B (2009) 'The Application of Law Within a Multicentric Legal System: Economic Analysis of Köbler and Traghetti' in T Buksinski and W Juchacz (eds), *Multicentrism as an Emerging Paradigm in Legal Theory* (Frankfurt am Main, Peter Lang) 173–96.

Gombos, K (2009) *Bírói jogvédelem az Európai Unióban* (Budapest, Complex, 2009).

—— (2011) 'Az uniós jogból fakadó bírói jogvédelmi eszközök szintjei és lépcsőfokai' 11 *Európai Jog* 35–45.

Göransson, F-L (2014) 'Rapport suédois' in L Coutron (ed), *L'obligation de renvoi préjudiciel à la Cour de justice une obligation sanctionnée?* Droit de l'Union européenne: Monographies 6 (Bruxelles, Bruylant) 479–496.

Gordon, RQC and Moffatt, R (2014) *EU Law in Judicial Review*, 2nd edn (Oxford, Oxford University Press).

Granger, M-PF (2007) 'National Applications of Francovich and the Construction of a European Administrative Jus Commune' 32 *European Law Review* 157–92.

—— (2017) 'Francovich Liability Before National Courts: 25 Years on, has Anything Changed?' in P Giliker (ed), *Research Handbook on EU Tort Law* (Cheltenham, Edward Elgar) 93–127.

Groussot, X and Minssen, T (2007) 'Res Judicata in the Court of Justice Case-Law: Balancing Legal Certainty with Legality?' 3 *European Constitutional Law Review* 385–417.

Gutman, K (2011) 'The Evolution of the Action for Damages Against the European Union and its Place in the System of Judicial Protection' 48 *Common Market Law Review* 695–750.

—— (2017) 'The Non-Contractual Liability of the European Union: Principle, Practice and Promise' in P Giliker (ed), *Research Handbook on EU Tort Law* (Cheltenham, Edward Elgar) 26–62.

—— (2019) 'The Essence of the Fundamental Right to an Effective Remedy and to a Fair Trial in the Case-Law of the Court of Justice of the European Union: The Best Is Yet to Come?' 20 *German Law Journal* 884–903.

Haba, M (2015) *The Case of State Liability: 20 Years After Francovich* (Wiesbaden, Springer Gabler).

Haket, SW (2015) 'Coherence in the Application of the Duty of Consistent Interpretation in EU Law' 8 *Review of European Administrative Law* 215–46.

Harlow, C (2000) 'A Common European Law of Remedies' in C Kilpatrick, T Novitz and P Skidmore (eds), *The Future of Remedies in Europe* (Oxford, Hart Publishing) 69–86.

Hartkamp, A, Sieburgh, CH, Keus, LAD and Kortmann, J (eds) (2014) *The Influence of EU Law on the National Private Law*, Onderneming en recht 81-1 (Deventer, Kluwer).

Heukels, T (1996) 'Joined Cases C-430/93 and C-431/93, Van Schijndel and Van Veen v Stichting Pensioenfonds Voor Fysiotherapeuten; and Case C-312/93, Peterbroeck, Van Campenhout & Cie SCS v Belgian State, Both Judgments of the Court of 14 December 1995 (Full Court)' 33 *Common Market Law Review* 337–53.

Hilson, C and Downes, A (1999) 'Making Sense of Rights: Community Rights in EC Law' 24 *European Law Review* 121–38.

Himsworth, C (1997) 'Things Fall Apart: The Harmonisation of Community Judicial Procedural Protection Revisited' 22 *European Law Review* 291–311.

Hofmann, HCH (2014) 'Art 47 – Right to an Effective Remedy. III. Specific Provisions (Meaning)' in S Peers, T Hervey, J Kenner, J and A Ward (eds), *The EU Charter of Fundamental Rights: A Commentary* (Oxford, Hart Publishing) 1211–28.

Hofstötter, B (2005) *Non-Compliance of National Courts: Remedies in European Community Law and Beyond* (The Hague, TMC Asser Press).

Holdgaard, R, Elkan, D and Schaldemose, GK (2018) 'From Cooperation to Collision: The ECJ's Ajos Ruling and the Danish Supreme Court's Refusal to Comply' 55 *Common Market Law Review* 17–53.

Hoskins, M (1996) 'Tilting the Balance: Supremacy and National Procedural Rules' 21 *European Law Review* 365–77.

Houyet, Y (2014) 'Rapport belge' in L Coutron (ed) *L'obligation de renvoi préjudiciel à la Cour de justice une obligation sanctionnée?* Droit de l'Union européenne: Monographies 6 (Bruxelles, Bruylant) 119–43.

Huet, A (2010) 'La France, le Comité des droits de l'Homme de l'ONU et la rétroactivité de la loi pénale plus douce: Note sous communication no 1760/2008 du 21 oct 2010, Cochet c France' *Recueil Dalloz* 2865–67.

Iliopoulos-Strangas, J, Biernat, S and Potacs, M (eds) (2014) *Verantwortung, Haftung und Kontrolle des Verfassungsstaates und der Europäischen Union im Wandel der Zeit = Responsibility, Accountability and Control of the Constitutional State and the European Union in Changing Times = Responsabilités et contrôle de l'État constitutionnel et de l'Union européenne au fil du temps* (Baden-Baden, Nomos).

Jacobs, FG (1993) 'Remedies in National Courts for the Enforcement of Community Rights' in M Díez de Velasco Vallejo and M Pérez González (eds) *Hacia Un Nuevo Orden Internacional Y Europeo: Estudios En Homenaje Al Profesor Don Manuel Díez de Velasco* (Madrid, Tecnos) 969–84.

Jakab, A and Kochenov, D (eds) (2017) *The Enforcement of EU Law and Values: Ensuring Member States' Compliance* (Oxford, Oxford University Press).

Jans, JH (2004) 'State Liability and Infringements Attributable to National Courts: A Dutch Perspective on the Köbler Case' in JW de Zwaan, JH Jans, FA Nelissen, and S Blockmans (eds), *The European Union: An Ongoing Process of Integration: Liber Amicorum Alfred E Kellermann* (The Hague, TMC Asser Press) 165–76.

Jans, JH and Marseille, A (2008) 'Joined Cases C-222–225/05, Van der Weerd and others v Minister van Landbouw, Natuur en Voedselkwaliteit, Judgment of the Court (Fourth Chamber) of 7 June 2007, [2007] ECR I-4233' 45 *Common Market Law Review* 853–62.

Jans, JH and Verhoeven, MJM (2015) 'Europeanisation via Consistent Interpretation and Direct Effect' in JH Jans, S Prechal and R Widdershoven (eds), *Europeanisation of Public Law*, 2nd edn (Groningen, Europa Law Publishing) 73–132.

Jans, JH, Prechal, S and Widdershoven, R (eds) (2015) *Europeanisation of Public Law*, 2nd edn (Groningen, Europa Law Publishing).

Jarukaitis, I (2010) 'Lithuania's Membership in the European Union and Application of EU Law at National Level' in A Łazowski (ed), *The Application of EU Law in the New Member States* (The Hague, TMC Asser Press) 209–41.

Jenkins, T and Bushell, G (2015) 'Justice Denied or Simply Delayed? Consequences of Excessive Delay at the EU's General Court' 6 *Journal of European Competition Law & Practice* 3–14.

Jeuland, E (2008) 'Le droit au juge naturel et l'organisation judiciaire' 125 *Revue française d'administration publique* 33–42.

Kakouris, CN (1997) 'Do the Member States Possess Judicial Procedural "Autonomy"?' 34 *Common Market Law Review* 1389–1412.

Kanninen, H (2014) 'Rapport finnois' in L Coutron (ed), *L'obligation de renvoi préjudiciel à la Cour de justice une obligation sanctionnée?* Droit de l'Union européenne: Monographies 6 (Bruxelles, Bruylant) 183–199.

Kawczyńska, M (2014) 'Concurrent Liability of the European Union and the Member States' in J Iliopoulos-Strangas, S Biernat and M Potacs (eds), *Verantwortung, Haftung und Kontrolle des Verfassungsstaates und der Europäischen Union im Wandel der Zeit = Responsibility, Accountability and Control of the Constitutional State and the European Union in Changing Times = Responsabilités et contrôle de l'État constitutionnel et de l'Union européenne au fil du temps* (Baden-Baden, Nomos) 73–92

Kilpatrick, C, Novitz, T and Skidmore, P (eds) (2000) *The Future of Remedies in Europe* (Oxford, Hart Publishing).

Klamert, M (2006) 'Judicial Implementation of Directives and Anticipatory Indirect Effect: Connecting the Dots' 43 *Common Market Law Review* 1251–75.

Kofler, G (2014) 'Direct Applicability and Direct Effect' in Brokelind, C (ed), *Principles of Law: Function, Status and Impact in EU Tax Law* (Amsterdam, IBDF) 273–301.

Kokott, J and Sobotta, C (2010) 'The Charter of Fundamental Rights of the European Union after Lisbon' EUI Working Paper AEL 6 (Florence, Academy of European Law).

Komárek, J (2005a) 'Inter-Court Constitutional Dialogue after the Enlargement – Implications of the Case of Professor Köbler' 1 *Croatian Yearbook of European Law and Policy* 75–94.

—— (2005b) 'Federal Elements in the Community Judicial System: Building Coherence in the Community Legal Order' 42 *Common Market Law Review* 9–34.

—— (2013) 'The Place of Constitutional Courts in the EU' 9 *European Constitutional Law Review* no 9, 420–450

—— (2014) 'Why National Constitutional Courts Should not Embrace EU Fundamental Rights' (Social Science Research Network), https://papers.ssrn.com/sol3/papers.cfm?abstract_id=2510290

Komninos, AP (2000) 'Case C-126/97, Eco Swiss China Time Ltd v Benetton International NV, Judgment of 1 June 1999, Full Court' 37 *Common Market Law Review* 459–78.

Kornezov, A (2014a) 'Res Judicata of National Judgments Incompatible with EU Law: Time for a Major Rethink?' 51 *Common Market Law Review* 809–842.

—— (2014b) 'Shaping the New Architecture of the EU System of Judicial Remedies: Comment on Inuit' 39 *European Law Review* 251–63.

—— (2016) 'The New Format of the Acte Clair doctrine and its Consequences' 53 *Common Market Law Review* 1317–42.

Krommendijk, J (2016) 'Is There Light on the Horizon? The Distinction Between "Rewe Effectiveness" and the Principle of Effective Judicial Protection in Art 47 of the Charter after Orizzonte' 53 *Common Market Law Review* 1395–1418.

—— (2017) '"Open Sesame!": Improving Access to the ECJ by Obliging National Courts to Reason Their Refusals to Refer' 42 *European Law Review* 46–62.

Lacchi, C (2015a) 'The ECrtHR's Interference in the Dialogue Between National Courts and the Court of Justice of the EU: Implications for the Preliminary Reference Procedure' 8 *Review of European Administrative Law* 95–125.

—— (2015b) 'Review by Constitutional Courts of the Obligation of National Courts of Last Instance to Refer a Preliminary Question to the Court of Justice of the EU' 16 *German Law Journal* 1663–1700.

—— (2016) 'Multilevel Judicial Protection in the EU and Preliminary References' 53 *Common Market Law Review* 679–707.

Laffranque, J (2010) '"Community, Identity, Stability": Ideals and Practice in Building a Bridge Between the Legal Systems of the European Union and one of the Smallest of the "Brave New Word"' in A Łazowski (ed), *The Application of EU Law in the New Member States* (The Hague, TMC Asser Press) 157–207.

—— (2018) '(Just) Give Me a Reason' 27 *Juridica International* 12–35.

Łazowski, A (ed) (2010) *The Application of EU Law in the New Member States* (The Hague, TMC Asser Press).

Lazzerini, N (2014) '(Some of) the Fundamental Rights Granted by the Charter May Be a Source of Obligations for Private Parties: AMS' 51 *Common Market Law Review* 907–34.

Leczykiewicz, D (2012) 'Enforcement or Compensation? Damages Actions in EU Law after the Draft Common Frame of Reference' Legal Research Paper Series 59 (University of Oxford) 1–19.

—— (2015) 'Effectiveness of EU Law Before National Courts: Direct Effect, Consistent Interpretation and Member State Liability' in A Arnull and D Chalmers (eds), *The Oxford Handbook of European Union Law* (Oxford, Oxford University Press) 212–48.

—— (2017) 'Compensatory Remedies in EU Law: The Relationship Between EU Law and National Law' in P Giliker (ed), *Research Handbook on EU Tort Law* (Cheltenham, Edward Elgar) 63–92.

Leczykiewicz, D and Weatherill, S (eds) (2013) *The Involvment of EU Law in Private Relationships*, Studies of the Oxford Institute of European and Comparative Law 16 (Oxford, Hart Publishing).

Lenaerts, K (2003) 'Interlocking Legal Orders in the European Union and Comparative Law' 52 *International & Comparative Law Quarterly* 873–906.

—— (2007) 'The Rule of Law and the Coherence of the Judicial System of the European Union' 44 *Common Market Law Review* 1625–59.

Lenaerts, K, Maselis, I, Gutman, K (authors) and Nowak, JT (ed) (2014) *EU Procedural Law* (Oxford, Oxford University Press).

Lock, T (2011) 'Taking National Courts More Seriously? Comment on Opinion 1/09' 36 *European Law Review* 576588.

—— (2012) 'Is Private Enforcement of EU Law Through State Liability a Myth? An Assessment 20 Years after Francovich' 49 *Common Market Law Review* 1675–1702.

Lomnici, Z, Nagy, G and Zanathy, J (eds) (1997) *Az Európai Bíróság gyakorlata: A Bírósági Határozatok melléklete* (Budapest, HVG-Orac).

Lonbay, J and Biondi, A (eds) (1997) *Remedies for Breach of EC Law* (Chichester, John Wiley).

Loth, M (2017) 'Who Has the Last Word? On Judicial Lawmaking in European Private Law' 25 *European Review of Private Law* 45–70.

Maduro, LMP and Azoulai, L (eds) (2010) *The Past and Future of EU Law: The Classics of EU Law Revisited on the 50th Anniversary of the Rome Treaty* (Oxford, Hart Publishing).

Maisto, G (2014) 'The Principle of Effectiveness' in C Brokelind (ed) *Principles of Law: Function, Status and Impact in EU Tax Law* (Amsterdam, IBDF) 163–82.

Marguery, TP and van Harten, HJ (2014) 'Rapport néerlandais' in L Coutron (ed), *L'obligation de renvoi préjudiciel à la Cour de justice une obligation sanctionnée?* Droit de l'Union européenne: Monographies 6 (Bruxelles, Bruylant) 335–55.

Marktler, T (2008) 'The European Court of Justice as Lawful Judge. Austrian Constitutional Court Judgement from December 11th, 1995 VfSlg 14.390' 2 *Vienna Online Journal on International Constitutional Law* 294–300.

Menyhárd, A (2004) 'A kártérítési jog egyes kérdései' 6 *Polgári Jogi Kodifikáció* 47–49.

Metzinger, P (2014) 'A tagállamok felelőssége az európai jog megsértéséért – a magyar jogalkalmazás szempontjából' in A Osztovits (ed), *A magyar bírósági gyakorlat az előzetes döntéshozatali eljárások kezdeményezésének tükrében, 2004–2014* (Budapest, HVG-Orac) 70–86.

—— (2015) 'A tagállamok kötelezettségei az uniós jog érvényesülése érdekében' in A Osztovits (ed), *EU-jog* (Budapest, HVG-Orac) 257–270.

Micklitz, H-W (2012) 'The ECJ Between the Individual Citizen and the Member States: A Plea for a Judge-Made European Law on Remedies' in H-W Micklitz and BEFM de Witte (eds), *The European Court of Justice and the Autonomy of the Member States* (Cambridge, Intersentia) 349–400.

Micklitz, H-W and de Witte, BEFM (eds) (2012) *The European Court of Justice and the Autonomy of the Member States* (Cambridge, Intersentia).

Mikłaszewicz, P (2014) 'Rapport polonais' in L Coutron (ed), *L'obligation de renvoi préjudiciel à la Cour de justice une obligation sanctionnée?* Droit de l'Union européenne: Monographies 6 (Bruxelles, Bruylant) 357–88.

Muir, E (2011) 'Of Ages in – and Edges of – EU Law' 48 *Common Market Law Review* 39–62.

Nassimpian, D (2007) 'And We Keep on Meeting: (De)Fragmenting State Liability' 32 *European Law Review* 819–38.

Naszladi, G (2014) 'Az Alkotmánybíróság esete az előzetes döntéshozatali eljárással – egy visszautasító végzés margójára' 14 *Európai Jog* 12–16.

—— (2015) The Hungarian Constitutional Court's Judgment Concerning the Preliminary Ruling Procedure: Comments on a Rejection Order' 3 *Pécs Journal of International and European Law* 37–43.

Neamt, VP (2016) 'Member States' liability for judicial error resulting in breaches of European Union Law' 17 *Journal of Legal Studies* 1–13.

Nollkaemper, A (2011) 'Joint Responsibility Between the EU and Member States for Non-Performance of Obligations under Multilateral Environmental Agreements' (Social Science Research Network), https://papers.ssrn.com/sol3/papers.cfm?abstract_id=1966933

—— (2012) 'The Role of National Courts in Inducing Compliance with International and European Law' in M Cremona, BEFM de Witte and F Francioni (eds), *Compliance and the Enforcement of EU Law*, Collected Courses of the Academy of European Law 20/2 (Oxford, Oxford University Press) 157–94.

O'Keeffe, D and Bavasso, A (eds) (2000) *Judicial Review in European Union Law: Liber amicorum in honour of Lord Slynn of Hadley*, vol I (The Hague, Kluwer Law International).

O'Reilly, S (2014) 'Köbler in the Common Law Courts: Cooper v Attorney General' 17 *Irish Journal of European Law* 87–101.

Oliver, P (2011) 'Case Note on Case C-279/09 DEB v Germany (Judgment of the Grand Chamber of 22 December 2010)' 48 *Common Market Law Review* 2023–40.

Ormerod, D and Laird, Karl (2014) *Smith and Hogan's Text, Cases, and Materials on Criminal Law*, 11th edn (Oxford, Oxford University Press).

Ortlep, R and Widdershoven, R (2015) 'Judicial Protection' in JH Jans, S Prechal and R Widdershoven (eds), *Europeanisation of Public Law*, 2nd edn (Groningen, Europa Law Publishing) 333–434.

Osztovits, A (ed) (2014) *A magyar bírósági gyakorlat az előzetes döntéshozatali eljárások kezdeményezésének tükrében, 2004–2014* (Budapest, HVG-Orac).

—— (ed) (2015) *EU-jog* (Budapest, HVG-Orac).

Pákozdi, Z (2011) 'A bírói jogkörben okozott károk megtérítése és a tisztességes eljárás' 6 *Miskolci Jogi Szemle* 87–100.

—— (2013) 'Problémás kérdések a jogerő intézményével összefüggésben' 68 *Jogtudományi Közlöny* 183–91.

Panagis, Y and Šadl, U (2015) 'What Is a Leading Case in European Union Law: An Empirical Analysis' 40 *European Law Review* 15–34.

Paris, M-L (2014) 'Rapport irlandais' in L Coutron (ed), *L'obligation de renvoi préjudiciel à la Cour de justice une obligation sanctionnée?* Droit de l'Union européenne: Monographies 6 (Bruxelles, Bruylant) 239–266.

Paunio, E (2014) 'Art 47 – Right to an Effective Remedy. IV. Effective Remedies Before Member State Courts and the Principle of Non-Discrimination (Meaning)' in S Peers, T Hervey, J Kenner and A Ward (eds), *The EU Charter of Fundamental Rights: A Commentary* (Oxford, Hart Publishing), 1228–34.

Peers, S, Hervey, T, Kenner, J and Ward, A (eds) (2014) *The EU Charter of Fundamental Rights: A Commentary* (Oxford, Hart Publishing).

Pelzl, A (2014) 'Rapport autrichien' in L Coutron (ed) *L'obligation de renvoi préjudiciel à la Cour de justice une obligation sanctionnée?* Droit de l'Union européenne: Monographies 6 (Bruxelles, Bruylant) 83–118.

Pérez de Nanclares, JM y (2010) 'Case C-118/08, Transportes Urbanos y Servicios Generales SAL v Administración del Estado, Judgment of the Court of Justice (Grand Chamber) of 26 January 2010, Not Yet Reported' 47 *Common Market Law Review* 1847–60.

Pernice, I (2013) 'The Right to Effective Judicial Protection and Remedies in the EU' in A Rosas, E Levits and Y Bot (eds), *The Court of Justice and the Construction of Europe: Analyses and Perspectives on Sixty Years of Case-Law = La Cour de Justice et la Construction de l'Europe: Analyses et Perspectives de Soixante Ans de Jurisprudence* (Berlin, Springer, The Hague, TMC Asser Press) 381–95.

Petrlík, D (2014) 'Rapport tchèque' in L Coutron (ed), *L'obligation de renvoi préjudiciel à la Cour de justice une obligation sanctionnée?* Droit de l'Union européenne: Monographies 6 (Bruxelles, Bruylant) 409–431.

Pfander, JE (2006) 'Köbler v Austria: Expositional Supremacy and Member State Liability' 17 *European Business Law Review* 275–297.

Piqani, D (2012) 'Arguments for a Holistic Approach in European Constitutionalism: What Role for National Institutions in Avoiding Constitutional Conflicts between National Constitutions and EU Law' 8 *European Constitutional Law Review* 493–522.

—— (2016) 'The Simmenthal Revolution Revisited: What Role for Constitutional Courts?' in BEFM De Witte et al (eds), *National Courts and EU Law: New Issues, Theories and Methods* (Cheltenham, Elgar) 26–48.

Plaza, C (2010) 'Member States Liability for Legislative Injustice. National Procedural Autonomy and the Principle of Equivalence: Going Too Far in Transportes Urbanos?' 3 *Review of European Administrative Law* 27–51.

Półtorak, N (2012) 'State Liability for Violation of European Union Law: A Polish Perspective' 13 ERA Forum (Trier, Springer) 185–97.

—— (2014) 'State Liability in EU Law – Have the Member States Learnt Anything in 20 Years after "Francovich"? in J Iliopoulos-Strangas, S Biernat and M Potacs (eds) *Verantwortung, Haftung und Kontrolle des Verfassungsstaates und der Europäischen Union im Wandel der Zeit = Responsibility, Accountability and Control of the Constitutional State and the European Union in Changing Times = Responsabilités et contrôle de l'État constitutionnel et de l'Union européenne au fil du temps* (Baden-Baden, Nomos) 181–94.

—— (2015) 'Changes in the Level of the National Judicial Protection Under the EU Influence on the Example of the Polish Legal System' in M Bobek (ed), *EU Law in the Member States: Central European Judges Under the European Influence. The Transformative Power of the EU Revisited* (Oxford, Hart Publishing) 223–41.

Potacs, M and Mayer, C (2013) 'Changes in Austrian State Liability Law under the Influence of European Law' 19 *European Public Law* 51–59.

Prechal, S (1990) 'Remedies after Marshall' 27 *Common Market Law Review* 451–73.

—— (1997) 'EC Requirements for an Effective Remedy' in J Lonbay and A Biondi (eds), *Remedies for Breach of EC Law* (Chichester, John Wiley) 3–13.

—— (1998) 'Community Law in National Courts: The Lessons from Van Schijndel' 35 *Common Market Law Review* 681–706.

—— (2000) 'Does Direct Effect Still Matter?' 37 *Common Market Law Review* 1047–69.

—— (2005) 'Joined Cases C-397/01 to C-403/01, Bernhard Pfeiffer et al' 42 *Common Market Law Review* 1445–63.

—— (2006A) 'Member State Liability and Direct Effect: What's the Difference After All?' 17 *European Business Law Review* 299–316.

—— (2006B) 'National Courts in EU Judicial Structures' 25 *Yearbook of European Law* 429–50.

Prechal, S and Shelkoplyas, N (2004) 'National Procedures, Public Policy and EC Law: From Van Schijndel to Eco Swiss and Beyond' 12 *European Review of Private Law* 589–611.

Prechal, S and Widdershoven, R (2011) 'Redefining the Relationship Between "Rewe-Effectiveness" and Effective Judicial Protection' 4 *Review of European Administrative Law* 31–50.

Prete, L (2017) *Infringement Proceedings in EU Law*, European Monographs 98 (Alphen aan den Rijn, Kluwer Law International).

Prete, L and Smulders, B (2010) 'The Coming of Age of Infringement Proceedings' 47 *Common Market Law Review* 9–61.

Procházka, R (2013) 'To Decide or Not to Decide: On the Political Theology of Simmenthal, Lyckeskog et al' in A Rosas, E Levits and Y Bot (eds), *The Court of Justice and the Construction of Europe: Analyses and Perspectives on Sixty Years of Case-Law = La Cour de Justice et La Construction de l'Europe: Analyses et Perspectives de Soixante Ans de Jurisprudence* (Berlin, Springer, The Hague, TMC Asser Press) 337–65.

Rauchegger, C and Wallerman, A (eds) (2019) *The Eurosceptic Challenge: National Implementation and Interpretation of EU Law* (Oxford, Hart Publishing).

Ravarani, G (2014) 'Rapport luxembourgeois' in L Coutron (ed), *L'obligation de renvoi préjudiciel à la Cour de justice une obligation sanctionnée?* Droit de l'Union européenne: Monographies 6 (Bruxelles, Bruylant) 309–333.

Regueiro, PVF (2002) 'Invocability of Substitution and Invocability of Exclusion. Bringing Legal Realism to the Current Developments of the Case-Law of "Horizontal" Direct Effect of Directives' Jean Monet Working Paper 7/2002 (New York, New York School of Law).

Reich, N (2007) 'Horizontal Liability in EC Law: Hybridization of Remedies for Compensation in Case of Breaches of EC Rights' 44 *Common Market Law Review* 705–42.

—— (2013) The Principle of Effectiveness and EU Private Law, in U Bernitz, X Groussot and F Schulyok (eds), *General Principles of EU Law and European Private Law*, European Monographs 84 (Alphen aan den Rijn, Kluwer Law International) 301–326.

—— (2017) 'Francovich Enforcement Analyzed and Illustrated by German (and English) Law' in A Jakab and D Kochenov (eds), *The Enforcement of EU Law and Values: Ensuring Member States' Compliance* (Oxford, Oxford University Press) 112–127.

Rodríguez, PM (2004–05) 'State Liability for Judicial Acts in European Community Law: The Conceptual Weaknesses of the Functional Approach' 11 *Columbia Journal of European Law* 605–621.

Rosas, A, Levits, E and Bot, Y (eds) (2013) *The Court of Justice and the Construction of Europe: Analyses and Perspectives on Sixty Years of Case-Law = La Cour de Justice et La Construction de l'Europe: Analyses et Perspectives de Soixante Ans de Jurisprudence* (Berlin, Springer, The Hague, TMC Asser Press).

Rossi, LS and Di Federico, G (2005) 'Case C-129/00, Commission v Repubblica Italiana, Judgment of 9 December 2003, Full Court, nyr' 42 *Common Market Law Review* 829–49.

Ruiz-Jarabo Colomer, D (2010) 'Once Upon a Time, Francovich: From Fairy Tale to Cruel Reality?' in LMP Maduro and L Azoulai (eds). *The Past and Future of EU Law: The Classics of EU Law Revisited on the 50th Anniversary of the Rome Treaty* (Oxford, Hart Publishing) 405–12.

Ryan, B (2000) 'A Private Enforcement of European Union Labour Laws' in C Kilpatrick, T Novitz and P Skidmore (eds), *The Future of Remedies in Europe* (Oxford, Hart Publishing) 141–63.

Šadl, U (2016) 'National Courts and the Effectiveness of EU Law' in BEFM De Witte et al (eds), *National Courts and EU Law: New Issues, Theories and Methods* (Cheltenham, Edward Elgar) 68–101.

Šadl, U and Mair, S (2017) 'Mutual Disempowerment: Case C-441/14 Dansk Industri, acting on behalf of Ajos A/S v Estate of Karsten Eigil Rasmussen and Case no 15/2014 Dansk Industri (DI) acting for Ajos A/S v The Estate Left by A' 13 *European Constitutional Law Review* 347–68.

Safjan, M (2014) A Union of Effective Judicial Protection: Addressing a Multi-Level Challenge through the Lens of Art 47 CFREU' 33 *Yearbook of European Law* 3–40.

Sánchez, SI (2012) 'The Court and the Charter: The Impact of the Entry into Force of the Lisbon Treaty on the ECJ's Approach to Fundamental Rights' 49 *Common Market Law Review* 1565–11.

Sarmiento, D (2014) 'Rapport espagnol' in L Coutron (ed), *L'obligation de renvoi préjudiciel à la Cour de justice une obligation sanctionnée?* Droit de l'Union européenne: Monographies 6 (Bruxelles, Bruylant) 165–81.

Schebesta, H (2010) 'Does the National Court Know European Law? A Note on Ex Officio Application after Asturcom' 18 *European Review of Private Law* 847–80.

Scherr, KM (2008) 'The Principle of State Liability for Judicial Breaches: The Case Gerhard Köbler v Austria under European Community law and from a Comparative National Law Perspective' PhD thesis (Florence, European University Institute).

—— (2012) 'Comparative Aspects of the Application of the Principle of State Liability for Judicial Breaches' 12 ERA Forum (Trier, Springer) 565–88.

Schmauch, M (2005) 'Lack of Preliminary References as an Infringement of Art 234 EC?' 11 *European Law Reporter*, no 11, 445–54.

Schmitt, Carl (2005) *Political Theology: Four Chapters on the Concept of Sovereignty*, trans G Schwab (Chicago, University of Chicago Press).

Sieburgh, CH and Devroe, W (eds) (2017) *Cases, Materials and Text on European Law and Private Law* (Oxford, Hart Publishing).

Silveira, AAS and Fernandes, SP (2016) 'Preliminary References, Effective Judicial Protection and State Liability: What if the Ferreira da Silva Judgement Had Not Been Delivered?' 20 *Revista de derecho comunitario europeo* 631–66.

Sjöstrand, C (2013) 'Effective Judicial Protection of Individuals: A Duty for the Court of Justice or the National Courts?' in A Rosas, E Levits and Y Bot (eds), *The Court of Justice and the Construction of Europe: Analyses and Perspectives on Sixty Years of Case-Law = La Cour de Justice et la Construction de l'Europe: Analyses et Perspectives de Soixante Ans de Jurisprudence* (Berlin, Springer, The Hague, TMC Asser Press) 64–78.

Slaughter, A-M, Sweet, AS and Weiler, J (eds) (1998) *The European Court and National Courts: Doctrine and Jurisprudence: Legal Change in Its Social Context* (Oxford, Hart Publishing).

Snijders, HJ (2014) 'New Developments in National Rules for ex Officio Raising of Points of Community law by National Courts' in A Hartkamp, CH Sieburgh, LAD Keus, J Kortmann (eds), *The Influence of EU Law on the National Private Law*, Onderneming en recht 81-1 (Deventer, Kluwer) 95–117.

Sowery, K (2016) 'Equivalent Treatment of Union rights under national procedural law: Târsia' 53 *Common Market Law Review* 1705–26.

Spaventa, E (2018) 'Should We "Harmonize" Fundamental Rights in the EU? Some Reflections About Minimum Standards and Fundamental Rights Protection in the EU Composite Constitutional System' 55 *Common Market Law Review* 997–1023.

Steiner, J (1993) 'From Direct Effects to Francovich: Shifting Means of Enforcement of Community Law' 18 *European Law Review* 3–22.

Storme, M (ed) (1994) *Rapprochement du droit judiciaire de l'Union européenne = Approximation of Judiciary Law in the European Union*, Bibliotheek van gerechtelijk recht 19 (Dordrecht, Martinus Nijhoff).

Szyszczak, E (1992) 'European Community Law: New Remedies, New Directions? Joined Cases C-6/90 and C-9/90, Francovich and Bonafaci v Italy' 55 *Modern Law Review* 690–97.

Taborowski, M (2012) 'Infringement proceedings and non-compliant national courts' 49 *Common Market Law Review* 1881–1914.

Temple Lang, J (1997) 'The Duties of National Courts under Community Constitutional Law' 22 *European Law Review* 3–18.

—— (2007) 'The Development by the Court of Justice of the Duties of Cooperation of National Authorities and Community Institution under Art 10 EC' 31 *Fordham International Law Journal* 1483–1532.

Ter Kuile, BH (1994) 'To Refer or Not to Refer: About the Last Paragraph of Art 177 of the EC Treaty' in D Curtin and T Heukels (eds) *Institutional Dynamics of European Integration: Essays in Honour of Henry G Schermers*, vol II (Dordrecht, Nijhoff) 381–89.

Terhechte, JP (2012) 'Judicial Accountability and Public Liability: The German "Judges Privilege"' Under the Influence of European and International Law' 13 *German Law Journal* 313–39.

Tesauro, G (2013) 'Reasonableness in the European Court of Justice Case-Law' in A Rosas, E Levits and Y Bot (eds), *The Court of Justice and the Construction of Europe: Analyses and Perspectives on Sixty Years of Case-Law = La Cour de Justice et La Construction de l'Europe: Analyses et Perspectives de Soixante Ans de Jurisprudence* (Berlin, Springer, The Hague, TMC Asser Press) 307–27.

Timmermans, C (2004) 'Use of the Infringement Procedure in Cases of Judicial Errors' in JW de Zwaan, JH Jans, FA Nelissen, and S Blockmans (eds), *The European Union: An Ongoing Process of Integration: Liber Amicorum Alfred E. Kellermann* (The Hague, TMC Asser Press) 155–163.

—— (2016) 'Horizontal Direct/Indirect Effect of Direct/Indirect Horizontal Effect: What's in a Name?' 24 *European Review of Private Law* 673–85.

Tomkin, J (2012) 'Case C-243/09, Günter Fuß, Judgment of the Court of Justice (Second Chamber) of 14 October 2010; Case C-429/09, Günter Fuß, Judgment of the Court of Justice (Second Chamber) of 25 November 2010' 49 *Common Market Law Review* 1423–42.

Tomkins, A (2003) 'Of Institutions and Individuals: The Enforcement of EC Law' in PP Craig and R Rawlings (eds), *Law and Administration in Europe: Essays in Honour of Carol Harlow* (Oxford, Oxford University Press) 273–95.

Tridimas, T (1994) 'Horizontal Effect of Directives: A Missed Opportunity?' 19 *European Law Review* 621–36.

—— (2000) Enforcing Community Rights in National Courts: Some Recent Developments, in D O'Keeffe and A Bavasso (eds), *Judicial Review in European Union Law: Liber amicorum in honour of Lord Slynn of Hadley*, vol I (The Hague, Kluwer Law International) 465–479.

—— (2001) 'Black, White, and Shades of Grey: Horizontality of Directives Revisited' 21 *Yearbook of European Law* 327–54.

—— (2001) 'Liability for Breach of Community Law: Growing Up and Mellowing Down?' 38 *Common Market Law Review* 301–32.

—— (2006) *The General Principles of EU Law*, 2nd edn (Oxford, Oxford University Press).

—— (2007) 'State Liability for Judicial Acts Remedies Unlimited?' in P Demaret, I Govaere, and D Hanf (eds), *European Legal Dynamics: Revised and Update Edition of 30 Years of European Legal Studies at the College of Europe? = Dynamiques juridiques européennes: Édition revue et mise à jour de 30 ans d'études juridiques européennes au Collegue d'Europe*, College of Europe Studies 2 = Cahiers du Collège d'Europe no 2 (Bruxelles, PIE Peter Lang) 147–61.

—— (2013) 'Bifurcated Justice: The Dual Character of Judicial Protection in EU Law' in A Rosas, E Levits and Y Bot (eds), *The Court of Justice and the Construction of Europe: Analyses and Perspectives on Sixty Years of Case-Law = La Cour de Justice et La Construction de l'Europe: Analyses et Perspectives de Soixante Ans de Jurisprudence* (Berlin, Springer, The Hague, TMC Asser Press) 367–337.

—— (2015) 'The ECJ and the National Courts: Dialogue, Cooperation and Instability' in A Arnull and D Chalmers (eds), *The Oxford Handbook of European Union Law* (Oxford, Oxford University Press) 403–30.

Trstenjak, V and Plaustajner, K (2014) 'Slovenian Rapport' in L Coutron (ed), *L'obligation de renvoi préjudiciel à la Cour de justice une obligation sanctionnée?* Droit de l'Union européenne: Monographies 6 (Bruxelles, Bruylant) 459–78.

Turmo, A (2017) *L'autorité de la chose jugée en droit de l'Union européenne*, Droit de l'Union européenne: Thèses 49 (Bruxelles, Bruylant).

—— (2019) 'A Dialogue of Unequals: The European Court of Justice Reasserts National Courts' Obligations under Article 267(3) TFEU' 15 *European Constitutional Law Review* 340–58.

Oliver, P (2011) 'Case Note on Case C-279/09 DEB v Germany (Judgment of the Grand Chamber of 22 December 2010)' 48 *Common Market Law Review* 2023–40.

Valutyté, R (2011) 'Concept of Court's Fault in State Liability Action for Infringement of European Union Law' 18 *Jurisprudencija* 33–50.

—— (2012a) 'Legal Consequences for the Infringement of the Obligation to Make a Reference for a Preliminary Ruling under Constitutional Law' 19 *Jurisprudencija* 1171–86.

—— (2012b) 'State Liability for the Infringement of the Obligation to Refer for a Preliminary Ruling under the European Convention on Human Rights' 19 *Jurisprudencija* 7–21.

—— (2014) 'Lithuanian Report' in L Coutron (ed), *L'obligation de renvoi préjudiciel à la Cour de justice une obligation sanctionnée?* Droit de l'Union européenne: Monographies 6 (Bruxelles, Bruylant) 283–307.

Van Cleynenbreugel, PJMM (2012A) 'The Confusing Constitutional Status of Positive Procedural Obligations in EU Law' 5 *Review of European Administrative Law* 91–114.

—— (2012B) 'Judge-Made Standards of National Procedure in the Post-Lisbon Constitutional Framework' 37 *European Law Review* 90–100.

Van Dam, JJ, and van Eijsden, JAR (2009) 'Ex Officio Application of EC Law by National Courts of Law in Tax Cases, Discretionary Authority or an Obligation?' 1 *EC Tax Review* 16–28.

Van den Bossche, A-M (2014) 'Private Enforcement, Procedural Authonomy and Art 19(1) TEU: Two's Company, Three's a Crowd' 33 *Yearbook of European Law* 41–83.

Van Gerven, W (1995) 'Bridging the Gap Between Community and National Laws: Towards a Principle of Homogeneity in the Field of Legal Remedies?' 32 *Common Market Law Review* 679–702.

—— (2000) 'Of Rights, Remedies and Procedures' 37 *Common Market Law Review* 501–36.

Varga, Zs (2014a) 'A Kúria ítélete a bíróságoknak az uniós jog megsértéséért fennálló felelősségéről' 5 *Jogesetek Magyarázata* 27–35.

—— (2014b) 'Az Alkotmánybíróság végzése az előzetes döntéshozatali kérelem előterjesztésének elmulasztásáról' 5 *Jogesetek Magyarázata* 1–27.

—— (2015) 'A Köbler-doktrína magyarországi alkalmazása' 15 *Európai Jog* 1–25.

—— (2016a) 'Why Is the Köbler Principle not Applied in Practice?' 23 *Maastricht Journal of European and Comparative Law* 984–1008.

—— (2016b) 'In Search of a "Manifest Infringement of the Applicable Law" in the Terms Set Out in Köbler' 9 *Review of European Administrative Law* 5–40.

—— (2016c) 'The Application of the Köbler Doctrine by Member State Courts' 4 *ELTE Law Journal* 71–93.

—— (2017a) 'Köbler and Francovich: What Is their Relationship?' 15 *Evropeiski Praven Pregled*

—— (2017b) 'National Remedies in the Case of Violation of EU Law by Member State Courts' 54 *Common Market Law Review* 51–80.

—— (2017c) 'Retrial in the Member States on the Ground of Violation of EU Law' 5 *ELTE Law Journal* 55–99.

—— (2019) 'Retrial and Principles of Effectiveness and Equivalence in case of Violation of the ECHR and of the Charter: XC' 56 *Common Market Law Review* 1673–96.

Varju, M (2014) 'The Judicial Reception of EU Law' in M Varju and E Várnay (eds), *The Law of European Union in Hungary: Institutions, Processes and Law* (Budapest, HVG-Orac) 183–222.

Varju, M and Kovács, AGy (2015) 'The Impossibility of Being a National and a European Judge at the Same Time: Doctrinal Rifts Between Hungarian and EU Administrative Law' in M Bobek (ed), *EU Law in the Member States: Central European Judges Under the European Influence. The Transformative Power of the EU Revisited* (Oxford, Hart Publishing) 197–221.

Varju, M and Várnay, E (eds) (2014) *The Law of European Union in Hungary: Institutions, Processes and Law* (Budapest, HVG-Orac).

Várnay, E (2015) 'Discretion in Articles 258 and 260(2) TFEU Procedures' 22 *Maastricht Journal of European and Comparative Law* 836–61.

Várnay, E and Papp, M (2010) *Az Európai Unió joga*, 3rd edn (Budapest, Complex).

Várnay, E, Papp, M, Varju, M and Bartha, I (2006) *A tagállamokkal szembeni kötelezettségszegési eljárások* (Budapest, Complex).

Vehovec, MT (2012) 'The Cause of Member State Liability' 20 *European Review of Private Law* 851–80.

Venice Commission (2011) *Study on Individual Access to Constitutional Justice*, 30 May 2011, Strasbourg, CDL-AD(2010)039 rev

Verbruggen, P and Kryla-Cudna, K (2020) 'Court of Justice The Union's Liability for Failure to Adjudicate Within a Reasonable Time: EU Tort Law after Gascogne, Kendrion and ASPLA' 57 *Common Market Law Review* 191–226.

Wallerman, A (2016a) 'Towards an EU Law Doctrine on the Exercise of Discretion in National Courts? The Member States' Self-Imposed Limits on National Procedural Autonomy' 53 *Common Market Law Review* 339–60.

—— (2016b) 'Harmonization of Civil Procedure: Can the European Union Learn from Swiss Experiences?' 24 *European Review of Private Law* 855–876.

Ward, A (2011) 'Damages under the EU Charter of Fundamental Rights' 12 ERA Forum (Trier, Springer) 589–611.

Wattel, PJ (2004) 'Köbler, CILFIT and Welthgrove: We Can't Go on Meeting Like This' 41 *Common Market Law Review* 177–90.

—— (2008) 'National Procedural Autonomy and Effectiveness of EC Law: Challenge the Charge, File for Restitution, Sue for Damages?' 35 *Legal Issues of Economic Integration* 109–32.

—— (2014) 'Access to Effective Legal Remedy' in C Brokelind (ed), *Principles of Law: Function, Status and Impact in EU Tax Law* (Amsterdam, IBDF) 183–204.

Weiler, JHH (1991) 'The Transformation of Europe' 100 *Yale Law Journal* 2403–83.

Wennerås, P (2006) 'A New Dawn for Commission Enforcement under Articles 226 and 228 EC: General and Persistent (gap) Infringements, Lump Sums and Penalty Payments' 43 *Common Market Law Review* 31–62.

—— (2012) 'Sanctions Against Member States under Art 260 TFEU: Alive, But Not Kicking?' 49 *Common Market Law Review* 145–75.

Whittaker, S (2013) 'Who Determines What Civil Courts Decide? Private Rights, Public Policy and EU Law' in D Leczykiewicz and S Weatherill (eds), *The Involvment of EU Law in Private Relationships*, Studies of the Oxford Institute of European and Comparative Law 16 (Oxford, Hart Publishing) 89–129.

Williams, D and Tushingham, M (2014) 'The Application of the Henderson v Henderson Rule in International Arbitration' 26 *Singapore Academy of Law Journal* 1036–58.

Wilman, FG (2015) *Private Enforcement of EU law Before National Courts: the EU Legislative Framework* (Cheltenham, Edward Elgar).

—— (2016) 'The End of the Absence? The Growing Body of EU Legislation on Private Enforcement and the Main Remedies it Provides For' 53 *Common Market Law Review* 887–935.

Wissink, MH (2005) 'EuGH, 30.9.2003, C-224/01, Gerhard Köbler v Republik Österreich-Liability of a Member State for Damage Caused to Individuals by Infringements of Community Law for Which it is Responsible' *European Review of Private Law = Revue Européenne de Droit Privé = Europäische Zeitschrift Für Privatrecht* 419–42.

Wyatt, D (1997) 'The Relationship Between Actions for Annulment and References on Validity after TWG Deggendorf' in J Lonbay and A Biondi (eds), *Remedies for Breach of EC Law* (Chichester, John Wiley) 55–66.

Xanthaki, H (2003) 'Effective Judicial Protection at the National Level against Breaches of EC Law: The Current Nightmare of Procedural Hurdles' 5 *European Journal of Law Reform* 409–46.

Zbíral, R (2012) 'Czech Constitutional Court, Judgment of 31 January 2012, Pl ÚS 5/12: A Legal Revolution or Negligible Episode? Court of Justice Decision Proclaimed Ultra Vires' 49 *Common Market Law Review* 1475–91.

Zukova, G (2010) 'The Application of EU Law in Latvia' in A Łazowski (ed), *The Application of EU Law in the New Member States* (The Hague, TMC Asser Press) 243–76.

Index

***acte clair* doctrine,** 36–38, 150–51, 154, 158–59, 162–63, 169–70, 179, 192, 203
***acte éclairé* doctrine,** 36–37, 39–40, 80, 150–51, 162, 167, 169–70, 203
allocation of responsibility, in liability actions:
- causation, 62
- concurrent liability of several branches of government, 60–62
- identification of responsible branch of government:
  - causation, 62–64
  - *Commission v Italy* case, 63
  - mitigation, 64–69
- mitigation, 64–65
  - effectiveness principle, 65–66
  - equivalence principle, 67
  - national procedural autonomy, 67–69

alternative actions to *Köbler*, 174–75, 179–80, 215–16
- constitutional complaint, 169–71
  - comparative analysis of rules, 148–51
  - breach of referral duty, 148–56
  - lawful judge principle, application to ECJ, 148–51, 156–69
- doctrine, 188
- ECJ case law, 182–88
  - action for annulment and preliminary ruling on validity, as alternative remedies, 183
  - actions for damages in general, as alternative to *Köbler*, 184–85
  - alternative remedies, acceptance of, 182–88
  - complete system of EU remedies, 183
  - creation of new national remedies, 185–86
  - direct effect, as alternative to *Köbler*, 184–85
  - effectiveness and effective judicial protection, 182
  - EU remedial system, 186–87
  - national remedial system, 182–86
  - national procedural autonomy, 182, 186–87
  - nullity and reinstatement, as alternative to *Köbler*, 184
  - recovery of tax, as alternative action to *Köbler*, 173–74, 183
  - retrial, as alternative to *Köbler*, 185
  - retroactive and proper application, as alternative to *Köbler*, 182–83
- retrial, 119–20
  - comparative analysis of rules, 125–27, 143–45
  - ECJ case law, 120–24
  - ECtHR case law, 124–25
  - prior/subsequent judgement, 147–48
  - state liability, relationship with, 145–47
  - states with retrial not available, 139–43
  - states with retrial in extraordinary situations only, 127–31
  - states with retrial under certain circumstances, 131–36
- special remedies:
  - *Amtshaftungsanspruch* (Austrian law), 171–72
  - *Anhörungsrüge* (German law), 172
  - *domvilla* (Swedish law), 172
  - *Drittwiderspruchsklage* (German law), 172–73
  - *recours dans l'intérêt de la loi* (French law), 173
  - recovery of tax, 173–74, 183
  - *Vollstreckungsabwehrklage* (German law), 172–73
  - *wytyk* (Polish law), 173

application of EU law in national courts, 3–7
- *see also* procedural obligations of national courts to apply EU law

application of *Köbler* liability, 81–82
- consequences:
  - impact of *Köbler* on national law, 81–82, 117–18, 213–15
  - duplication of liability regimes, 117–18
  - spill-over, 117–18
- national legislative restrictions, 82–83, 118, 176
  - declaration of unlawfulness, 83

exclusion of liability for judicial activity, 82
establishment of criminal liability, 82
res judicata, 82
reversal of contested judgments, 82–83
states implementing *Köbler* through case law, 87–104
states implementing *Köbler* through legislation, 104–8
states refusing to implement *Köbler*, 108–13
states with no accommodation to *Köbler*, 113–17
states with regimes compatible with *Köbler*, 83–87
see also breach of EU law by courts, damages for breach of EU law by courts
Austria:
Amtshaftungsanspruch, 171–72
lawful judge principle, application to ECJ, 162–64
retrial, not available for EU law breaches, 142
state liability for judicial breaches of *Köbler*, 99–100
autonomy, *see* **national procedural autonomy**

Belgium:
retrial, not available for EU law breaches, 136
state liability for judicial breaches of *Köbler*, 88–90
branches of government, liability of:
administration, 78
judicature, 78–79
violation of CFREU, 80
violation of referral duty, 79–80
violation of substantive law, 79
legislature, 77–78
several branches of government, 60–62, 80–81
sole breach by one body, 77
liability of administration, 78
liability of judicature, 78–80
liability of legislature, 77–78
breach of EU law by courts, 7
ECJ case law, 8–13
Commission v France case, 79–80
Commission v Italy case, 63
Commission v Spain case, 79
Ferreira da Silva e Brito e.a. case, 10–11
Köbler case, 8–9
Tomášová case, 12–13
Traghetti del Mediterraneo case, 9–10
national case law:
retrial in extraordinary situations only, 127–31
retrial not available, 139–43
retrial under certain circumstances, 131–36
state liability as a remedy for, 83–87, 153–54
state liability as a remedy for, despite limitations, 88–102
state liability as a remedy for, due to legislative amendments, 104–8
state liability not available for, 9, 108–117
special remedies, 171–74
see also alternative remedies to *Köbler*; application of *Köbler* liability; damages for breach of EU law by courts
breach of referral duty, 40–41
ECJ case law, 38–41, 79–80, 191–93, 200–1, 205–8
Commission v France case, 39–40, 43, 79–80, 192
Ferreira da Silva e Brito e.a. case, 10–11, 38–40
ECtHR case law, 151–56, 198–99, 203–4
grounds for liability claims, 35–45, 195–98, 218–19
breach of substantive law, relationship with, 41–45
impact on gravity of breach, 44–45
manifest breach of applicable law, considered as, 41–44
separate grounds for liability, 195–201
serious breach, 38
simple breach, 38
national case law, 48–50, 52–53, 194–95, 199–200, 204–5
constitutional complaints, 150–51, 156–71
unsuccessful liability claims:
no violation of referral duty, 48–50
no violation of referral duty and substantive EU law, 52–53
see also duty to refer
Bulgaria:
res judicata, 91
retrial, available under certain circumstances, 131–32
state liability for judicial breaches of *Köbler*, 90–92

causation, as condition of *Köbler* actions, 1, 59
disassociation of liability from conduct of national courts, 64
identification of responsible state body, 59–60
liability of several branches of government, 60–62, 80–81
mitigation of damages, 64–69
multiple breaches, 62–64
sole breach, 77–80
VAT Directives case law, 69–77
mitigation of damages, 64–65
effectiveness principle, 65–66
equivalence principle, 67
national procedural autonomy principle, 67–69
multiple breaches, 62–63
Commission v Italy case, 63
Charter on Fundamental Rights of the EU (CFREU):
duty to refer, 201–3, 211–12
ECJ case law, 205–8
ECtHR case law, 203–4
national case law, 204–5
right to an effective remedy and to a fair trial (Art. 47), 208
right to statements of reasons:
ECJ case law, 205–8
ECtHR case law, 203–4
national case law, 204–5
scope of application, 201–2
undue delay in proceedings, 208–11
see also European Court of Justice (ECJ)
compensation:
successful *Köbler* actions, 61–62
Bulgaria, 54–55
Finland, 54
Italy, 55–56
Portugal, 57
Sweden, 56–57
Tomášová case, 12–13
Traghetti del Mediterraneo case, 55–56
unsuccessful *Köbler* actions, 46–53
see also application of *Köbler* liability; damages for breach of EU law by courts
competence regarding remedies, ***see*** **remedial competence**
concurrent liability, of several branches of government, 60–62, 69, 80–81
conforming interpretation principle, 29–32, 34, 53, 77
manifest infringement, 32–33
consistent interpretation doctrine, ***see*** **conforming interpretation principle**
constitutional complaint, on grounds of violation of referral duty,
availability in national laws, 148–51
lawful judge principle, application to ECJ, 156–67
correct interpretation principle, 33, 35, 39–40, 80, 111, 149, 157, 160, 195–96
manifest infringement, 33–34
Croatia:
retrial, not available for EU law breaches, 139
state liability, no accommodation for *Köbler*, 114
Cyprus:
retrial, available in extraordinary situations, 127
state liability, no accommodation for *Köbler*, 113–14
Czech Republic:
lawful judge principle, application to ECJ, 156–57
res judicata, 136–37
retrial, not available for EU law breaches, 136–37
state liability, refusal to apply *Köbler*, 109–10
damages for breach of EU law by courts, 7
ECJ case law, 7–12
national case law, 83–117
successful claims, 61–62
Bulgaria, 54–55
Finland, 54
Italy, 55–56
Portugal, 57
Sweden, 56–57
Tomášová case, 12–13
Traghetti del Mediterraneo case, 55–56
unsuccessful claims, 46–53
no manifest infringement due to ambiguity of EU law, 46–48
no violation of referral duty and substantive EU law, 52–53
no violation of referral duty, 48–50
no violation of substantive EU law, 50–52
see also application of *Köbler* liability; breach of EU law by courts

Denmark:
res judicata, 83
retrial, available in extraordinary situations, 127
state liability, regime conforming to *Köbler*, 83
direct effect, 6, 23–25
manifest infringement, 25–26
disapplication remedy and primacy principle, 26–28
manifest infringement, 28–29
discretion of national courts, *see* **judicial discretion**
duty to refer, 35–38, 40–41
correct application of EU law, relationship with, 35
doctrine, 193
ECJ case law, 38–41, 79–80, 191–93, 200–1, 205–8
ECtHR case law, 151–56, 198–99, 203–4
national case law, 194–95, 199–200, 204–5
procedural obligation to apply EU law, seen as, 196–97
TFEU, substantive norm of, seen as, 197–98
see also acte clair doctrine, *acte éclairé* doctrine, breach of referral duty

effective judicial protection, 7, 217–18
duty to refer, 198
ECJ case law, 182–88, 208
ECtHR case law, 189, 209
effectiveness, relationship with, 182, 183–87
EU law in general, 5–7, 178, 180–82, 193, 208, 216
EU remedial system, 186–87
grounds for liability, violation of, 208, 211
national case law, 101, 157, 161, 165–67, 171
national remedial system, 119, 175, 182–88, 190, 198
right to statement of reasons, 205
effectiveness principle:
ECJ case law, 12, 65–66, 182–88
ECtHR case law, 189
effective judicial protection, relationship with, 182, 183–87
EU law in general, 21, 22, 61, 119, 175, 181, 182, 208, 216
EU remedial system, 186
Köbler liability, effectiveness of, 3–4, 9, 48, 50, 59, 112
limitation on procedural autonomy, 21
mitigation of damages, 67
Metallgesellschaft case, 65–66
Fuß case, 65–66
national remedial system, 182–88
retrial, 122, 123, 136
***effet utile* principle,** 7, 187, 188
equivalence principle, 12, 21, 69
ECJ case law, 12, 67, 182–88
limitation on procedural autonomy, 21
national case law, 71–72, 85
national remedial system, 59, 67–69, 181, 183–87
retrial, 123
Transportes Urbanos case, 67–69
Estonia:
retrial, not available for EU law breaches, 137
state liability, no accommodation for *Köbler*, 114
European Convention on Human Rights (ECHR), 89, 95–96, 146–47, 211
retrial, 123, 126–27
right to a fair trial (Art. 6(1)), 119, 129, 151–56, 203–4, 207, 209–10
right to effective remedy (Art. 13), 189, 209–10, 218
right to statements of reasons, 203–4
see also European Court of Human Rights (ECtHR)
European Court of Human Rights (ECtHR):
duty to refer case law, 151–56, 198–99
right to statements of reasons case law, 203–4
effective judicial protection case law, 189, 209
res judicata case law, 124
see also European Convention on Human Rights (ECHR)
European Court of Justice (ECJ), case law:
alternative remedies to *Köbler*, acceptance of, 182–88
complete system of EU remedies, 183
creation of new national remedies, 185–86
EU remedial system, 186–87
national remedial system, 182–86
application of EU law, obligations of national courts, 20–50
direct effect, 23–25
duty to refer, 38–41, 79–80, 191–93, 200–1, 205–8
conforming interpretation, 29–32
primacy and disapplication remedy, 26–28

causation, in liability actions, 63
effective judicial protection, 182–88, 208
effectiveness principle, 12, 65–66, 182–88
equivalence principle, 12, 67, 182–188
national procedural autonomy, 20–21, 182, 186–87
state liability for EU law violation by courts, 7–13
manifest breach of applicable law, 15–17, 19–20
retrial, 120–24
scope of application of the Charter, 205–6
statements of reasons, 206–8
undue delay in proceedings, 208–9
see also Charter on Fundamental Rights of the EU (CFREU)
ex officio application of EU law, 20–21, 113, 115
national procedural autonomy and *Köbler* doctrine, 21–23
procedural rule of reason, 20–21

fair trial, *see* right to a fair trial
Finland:
res judicata, 130–31
retrial, available in extraordinary situations, 129–31
state liability for judicial breaches of *Köbler*, 102–3
France:
recours dans l'intérêt de la loi, 173
res judicata, 139
retrial, not available for breaches of EU law, 139
state liability for judicial breaches of *Köbler*, 93–96
***Francovich* liability,** 2–3, 8, 61, 68, 81, 88, 91, 98–99, 114, 174, 179, 182, 187–88

Germany:
Anhörungsrüge, 172
Drittwiderspruchsklage, 172–73
lawful judge principle, application to ECJ, 157–62
retrial, not available for breaches of EU law, 137
state liability for judicial breaches of *Köbler*, 92–93
Vollstreckungsabwehrklage, 172–73
Greece:
retrial, not available for breaches of EU law, 138
state liability, no accommodation for *Köbler*, 114

harmonious interpretation, *see* conforming interpretation principle
harmonisation of remedies, 5, 190, 216–17
Hungary:
lawful judge principle, refusal to apply to ECJ, 168–69
res judicata, 108, 110–12, 117–18
retrial, not available for breaches of EU law, 140–41
state liability, to apply *Köbler*, 110–12

indirect effect, *see* conforming interpretation principle
interference by ECJ, in national remedial systems, 6, 81, 185, 188
see also national procedural autonomy
Ireland:
res judicata, 113
retrial, not available for breaches of EU law, 138
state liability, refusal to apply *Köbler*, 112–13
Italy:
res judicata, 104, 139–40
restricting state liability for judicial errors, 63, 79, 82
retrial, not available for breaches of EU law, 139–40
state liability, introduced through legislation, 104–5

judicial errors in applying EU law, 1, 151
see also **breach of EU law by courts**

Latvia:
retrial, not available for breaches of EU law, 140
state liability, regime conforming to *Köbler*, 84
lawful judge principle, application to ECJ, 148–49
limitations, 148–50
national case law, 156–67
refusal, 167–69
legal uncertainty, 59, 66
Portugal, 100–1

legality principle, 120, 185
liability for manifest breach of EU law, 175–76
manifest breach, 15–45
successful claims, 53
infringement by several branches of government, 54–55
liability established by lower court, 57
liability established following preliminary ruling, 55–56
relevant national rules, 56–57
unsuccessful claims, 46
no manifest infringement due to ambiguity of EU law, 46–48
no violation of referral duty and substantive EU law, 52–53
no violation of referral duty, 48–50
no violation of substantive EU law, 50–52
see also damages for breach of EU law by courts
Lithuania:
retrial, available in extraordinary situations, 127–29
state liability for judicial breaches of *Köbler*, 96–97
Luxembourg:
res judicata, 115
retrial, not available for breaches of EU law, 140
state liability, no accommodation for *Köbler*, 115

Malta:
retrial, available in extraordinary situations, 129
state liability, no accommodation for *Köbler*, 115
manifest breach of applicable law, as condition of *Köbler* actions, 1–2, 58–59, 175–76
conforming interpretation principle, manifest breach of, 32–33
correct interpretation principle, manifest breach of, 33–34
direct effect, manifest breach of, 25–26
duty to refer,
manifest breach of, 41–44
impact on gravity of breach, 44–45
ECJ interpretation, 15–16
factors to consider:
clarity and precision of rule infringed, 17, 19
disregard of duty to refer, 17, 19–20
intentional nature of infringement, 19
whether error in law excusable, 19
gravity of violation, 34–35
violation of applicable EU law defined, 17–19
unsuccessful *Köbler* actions:
no manifest infringement due to ambiguity of EU law, 46–48
margin of discretion, *see* **judicial discretion**
mitigation of damages:
duty of mitigation, 64–65
effectiveness principle case law:
Metallgesellschaft case, 65–66
Fuß case, 65–66
equivalence principle case law, 67
Transportes Urbanos Case, 67
national procedural autonomy principle, 67–68
Tomašova case, 68–69

national law:
impact of *Köbler*, 213–15
duplication and spill-over, 117–18
interference by ECJ, 6, 81, 185, 188
national legislative restrictions to application of Köbler, 118, 176
declaration of unlawfulness, 83
exclusion of liability for judicial activity, 82
establishment of criminal liability, 82
impact of *Köbler* on national law, 81–82, 213–15
duplication and spill-over, 117–18
res judicata, 82
reversal of contested judgments, 82–83
national procedural autonomy, 1, 3, 6, 12, 190, 192
Köbler doctrine, 21–23
limitations, 20–21
effectiveness principle, 65–66
equivalence principle, 67
mitigation of damages, 67–68
national case law, 86, 97, 107, 116
Tomašova case, 12, 68–69
Netherlands:
res judicata, 141
retrial, not available for breaches of EU law, 141–42
state liability for judicial breaches of *Köbler*, 97–99, 142

obligation to apply EU law, *see* **procedural obligations of national courts to apply EU law**
obligation to submit referral to preliminary ruling, *see* **referral duty**

Poland:
res judicata, 108
retrial, available under certain circumstances, 132–33
state liability introduced through legislation, 105–8
wytyk, 173
Portugal:
res judicata, 101
retrial, not available for breaches of EU law, 142
state liability for judicial breaches of *Köbler*, 100–2
legal uncertainty, 100–1
procedural obligations of national courts to apply EU law, 20, 34–35
conforming interpretation, 29–33
correct interpretation, 33–34
direct effect, 23–26
primacy principle and disapplication remedy, 26–29
referral duty, 35–45
procedural rule of reason, 20–21, 22, 216–17
preliminary reference procedure, *see* **duty to refer; breach of referral duty**
primacy principle and disapplication remedy, 6, 26–28, 133–34, 187
manifest infringement, 28–29

referral duty, *see* **duty to refer**
refusal to submit referral to preliminary ruling, *see* **breach of referral duty**
remedial competence, 5–7, 188, 190
reparation, 11, 16, 102, 182–83, 188, 204
see also compensation; damages for breach of EU law by courts
***res judicata*,** 1, 118, 187
Bulgaria, 91
Czech Republic, 136–37
Denmark, 83
ECJ case law, 120–23
ECtHR case law, 124
Finland, 130–31
France, 139
Hungary, 108, 110–12, 117–18
Ireland, 113
Italy, 104, 139–40
Luxembourg, 115
Netherlands, 141
Poland, 108
Portugal, 101
Romania, 134
Slovenia, 143
restitution, 7, 69, 124, 174
retrial, on grounds of violation of EU law, 119–20
comparative analysis of rules, 125–27, 143–45
ECJ case law, 120–24
ECtHR case law, 124–25
prior/subsequent judgement, 147–48
states with retrial not available, 139–43
states with retrial in extraordinary situations only, 127–31
states with retrial under certain circumstances, 131–36
state liability, relationship with, 145–47
retroactivity principle, 51, 57–58, 147, 182–83
right to a fair trial (Art. 6(1) ECHR; Art. 47 CFREU), 119, 129, 151–56, 203–4, 207, 209–10
right to effective remedy (Art. 13 ECHR; Art. 47 CFREU), 189, 209–10, 218
right to statements of reasons:
ECJ case law, 205–8
ECtHR case law, 203–4
national case law, 204–5
Romania:
res judicata, 134
retrial, available under certain circumstances, 133–34
state liability, no accommodation for *Köbler*, 115–16
rule of reason, *see* **procedural rule of reason**

***Simmenthal* doctrine,** 6, 26–27
Slovakia:
lawful judge principle, application to ECJ, 165–66
retrial, available under certain circumstances, 134–35
state liability, no accommodation for *Köbler*, 116
Slovenia:
lawful judge principle, application to ECJ, 162–65
res judicata, 143

retrial, not available for breaches of EU law, 142–43
state liability, no accommodation for *Köbler*, 116–17

Spain:
lawful judge principle, application to ECJ, 166–67
retrial, not available for breaches of EU law, 138–39
state liability, regime conforming to *Köbler*, 84–87

standard of liability, 5, 19, 63, 175–76
adequacy of current system, 177–78
lack of coherence, 178
compensation-focused regime, 178–79
enforcement-focused regime, 178–79
manifest infringement, *see* manifest breach of applicable law

state liability principle generally:
effective judicial protection principle, 180, 181–82
effectiveness principle, 180, 181–82
origins, 180

state liability regimes conforming to *Köbler*:
Denmark, 83
Latvia, 84
Spain, 84–87
Sweden, 87

state liability for judicial breaches of *Köbler*, 87–88
Austria, 99–100
Belgium, 88–90
Bulgaria, 90–92
Finland, 102–3
France, 93–96
Germany, 92–93
Lithuania, 96–97
Netherlands, 97–99
Portugal, 100–2
UK, 103–4

state liability introduced through legislation, 104
Italy, 104–5
Poland, 105–8

state refusal to apply *Köbler*, 108–9
Czech Republic, 109–10
Hungary, 110–12
Ireland, 112–13

state unity doctrine, 61–62, 81

states with no accommodation for *Köbler*:
Croatia, 114
Cyprus, 113–14
Estonia, 114
Greece, 114
Luxembourg, 115
Malta, 115
Romania, 115–16
Slovakia, 116
Slovenia, 116–17

successful *Köbler* actions, 53
infringement by several branches of government, 54–55
liability established by lower court, 57
liability established following preliminary ruling, 55–56
relevant national rules, 56–57

sufficiently serious breach, *see* **manifest breach of applicable law**

supremacy principle, *see* **primacy principle and disapplication remedy**

Sweden:
domvilla, 172
retrial, available in extraordinary situations, 131
state liability, regime conforming to *Köbler*, 87

United Kingdom:
retrial, available under certain circumstances, 135–36
state liability for judicial breaches of *Köbler*, 103–4

undue delay in proceedings, 208–11

unsuccessful *Köbler* actions, 46
no manifest infringement due to ambiguity of EU law, 46–48
no violation of referral duty and substantive EU law, 52–53
no violation of referral duty, 48–50
no violation of substantive EU law, 50–52

VAT Directives:
breach of rights under, 69–70
allocation of responsibility, 76
breach by judiciary cases, 73–75
breach by several branches of government, 75–76
breach by tax administration cases, 72–73
ECJ case law, 183
legislative omission cases, 70–72

www.ingramcontent.com/pod-product-compliance
Lightning Source LLC
Chambersburg PA
CBHW071302180926
51613CB00001B/104
* 9 7 8 1 5 0 9 9 3 9 1 9 0 *